COMMUNITIES

second edition **COMMUNITIES**

A Survey of Theories and Methods of Research

DENNIS E. POPLIN

Murray State University
Murray, Kentucky

MACMILLAN PUBLISHING CO., INC.
New York
COLLIER MACMILLAN PUBLISHERS
London

To my Wife,
Kay Brandon Poplin

Macmillan Publishing Co., Inc.
866 Third Avenue, New York, New York 10022

Collier Macmillan Canada, Ltd.

Library of Congress Cataloging in Publication Data

Poplin, Dennis E
  Communities.

  Includes bibliographies and index.
  1. Community. 2. Community life—Research.
I. Title.
HM131.P67   1979   301.34'07'2   78-3571
ISBN 0-02-396160-0

Printing: 1 2 3 4 5 6 7 8   Year: 9 0 1 2 3 4 5

PREFACE

□□□□□□□□□
to the second edition

□   The reactions to the first edition of this book have been extremely gratifying. Because of this, the basic format of this edition remains essentially unchanged. However, major modifications have been made in the book itself. First, two completely new chapters have been added. One of these (Chapter 3) deals with communes, new communities, and total institutions. Although these three communal types differ greatly from one another, they do have one thing in common: they are established with a purpose in mind. The second new chapter (Chapter 7) deals with community conflict. The first edition was seriously deficient in that it almost totally ignored conflict as a basic part of community life.

In addition to preparing two entirely new chapters for this edition, I have tried to do several other things. Every chapter has, to a greater or lesser degree, been revised. New developments in community theory and research have been considered, and every effort has been made to clarify difficult sections of the text. The footnotes and bibliographic references have also been updated, a task that proved to be particularly formidable. The body of literature on communities continues to grow so rapidly that it is almost impossible to put one's fingers on it all. I am sure that I have overlooked some very important contributions made by other students of community life. I regret this and hope that those people whom I have slighted will accept my apologies.

My debt to those who were acknowledged in the first edition still stands. In addition, there are several people who made major contributions to the second edition. Annabel Kirschner Cook of the University of Puget Sound and Forrest W. Graves of Eastern Michigan University made comments on the first edition that were very helpful in strengthening this edition. I also owe a very heavy debt to Professors Larry M. Landis of Drake University and Russell E. Lewis of the University of Evansville. Professor Landis reviewed the entire first edition and made perceptive suggestions, comments, and criticisms on almost every page of the manuscript. Professor Lewis was kind enough to perform the same time-consuming and laborious task on a rough draft of the second edition. If this edition represents a significant improvement over the first edition, certainly Professors Landis and Lewis deserve a large share of the credit. Also, I must extend my deepest appreciation to Kenneth J. Scott of the Macmillan Publishing Co., Inc. Throughout the preparation of this edition Mr. Scott has been extremely helpful, patient, and supportive. Finally, I shall close this preface with the same words with which I closed the preface to the first edition: Without my wife's encouragement, patience, and concrete assistance, this edition, like the first edition, would never have reached completion.

D. E. P.

PREFACE

□ □ □ □ □ □ □ □ □

to the first edition

□   During the last few years I have had responsibility for teaching courses entitled "The Community" or "The Urban Community." Perhaps the thing which has bothered me most often is that it is extremely difficult to decide what approach to take in teaching these courses. One approach the writer has tried is essentially descriptive, i.e., the student is asked to familiarize himself with the basic characteristics of rural and urban communities, with the spatial organization of cities, and with a variety of other features of the modern community. This approach has some real merits, but it has one crucial drawback: it does not necessarily help the student to adopt the thought patterns of the professional sociologist. Today's sociologist is not content to engage in armchair description. Rather, he develops concepts, advances theories, and conducts research. It is the goal of this book to give the student an opportunity to follow the sociologist as he seeks knowledge about the community.

Thus, in Part I of this book the student is asked to think about the concept of community. This is one of the most confusing terms that sociologists use. If the student does not grasp some of the meanings we attach to it, he will gain little from our efforts to instruct him. His confusion will become even greater if he tries to distinguish among various types of communities. This is our fault. We use such terms as *village, city,* and *metropolitan area* with alacrity, but sometimes we fail to define them precisely.

Sociology has become both theory conscious and research oriented. The sociology of community life has not been exempted from this trend. Hence, Part II of this book draws together and summarizes various theories of community. Specifically, consideration is given to social system theory and functionalism as they apply to the study of communities, as well as to some of the more traditional types of community theory. Likewise, in Part III the student is introduced to methods of community research. We do not attempt to teach him how to conduct a community study. Rather, he is encouraged to think about the ways we gain knowledge about community life.

One of the things which might be considered new about this book is its organization. I have attempted to summarize and evaluate some of the most significant contributions of those sociologists who have seen the community as a worthy object of study. An undertaking of this type has its dangers. It is challenging enough to put one's own thoughts into writing. To summarize and evaluate the work of others is difficult indeed. Nonetheless, I have attempted to deal fairly and accurately with the articles, books, and other publications considered in this text. If I have at times failed, those whom I have slighted might bear one thing in mind: it is my fault, not theirs!

To express my appreciation to everyone who has lent a hand in the preparation of this manuscript is impossible. Nonetheless, a special note of thanks must be extended to Professors Walter J. Cartwright and John H. Watson, both of whom provided that kind of encouragement which is so necessary if a project of this type is to be completed. Likewise, I owe a heavy intellectual debt to Professors Therel R. Black, Evelyn H. Lewis, and George A. Hillery, Jr. Only they can understand the nature of this debt. Many of my colleagues and students have been kind enough to read portions of the manuscript and to make a number of comments and suggestions. They include Francis B. Collins, Harry J. Hale, Jr., Harold R. Hepler, George A. Hillery, Jr., David R. Rodnick, Jon P. Tyner, John H. Watson, and Robert Whitten. Personnel of The Macmillan Company, and especially Charles E. Smith, have been thoroughly helpful and deserve much credit. Mrs. Joycelyn Graves and several of her student assistants rendered invaluable help in typing a complete draft of the manuscript and in otherwise assisting me with the details of its preparation. Finally, without my wife's encouragement, patience, and concrete assistance this manuscript would have never reached completion. To all of these people I extend my deepest gratitude.

D. E. P.

CONTENTS

□□□□□□□□□□□□

COMMUNITIES

□□□□□□□□□□□□□□□□□□□□□□□□

□□□□□□
□
□
□
□
□
□
□
□
□
□
□

PART I

The Concept of Community

□ The purpose of this book is to present college and university students with a survey of the most significant theories of community and to introduce them to methods of community research. Before this can be done, however, it is necessary to examine the word *community* itself. Unfortunately, it is not easy to say just what sociologists mean by this term.

Hence in Chapter 1 the concept of community is examined. It is argued that sociologists used the word *community* in essentially three ways. First, it is often used as a synonym: at one time or another, prisons, religious organizations, minority groups, members of the same profession, and even military establishments have been referred to as communities. Second, *community* is often used to refer to a moral or spiritual phenomenon. Today men and women the world over are supposedly engaged in a "search for community" (i.e., a quest for unity and involvement with other human beings). Finally, *community* is used to refer to those units of social and territorial organization that dot the face of the earth and that can also be called hamlets, villages, towns, cities, or metropolitan areas. It is an interest in these units of social and territorial organization that has prompted the writing of this book.

In Chapters 2 and 3 the reader's attention is focused on some of the forms that territorial communities can assume. More specifically, Chapter 2 spells out some of the characteristics of rural, urban, and metropolitan communities. Are there major and significant differences among these three communal types? If so, what are they? Once these questions are answered, we shall be in a good position to examine theories of community structure and process. Likewise, in Chapter 3 we examine communes, new communities, and total institutions. No attempt is made to argue that these are like units of social organization. However, it is suggested that these three units of organization have at least one thing in common: they are established with a goal or a purpose in mind.

CHAPTER 1

□□□□□□□□
□
□
□
□
□
□
□
□
□
□

The Concept of Community

From its inception as a discipline, sociology has been plagued by inconsistency and ambiguity in some of its basic terminology. Indeed, some words that are used almost daily by the sociologist take on so many shades of meaning that it is difficult to endow them with scientific precision. The word *community* falls into this category. As an element in the sociological vocabulary, this term has been used in so many ways that it has been described as an omnibus word.[1] In this book, however, we shall use the word *community* to refer to those units of social and territorial organization that, depending on their size, may also be called hamlets, villages, towns, cities, or metropolitan areas. Before we examine this concept of community, perhaps we need to look at some of the other ways in which this illusive term has been used.

□ COMMUNITY: A WORD OF MANY USES

One need not go far into the literature of sociology before encountering the term *community*. For alert readers this can become a source of utmost confusion. David W. Minar and Scott Greer, for example, refer to factories, trade unions, corporations, and professions as communities,[2]

---

[1] George A. Hillery, Jr., "Villages, Cities, and Total Institutions," *American Sociological Review*, **28** (October, 1963), 779. In a similar vein, Freilich tells us that "since a requisite of science is specificity of terminology, we must conclude . . . that at this time 'community' is a non-scientific term unless separately defined in every paper which uses it." See Morris Freilich, "Toward an Operational Definition of Community," *Rural Sociology*, **28** (June, 1963), 118.

[2] David W. Minar and Scott Greer, *The Concept of Community: Readings with Interpretations* (Chicago: Aldine Publishing Company, 1969), p. 140.

and at various times reference is made to prison communities, military communities, religious communities, academic communities, and so on, through a seemingly endless array of social phenomena. These multiple usages of *community* may be unavoidable, but they make things difficult for those who seek to study communities as a distinct form of social and territorial organization. Furthermore, the fact that a word can be used in several different ways diminishes its usefulness for purposes of scientific communication. For example, Herbert J. Gans has described the emergence of a small "community" of Jewish families in a predominantly Gentile suburb of Chicago.[3] The way Gans uses the term *community* seems to be perfectly appropriate. However, if this or any other small, closely knit minority group constitutes a community, then a great deal of mental gearshifting must occur before one can refer to the great cities of the world or the thousands of smaller towns and villages scattered across the face of the earth as communities. Likewise, if the American military establishment represents a community,[4] then one can question whether a small group of Jewish families also constitutes a community. Are we not stretching the concept of community to the point where it loses all meaning and becomes useless for scientific purposes? Do a minority group, a large city, and complex military organization have enough in common that they can be referred to by the same term? They should be called the same thing only if they constitute *like* units of social organization.

These remarks rest on theoretical rather than practical grounds. Sociologists will, undoubtedly, continue to use *community* as a catchall term for a long time to come. However, this practice can only cause confusion. Furthermore, in many cases the use of the term *community* indicates a lack of conceptual rigor. If the sociologist is talking about a social group, then he or she should refer to it as such and fit it into one of the many typologies of social groups. Likewise, if the object of investigation is a subculture (e.g., the "academic community"), then the vocabulary of subcultural analysis should be used. This is not to deny, of course, that there are some units of social organization that do not

[3] See Herbert J. Gans, "Park Forest: The Birth of a Jewish Community," *Commentary*, 11 (April, 1951), 330–39. In a more recent work, Gerald Suttles uses the term *community* in much the same way as Gans. In particular, Suttles refers to various ethnic neighborhoods in Chicago as communities. Sometimes these "communities" occupy both sides of only one city block and do not include a school, church, business establishment, or anything else that we usually associate with territorial communities. See Gerald Suttles, *The Social Construction of Communities* (Chicago: University of Chicago Press, 1972).

[4] For a discussion of "military communities" see Maurice R. Stein, *The Eclipse of Community: An Interpretation of American Community Studies* (New York: Harper Torchbooks, 1964), pp. 175–98.

seem to fit anywhere in the landscape of sociological terminology. Among the examples that can be cited are prisons, convents, mental hospitals, orphanages, and army barracks. We need more research that focuses on these entities so that their basic properties can be determined. Erving Goffman, for example, has suggested that prisons, convents, mental hospitals, and kindred organizations share so many characteristics that they can be lumped into one category. He suggests that the term *total institution* be assigned to this category.[5]

☐ MORAL COMMUNITIES AND MASS SOCIETY

Whenever we encounter the term *community* we should ask ourselves whether the writer is guilty of using an illusive concept in a careless, imprecise way. At the same time, we must also be aware of the fact that the writer may be using the word *community* in a philosophical sense. Indeed, *community* is sometimes used to refer to a moral or a spiritual phenomenon. This seems to be true in the case of Minar and Greer. In discussing their concept of community, they tell us that "it expresses our vague yearnings for a commonality of desire, a communion with those around us, an extension of the bonds of kin and friend to all those who share a common fate with us." [6]

Table 1-1 provides us with a preliminary overview of this concept of community and contrasts it with its opposite, mass society. In the left-hand column of this table a few basic characteristics of "moral communities" are listed; the right-hand column gives the reader a clue to some of the characteristics of mass societies. Our listing of characteristics is by no means complete. Many other characteristics of "moral communities" and "mass societies" could be delineated.

Table 1-1 makes it apparent that this concept of community is far from unidimensional. Rather, community as a moral phenomenon seems to involve a sense of identity and unity with one's group and a feeling of involvement and wholeness on the part of the individual. In short, *community* has been used to refer to a condition in which human beings find themselves enmeshed in a tight-knit web of meaningful relationships with their fellow human beings. In contrast to this "sense of community" are the conditions that supposedly prevail in modern society. During recent years scholars have become increasingly concerned with the place

[5] See Erving Goffman, "Characteristics of Total Institutions," in Maurice R. Stein, Arthur J. Vidich, and David Manning White (eds.), *Identity and Anxiety: Survival of the Person in Mass Society* (New York: The Free Press, 1960), pp. 499–79. For further discussion of total institutions see Chapter 3.

[6] Minar and Greer, *The Concept of Community*, p. ix.

TABLE 1-1. Selected Characteristics of Moral Communities and Mass Societies

Moral Communities	Mass Societies
Identification Members of the moral community have a deep sense of belonging to a significant, meaningful group.	*Alienation* Members of mass society have a deep sense of being "cut off" from meaningful group associations.
Moral Unity Members of the moral community have a sense of pursuing common goals and feel a oneness with other community members.	*Moral Fragmentation* Members of mass society pursue divergent goals and feel no sense of oneness with other members of the mass society.
Involvement Members of the moral community are submerged in various groups and have a compelling need to participate in these groups.	*Disengagement* Members of mass society have no meaningful group membership and feel no compulsion to participate in the collective activities of various groups.
Wholeness Members of the moral community regard each other as whole persons who are of intrinsic significance and worth.	*Segmentation* Members of mass society regard each other as means to ends and assign no intrinsic worth or significance to the individual.

of the individual in mass society. From the prodigious amount of literature on the subject it might will be concluded, rightly or wrongly, that twentieth-century people are alienated, frustrated, and alone.[7] In any event, it is the opposite of this condition that several scholars choose to call community.

Among the sociologists who have championed this concept during recent years is Robert A. Nisbet. According to Nisbet, one of the funda-

---

[7] As a matter of fact, there have been several high-quality empirical studies that suggest that even in large urban areas most people do not feel particularly isolated, alienated, and alone. For example, see Albert Hunter, "The Loss of Community: An Empirical Test Through Replication," *American Sociological Review,* **40** (October, 1975), 537–52; Claude S. Fischer, "On Urban Alienation and Anomie: Powerlessness and Social Isolation," *American Sociological Review,* **38** (June, 1973), 311–26; John D. Kasarda and Morris Janowitz, "Community Attachment in Mass Society," *American Sociological Review,* **39** (June, 1974), 328–39. For a discussion of the consequences for urban sociology of research findings such as those of Hunter, Fischer, and Kasarda and Janowitz see Edward G. Armstrong, "The Crisis in Urban Sociology," *South Atlantic Urban Studies,* **1** (1977), 93–115. See also Chapter 2.

mental themes of the twentieth century is a "quest for community." This quest arises from the fact that conditions in modern society do not give the individual a sense of security and fulfillment. In commenting on the modern political state, for example, Nisbet points out that

> the state does not even serve the security need. No large scale organization can really meet the psychic demand of individuals because, by its very nature, it is too large, too complex, too bureaucratized, and altogether too aloof from the residual meanings which human beings live by. *The state can enlist popular enthusiasm, can conduct crusades, can mobilize on behalf of great "causes," such as wars, but as a regular and normal means of meeting human needs for recognition, fellowship, security, and membership, it is inadequate.*[8]

In short, although modern society can offer people the miracles of mass government, mass education, mass production, and mass communications, it cannot offer them the security and belongingness that seem to accompany a sense of well-being. Hence the only alternative to the continued spread of alienation in the twentieth century is "communities small in scale but solid in structure." [9] According to Nisbet, only "they and they alone can be the beginning of social reconstruction because they respond, at the grass roots, to fundamental human desires: living together, working together, experiencing together, being together." [10]

Baker Brownell adopts much the same perspective in his discussion of the human community.[11] Although the term *community* has several shades of meaning for Brownell, it is above all the "cooperative fullness of action, the sense of belonging, the face-to-face association with people well known." [12] Thus Brownell limits *community* to a "potentially or practically face-to-face group in which a member may be easily in another's presence and where in the day-by-day comings and goings of life they may and do 'run across' each other with familiarity and without surprise." [13] On the other hand, the large bureaucratic organization, the modern state, and the sprawling metropolitan region constitute something other than "community." Human relationships in entities of this

[8] Robert A. Nisbet, "Moral Values and Community," *International Review of Community Development*, No. 5 (1960), 82. Italics added. For a more complete statement of Nisbet's thesis see his *Community and Power: A Study in the Ethics of Order and Freedom* (New York: Oxford University Press, 1962).
[9] Nisbet, "Moral Values and Community," p. 82.
[10] Ibid., p. 82.
[11] See Baker Brownell, *The Human Community: Its Philosophy and Practice for a Time of Crisis* (New York: Harper & Row, Inc., 1950).
[12] Ibid., p. 209.
[13] Ibid., p. 199.

type are, according to Brownell, of a secondary, noncommunal nature.

It is clear that Nisbet and Brownell are representatives of a great intellectual tradition that views community as a source of the security and stability that people so desperately need. Certainly it cannot be denied that their concept of community points to conditions in modern society of the utmost significance. Along with urbanization, rapid population growth, and the increasing complexity of modern society has apparently come a heightened sense of alienation and anxiety. Furthermore, the term *community* seems to be the only one that fully captures the sense of oneness for which Nisbet and Brownell so convincingly appeal. The term *shared culture* will not do the job because it is too broad. Millions on millions of people can share a culture, that is, they can share common beliefs, norms, values, and so on. On the other hand, the term *primary group* will not work either because it is too concrete. When we think of primary groups we think immediately of such things as the nuclear family, our work group, or a gang of neighborhood kids who constantly play together. Hence for some time to come those who study territorial communities will probably have to share their term with scholars who take note of the continuous search on the part of people for meaning and security in an increasingly complex world.

☐ THE COMMUNITY IN SOCIOLOGICAL PERSPECTIVE

Today most sociologists use the word *community* to refer to such units of social and territorial organization as hamlets, villages, towns, cities, and metropolitan areas. In brief, *community* refers to the places where people maintain their homes, earn their livings, rear their children, and carry on most of their life activities. Thus Hillery has found that at least three major elements enter into most sociological definitions of community, including (1) geographic area, (2) social interaction, and (3) common tie or ties.[14] Because of its basis in careful research, we shall accept Hillery's contention that a "community consist of persons in social interaction within a geographic area and having one or more additional

[14] George A. Hillery, Jr., "Definitions of Community: Areas of Agreement," *Rural Sociology,* **20** (June, 1955), 118. In a more recent survey of some 125 definitions of community, Sutton and Munson found that definitions of community have undergone some changes since Hillery published his article. Nonetheless, a majority of definitions of community, in one form or another, still stress the idea that territoriality, social interaction or social interrelations, and common ties or activities are components of community. See Willis A. Sutton, Jr., and Thomas Munson, "Definitions of Community: 1954 through 1973," paper presented to the American Sociological Association, New York, August 30, 1976.

common ties." [15] It will be noted that this definition includes a territorial variable (geographic area), a sociological variable (social interaction), and a psychocultural variable (common ties).[16] Each of these must now be elaborated on.

The Community as a Territorial Unit

Hillery's definition reminds us that communities exist in a spatial milieu. Indeed, the community has been referred to as a spatial unit, as a cluster of people living within a specific geographic area, or simply as "a place." It is, however, somewhat difficult to analyze thoroughly all facets of the spatial dimension of communities. Perhaps some progress can be made in this direction by pointing out that (1) territorial factors help to account for the location, universality, and persistence of communities and (2) community members constantly modify the territorial milieu in which they live. Both the influence of territorial variables on community life and the influence of the community on its spatial milieu must be considered.

Territory as an Independent Variable. It seems clear that territorial and geographic variables help to account for the location and growth potential of communities. Generally speaking, communities are most likely to appear at locations where rich natural resources exist or where transportation routes make permanent settlement appropriate: an especially favored site for new settlements is where resources and potentially adequate transportation routes converge, provided that there is a population base for the new community to draw on. However, two qualifications must be attached to this statement. First, whether something constitutes a "resource" depends on social and cultural definitions. The "resource" may be physical (oil, water, and so on), recreational, climatic, or agricultural. Second, regardless of the resource potential of an area, neither will a new community appear nor an old one grow unless adequate transportation routes are present or can be developed. At the same time the transportation and community growth relationship has many of the features of the chicken or the egg dilemma. Accessibility is a major variable affecting the emergence of communities, but as communities grow, the transportation routes that link them to the outside world are constantly improved.

It is also clear that territorial and geographic factors help to explain

[15] Ibid., p. 11.
[16] Reiss includes essentially the same elements in his definition of community. See Albert J. Reiss, "The Sociological Study of Communities," *Rural Sociology*, **24** (June, 1959), 118.

the universality, growth, and persistence of communities. Although people have achieved much, they must still meet most of their needs in a local area. Modern transportation has made it possible to eat breakfast in New York City and dinner in Los Angeles. Yet during a more extended period of time the individual must work, eat, sleep, and acquire goods and services in a severely delimited area. The clustering of people in increasingly large communities was also a by-product of the industrial revolution and the development of modern economies (see Chapter 9). Industry must have a large, conveniently located pool of labor to draw on, and a modern economy needs large numbers of people to work in its banks, stores, hotels, governmental agencies, and so on. In short, communities appeared because human beings cannot transcend space. They also appeared because the satisfaction of people's social and psychological needs involves "nearness." According to Kingsley Davis, "it is no accident that people cluster together. Nearness facilitates contact, furnishes protection, and makes easier the organization and integration of the group." [17]

Territory as a Dependent Variable. Although territorial variables influence the location and growth dynamics of communities, the way in which people adjust and adapt to their territorial milieu still depends a great deal on their cultural heritage and technical know-how. Terrain is malleable and may be modified by direct action or as a latent consequence of other activities. Thus deserts have been made to bloom and brush-covered mountainsides have been converted into plush residential areas. In fact, the development of modern construction equipment has made it less necessary for people to choose their territorial milieu with care and more possible for them to shape diverse physical environments to meet their needs. Unfortunately, it has also made it possible for them to devastate timberland, gut mountain chains, and pollute air and water supplies. Because of people's apparent willingness and capacity to destroy their own physical environment, during recent years we have seen a countering upsurge of interest in improving the environment and in preserving natural resources.

Of even more importance are the many ways in which local territories have been modified as a latent consequence of laws and values. It is clear, for example, that both laws and values have influenced patterns of land settlement in the United States. Generally speaking, the United States has been settled along "isolated farmstead" lines, with its corollary, the village trade center. The dominance of this pattern of land settlement can be partly explained by the American pioneers' emphasis on in-

[17] Kingsley Davis, *Human Society* (New York: Macmillan Publishing Co., Inc., 1948), p. 311.

dividualism and partly by the Quadrangular Survey and Homestead Acts.[18] However, a value system unique to the Latter-Day Saints (Mormons) led to the emergence of the village pattern of land settlement in Utah and in scattered parts of Arizona, New Mexico, Idaho, and Alberta, Canada.[19] In Utah in particular, farmers live in small towns or even cities and commute to their outlying farmland in much the same way that someone else might commute from home to a factory or office building.

Academic Approaches to the Territorial Variable. Our comments should make it clear that territorial variables cannot be ignored in the sociological study of communities. In fact, several approaches have been used to study the community as a territorial entity. Among other things, attention has been centered on patterns of land settlement.[20] We have realized that people must live in proximity to their fellow human beings but that this need can be met in more than one way. Likewise, much research has focused on the delineation of community boundaries.[21] To several sociologists it has seemed significant to establish meaningful community boundaries and to study the ties that exist between the community and its hinterland. Finally, a rich body of theory and research has emerged that attempts to explain the "whys" and "hows" of city growth and the spatial relationships between people and their environment, their institutions, and their fellow human beings. This body of theory and research, called human ecology, is reviewed in Chapter 4 of the present text.

The Community as a Unit of Social Organization

There is equally widespread agreement that the community is a basic unit of social organization. However, even a cursory survey of the litera-

[18] Carl C. Taylor, Walter Goldschmidt, and Glen Taggart, *Patterns of Rural Settlement,* United States Department of the Interior, Bureau of Reclamation, Columbia Basin Joint Investigations Problem 10 (Washington, D.C.: U.S. Government Printing Office, 1947), p. 7.
[19] There are several good descriptions of the "Mormon village" pattern of land settlement. For example, see Lowry Nelson, *The Mormon Village: A Technique and Pattern of Land Settlement* (Salt Lake City: The University of Utah Press, 1952).
[20] See Taylor, Goldschmidt, and Taggart, *Patterns of Rural Settlement,* and Nelson, *The Mormon Village.* See also Lowry Nelson, Charles E. Ramsey, and Coolie Verner, *Community Structure and Change* (New York: Macmillan Publishing Co., Inc., 1960), pp. 33–45.
[21] About the earliest such research was that of Charles J. Galpin. See his *The Social Anatomy of an Agricultural Community* (Madison: Wisconsin Agricultural Experiment Station Bulletin 34, 1915).

11

ture suggests that there is little agreement on how best to describe the community as a sociological entity. Broadly speaking, there have been two approaches to this problem. First, the community has been viewed as a social group or, more recently, as a social system. Second, the community has been analyzed as a network of interaction. In reality, these are not two distinctly different approaches to the study of communities. Our subsequent discussion will show that they have much in common.

The Community as a Social Group. To E. T. Hiller must go the credit for suggesting that the community is one among many social groups. According to Hiller, social groups have several basic properties, including a body of members, one or more tests of membership, a collection of assigned roles, and a set of norms.[22] Presumably, all these properties are an integral part of community structure; hence it is legitimate to view the community as a social group.

Communities do possess these properties to some degree. All communities have a body of members (or a population) and demand certain things of those persons who want to enjoy full membership. Likewise, each community assigns various roles to its members and has a set of norms to which these members are expected to conform. However, if the community is to be viewed as a social group, then it must be differentiated from other types of social groups. One way to do this is to follow the lead of Reiss,[23] Lowry and Rankin,[24] and others who suggest that communities are somewhat unique in that they have a territorial dimension. To be specific, communities occupy a given area of land within which people maintain their homes, earn their livings, rear their children, and so on.

A more difficult question is whether it is scientifically profitable to view the community as a social group. Is the most to be learned about communities by treating them as a special form of social group, or should they, for purposes of analysis, be treated as distinct forms of social organization? The answer to this question depends on the leanings of the individual sociologist. On the one hand, much is to be gained by pinpointing the similarities among what may at first glance appear to be dissimilar units of social organization. The community does have something in common with other types of social groups, and these common elements should be identified. On the other hand, if we refer to the community as a social group, we may be stretching the term *social group* to the point where it loses much of its conceptual power. If both an in-

[22] E. T Hiller, "The Community as a Social Group," *American Sociological Review,* **6** (April, 1941), 189.

[23] Reiss, "The Sociological Study of Communities," p. 127.

[24] Richie P. Lowry and Robert R. Rankin, *Sociology: The Science of Society* (New York: Charles Scribner's Sons, 1969), esp. pp. 366–68.

formal gathering of two or three persons and a large metropolitan area can be referred to as social groups, then the term loses much of its usefulness for purposes of scientific communication.

Today the social group approach to community analysis has relatively few adherents. Instead, it has become fashionable to analyze the community as a social system.[25] Roland L. Warren, for example, defines the community as "that combination of social units and systems which perform the major social functions having locality relevance."[26] Although the approach to community analysis suggested by Warren is complex and multifaceted, his argument seems to be that the community is a total system consisting of smaller subsystems. These subsystems, in turn, perform the "locality-relevant" functions of socialization, social control, social participation, mutual support, and production, distribution, and consumption.[27]

In reality, the social system approach is probably most accurately viewed as a refined version of the "community as a social group" approach. Social systems, like social groups, have a body of members, a normative structure, and one or more tests of membership. In social system theory the latter take the form of geographic, psychological, and social boundaries. All of this adds up to one thing: The application of social system theory to the community does not appear to be an entirely new innovation as it might first be thought. Rather, social system theory incorporates the social group approach into a more comprehensive frame of reference.

Regardless of whether or not the social system approach to community analysis represents a major breakthrough, it does make clear the importance of the community as a unit of social organization. As we examine the hierarchy that begins with the two-person group and ends with national societies, the community emerges as the first subsystem that can potentially meet the full range of people's physiological, psychological, and social needs.[28] The small group cannot do this, nor can the nuclear family, the church, the government, or a voluntary association. This may well be what Robert M. MacIver had in mind when he said that

[25] For example, see Roland L. Warren, *The Community in America*, 2nd ed. (Chicago: Rand McNally & Company, 1972); Irwin T. Sanders, *The Community*, 3rd ed. (New York: The Ronald Press, 1975), esp. Part III; Frederick L. Bates and Lloyd Bacon, "The Community as a Social System," *Social Forces*, 50 (March, 1952), 371–79; John E. Bebout and Harry C. Bredmeier, "American Cities as Social Systems," *American Institute of Planners Journal*, 29 (May, 1963), 64–76.

[26] Ibid., p. 9.

[27] Ibid., pp. 9–10.

[28] This perspective on the community was first brought to the author's attention in an article by Conrad M. Arensberg. See Conrad M. Arensberg, "The Community as Object and as Sample," *American Anthropologist*, 63 (April, 1961), 241–61.

Any circle of people who live together, who belong together so that they share not this or that particular interest, but a whole set of interests wide enough and complete enough to include their lives, is a community. . . . The mark of a community is that one's life may be lived wholly within it, that all one's relationships may be found within it.[29]

Although this fullness of scope is seldom found in modern American communities, it is the rule in many primitive communities. Furthermore, although it might prove stifling, many Americans can potentially meet all of their basic needs in their home community. This is not true of any social unit of less complexity than the community.[30]

The Community as a Network of Interaction. As an alternative to the social system approach, some writers prefer to view the community as a network of interaction. Before we examine the interactional approach, two things should be noted. First, the social system and interactional approaches are not discrete, distinct ways of analyzing the community. Rather, they have much in common. As a matter of fact, the chief point of articulation between the two approaches lies in the postulate that interaction occurs not only between individuals but also between groups and institutions. Second, a distinction must be made between the approach that views the community as a network of interaction and what is known as community action theory. Interaction is, of course, a rather standard conceptual tool in sociology, and it is quite understandable that sociologists use it in their efforts to analyze the community. On the other hand, community action theory seeks to distinguish activities that are communal in nature from those that are not.[31] Quite often, community action theorists have the explicit goal of shedding light on the dynamics of planned community change and development. Thus a leading writer on community action concludes one of his discussions by stating that his concern has been "with the development of theory which would support research that would contribute effectively to the growing community organization and development movement." [32]

With these comments in mind, we can examine the community as a

[29] Robert M. MacIver, *Society: Its Structure and Changes* (New York: Ray Long & Richard R. Smith, Inc., 1931), p. 9.

[30] Some persons, of course, may spend their entire lives in "total institutions." This is possible, however, only because others, in this case the staff, play roles that link the institution to the larger community.

[31] See Willis A. Sutton, Jr., "Toward a Universe of Community Actions," *Sociological Inquiry*, 34 (Winter, 1964), 48–59. For a more detailed examination of community action theory see Chapter 8.

[32] Harold F. Kaufman, "Toward an Interactional Conception of Community," *Social Forces*, 38 (October, 1959), 17.

network of interaction. One of the chief problems inherent in the interactional approach to community analysis is that conditions in the modern community do not completely square with the definitions of interaction accepted by most sociologists. In brief, interaction is usually defined as a face-to-face encounter between two or more people in which each person takes the other into account. Obviously the involvement of every member of the community in a network of interaction of this type never occurs, except perhaps in the smallest rural hamlet. In most communities the number of actors (i.e., large population) and a lack of common interests prevent such contact from occurring.

Those who view the community as a network of interaction attempt to overcome this conceptual problem in one of two ways. As we noted before, one solution is to maintain not only that individuals interact but also that interaction occurs among the various groups and institutions of which the community is composed. Those who take this position usually view the community as a chain of input-output relationships in which each subsystem receives needed inputs from other subsystems and, in turn, contributes to the other subsystems and to the total community system. These inputs and outputs may take the form of financial contributions, physical resources, social pressures, a labor force, and so forth.[33] Likewise, those who view the community as a network of interacting subsystems often refer to the community's horizontal and vertical axes. The horizontal axis "involves the relationship of individual to individual or of group to group within the locality," whereas the vertical axis "involves the relationship of the individual to a local interest group and of that interest group to a regional, state, or national organization." [34] This is simply a shorthand way of indicating that interaction can occur between two social units that occupy a similar level in the total community system or between two social units one of which is more inclusive than the other.

An insightful analysis of networks of interaction at the community level has been developed by Norton E. Long.[35] Basically, Long compares interaction at the community level to a series of games. He tells us, for example, that "in the territorial system there is a political game, a banking game, a contracting game, a newspaper game, a civic organization game, an ecclesiastical game, and many others." [36] Furthermore, even

---

[33] Warren, *The Community in America*, pp. 193–94.
[34] Roland L. Warren, "Toward a Reformulation of Community Theory," *Human Organization*, **15** (Summer, 1956), 8.
[35] See Norton E. Long, "The Local Community as an Ecology of Games," in Roland L. Warren, *New Perspectives on the American Community: A Book of Readings*, 3rd ed. (Chicago: Rand McNally & Company, 1977), pp. 58–74.
[36] Ibid., p. 60.

though all these game players are pursuing their own goals, Long maintains that the "ecology of games in the local territorial system accomplishes unplanned but largely functional results." [37] For example, politicians, bankers, and contractors may each be pursuing different goals when they push for the development of a new suburban residential area. Yet, as a result of their interaction and the games that they play, the housing needs of the community may be more adequately met.

Morris Freilich has also analyzed networks of interaction in his efforts to identify communities.[38] Basically, Freilich conceives of communities as consisting of a series of centers where people congregate. For example, in a large urban slum, there may be certain bars, churches, and other meeting places where local people gather. However, as one moves outward from these centers one gradually finds that people do not frequent the first set of centers but go in another direction to another set of centers. This amorphous line, Freilich implies, represents the boundaries of the community.[39] The fact that there are centers of interaction in each community means that members of the community, to some extent, develop a subculture and a specialized body of information and knowledge.

There is at least one major advantage in viewing the community as a network of interaction: It serves well as a tool by which to describe systematically the interrelationships of the various units that compose the community. This alone can help increase our understanding of community structure and process.

There have, of course, been other approaches to analyzing the community as a network of interaction. For example, it has been pointed out that interaction at the community level often displays characteristic themes and patterns. When these become generalized to the point that they are characteristic of the interaction of both individuals and groups, they are referred to as the basic social processes. The basic social processes are cooperation, competition, and conflict. The subprocesses by which cooperation is furthered and competition and conflict are mitigated are accommodation, amalgamation, and assimilation. Those who use these concepts to analyze the American community are heavily in debt to the pioneering work of Park and Burgess, in which the significance of the social processes was made clear.[40]

---

[37] Ibid., p. 62.
[38] Freilich, "Toward an Operational Definition of Community," pp. 117–27.
[39] It should be noted that Freilich, like Suttles (see footnote 3), uses the term *community* in a somewhat different sense than used in this book. Thus, in Freilich's thinking, even a large slum might contain a number of different communities.
[40] Robert E. Park and Ernest W. Burgess, *Introduction to the Science of Sociology* (Chicago: University of Chicago Press, 1921).

To be more specific, it has been suggested many times that the American community is an arena of competition and that competition is the key to progress at both the local and the national level. Similarly, it has become rather common to view the American community as an arena of conflict, and a number of studies have focused on specific instances of community conflict (see Chapter 7). However, those who study communities in terms of the social processes often overlook the central role of cooperation in community life. In actuality, it is only because people cooperate with each other that viable communities are maintained. This follows from the fact that conflict can become costly and dysfunctional for the community system whereas competition does not always lead to the solution of basic community problems. Whenever competition or conflict is encountered, further exploration usually reveals an underlying dimension of cooperation. In even the most conflict-ridden communities most people still cooperate with the police, still support their churches and schools, and still subscribe to basic social norms. Likewise, competition rarely occurs in raw, cutthroat form. In the final analysis, competition is an essentially cooperative process in which the parties to the interaction agree on which goals to compete for and on the ways by which these goals may be legitimately achieved.

The study of villages, cities, and metropolitan areas in terms of cooperation, competition, and conflict can yield significant insight into the sociological dimensions of community life. Among other things, it forces one to explore the very basis on which communities rest: Cooperation is seemingly the fundamental theme underlying all other social processes at the community level. Furthermore, the "social processes" approach provides a useful tool for analyzing the dynamics of any given community. Social relationships in some communities may be of a cooperative nature, whereas in other communities competition or even conflict may reign. For example, it would not be surprising to find that there is more internal conflict in a lower-class urban slum or ghetto that is populated by people of all races, ethnic backgrounds, and religions than in an affluent retirement community located in Arizona or Florida. In many cases, however, these three processes are so interwoven that it is meaningless to characterize the community as being an arena of cooperation, competition, or conflict. All three processes are present in varying degrees.

Miscellaneous Approaches. In addition to these general approaches, there are more specialized approaches that have been used to analyze communities. Two of these require brief mention. First, a number of books and articles have focused on social class at the community level, and, indeed, among the most widely hailed community studies are those concerned chiefly with local stratification systems.[41] For the most part, these studies have not led to a comprehensive theory of community structure and process. Rather, their authors have sought insight into a phenomenon that has national as well as local dimensions. Second, during recent years students of community life have developed a keen interest in community power and in the processes by which decisions are made at the local level.[42] Although some of these studies are both insightful and interesting, a theory of community that has power as its key variable has yet to be developed. For the most part, the frequently heated debates concerning community power have centered around methodological rather than theoretical questions.[43]

The Community as a Psychocultural Unit

The third element in many sociological definitions of community stresses the idea that there are common ties or bonds among community members. As a matter of fact, sociologists have not been totally insensitive to the dimensions of community explored in depth by Nisbet, Brownell, and others. However, sociologists of an empirical bent do insist that common ties and bonds are but one aspect of the complex reality subsumed under the term *community*. To their way of thinking, the term should be used only to refer to those units of social organization that have a territorial dimension.

[41] Among the best-known studies are Allison Davis and Burleigh Gardner, *Deep South* (Chicago: University of Chicago Press, 1941); John Dollard, *Class and Caste in a Southern Town* (New Haven: Yale University Press, 1937); A. B. Hollinghead, *Elmtown's Youth* (New York: John Wiley & Sons, 1949); W. Lloyd Warner and associates, *Democracy in Jonesville* (New York: Harper & Row, Inc., 1949); W. Lloyd Warner and Paul S. Lunt, *The Social Life of a Modern Community* (New Haven: Yale University Press, 1946).

[42] One of the best-known accounts of a community power structure was made by Robert S. and Helen M. Lynd in their *Middletown in Transition: A Study in Cultural Conflicts* (New York: Harcourt Brace Jovanovich, Inc., 1937), Chapter 3. Another well-known study is Floyd Hunter's *Community Power Structure: A Study of Decision Makers* (Chapel Hill: University of North Carolina Press, 1953).

[43] For a sampling of this literature see William V. D'Antonio and Eugene E. Ericksen, "The Reputational Technique as a Measure of Community Power: An Evaluation Based on Comparative and Longitudinal Studies," *American Sociological Review,* 27 (June, 1962), 362–76; M. Herbert Danzgar, "Community Power Structure: Problems and Continuities," *American Sociological Review,* 29 (October, 1964), 707–17; Nelson W. Polsby, "Three Problems in the Analysis of Community Power," *American Sociological Review,* 24 (December, 1959), 796–802; John Walton, "Substance and Artifact: The Current Status of Research on Community Power Structure," *American Journal of Sociology,* 71 (January, 1966), 430–38; Raymond E. Wolfinger, "Reputation and Reality in the Study of Community Power," *American Sociological Review,* 25 (October, 1960), 363–44.

There is little agreement as to whether these common ties are psychological or cultural. Roland L. Warren suggests that the degree to which persons psychologically identify with local social systems varies from community to community,[44] whereas Irwin T. Sanders devotes a chapter of his text to a discussion of community traditions and values.[45] According to the psychological perspective, people gain a sense of security because they identify with their community; however, advocates of the cultural perspective maintain that this identification exists because community members share common values, norms, and goals. Both of these ideas are encompassed in the concept of community sentiment as used by MacIver and Page, that is, "an awareness of sharing a way of life as well as the common earth."[46]

The Psychocultural Dimension. Before we examine the functional consequences of community sentiment, it might be well to indicate some of its elements. As a cultural variable, community sentiment involves, first, a sharing of common values, beliefs, and goals. These may arise from many sources, especially from the historical milieu out of which the community grew.[47] These values, beliefs, and goals may of course be focused on many things. Florence Kluckhohn and Fred Strodtbeck, for example, suggest that most cultural systems have value orientations pertaining to people's relationship to nature, to the supernatural, to time, to the modality of human activity, and to other human beings.[48] Likewise, as a cultural variable, community sentiment also involves norms; that is, community members have a set of shared behavioral expectations to which they supposedly conform. As a psychological concept, community sentiment encompasses many things, including a feeling of "we-ness." Presumably, many community members think of each other as "we" and of other persons as "they." It has also been argued that whatever psychological security and stability individuals enjoy come to them by virtue of their community membership. Perhaps in an era when family names mean little and society is extremely complex, the only way that individuals can place themselves in the larger scheme of things is by claiming their identity from their home community.

[44] Warren, *The Community in America*, p. 13.
[45] Sanders, *The Community*, esp. pp. 95–104.
[46] Robert M. MacIver and Charles H. Page, *Society: An Introductory Analysis* (New York: Holt, Rinehart and Winston, 1949), p. 10.
[47] For an example of how historically rooted values can affect community structure see Walter Firey, "Sentiment and Symbolism as Ecological Variables," *American Sociological Review*, 10 (April, 1945), 140–48.
[48] Florence R. Kluckhohn and Fred L. Strodtbeck, *Variations in Value Orientation* (New York: Harper & Row, 1961), pp. 11–20.

Most of the statements in the preceding paragraph are, in the present writer's opinion, quite debatable. For one thing, few twentieth-century communities have a cultural system completely distinct from that of the larger society. Rather, people today are confronted both with cultural phenomena that originate at the local level and with those that have their origin in the larger society. Similarly, given the heterogeneity and complexity of most twentieth-century communities, particularly urban communities, it seems unlikely that their members share a great many common values originating at the local level or that they feel a close psychological identification with their community. Theoretically, the existence of common values and psychological identification should effectively stifle deviancy and disorganization, but crime, mental illness, and social unrest are among the most basic problems confronting modern communities. In sum, the inclusion of common ties and/or psychological identification in sociological definitions of community needs careful examination, qualification, and documentation. Is the modern community characterized by a set of common values and norms originating at the local level? Do most people actually identify with their community? Unfortunately, not enough empirical research has been carried out to answer these questions fully.

Consequences and Implications. Even though psychocultural variables have a questionable place in definitions of community, it might be well to indicate some of the potential consequences and implications of community sentiment for individuals and for the community as a social system.

Community sentiment potentially gives the individual something to draw on for pattern and stability in a complex world and is, theoretically, the opposite of alienation and insecurity. Yet it is entirely possible that strong community sentiment can hamper individual growth and achievement. In modern societies a high degree of commitment to one's local community may be dysfunctional for a person, for he or she must survive in a social milieu that places a premium on mobility. This may be especially true in rural areas. For example, the present writer has spent most of his teaching career at universities located in essentially rural areas. During that time he has been frustrated time and time again by bright, able students who refuse to pursue graduate degrees at major universities because they do not want to venture far away from their family, home, and community. This is probably less of a problem in major urban communities because young people have the opportunity to develop their potentials (e.g., go to graduate school) without leaving their family, friends, and community behind. In the final analysis, a high degree of community sentiment may underlie a dilemma that many people face today. Presumably, people need the security and acceptance that come from being wholly committed to an identifiable social system such as their home community, but this commitment may occasionally retard personal development and frustrate the achievement of other potentials.

The possible breakdown of community sentiment also has tremendous implications for the community itself. Certainly all communities have a crucial interest in the development of healthy, stable personalities. Crime, mental illness, divorce, and social unrest not only are personal tragedies but also entail multiple costs for the community. It might be argued that one way to avert such tragedies is to give individuals a sense of identification with their community. However, the achievement of widespread community sentiment involves a seemingly hopeless paradox. The key to psychological identification is *involvement*, that is, a willingness on the part of the individual to participate in local community affairs. At the same time, meaningful community involvement, if it develops at all, occurs only among those who readily identify with their communities. We have already questioned whether many people fall into this category.

Community sentiment also has a number of implications for social control. Indeed, community sentiment can be a powerful force that leads the individual to conform to community values, beliefs, and norms. Alan Wheelis makes this clear:

> One who lives out his life in the town of his birth derives much superego support from proximity to family and relatives, and from their continuing expectations of him. They know what kind of person he is, and they expect him to continue being that kind of person. If the culture of the community is relatively homogeneous, conscience is strengthened also by the continuing pattern of known traditions, customs, and values. Unopposed mores are not subject to critical scrutiny, but they are taken for granted. . . . Life under such conditions is orderly and predictable.[49]

Wheelis continues by pointing out that

> Probably there is no one who is not more liable to steal, to lie, or commit adultery in a foreign land than at home. Some persons, indeed, travel for just this purpose—to lose an unwanted reinforcement of conscience. For them wanderlust is not a lust for wandering, but a wandering for lust—an effort to achieve abroad a license for which one could not forgive himself at home. Many persons do not need to go far: the annual business convention in America is notorious in this respect. Things happen in motels that do not happen in homes, and towels are swiped in distant hotels by persons who would not steal a pin in their own home

[49] Alan Wheelis, *The Quest for Identity* (New York: W. W. Norton & Company, Inc., 1958), p. 100.

towns. In these ways our increased mobility diminishes the external support for conscience.[50]

It should be clear that Wheelis grossly overstates the case. Most Americans are not so poorly socialized that they cannot wait to leave their home communities so that they can steal, go on drunken binges, and commit atrocities! Nonetheless, Wheelis makes the interrelationship of common values, psychological identification, and social control so clear that further comment is unnecessary.

Community and The Community

We have seen that the word *community* has been used in a variety of different ways: It has been used to refer to social groups, total institutions, and neighborhoods; it has been used in a philosophical sense, and, of course, it has been used as a generic term that includes villages, cities, and metropolitan areas. Furthermore, each usage of *community* that we have described in this chapter can be defended by its user. For example, students and their professors interact with each other to pursue common goals, and a sense of unity and cohesiveness develops between them. Hence the phrase *academic community* has been coined.

Yet we have argued that the use of a term in so many different ways can be confusing. Jessie Bernard has suggested one way to resolve this dilemma.[51] She suggests that we use the word *community* to refer to the common ties and esprit de corps that can develop among people in diverse settings. Thus we can refer to scientific communities, academic communities, prison communities, and so on. On the other hand, Bernard suggests that the term *the community* be reserved for those units of social organization that have a territorial dimension. For example, if we saw a book entitled *The Community* we would know that it deals with hamlets, villages, towns, cities, and so on. In this book we are more concerned with *the* community than with community.

☐ SUMMARY

In this chapter we have indicated some of the different ways in which the term *community* has been used. At times, it is used to refer to social groups, total institutions, neighborhoods, and so forth. The term *com-*

[50] Ibid., p. 101.
[51] See Jessie Bernard, *The Sociology of Community* (Glenview, Ill.: Scott, Foresman and Company, 1973), 3–5.

munity has also been adopted by some writers to refer to the condition in which people enjoy meaningful fellowship with other people. These writers are, of course, concerned with matters of the highest significance, and *community* seems to be the only term that fully encompasses the condition for which Nisbet, Brownell, and others so forcefully appeal. Finally, *community* has been used as a generic term to encompass those units of social and territorial organization that, depending on their size, may also be called hamlets, villages, towns, cities, or metropolitan areas. It should be clear that the present writer's interest is in the analysis of these units.

We have also attempted to present an analysis of the term *community* as it is used in this book. That many sociologists agree on the inclusion of geographic area, social interaction, and common ties in definitions of the term need not be demonstrated. This has already been done by Hillery, Sutton and Munson, and others. However, the validity of including these elements in definitions of the community does require exploration, especially in light of the fact that sociologists have experienced difficulty in differentiating the community from other units of social organization. Although some of the statements made in this chapter are tentative, the following observations seem to be warranted:

1. The community differs from other units of social organization in that it has a firm territorial base. Above all, the community represents an organizational pattern through which persons meet their daily needs in a local area. This is perhaps the major criterion by which the community can be delineated from other units of social organization. Although it is true that families, churches, schools, and so forth, exist in a territorial milieu, we do not usually think of them as units of territorial organization. Rather they are a part of a larger territorial unit, the community, that is potentially able to meet the full range of people's physiological, psychological, and social needs.

2. Although there is some disagreement concerning the best way to describe the community as a unit of social organization, there is no question that the community must be analyzed in terms of interaction, as a social group, or as a social system. The community consists of people in interaction with other people. This implies that communities do have definite patterns of social organization. Furthermore, the community is a rather unique form of social organization, again because it is potentially able to meet the full range of people's needs. Families meet some needs, as do churches, governments, and schools, but none of these institutions can simultaneously provide people with food, clothing, and shelter, with a marriage partner, with a sense of belonging, with intellectual stimulation, and so on through the seemingly endless list of human wants. In

the hierarchy of social organization the community emerges as the first social unit that can claim such all-inclusiveness as a needs-meeting facility.

3. For the sake of agreement with other sociologists it would be desirable if we could argue that the community is a basic unit with which people identify and from which they gain a sense of security and belonging. However, the preceding discussion suggests that this may not be the case. The contention that members of the modern community share common ties and bonds needs to be carefully examined. If these ties and bonds do exist, we have been seriously misled by many, many scholars who claim that people in the twentieth century are alienated, frustrated, and alone.[52] Nonetheless, it would seem quite safe to suggest that the common ties that bind people together at the community level have been weakened and that the answer to many of our problems is to try to strengthen whatever common ties that still do exist at the local level.

BIBLIOGRAPHY

Baltzell, E. Digby. *The Search for Community in Modern America.* New York: Harper & Row, 1968.

Bates, Frederick L., and Lloyd Bacon. "The Community as a Social System," *Social Forces,* **50** (March, 1972), 371–79.

Bernard, Jessie. *The Sociology of Community.* Glenview, Ill.: Scott, Foresman and Company, 1973.

Brownell, Baker. *The Human Community: Its Philosophy and Practice for a Time of Crisis.* New York: Harper & Row, 1950.

Dewors, Richard E. "Explanation of Community Persistence and Change as a Form of Symbolic Interaction," *International Review of Sociology,* **7** (August, 1971), 787–819.

Effrat, Marcia Pelly. "Approaches to Community: Conflicts and Complementaries," *Sociological Inquiry,* **43** (1973), 1–32.

Fischer, Claude S. "On Urban Alienation and Anomie: Powerlessness and Social Isolation," *American Sociological Review,* **38** (June, 1973), 311–26.

Freilich, Morris. "Toward an Operational Definition of Community," *Rural Sociology,* **28** (June, 1963), 117–27.

Hiller, E. T. "The Community as a Social Group," *American Sociological Review,* **6** (April, 1941), 189–202.

Hillery, George A., Jr. "Definitions of Community: Areas of Agreement," *Rural Sociology,* **20** (June, 1955), 111–23.

———. "Selected Issues in Community Theory," *Rural Sociology,* **37** (December, 1972), 534–52.

[52] See footnote 7.

————. "Villages, Cities, and Total Institutions," *American Sociological Review*, **28** (October, 1963), 779–91.

Hunter, Albert. "The Loss of Community: An Empirical Test Through Replication," *American Sociological Review*, **40** (October, 1975), 537–52.

Kasarda, John D., and Morris Janowitz. "Community Attachment in Mass Society," *American Sociological Review*, **39** (June, 1974), 328–39.

Long, Norton E. "The Local Community as an Ecology of Games," in Roland L. Warren (ed.), *New Perspectives on the American Community: A Book of Readings*, 3d ed. Chicago: Rand McNally & Company, 1977, 58–74.

Minar, David W., and Scott Greer (eds.). *The Concept of Community.* Chicago: Aldine Publishing Company, 1969.

Nelson, Lowry. *The Mormon Villages: A Technique and Pattern of Land Settlement.* Salt Lake City: The University of Utah Press, 1952.

Nisbet, Robert A. *Community and Power: A Study in the Ethics of Order and Freedom.* New York: Oxford University Press, 1962.

————. "Moral Values and Community," *International Review of Community Development*, **5** (1960), 77–85.

Reiss, Albert J. "The Sociological Study of Communities," *Rural Sociology*, **24** (June, 1959), 118–30.

Sanders, Irwin T. *The Community*, 3rd ed. New York: The Ronald Press, 1975.

Schnore, Leo R. "The Community," in Neil J. Smelser (ed.), *Sociology: An Introduction.* New York: John Wiley & Sons, 1967.

Suttles, Gerald D. *The Social Construction of Communities.* Chicago: University of Chicago Press, 1972.

————. *The Social Order of the Slum: Ethnicity and Territory in the Inner City.* Chicago: University of Chicago Press, 1968.

Sutton, Willis A., Jr., and Thomas Munson. "Definitions of Community: 1954 through 1973." Paper presented to the American Sociological Association, New York, August 30, 1976.

Warren, Roland L. *The Community in America*, 2nd ed. Chicago: Rand McNally & Company, 1972.

————. "Toward a Reformulation of Community Theory," *Human Organization*, **15** (Summer, 1956), 8–11.

CHAPTER 2

□ □ □ □ □ □ □ □ □
□
□
□
□
□
□
□
□
□
□

Major Community Types

We have faced the task of indicating what we shall mean by the term *community*. In essence, we have said that a community is a unit of social and territorial organization in which people live, work, attend church and school, and carry on a host of other activities that are a part of daily living. Indeed, communities are unique in that they are linked to the larger society in such a way that all of a person's needs can potentially be met within them. At the same time, it is apparent that communities differ greatly from one another. Thus both Houston and New Deal have at least one thing in common: They are both communities in the state of Texas. Yet the differences between Houston and New Deal appear to be much more significant than their similarities. The same is true of Los Angeles and Pumpkin Center, California, or Louisville and Possum Trot, Kentucky. Hence in this chapter we must take a close look at major community types.

□ RURAL AND URBAN COMMUNITIES: A SURVEY OF DIFFERENCES

In this chapter we should be able to derive a scheme for classifying communities by type that is simple, theoretically relevant, and unambiguous. Unfortunately, this is probably impossible. For one thing, there are literally hundreds of variables that could be used to differentiate among types of communities.[1] We could, for example, classify com-

[1] In a highly sophisticated piece of research using factor analysis, Christen D. Jonassen has isolated seven factors that systematically differentiate among types of communities. For a description of these factors see Christen D. Jonassen, "Functional Unities in Eighty-eight Community Systems," *American Sociological Review*, 26

munities according to the size and density of their population, their ecological characteristics, their legal status, their sociocultural characteristics, or their predominant economic activity. Furthermore, there is no foolproof way to decide whether the variables we might choose to distinguish among types of communities are meaningful and important. Other variables might do the job better. To make matters even worse, if a combination of two or more variables was used to distinguish among types of communities there would be no guarantee that they would correlate with one another: on one variable community A might be urban whereas on other variables it might be rural. Nonetheless, in this chapter we shall attempt to derive a tentative classification of types of communities. In so doing, we shall examine some of the chief differences between rural and urban communities and look rather closely at the metropolitan area and the communities drawn into its orbit. A good place to begin is by examining some of the demographic differences between rural and urban communities.

Demographic Differences

Population size is often cited as one of the most important differences between rural and urban communities. There are several advantages to differentiating among types of communities on the basis of this variable, including the fact that accurate data on population size are readily available in many countries. Moreover, population size sometimes has a profound effect on other facets of community life.[2] Within a given culture, we can often make some crude hypotheses about the nature of a community by simply knowing the number of people who live there. It is, however, extremely risky to do this when one is conducting cross-cultural research. A community with 20,000 population located in an underdeveloped country may be much more rural than a community

---

(June, 1961), 399–407. Likewise, Frank D. Alexander has suggested that locality groups, or communities, should be classified in terms of the number of services they provide and the degree to which residents identify with the locality ("group identification"). Presumably, urban areas would be characterized by a high service rating and a low group identification score. See Frank D. Alexander, "The Problem of Locality-Group Classification," *Rural Sociology,* 17 (September, 1952), 236–44.

2 For example, Mayhew and Levinger's work strongly suggests that there is a direct and meaningful relationship between violence and the size of a community: the larger the community, the higher the rate of violent crime. Their work also suggests a direct relationship between population size and other community-related phenomena. See Bruce H. Mayhew and Roger L. Levinger, "Size and Density of Interaction in Human Aggregates," *American Journal of Sociology,* 82 (July, 1976), 86–110.

of 10,000 population located within the United States.[3] This suggests of course that there are difficulties associated with the use of population size in classifying communities as rural or urban. For one thing, it cannot be assumed that population size always correlates with the more complex cluster of traits implied by the terms *rural* and *urban*.[4] In the final analysis, these broad rural-urban differentials must be built into an adequate classification of communities. Likewise, on the surface it might appear that the use of population size in differentiating among types of communities would involve no methodological problems. This is partially true in the United States, where the Bureau of the Census has, to some extent, devised standardized techniques for enumerating community populations. On the other hand, the dangers of making international comparisons of communities on the basis of population size are great. Gibbs and Davis, for example, point out that "there is no assurance that persons included as city residents in one country are not excluded in other countries, and vice-versa." [5] Furthermore, they suggest that "even within the same country there may be little uniformity from one province or state to another or from one city to another in drawing the urban boundaries." [6] Even in the United States this can become a problem because some communities are underbounded, others overbounded, and yet others bounded in a realistic manner.

Another major difficulty inherent in differentiating among types of communities on the basis of population size is that communities fall along a continuum in terms of this variable. Hence the choice of cutting points between rural and urban communities is arbitrary. For research personnel in the United States, 2,500 and 50,000 constitute the most familiar cutting points. The United States Bureau of the Census uses a population of 2,500 as the basic figure for differentiating between

---

[3] Because of this, Gideon Sjoberg tells us that "in practice it is difficult, if not impossible, in cross-cultural research to take size as the sole criterion of what is urban. It is evident, for instance, that communities of say, 5,000, differ considerably in India, Mexico, and the United States, and any analysis predicated on size alone is a poor one. . . . In other words, it is often essential to specify the social conditions under which size is taken as the criterion for urban centers." Gideon Sjoberg, "Theory and Research in Urban Sociology," in Philip M. Hauser and Leo F. Schnore (eds.), *The Study of Urbanization* (New York: John Wiley & Sons, Inc., 1965), p. 164.

[4] See Otis Dudley Duncan, "Community Size and the Rural-Urban Continuum," in Paul K. Hatt and Albert J. Reiss, Jr. (eds.), *Cities and Society* (New York: The Free Press, 1957), pp. 35–45; Richard Dewey, "The Rural-Urban Continuum: Real but Relatively Unimportant," *American Journal of Sociology,* **66** (July, 1960), 60–66; Hauser and Schnore, *The Study of Urbanization,* esp. p. 511.

[5] Jack P. Gibbs and Kingsley Davis, "Conventional Versus Metropolitan Data in the International Study of Urbanization," *American Sociological Review,* **23** (October, 1958), 505.

[6] Ibid.

rural and urban territories, and the concept of Standard Metropolitan Statistical Area as defined by the same agency hinges on the requirement that the community in question have a central city of at least 50,000 inhabitants. However, it has been argued that both the rural-urban and the metropolitan cutting points are unrealistically low. At a later point in this chapter we shall examine these arguments.

Another index of rurality or urbanity frequently used is the ratio of population to land area (i.e., population density). Some years ago Louis Wirth argued that density of population has a profound impact on community structure,[7] and more recently Smith and Zopf have argued that "differences in the density of population color many important features of rural and urban life."[8] Again, however, it cannot be assumed that population density always correlates with degrees of "rurality" or "urbanity" or, for that matter, with size of population. A high population density, like a large population size, does not necessarily mean that the members of the community are "urbane" in their attitudes and behavior. Kingsley Davis is undoubtedly correct when he points out that

> A hundred people may happen to live very close together, separated by open country from other dense settlements, but the place would ordinarily be called a "hamlet" or "village" rather than a town or city. To qualify as an urban place in the eyes of most observers, a settlement would have to embrace a more substantial population and a larger area. In other words, we implicitly recognize not only the factor of density but also the absolute population and the absolute area.[9]

The researcher who uses population density to differentiate between rural and urban communities must bear two things in mind. First, even though population density may be a satisfactory measure of urbanity in the developed countries, it is not in the underdeveloped world. In many of the emerging nations population densities are extremely high in essentially rural, agricultural areas.[10] Second, if population density is used as a measure of urbanity, it must always be in conjunction with population size or some other variable. Otherwise, data on population density tell us nothing about the community. There are also methodological problems entailed in the use of population density as a device for

---

[7] See Louis Wirth, "Urbanism as a Way of Life," *American Journal of Sociology*, 44 (July, 1938), 14–16.

[8] T. Lynn Smith and Paul E. Zopf, Jr., *Principles of Inductive Rural Sociology* (Philadelphia: J. A. Davis Company, 1970), p. 26.

[9] In Jack P. Gibbs, *Urban Research Methods* (New York: Van Nostrand Reinhold, 1961), p. xvii.

[10] For one example see Joel M. Halpern, *The Changing Village Community* (Englewood Cliffs, N.J.: Prentice-Hall, Inc., 1967), pp. 83–86.

differentiating among types of communities. For example, the population density of an underbounded community should not be compared with that of another community whose boundaries extend far into the adjacent rural territory.

Ecological Differences: The Community and Its Hinterland

Several writers have suggested that cities and metropolitan areas could not emerge until working relationships were established between the community and its hinterland.[11] Among other things, the urbanite has always had to obtain food, fuel, and fiber from the hinterland population. More recently, the urbanite has had to look to the hinterland for choice residential sites, and commercial and business ventures on the scale that we find them in the modern urban community can thrive only if they get the trade of persons who live far out in the hinterland. This suggests that a second major difference between rural and urban communities lies in the nature of their hinterlands. Generally speaking, rural communities have hinterlands that are small and underdeveloped whereas urban communities have large, well-developed hinterlands. In fact, this may be one of the most accurate ways of distinguishing between rural and urban communities.

Hinterlands may be conceptualized in several ways. One possibility is to conceive of hinterlands in demographic and ecological terms, which involves an inquiry into the number of inhabitants in the territory surrounding a community and into the size and shape of this territory. However, it is nonsensical to delineate a hinterland of this type unless the inhabitants of the territory have viable relationships with the community in question. These relationships may be of various kinds. First, they may entail exchange between the community and the surrounding territory. This exchange may be manifested in periodic shopping trips to the community center, visits to friends who live in the community center, and the utilization of community-based facilities by the hinterland population. Second, the community-hinterland relationship may involve economic ties. Indeed, the traditional concept of *hinterland* implies economic interdependency between a city with its commerce and industry and the agricultural hinterland. Finally, the hinterland can be delineated in terms of patterns of influence. With the emergence of mass media of communication the urban community can, and often does, influence a vast geographic area, at least in terms of shaping values, opinions, attitudes, and knowledge.

It is no easy task to measure the size and degree of development of

[11] See, for example, Hauser and Schnore, *The Study of Urbanization*, p. 2.

a community's hinterland, and one must keep his or her definition of hinterland constant from community to community. One way to meet the latter requirement is through the use of Hawley's concepts of primary, secondary, and tertiary community areas.[12] The primary community area is the relatively small area that surrounds the central community. Its residents work, purchase groceries, and meet other recurrent needs in the central community. It seems safe to assume that all U.S. communities have primary areas, although their nature depends partly on the size of the community: the primary area associated with a rural community is often sparsely settled and accessible only by poor roads, whereas the primary area of a large city may be densely settled and crisscrossed by freeways running in all directions. On the other hand, small rural communities simply do not have secondary and tertiary areas. Basically, a secondary community area is one in which the exchange between the community center and the hinterland occurs on a sporadic, irregular basis and pertains to "the retail purchase of durable goods, wholesale distribution, specialized medical, legal, and financial services, rare forms of entertainment, etc."[13] More often than not, the rural community lacks a highly developed secondary area and is instead located within the secondary area of a more urban community. Finally, a tertiary community area is found only in conjunction with the most metropolitan of communities. Quite often these communities perform specialized services for an extremely large hinterland or tertiary area. For instance, Hawley points out that "Chicago is the transportation hub and the livestock market for the whole of the United States; New York and London are the world's financial centers; and Hollywood, New York, and Paris are fashion centers for the world."[14]

It would seem that the presence or absence of a highly developed secondary area surrounding the community center constitutes an excellent basis for distinguishing between rural and urban communities, especially in cultural areas where emphasis is placed on trade and commerce. If a particular community serves as a retail, financial, wholesale, medical, and legal center for a large area, we would undoubtedly think of it as urban regardless of its size or density of population. During recent years urban geographers, under the leadership of Walter Cristaller, have apparently arrived at essentially the same conclusion. In reference to the work of these urban geographers in classifying communities by type, Raymond Murphy points out that "most of these studies, like

[12] Amos H. Hawley, *Human Ecology: A Theory of Community Structure* (New York: The Ronald Press Company, 1950), pp. 255–58. Hawley's concept of *Community area* and our concept of *hinterland* appear to be identical.
[13] Ibid., p. 256.
[14] Ibid., p. 257.

Cristaller's theoretical one, are based on the idea that the services a city performs for the surrounding area—its central services—rather than its size or governmental status should determine its position in the [rural-urban] hierarchy." [15] This is simply another way of saying that an urban community is one that has a highly developed secondary area.

Sociocultural Differences

When people ask whether a community is rural or urban, they are partly interested in its size and the density of its population. However, they are probably more interested in the life-styles of its residents, how they earn their livings, how they relate to each other, and so on. In short, what are the social and cultural characteristics of the community?

There have been many analyses of social and cultural differences between rural and urban communities, some of them rather elaborate. Agreement is rather widespread that there are at least five major sociocultural differences between rural and urban communities.

First, a number of writers have suggested that the urbanite enjoys more anonymity than the ruralite.[16] By going downtown, to an amusement park, or to a theater, for example, the urbanite can completely escape the scrutiny of family and friends. Sometimes a person may live in an apartment house for years and never get acquainted with his or her nextdoor neighbor. On the other hand, rural dwellers are known by most of the other members of their community. In order to escape the scrutiny of family and neighbors rural dwellers may have to leave their hamlet, village, or town.

Second, there are definite differences in the occupational structure of rural and urban communities. To be specific, urban areas are characterized by a high division of labor.[17] Thus in a rural community considerably over one half of the labor force may be engaged in farming or selling goods and services to the farm population, whereas in the city people are literally employed in thousands of different occupations and only a fraction of the total labor force is engaged in any one occupation. Richard Dewey puts it well when he says that "whereas a small rural

[15] Raymond E. Murphy, *The American City: An Urban Geography* (New York: McGraw-Hill Book Company, 1966), pp. 83–84.

[16] For example, see Wirth, "Urbanism as a Way of Life," esp. pp. 10–14; Stanley Milgram, "The Experience of Living in Cities," *Science,* **167** (March, 1970), 1464; Dewey, "The Rural-Urban Continuum," p. 65.

[17] See Emile Durkheim, *The Division of Labor in Society* (New York: The Free Press, 1964), esp. pp. 256–82; Georg Simmel, "The Metropolis and Mental Life," in Roland L. Warren (ed.), *New Perspectives on the American Community: A Book of Readings,* 3rd ed. (Chicago: Rand McNally & Company, 1977), esp. pp. 41–42; Dewey, "The Rural-Urban Continuum," p. 65.

community can present an undifferentiated occupational pattern, a city of a million most certainly cannot. Great complexity in the division of labor can exist in an industrial culture's city, but a certain minimum must exist." [18]

Third, urban communities tend to be much more heterogeneous than rural communities.[19] We have already suggested, for example, that rural communities are relatively homogeneous in their occupational composition. In addition, a large percentage of the population of a small rural community may belong to the same political party, attend the same church, share the same ethnic background, and so on. On the other hand, in the urban community one encounters people of all types and from all walks of life. The urban community is also characterized by a multitude of organizations and associations.

Fourth, people who live in rural communities relate to each other in a somewhat different manner than do the residents of urban communities. Impersonal and formally prescribed relationships are likely to flourish in the urban milieu.[20] Certainly it is impossible for urbanites to develop primary relationships with all the people with whom they come into contact. On the other hand, ruralites may know most of the people with whom they interact. Even when they do run across strangers, ruralites may feel quite free to greet them, offer them assistance, or ask them what their names are, where they live, and what they do for a living.

Finally, to a great extent urbanites rank each other on the basis of overt symbols of status.[21] In cities and metropolitan areas people frequently "size" each other up in terms of the neighborhood where they live, the make and model of the car they drive, and the type of clothes they wear. On the other hand, in rural communities, people know each other and therefore are able to judge, rank, and evaluate each other on the basis of their personal characteristics.

Louis Wirth: A Further Look at Urbanism. In the preceding discussion we have leaned heavily on Louis Wirth. This is entirely proper because Wirth's paper entitled "Urbanism as a Way of Life" represents a basic

[18] Dewey, "The Rural-Urban Continuum," p. 65.
[19] See Robert Redfield, *The Folk Culture of Yucatan* (Chicago: University of Chicago Press, 1941), esp. 23–24; Wirth, "Urbanism as a Way of Life," pp. 16–18; Milgram, "The Experience of Living in Cities," pp. 1464–65.
[20] See Wirth, "Urbanism as a Way of Life," esp. 11–12, Milgram, "The Experience of Living in Cities," esp. p. 1462; Simmel, "The Metropolis and Mental Life," esp. pp. 34–38.
[21] See Dewey, "The Rural-Urban Continuum," p. 65; T. E. Lasswell, "Social Class and Size of Community," *American Journal of Sociology*, **64** (March, 1959), 505–8; Bernard Berelson and Gary A. Steiner, *Human Behavior: An Inventory of Scientific Findings* (New York: Harcourt Brace Jovanovich, Inc., 1964), p. 462.

contribution to our understanding of urban communities. Wirth agrees that urban areas are characterized by anonymity, a high division of labor, heterogeneity, and impersonality. He also identifies a number of other characteristics that are supposedly associated with urbanism. By summarizing these characteristics we can enhance our understanding of the urban community.

However, first we should note that this University of Chicago sociologist said nothing about the rural community. Although it may be safe to make inferences about the rural community from Wirth's analysis of urbanism, it must be stressed that these are no more than inferences. Furthermore, Wirth maintains that the characteristics of the city are the function of large population size, high density of population, and the heterogeneous character of urban populations. On the last variable, heterogeneity, Wirth's thinking appears to be somewhat confused. On the one hand, he clearly views the heterogeneity of urban populations as an independent variable that influences the sociocultural characteristics of cities. After examining Wirth's article, however, one must conclude that heterogeneity itself is partly attributable to high population size and density.

In any event, Wirth's description of urbanism is detailed and multifaceted. In his critique of Wirth's work, Richard Dewey, for example, lists nearly fifty traits that Wirth ascribes to urbanism or to the urban personality.[22] This multitude of specific traits can be summarized as follows:

1. Urbanism is characterized by the segmentalization of human relationships. This entails the predominance of secondary over primary contacts and a means-end-oriented form of role playing.
2. Urbanism fosters sophistication, rationality, and a utilitarian accent in interpersonal relationships. In turn, this cluster of traits leads to reserve, indifference, and a blasé outlook and to anonymity and depersonalization.
3. Urbanism is characterized by a high division of labor and a high degree of role specialization.
4. Urbanism depends on communication via the mass media and the expression of individual interests by a process of delegation. Wirth maintains that the "individual counts for little but the voice of the representative is heard with a deference roughly proportional to the numbers for whom he speaks."[23]
5. Urbanism is characterized by formal mechanisms of social control.

[22] Dewey, "The Rural-Urban Continuum," pp. 61–62.
[23] Wirth, "Urbanism as a Way of Life," p. 14.

6. Urbanism encourages the individual to develop a relativistic perspective and a tolerant stance toward individual differences.
7. Urbanism implies a complicated and multidimensional class structure. High rates of vertical mobility are typical of the city.
8. Finally, we have noted that Wirth associates heterogeneity with urbanism. According to him, the large population found in urban areas leads to a heightened range of individual variation, and the urban milieu, for various reasons, encourages and rewards individuality.

The fact that Wirth associates so many traits with urbanism makes it difficult to indicate briefly the traits that would, by inference, be associated with rurality. Presumably, a rural community would display such features as homogeneity of population, a predominance of primary relationships, and social control on an informal basis.

Wirth's and similar analyses have been subject to rather heavy criticism. Among others, Harold L. Wilensky and Charles N. Lebeaux question the "traditional view" and argue that the form of urbanism described by Wirth was a passing, transitional phenomenon resulting from high rates of industrialization and immigration.[24] Today, they maintain, a mature industrial order is emerging that does not have secondary contacts, superficiality, and subjugation of the individual as its hallmarks. Indicative of the type of evidence with which Wilensky and Lebeaux support their thesis is the following comment about the modern family:

> With striking consistency the recent studies of urban life underscore the nuclear family as the basic area of involvement for all type of urban populations. *We find not a madly mobile, restless mass, disintegrating for want of intimate ties,* but an almost bucolic contentment with the narrow circle of kin and close friends, with the typical urbanite spending most of his leisure with the family at home, caring for the children, watching television, maintaining the home, reading.[25]

This image of urbanism clearly contradicts the traditional view of urbanism as articulated by Wirth.

Richard Dewey has also criticized Wirth's analysis of urbanism.[26] In particular, Dewey maintains that many of the traits that Wirth

---

[24] See Harold L. Wilensky and Charles N. Lebeaux, *Industrial Society and Social Welfare* (New York: The Free Press, 1965), pp. 121–33. See also Claude S. Fischer, "On Urban Alienation and Anomie: Powerlessness and Social Isolation," *American Sociological Review*, 38 (June, 1973), 311–26; John D. Kasarda and Morris Janowitz, "Community Attachment in Mass Society," *American Sociological Review*, 39 (June, 1974), 328–39.
[25] Wilensky and Lebeaux, op. cit., p. 129. Italics added.
[26] Dewey, "The Rural-Urban Continuum," pp. 60–66.

associates with urbanism are not a product of large population size and high density at all. Rather, they are part of the general cultural setting within which cities appear. Urbanism, so Dewey's argument runs, is a trait associated with entire societies rather than with communities of a specific size. This is why one finds "small rural communities which are secular, civilized, dynamic, and highly literate as well as large, sacred, essentially primitive, illiterate, and relative static urban communities." [27] At the same time, however, Dewey does not argue that the size and density of their populations are the only major differences between rural and urban communities. Rather, he concurs that cities are characterized by anonymity, heterogeneity, a high division of labor, impersonality, and status ranking on the basis of overt symbols of status.

☐ MAJOR COMMUNITY TYPES

We have enumerated some of the variables that can be used to distinguish among different types of communities. These variables can now be utilized in a discussion of some of the forms that the community actually takes. Specifically, we shall explore rural and urban communities in more detail. Within the latter category we must look at both the city and the metropolitan area. It could easily be argued that this classification of types of communities is grossly oversimplified. Certainly it is possible to draw fine distinctions among hamlets, villages, towns, cities, and metropolitan areas. It is not necessary to do so, however, in order to understand the concept of community itself.

The analysis that follows was written for the first edition of this book, published in 1972. Since that time, Edgar W. Butler has neatly summarized the following discussion in the form of a typology (see Table 2-1). Butler's work will serve as a useful guide as we discuss the differences among villages, cities, and metropolitan areas.

Rural Communities

Demographic Characteristics. To Americans the most obvious feature of the rural community is its small population. However, the point at which a community ceases to be rural and becomes urban is open to debate. In the United States some students of community life follow

[27] Ibid., p. 65. Today most sociologists accept the idea that "urbanism" is a trait associated with entire societies rather than with communities of a specific population size. However, Smith and Zopf maintain that differences between the "country and the city" are still strong and important. See Smith and Zopf, *Principles of Inductive Rural Sociology,* Chapter 2.

TABLE 2-1. A Typology of Communal Units

| | Communal Unit | | |
	Village	City	Metropolitan Area
Demographic Characteristics			
Size of population	small (under 10,000?)	intermediate (10–50,000?)	large (over 50,000?)
Density of population	low	intermediate	high
Community-Hinterland Relations			
Hinterland population	small	variable	large
Community's influence over hinterland	limited	variable	extensive
Number of community-hinterland ties	few	variable	many
Sociocultural Characteristics			
Heterogeneity of population	low	intermediate	high
Availability of organizations and services	limited	intermediate	extensive
Division of labor	low	intermediate	high
Potential anonymity of the individual	low	variable	high
Predominant character of social relations	primary	secondary	secondary
Predominant type of social control	primary	secondary	secondary
Degree of status ranking on basis of overt symbols	low	intermediate	high

Source: Edgar W. Butler, *Urban Sociology: A Systematic Approach* (New York: Harper & Row, 1976), p. 266.

the practice employed by the U.S. Bureau of the Census and designate a population of 2,500 as the cutoff point between rural and urban. Thus all communities of under 2,500 population, whether incorporated or not, might be classified as rural whereas those with a population of 2,500 or more might be classified as urban. There is fairly widespread agreement, however, that the figure of 2,500 is unrealistically low. It is indeed difficult to think of communities with 2,500 inhabitants as being urban, especially when they are compared to large cities with their millions of people. Gibbs and Davis suggest that for purposes of international comparison a population of 10,000 represents a more satisfactory cutoff point between rural and urban,[28] whereas Fenton Keyes presents data indicating that 25,000 might represent a good cutoff point between rural and urban communities, at least in the United States.[29] Similarly, Philip M. Hauser maintains that "in practice, many comparative international studies use populations in places of 20,000 or more as urban because the data are generally available on that basis and because an agglomeration of this size is not likely to retain rural characteristics."[30] The latter portion of Hauser's statement is, of course, debatable.

It is not the intention of the present writer to resolve this question. The present discussion does, however, raise again the possibility that population size is not of intrinsic significance in distinguishing among types of communities. At the risk of being repetitious, it must be reiterated that a large population by itself does not guarantee that a community will be "urbanlike" in its social and cultural characteristics. About the best that can be said is that as a community gains in population the likelihood that its members will be urban in their values, attitudes, and behavior is increased. In any event, if we must select a cutoff size, it should be at that population size at which the social and cultural characteristics of the community change from rurallike to urbanlike. This is more easily said than done. We would first have to specify clearly what we mean by "rurallike" and "urbanlike." Then we would have to do research on a number of communities of different sizes to determine the approximate population size at which communities display a preponderance of urbanlike traits.

It is even more difficult to offer a definitive proposition concerning the population densities of rural communities. In the United States, rural communities generally are characterized by relatively low population densities. This is the result of many things, including the fact that in rural America one simply does not find many plots of land that are crowded with multiple-family dwelling units. In countries where land is in extremely short supply, however, one can find communities with an extremely high density of population that are essentially rural. Halpern,

[28] Gibbs and Davis, "Conventional Versus Metropolitan Data," p. 511.
[29] Fenton Keyes, "The Correlation of Social Phenomena with Community Size," *Social Forces*, 36 (May, 1958), 311–15.
[30] Hauser and Schnore, *The Study of Urbanization*, p. 10.

for instance, describes one Indian village that had, as of 1951, a population density of approximately 4,700 per square mile.[31] This is as high as or higher than the average population density of many large American cities. Again, population density, taken alone, may be almost worthless as a measure of degrees of urbanization. It is debatable whether one can even hypothesize that there is a direct correlation between population density and the probability that a community will be urban in its social and cultural characteristics.

The Rural Community and Its Hinterland. A second characteristic of the rural community is its small and sometimes undeveloped hinterland.[32] Indeed, we have already discussed the possibility that most rural communities have only a primary community area. The evidence at hand seems to bear this out. Normally, the rural community serves as a shopping and service center for its own residents and for the surrounding farm population, and both of these groups sometimes trade in larger communities.[33] Furthermore, the ties between the village and its hinterland may be weak. Aside from serving as a center where they purchase their daily commodities, worship, and send their children to school, the village may perform few other functions for families who live in its hinterland. Their thoughts, attitudes, and opinions are at least partially shaped and formed by people with whom they interact at the local level, but they are also profoundly influenced by messages diffused from larger communities. Likewise, today most people "buy" durable goods, expert medical attention, legal advice, and financial services from "sellers" in a nearby, but nonetheless large, city.

Sociocultural Characteristics. We have already suggested that urbanism is a trait associated with entire societies. It is because of this fact that a particular community may clearly be rural in terms of population size but still display many of the characteristics associated with urbanism. In large measure the entire population of the United States, as well as the populations of other developed countries, is urbanized, and the differences we shall now discuss are a matter of degree.

Residents of a rural community are supposedly enmeshed in a tight-knit web of social relationships. This makes it impossible for them to

[31] Halpern, *The Changing Village Community*, p. 68.
[32] For a description of several rural villages and their hinterlands see Irwin T. Sanders and Douglas Ensminger, *Alabama Rural Communities: A Study of Chilton County* (Montevallo, Ala.: Alabama College Bulletin No. 1A, July, 1940).
[33] See Arthur J. Vidich and Joseph Bensman, *Small Town in Mass Society: Class, Power and Religion in a Rural Community* (Princeton, N.J.: Princeton University Press, 1958).

remain anonymous for very long. Newcomers to a rural community often find that their neighbors know a great deal about them even before they take up residence in the community, and rural youth often lament the fact that they cannot escape the ever-watchful eyes of kin and neighbors. In short, rural dwellers are both visible and known. This means that they normally do not experience that type of anonymity that leaves one feeling isolated and alone, but they may not enjoy the freedom and privacy enjoyed by the urban dweller. Furthermore, rural dwellers are also likely to become one strand in a web of informal primary relationships. They are on a friendly, first-name basis not only with their next-door neighbors but also with most other people with whom they come into contact.

Because primary relationships predominate, rural dwellers are frequently ranked on the basis of personal characteristics as well as on the basis of overt symbols of status. It is true, of course, that one's position in the class structure is partly determined by his or her occupation, education, and income. However, the values that people hold and the practices that they engage in are equally strong determinants of social rank in the rural community.[34] The end product of social ranking in the rural community is a simple stratification system as compared to that of the city, although the class system of small towns is apparently more complex than might be thought.[35]

In most cases the rural community is characterized by homogeneity in both people and institutions. In many rural communities the surnames of most residents reveal their common ethnicity, and, by national standards, the vast majority of residents may belong to the same social class. Similarly, the range of organizations and services available in the rural community is limited.[36] Some rural communities have only a few churches and a few small business concerns. Because of the post-World War II trend toward consolidation and centralization, they may lack even a local school and a viable unit of government. This restricted range of organizations and services is simply not encountered in the city. Indeed, if a community's facilities are this limited, it might properly be classified as rural even though it has a large population.

Another dimension of this homogeneity is the low division of labor that typifies most rural communities. In fact, the entire economic system

[34] For evidence bearing on this point see ibid., esp. Chap. 3.

[35] For a superb description of the class structure of one small rural community see James West, *Plainville, U.S.A.* (New York: Columbia University Press, 1945), pp. 115–41.

[36] See Keyes, "The Correlation of Social Phenomena with Community Size," pp. 311–15.

of the rural community is often built around meeting the needs of the farm population and of those people who serve the farm population such as bankers, farm equipment dealers, clothiers, feedstore operators, doctors, and dentists.[37] In a few rural communities the dominant economic activity shifts from agriculture to manufacturing or to the operation of resort and recreational facilities. This low division of labor must of course be measured in terms of the occupational structure of the rural community itself. Today, it is relatively common for individuals who are employed in the city to live in small hinterland communities. Thus a complete enumeration of the residents of an essentially rural community may uncover podiatrists, keypunch operators, and nuclear physicists as well as persons engaged in farming. The former are a part of the urban labor force even though they live in a rural setting.

Rural Communities: The Delineation of Subtypes. We have already hinted that rural communities can be classified on the basis of their dominant economic activity. Is the community primarily an agricultural center? A mining center? A manufacturing center? A resort and recreational center? When distinctions of this type contribute to one's study of community structure and process, it is perfectly legitimate to make them. Likewise, a leading student of rural community life, Lowry Nelson, has drawn a distinction among three types of rural communities: the hamlet, the small village, and the large village.[38] Nelson's classificatory scheme is based on population size alone. Thus he applies the term *hamlet* to all communities that have a population of 250 or less, the term *small village* to all communities that have a population of 250 to 1,000, and the term *large village* to all communities that have a population of 1,000 to 2,500. He also distinguishes between towns and small cities. Towns, according to Nelson, have a population greater than 2,500 but less than 5,000, whereas small cities have a population of between 5,000 and 10,000. Some of our earlier comments should, however, make it clear that this classificatory scheme, based as it is on population size alone, may not tell us much about rural communities as units of social and cultural organization. Only field research can reveal whether there are major social and cultural differences between hamlets and small villages, or between small villages and large villages.

[37] Because of this, Smith and Zopf maintain that "among all the differences which have been noted between the rural and urban portions of society, the occupational difference seems to have the most fundamental importance." Smith and Zopf, *Principles of Inductive Rural Sociology,* p. 24.

[38] See Lowry Nelson, *Rural Sociology,* 2nd ed. (New York: American Book Company, 1955), p. 87.

Urban Communities: Cities and Metropolitan Areas

Wirth's concept of urbanism as we have discussed it is quite comprehensive. However, there is something to be gained by examining further the more salient characteristics of the modern city and metropolitan area.

Demographic Characteristics. Little needs to be said about the size of urban communities. In terms of numbers, the urban community begins where the rural community leaves off. Population size might also be used to draw a distinction between minor urban communities and metropolitan communities. The U.S. Bureau of the Census, for example, classifies as urban all places, whether incorporated or not, that have a population of 2,500 or more.[39] However, if an urban place has 50,000 or more inhabitants, it is designated as a Standard Metropolitan Statistical Area. In addition to including the central city, a Standard Metropolitan Statistical Area includes the county in which the city is located, plus contiguous counties "if according to certain criteria they are essentially metropolitan in character and socially and economically integrated with the central city." [40]

In the United States, then, students of community life might be on fairly safe ground if they applied the term *metropolis* to communities that have a total population of 50,000 or more. They might, of course, want to use additional criteria that would assure that the community in question actually possesses metropolitan characteristics. At the same time, there is fairly widespread agreement that a population of 50,000 is really not large enough to distinguish between metropolitan communities and smaller urban places. William A. Robson, for instance, maintains that a community should have a central city with at least 300,000 population and a total population of at least 400,000 if it is to qualify for metropolitan status.[41] Similarly, Hans Blumenfeld defines a metropolis as "a concentration of at least 500,000 people living within an area in which the traveling time from the outskirts to the center is no more than about 40 minutes." [42]

Cities also tend to have high population densities. This can be attributed to tightly circumscribed city boundaries, a preponderance of

[39] For further discussion see Murphy, *The American City: An Urban Geography*, pp. 9–10.
[40] Ibid., p. 17.
[41] William A. Robson, *Great Cities of the World*, 2nd ed. (New York: Macmillan Publishing Co., Inc., 1957), p. 31.
[42] Hans Blumenfeld, "The Modern Metropolis," *Scientific American*, 213 (September, 1965), 64.

small lots, and a large number of multifamily dwelling units. Thus on occasion large cities have within their boundaries areas where population densities exceed 100,000 per square mile: The overall population densities of cities may run into the thousands. It is a bit more difficult to generalize about the population densities of metropolitan communities. They tend to be high near the center of the community and to decrease in an outward direction.

Ecological Characteristics. If we follow Hawley's analysis, relatively little needs to be said about the urban community and its hinterlands (i.e., community areas). One can presume that all cities and metropolitan communities have primary community areas, that is, areas immediately surrounding the central city whose residents still go downtown to purchase groceries, medications, clothing, and so on. Because of the suburban exodus, the people who live in the city's primary community area are often poor and disadvantaged. It also seems safe to assume that all except perhaps the smallest urban communities (assuming that the cut-off point between rural and urban communities is set at 2,500) have secondary community areas. Even though suburbanites meet their day-to-day needs in the suburban community where they live, they still make occasional trips to the central city to attend the theater, to have a "night on the town," or to obtain specialized medical, legal, and financial services. In addition, suburbanites are dependent on wholesale distributors located in the central city, and they are influenced by newspapers that are published in and television stations that broadcast from the central city. Finally, most large metropolitan communities have tertiary community areas. The nationwide and even worldwide influence of such great metropolitan centers as New York, London, Paris, Tokyo, and Moscow is obvious. Sometimes these huge metropolitan centers shape the social, economic, and political life of entire nations.

Sociocultural Characteristics. The social characteristics of urban communities can be easily summarized. Among other things, urban dwellers can supposedly remain anonymous if they so desire. This does not mean that urbanites necessarily feel cutoff from group ties but only that there are places where they can go and not be known by anyone. This, in turn, makes it necessary to rely on the police, courts, and other regulatory bodies to provide for social control. These agencies cannot deal with the minutia of human behavior. Therefore, minor patterns of deviance are sometimes ignored by urban dwellers. However, the fact that urban dwellers must rely on secondary mechanisms of social control does not mean that social control on a primary basis has disappeared completely. Most urbanites are still responsive to pressures exerted on them by family, friends, and even passing acquaintances. In fact, it is a rare person indeed who does not experience these pressures and respond to them in one way or another.

That the urban community is characterized by heterogeneity in people and organizations scarcely needs to be pointed out. It is in the urban community that one finds people of all races, religions, and creeds, people who hold a variety of value orientations and who have a variety of life-styles. Subcultures devoted to drug abuse, homosexuality, and other "deviant" activities frequently abound in urban areas. One way in which this heterogeneity is manifested is in a very high division of labor. In the urban community a range of occupational specialties is found that is unknown in the rural community. In addition, a wide range of organizations and services is found. If one desires a wide choice of churches or schools, if one wishes to patronize a podiatrist or a burlesque show, one would be best advised to look to the city rather than the country.

Finally, the class structure of the modern urban community is exceedingly complex, and the social rank of the individual is often determined on the basis of impersonal criteria. Such variables as education, income, and occupation often serve to determine with whom one associates and how one is evaluated by passing acquaintances. In daily encounters with strangers even less personal criteria are used to evaluate the individual. This is made clear by Richard Dewey:

> When people interact socially, they must, except on rare occasions, know the status of their associates, and the pervasive anonymity of the large city demands some means of identifying the functionaries essential to daily living there. The waitress, the clerk, the policemen, the priest, and others must be identified. Even the less uniform symbols of "good standing" are important in the city. A salesman whose clothes were soiled and ill pressed and whose face and hair were unkempt would stand little chance of gaining an audience with a prospective customer in the city.[43]

This is in marked contrast to the rural community. In the latter, one's status may not become fully crystallized until one's neighbors have the opportunity to study his or her behavior and values.

Megalopolis

The northeastern seaboard of the United States has, for many years now, had a heavy concentration of metropolitan areas such as New York City, Boston, Philadelphia, Washington, D.C., and Baltimore.

[43] Dewey, "The Rural-Urban Continuum," pp. 65–6.

Furthermore, the fringes of these metropolitan areas have grown to such a large size that they have merged. As a result, a continuous band of urban and suburban development has emerged that extends for about 600 miles from southern New Hampshire to northern Virginia.[44] A French geographer, Jean Gottman, has coined the term *megalopolis* to refer to regions of this type.[45]

The cities, suburban areas, and occasional patches of open land within a megalopolitan region are completely interdependent. They share a complex network of highways, they jointly provide residents of the region with goods, services, and jobs, and they share problems of crime, delinquency, mental illness, and so on. Yet the average resident of the megalopolis is not completely engulfed in the megalopolitan area. Rather, most of the individual's social activities are carried out in one of the thousands of smaller neighborhoods or suburban communities of which the megalopolis is composed.[46]

It is predicted that by the year 2000 about 41 per cent of the U.S. population will live in the megalopolitan region located on the northeastern seaboard of the United States and stretching as far west as Chicago. An additional 13 per cent will be residents of the emerging megalopolitan area that will stretch from San Francisco to San Diego, California.[47] Millions of other Americans will live in smaller megalopolitan regions located in Florida, Texas, Washington, Oregon, Arizona, and so on. It is quite likely that these people will enjoy an extremely high standard of living in a material sense. How megalopolitan living will affect their values, attitudes, beliefs, and behavior patterns is an open question.

Of course, during recent years small cities and areas that are technically classified as rural have been growing more rapidly than large metropolitan centers.[48] It is too early to hazard a guess as to whether this trend will slow down or even halt the growth of megalopolitan regions. On the one hand, some megalopolitanites apparently are abandoning the hectic, fast-paced life supposedly characteristic of metropolitan regions in order

[44] See Noel P. Gist and Sylvia Fleis Fava, *Urban Society*, 6th ed. (New York: Thomas Y. Crowell, 1974), p. 91.

[45] See Jean Gottman, *Megalopolis: The Urbanized Northeastern Seaboard of the United States* (New York: Twentieth Century Fund, 1961).

[46] Gist and Fava, *Urban Society*, p. 95.

[47] *Population and the American Future,* Report of the Commission on Population Growth and the American Future (Washington, D.C.: U.S. Government Printing Office, 1972), p. 37

[48] See James L. Freund, "Small Cities and Their Future," in Jacqueline Scherer (ed.), *Focus: Urban Sociology* (Guilford, Conn.: The Dushkin Publishing Group, 1978), pp. 226–32

to enjoy the purported amenities of living in smaller communities. At the same time, these people—and especially their children—will want good, high-paying jobs, good schools, good health and welfare services, a variety of recreational opportunities, and so on. It is almost inevitable that these things will be more readily available in large metropolitan communities and in megalopolitan regions. Hence it is hard for the present writer to get too excited about the current "back to small towns" movement. Furthermore, the fastest-growing communities are not small, isolated rural communities. Rather, they are communities adjacent to metropolitan areas.[49] These communities will eventually become absorbed into the megalopolitan orbit.

☐ A FURTHER LOOK AT THE METROPOLITAN COMMUNITY

The movement of the world's population from rural to urban areas has been going on for a long, long time. The gigantic metropolitan community is, however, a product of the twentieth century. Amos H. Hawley, for example, points out that "few phenomena are more representative of the trend of modern society with its increasing emphasis on large-scale organization than is the emergence and rapid development of the metropolitan community during the past fifty odd years." [50] Likewise, Philip M. Hauser presents data indicating that "by the end of the century 42 per cent of the world's people may be resident in places of 100,000 or more as contrasted with 20 per cent in 1960, 5.5 per cent in 1900, and 1.7 per cent in 1800." [51] Within the United States, trends in metropolitan growth are even more dramatic and the metropolitan community has indeed become the "city" of the twentieth century. It therefore behooves us to examine the metropolitan community in more detail. A good place to begin is with an analysis of some of the factors that have contributed to metropolitan growth.

The Logic of Metropolitan Growth: Edward C. Banfield

Edward C. Banfield has shed a good deal of light on some of the factors that have led to suburbanization and the growth of metropolitan

[49] Ibid., p. 232
[50] Amos H. Hawley, *The Changing Shape of Metropolitan America: Deconcentration Since 1920* (New York: The Free Press, 1956), p. 1.
[51] Philip M. Hauser, "The Chaotic Society: Product of the Social Morphological Revolution," *American Sociological Review*, **34** (February, 1969), 4.

regions in the United States.[52] One of these factors is demographic in nature; that is, there has been a steady stream of migrants (both from within the country and from overseas) into American cities during the twentieth century. Because of their sheer numbers, the urban community has expanded outward and become the sprawling entity that it is today. Banfield devotes considerable effort to explaining why it has been the "well-off" rather than the "not well-off" who have moved to the periphery of the metropolitan community, but this need not concern us here. At the same time, population pressure alone does not totally explain the outward expansion of the city. Rather, population pressure operated in combination with two other factors to make the emergence of the metropolitan community inevitable. The first of these factors was technological in nature. Banfield tells us that "if it is feasible to transport large numbers of people outward (by train, bus, and automobile) but not upward or downward (by elevators), the city must expand outward." [53] Another set of factors that made suburbanization and metropolitan growth possible, and indeed inevitable, was economic in nature, that is, "if the distribution of wealth and income is such that some can afford new housing and the time and money to commute considerable distances to work while others cannot, the expanding periphery of the city must be occupied by the first group (the 'well-off') while the older, inner parts of the city, where most of the jobs are, must be occupied by the second group (the 'not well-off')." [54]

The Structure of the Metropolitan Community

At first, it might appear that the metropolitan community is simply an extremely large city. However, students of the urban community see the "metropolis" as a series of interdependent communities, one of which exercises dominance over the rest. Indeed, one of the most famous students of the metropolitan community in America, Roderick D. McKenzie, has noted that the metropolitan community "absorbs varying numbers of separate local communities into its economic and cultural organization" [55] and further states that "the city of former days is really being replaced by a new entity, the metropolitan community, with a distribution of people shading off from extreme congestion to relative

---

[52] See Edward C. Banfield, *The Unheavenly City Revisited* (Boston: Little, Brown and Company, 1974), Chapter 2.
[53] Ibid., p. 25.
[54] Ibid.
[55] Roderick D. McKenzie, *The Metropolitan Community* (New York: McGraw-Hill Book Company, 1933), p. 7.

sparseness, yet with some uniformity of character." [56] Similar ideas lie behind the concept of Standard Metropolitan Statistical Area as it has been developed by the U.S. Bureau of the Census.[57]

When these threads of thought are drawn together, the image of the metropolitan area that emerges is of a very large central city surrounded by a number of smaller communities and residential areas. The boundaries of the central city, its satellites, and its suburbs may merge to such an extent that they have only legal significance. Nonetheless, students of the metropolitan community have found it helpful to analyze the "metropolis" in terms of three components: the central city, the suburban ring with its suburban and satellite communities, and the rural-urban fringe. These three components of the metropolitan community are shown in Figure 2-1.

The Central City. The heart of any metropolitan community is its central city. In fact, it would be hard to visualize a metropolitan community without a densely settled urban core.

The central city is utilized by two distinct types of occupants. The most prominent of these occupants are various business and commercial organizations. Even today, the huge skyscraper buildings found in the central city are the headquarters for large department stores, financial institutions, specialty shops, legal firms, giant corporations, medical specialists, and advertising agencies. And millions of people still live within the central city. In the United States these inner-city residents are often the most disadvantaged members of society. Scott Greer puts it well when he states that the central city "has exclusive possession of most nonassimilating ethnics (the darker-skinned migrants) and most of the very poor (the dwellers in congested, aged residential areas inherited from an earlier epoch)." [58]

Needless to say, the central city has, at least in the United States, been in a state of continuous flux. In the residential sector, this change has manifested itself in the steady movement of white persons out of the central city. As a result, the modern central city has become a community populated mainly by black Americans,[59] Puerto Ricans, Mexican-

[56] R. D. McKenzie, "The Rise of Metropolitan Communities," in President's Research Committee on Social Trends, *Recent Social Trends in the United States,* 1-vol. ed. (New York: McGraw-Hill Book Company, 1933), p. 444.

[57] For a discussion of "Standard Metropolitan Statistical Areas" see U.S. Bureau of the Census, *U.S. Census of Population 1960, Part A, Number of Inhabitants* (Washington, D.C.: U.S. Government Printing Office, 1961), pp. xxiii–xxviii.

[58] Scott Greer, *The Emerging City: Myth and Reality* (New York: The Free Press, 1962), p. 84.

[59] For documentation see Hauser and Schnore, *The Study of Urbanization,* Chapters 14 and 15.

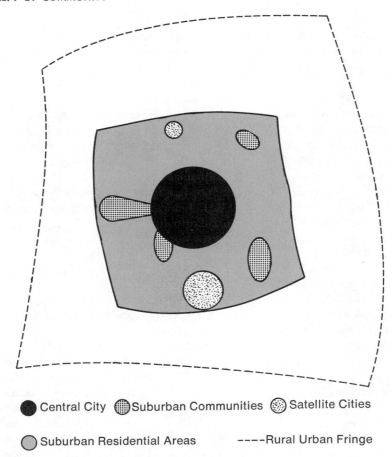

● Central City ⊛ Suburban Communities ⊛ Satellite Cities

◯ Suburban Residential Areas ----Rural Urban Fringe

FIGURE 2-1. Structure of the metropolitan community.

Americans, and other minority groups. Change in the central city, how-ever, has not been confined to the residental sector. At one time the central city, among other things, provided a locus for factories, ware-houses, railroad yards, and truck terminals. Like the more affluent white population, however, these organizations have long since moved to the periphery of the metropolitan area where open land is available for expansion, storage, and parking.[60]

The Suburban Ring and Suburban Communities. The typical metro-politan community is characterized by a suburban ring or fringe that surrounds the central city. Like the central city, the suburban ring consists of two components. First, it usually encompasses vast tracts of land devoted to residential uses. Indeed, Dobriner describes portions of

[60] For an analysis of changes in the central city see Blumenfeld, "The Modern Metropolis," p. 71.

the suburban ring well: "moving out into the inner (or suburban) ring the quality of the housing improves. The apartment houses all but disappear, and the modern single-family house on the 60 by 100 plot, the universal symbol of suburban America, stands triumphant everywhere." [61] Second, the suburban ring is dotted with suburban and satellite communities, two communal types that we shall explore in more detail.

The distinction between suburban communities and satellite cities is well established in the literature. In fact, as early as 1925 Harlan Paul Douglas recognized that a distinction can be made between "suburbs of production" and "suburbs of consumption." [62] The first of these terms reminds us that within the suburban ring of many metropolitan communities one can find subcenters where manufacturing and related types of activity are dominant. These centers of production that may dot the suburban ring are referred to as satellite cities. As such they provide jobs not only for their own residents but also for workers who commute from other communities within the metropolitan complex. Because jobs are available in the satellite community, its residents may not be particularly dependent on the central city.

The residents of suburban communities, on the other hand, are quite dependent on the central city. Thus Alvin Boskoff tells us that the "suburbs" consist of "those urbanized nuclei located outside (but within accessible range) of central cities that are politically independent but economically and psychologically linked with services and facilities provided by the metropolis," [63] whereas Walter T. Martin defines a "suburb" as "the relatively small but formally structured community adjacent to and dependent upon a larger central city." [64] Furthermore, he suggests that two features distinguish the suburban from other community types: physical and political separation from the central city and economic dependence on the central city.[65] The latter characteristic manifests itself in the fact that residents of suburban communities frequently work in the central city and make most of their major purchases there. It is because of this that Janowitz refers to the suburban community as a "community of limited liability." [66]

[61] William M. Dobriner, *Class in Suburbia* (Englewood Cliffs, N.J.: Prentice-Hall, Inc., 1963), p. 162.
[62] Harlan Paul Douglas, *The Suburban Trend* (New York: The Century Co., 1925), pp. 74–92. See also Leo F. Schnore, "Satellites and Suburbs," *Social Forces*, 36 (December, 1957), 121–29.
[63] Alvin Boskoff, *The Sociology of Urban Regions*, 2nd ed. (New York: Appleton-Century-Crofts, 1970), p. 109.
[64] Walter T. Martin, "The Structure of Social Relationships Engendered by Suburban Residence," *American Sociological Review*, 21 (August, 1956), 447.
[65] Ibid.
[66] Morris Janowitz, *The Community Press in an Urban Setting* (New York: The Free Press, 1951), pp. 222–25.

In 1971 *Time* magazine, in conjunction with the Louis Harris polling organization, developed a typology of suburban communities.[67] This typology was the outgrowth of a survey of over 1,600 people who lived in 100 different suburban communities across the United States. The first type of suburban community identified by *Time* was the *affluent bedroom community,* which comes closest to fitting our stereotype of what suburban communities are like. Among other things, the residents of affluent bedroom communities earn high incomes, many are professionals or executives, and a high percentage own their own homes. They are overwhelmingly white, Protestant, and Republican. It should be noted, however, that fewer than one half of the employed people of affluent bedroom communities work in large cities.[68] Some examples of affluent bedroom communities are New Canaan, Connecticut; Winnetka, Illinois; Leawood, Kansas; and Atherton, California. The second type of suburban community identified by *Time* is the *affluent settled community.* Incomes here are a little lower than in affluent bedroom communities, and there are slightly fewer homeowners. Protestants barely outnumber Catholics, and it appears that Republicans barely outnumber Democrats. Some examples of affluent settled surburban communities are Fairfield, Connecticut; Huntington, Long Island; Arlington, Virginia; and Evanston, Illinois. The third type of suburban community that the *Time* survey identified was the *low-income growing community,* which has a sizable population of skilled workers whose incomes are substantially lower than those of residents of the affluent suburban communities. Protestants far outnumber Catholics, and most people claim to be Democrats.[69] One such community is El Monte, California. In describing El Monte, *Time* reports that

> Even its defenders admit that El Monte is an eyesore, a blur of suburban sprawl 14 miles from downtown Los Angeles. Its boundaries meander without obvious aim or purpose. Tiny houses, usually stucco and rarely worth more than $30,000, are jumbled together with tacky businesses along its dismal streets. Some 70,000 people call it home, but only a city father could love it. . . .
>
> Within its 15 sq. mi., there is no college, no symphony orchestra, no art gallery, no country club, no good bookstore. There is one cinema. The bars run to beer, the churches to fundamentalism. . . . Western music flourishes in popular nightspots like Nashville West. The stores are mainly cut rate ("Crawford's: The Biggest Country Store in the World"). The citizens for the most part are unskilled or semiskilled workers from the South and the Midwest. They find jobs in places rang-

[67] "Suburbia: The New American Plurality," *Time,* 97 (March 15, 1971), 14–20.
[68] Ibid., p. 15.
[69] Ibid.

ing from the Clayton Manufacturing Co., a valve-making concern with more than 1,000 employees, to hundreds of small, ten- to twelve-man machine shops.[70]

The final type of surburban community identified by *Time* is the *low-income stagnant community*. *Time* reports that this type of suburban community "has the highest proportion of nonskilled and service workers —janitors, firemen, waiters, longshoremen, common laborers and the like—and the lowest proportion of commuters to the central city (34%)."[71] Some examples of low-income stagnant communities are Cambridge, Massachusetts; McKeesport, Pennsylvania; Joliet, Illinois; East Orange, New Jersey; and Compton and Bell Gardens, California.

Suburban Residential Areas

In addition to encompassing satellite cities and suburban communities, the suburban ring contains residential subdivisions that do not seem to be directly affiliated with any particular community. Indeed, the term *suburbia* conjures up the image of a housing development that is homogeneous both in architecture and in the characteristics of its inhabitants. However, in the first edition of his book Alvin Boskoff suggested that there are basically three types of residential suburbs.[72] The first, the traditional upper-class suburb, is inhabited by long-established, high-status families, and little turnover of population occurs. Upper-class suburbs tend to be concentrated in older sections of the country, such as near Boston, New York, and Philadelphia. The second type of residential development is what Boskoff calls the stable middle-class suburb. Suburban residential areas of this type are populated by middle-class families and are usually located in the newest sections of the suburban ring. The final type of suburban residential area that Boskoff identifies is the "packaged" surburb. These are mass-produced suburban housing developments intended for those families who wish to enjoy the amenities of suburban living but who cannot afford residences in the middle-class suburbs.[73]

[70] Ibid., p. 18.
[71] Ibid., p. 15.
[72] Alvin Boskoff, *The Sociology of Urban Regions* (New York: Appleton-Century-Crofts, 1962), pp. 134–35. Boskoff takes a somewhat different approach to the classification of types of suburbs in the second edition of his book. See pp. 113–19. Yet another classification of types of suburbs is offered by S. D. Clark. See his *The Suburban Society* (Toronto: University of Toronto Press, 1966), esp. pp. 15–18.
[73] For a thorough description of a "packaged" suburb see Bennett M. Berger, *Working Class Suburb: A Study of Auto Workers in Suburbia* (Berkeley: University of California Press, 1960).

One group of suburban dwellers, the "exurbanites," has been vividly described by A. C. Spectorsky.[74] Basically, exurbanites are upper-middle-class people who have migrated from the central city into prosperous suburban residential areas. They are motivated to move by a desire to get away from the hectic, fast-paced life of the central city. However, once they settle in the suburbs their free time is almost totally eaten up by parties and social activities, by chores such as mowing the lawn and shopping for food, and by long-distance commuting to and from work in the central city. In sum, the exurbanite often finds that the image of suburbia as a place of peace and tranquility is an illusion.

Rural-Urban Fringe. There is some confusion in the literature concerning whether there is one ring or two surrounding the central city. Some writers are content with drawing a distinction between the central city and the metropolitan ring. Most urban sociologists, however, argue that the metropolitan ring can and should be divided into the suburban ring and the rural-urban fringe.

There are some serious problems entailed in delineating both the inner and the outer boundaries of the rural-urban fringe.[75] Nonetheless, the nature of the rural-urban fringe itself is easily specified. The rural-urban fringe is that belt of land lying between the rather densely populated suburban fringe and that part of the city's rural hinterland devoted almost entirely to farming.[76] As such the rural-urban fringe is characterized by mixed land use; one can find scattered residential developments, small communities, industries that cannot operate in heavily populated areas, and of course farms and unused lands. Indeed, the rural-urban fringe is exactly what its name implies: it represents the fusion of rural and urban ways of life on the outskirts of large metropolitan communities.

Murphy suggests that at one time the rural-urban fringe had more than its fair share of problems.[77] In many cases people were drawn to the rural-urban fringe by the promise of inexpensive lots and low taxes. At the same time, the rural-urban fringe frequently lacked building codes and zoning ordinances and thus its development occurred in a random,

---

[74] See A. C. Spectorsky, *The Exurbanites* (Philadelphia: J. B. Lippincott Company, 1955).

[75] See Murphy, *The American City*, pp. 43–45.

[76] For a much more extensive and sophisticated definition and delineation of the rural-urban fringe see Robin J. Pryor, "Defining the Rural-Urban Fringe," *Social Forces*, 47 (December, 1968), 202–10.

[77] See Murphy, *The American City*, pp. 45–48. See also Walter Firey, "Ecological Considerations in Planning for Urban Fringes," *American Sociological Review*, 11 (August, 1946), 411–21.

haphazard fashion. Furthermore, the two units of government most typically found in the rural-urban fringe, the county government and the
school district, were often unable to provide a growing population with
adequate schools, police and fire protection, roads, and other public
facilities. Fringe residents, as a result, often found that they were paying
rather high taxes for services that were inferior to those received by
urban residents. During recent years, however, this picture may have
been improved considerably. Fringe residents have undoubtedly benefited
from the increased standard of living that most members of our society
enjoy and from the fact that the federal government has become more and
more willing to foot part of the bill for improvements made at the local
level.

☐ SUMMARY

We have attempted to do two things in this chapter. First, some of the
differences between rural and urban communities have been indicated
and discussed. Among other things, the rural community differs from the
urban community in its demographic characteristics, the nature of its
hinterlands, and its sociocultural features. Whether these differences are
of great importance is a matter that can be debated. Second, in the latter
half of this chapter we have tried, in effect, to give the reader a profile
of rural and urban communities. Special emphasis has been placed on the
metropolitan community, because it is the community of the twentieth
century and of the future. Most of the readers of this book will live and
work in huge metropolitan areas. Anyone who writes a chapter of this
type faces several risks. There is, of course, a danger that an ethnocentric
bias will intrude itself. For example, the present writer is entirely aware
that there are communities in every corner of the world and that a
sociologically acceptable discussion of community types should apply to
all communities, regardless of whether they are located in Asia, Africa
Europe, or the Americas. The fact of the matter is, however, that our
comments probably apply with most accuracy to communities within the
United States. This is inevitable given the fact that most of the literature
that we have had to draw on is written for the American student of
American community life. Likewise, our discussion may convey the impression that there is a great gulf between the rural and the urban community and that these are two totally distinct forms of territorial and
social organization. This simply is not the case. We must always remember
that all Americans, regardless of whether they live in small villages or
large cities, are a part of a larger society in which urbanism is the order
of the day. There is every reason to think that in virtually every country

of the world the differences between rural and urban become less significant with each passing decade.

BIBLIOGRAPHY

Banfield, Edward C. *The Unheavenly City Revisited*. Boston: Little, Brown and Company, 1974.

Bell, Wendell, and Marion T. Boat. "Urban Neighborhoods and Informal Social Relations," *American Journal of Sociology, 26* (January, 1967), 391–98.

Berger, Bennett M. *Working Class Suburb: A Study of Auto Workers in Suburbia*. Berkeley: University of California Press, 1960.

Birch, David L. "From Suburb to Urban Place," *The Annals of the American Academy of Political and Social Science, 422* (November, 1975), 25–35.

Blumenfeld, Hans. "The Modern Metropolis," *Scientific American, 213* (September, 1965), 64–74.

Bogue, Donald J. *The Structure of the Metropolitan Community*. Ann Arbor: University of Michigan Press, 1950.

Bollens, John C., and Henry J. Schmandt. *The Metropolis,* 3rd ed. New York: Harper & Row, 1975.

Boskoff, Alvin. *The Sociology of Urban Regions*, 2nd ed. New York: Appleton-Century-Crofts, 1970.

Clark, S. D. *The Suburban Society*. Toronto: University of Toronto Press, 1966.

Dewey, Richard. "The Rural-Urban Continuum: Real but Relatively Unimportant," *American Journal of Sociology, 66* (July, 1960), 60–66.

Dobriner, William M. *Class in Suburbia*. Englewood Cliffs, N.J.: Prentice-Hall, Inc., 1963.

———. (ed.). *The Suburban Community,* New York: G. P. Putnam's Sons, 1958.

Duncan, Otis Dudley. "Community Size and the Rural-Urban Continuum," in Paul K. Hatt and Albert J. Reiss, Jr. (eds.), *Cities and Society: The Revised Reader in Urban Sociology*. New York: The Free Press, 1957.

——— et al. *Metropolis and Region*. Baltimore: The Johns Hopkins Press, 1960.

Fava, Sylvia F. "Beyond Suburbia," *The Annals of the American Academy of Political and Social Science, 422* (November, 1975), 10–24.

Firey, Walter. "Ecological Considerations in Planning for Urban Fringes," *American Sociological Review, 11* (August, 1946), 411–21.

Fischer, Claude S. "On Urban Alienation and Anomie: Powerlessness and Social Isolation," *American Sociological Review, 38* (June, 1973), 311–26.

Gans, Herbert J. *The Levittowners: How People Live and Politic in Suburbia*. New York: Pantheon Books, 1966.

Gibbs, Jack P., and Kingsley Davis. "Conventional Versus Metropolitan Data in the International Study of Urbanization," *American Sociological Review, 23* (October, 1958), 504–14.

Goldfield, David R. "The Limits of Suburban Growth: The Washington, D.C. SMSA," *Urban Affairs Quarterly*, **12** (September, 1976), 83–102.

Gottman, Jean. *Megalopolis: The Urbanized Northeastern Seaboard of the United States.* New York: The Twentieth Century Fund, 1961.

Green, Constance McLaughlin. *The Rise of Urban America.* New York: Harper & Row, 1965.

Greer, Scott. *The Emerging City: Myth and Reality.* New York: The Free Press, 1962.

Halpern, Joel M. *The Changing Village Community.* Englewood Cliffs, N.J.: Prentice-Hall, Inc., 1967.

Hauser, Philip M., and Leo F. Schnore (eds.). *The Study of Urbanization.* New York: John Wiley & Sons, 1965.

Kasarda, John D., and Morris Janowitz. "Community Attachment in Mass Society," *American Sociological Review*, **39** (June, 1974), 328–39.

Keller, Suzanne. *The Urban Neighborhood: A Sociological Perspective.* New York: Random House, Inc., 1968.

Keyes, Fenton. "The Correlation of Social Phenomena with Community Size," *Social Forces*, **36** (May, 1958), 311–15.

Lasswell, T. E. "Social Class and Size of Community," *American Journal of Sociology*, **64** (March, 1959), 508–9.

Mann, Peter H. "The Concept of Neighborliness," *American Journal of Sociology*, **60** (September, 1954), 163–68.

Martin, Walter T. "The Structure of Social Relationships Engendered by Suburban Residence," *American Sociological Review*, **21** (August, 1956), 446–53.

McKelvey, Blake. *The Emergence of Metropolitan America 1915–1966.* New Brunswick, N.J.: Rutgers University Press, 1968.

McKenzie, Roderick D. *The Metropolitan Community.* New York: McGraw-Hill Book Company, 1933.

————. "The Rise of Metropolitan Communities," in President's Research Committee on Social Trends, *Recent Social Trends in the United States.* 1-vol. ed. New York: McGraw-Hill Book Company, 1933.

Milgram, Stanley. "The Experience of Living in Cities," *Science*, **167** (March, 1970), 1461–68.

Murphy, Raymond E. *The American City: An Urban Geography.* New York: McGraw-Hill Book Company, 1966.

Pryor, Robin J. "Defining the Rural-Urban Fringe," *Social Forces*, **47** (December, 1968), 105–15.

Schnore, Leo F. "Satellites and Suburbs," *Social Forces*, **36** (December, 1957), 121–29.

Sherbenou, Edgar L., and Victor E. Glango. "An Empirical Test of Size as a Measure of Urbanism," *Urban Affairs Quarterly*, **12** (September, 1976), 3–17.

Simmel, Georg. "The Metropolis and Mental Life," in Roland L. Warren (ed.), *New Perspectives on the American Community: A Book of Readings*, 3rd ed. Chicago: Rand McNally & Company, 1977, 33–44.

Smith, Joel, William H. Form, and Gregory P. Stone. "Local Intimacy in a Middle-Sized City," *American Journal of Sociology*, **60** (November, 1954), 276–84.

Spectorsky, A. C. *The Exurbanites*. Philadelphia: J. B. Lippincott, 1955.

Stein, Benjamin. "Whatever Happened to Small-Town America?" *The Public Interest*, **44** (Summer, 1976), 17–26.

"Suburbia: The New American Plurality," *Time*, **97** (March, 1971), 14–20.

West, James. *Plainville, U.S.A.* New York: Columbia University Press, 1945, esp. pp. 115–41.

Wilensky, Harold L., and Charles N. Lebeaux. *Industrial Society and Social Welfare*. New York: The Free Press, 1965, esp. Chapter V.

Wirth, Louis. "Urbanism as a Way of Life," *American Journal of Sociology*, **44** (July, 1938), 8–20.

Wood, Robert C. *Suburbia: Its People and Their Politics*. Boston: Houghton Mifflin Company, 1958.

Zimmerman, Joseph F. "The Metropolitan Area Problem," *The Annals of the American Academy of Political and Social Sciences*, **416** (November, 1974), 133–47.

CHAPTER 3

□□□□□□□□□
□
□
□
□
□
□
□
□
□
□

Purposeful Communities: Communes, New Communities, and Total Institutions

Most Americans live in largely unplanned villages, cities, and metropolitan areas such as the ones that were described in Chapter 2. However, a few people live in communes, and a small number of Americans live in completely planned "new communities." Likewise, millions of Americans spend at least part of their lives in total institutions, that is, in prisons, mental hospitals, convents, orphanages, and so on. There is a large body of literature pertaining to these alternative communal types. It is to this body of literature that we turn in this chapter.

In this chapter we shall not attempt to argue that communes, new communities, and total institutions have a great deal in common. As a matter of fact, these three communal types differ greatly from one another. Rather, we seek only to describe and discuss communes, new communities, and total institutions. It should be noted, however, that these three communal types have at least one thing in common: *They are established with a purpose in mind.* This is true whether we are talking about a hippie commune in the New Mexico desert, a new community in Maryland, or a prison in Mississippi. It is for this reason that this chapter's title includes the phrase *purposeful communities.* The purposes of communes, new communities, and total institutions are indicated throughout this chapter.

□ COMMUNES [1]

Communes have a very long history, and one writer suggests that com-

---

[1] Communes are often referred to as intentional communities. The use of this term has its merits because it does draw our attention to the fact that communes are started with a purpose in mind. However, one argument put forth in this chapter is that

munes date back to before the birth of Christ.[2] The Hutterites have practiced communal living since the 1500s, and hundreds of communes came into being in the United States during the mid-nineteenth century (e.g., Oneida, New York [1848–1881]; Brook Farm, near Boston [1841–1847]; and Amana, Iowa [1843–1933]).[3]

Even though these communes differed greatly from one another, they seem to have had at least two things in common. First, their members desired to escape the pressures and corrupting influences of the larger society. Second, their members sought a more perfect life. Many communes have been founded on the assumption that a more perfect life can be found by pooling resources and doing away with private property and by reestablishing meaningful ties with one's fellow human beings. Even today, many communes simply refer to themselves as "the Family."

The period from the late 1960s to the present has been marked by a renewed interest in communes. This can in part be traced to the death of the hippie movement.[4] The collapse of the hippie movement left many young, middle-class Americans in the awkward position of being alienated from the larger society but having nowhere to go. It is not surprising that some of these youth sought refuge in isolated rural communes: communal living has always been part of the American heritage. As of 1970–1971 it was estimated that there were between two and three thousand communes in the United States, most of which had no more than thirty members.[5] Kephart suggests that, on the whole, com-

---

there are other community-like organizations that are also purposefully or intentionally established. Hence to avoid confusion we shall use the term *communes* rather than *intentional communities*.

[2] See Calvin Redekop, "Communal Groups: Inside or Outside the Community," in Jack Kinton (ed.), *The American Community: Creation & Revival* (Aurora, Ill.: Social Science and Sociological Resources, 1975), p. 140.

[3] For a history of communes in the United States see Charles Nordhoff, *The Communistic Societies of the United States* (New York: Hillery House, 1960); Mark Holloway, *Heavens on Earth: Utopian Communities in America, 1680–1880,* 2nd rev. ed. (New York: Dover, 1966). See also William M. Kephart, *Extraordinary Groups: The Sociology of Unconventional Life-Styles* (New York: St. Martin's Press, 1976).

[4] See John R. Howard, *The Cutting Edge: Social Movements and Social Change in America* (Philadelphia: J. B. Lippincott Company, 1974), pp. 199–205.

[5] See Rosabeth Moss Kanter, *Commitment and Community: Communes and Utopias in Sociological Perspective* (Cambridge, Mass.: Harvard University Press, 1974), p. 166. For additional estimates of the number of communes in the United States see Patrick W. Conover, "An Analysis of Communes and Intentional Communities with Particular Attention to Sexual and Genderal Relations," *The Family Coordinator,* 24 (October, 1975), 454; Hugh Gardner, "Dropping into Utopia," *Human Behavior,* 7 (March, 1978), 43. Gardner estimates that between 1965 and 1975 at least 5,000 and perhaps as many as 10,000 rural communes were formed in the United States. How many of these communes still exist is unknown.

munes are more likely to meet the needs of their members—and hence survive—if they are kept small. Specifically, everybody needs to enter into primary group relationships with a few individuals who will listen and talk to them and who will give them sympathy, support, and a feeling of belonging. If the commune becomes too large it cannot meet these needs itself. As a result, cliques and factions may arise to meet these needs.[6] Over the course of time, these cliques and factions may lose interest in the commune as a whole and become more concerned with self-preservation, which could lead to the demise of the commune.

For a few Americans, then, communes have emerged as an alternative to living in a more usual type of community (e.g., in a metropolitan area). Because this is the case, we must look more closely at the nature and characteristics of communes. We must also examine the problems that seem to be common to almost all communes.

The Nature of Communes

Communes differ greatly from one another. On the surface, for example, there appears to be no resemblance between Morningstar East, a small, drug-using rural commune near Taos, New Mexico,[7] and the three highly structured, religiously oriented Bruderhof communes located in New York, Connecticut, and Pennsylvania.[8] Nonetheless, all communes have at least two things in common.

1. The members of a commune live together in a common geographic area: It would be nonsensical to talk about a commune whose members are scattered all over the country. Communes are found in urban areas,[9] but the posthippie communes are for the most part located in isolated or semi-isolated rural areas. There are probably two reasons for this. First, communes are frequently established by people who seek independence

[6] Kephart, *Extraordinary Groups*, pp. 296–99. The points that Kephart make seem, of course, to apply mainly to hippielike retreatist communes. Many religiously oriented communes have far more than thirty members. These communes are probably able to survive partly because of their authoritarian leadership structure and partly because all of their members believe strongly in the ideologies and doctrines of the commune.

[7] For a brief discussion of Morningstar East see Keith Melville, *Communes in the Counter Culture: Origins, Theories, Styles of Life* (New York: William Morrow & Company, 1972), p. 26.

[8] For an excellent study of the Bruderhof communes see Benjamin Zablocki, *The Joyful Community* (Baltimore: Penguin Books, 1971).

[9] Gardner, however, points out that "for the most part the urban groups could be more accurately described as shared apartment houses, co-ops, crashpads, issue-oriented action groups and service organizations." See Gardner, "Dropping into Utopia," p. 43.

from the larger society. This means that they must have land to cultivate and must have a place where they can avoid constant contact with the larger society. Second, quite often the values of the commune are in conflict with those of the larger society: Many hippie communes are drug oriented and some communes espouse greater sexual freedom than is tolerated by mainstream America. Similarly, almost all communes, regardless of type, reject the value that American society places on individual success and achievement. Value orientations such as these sometimes engender extreme hostility from the larger society. One way to escape the wrath of mainstream America is to settle in an isolated, hard-to-reach area.

2. Another characteristic of communes is that their members usually "desire to subordinate individual ends for group or collective goals." [10] Redekop says: "the basic reason for existence of the intentional community [or commune] is the breaking down of the myriad barriers that isolate individuals; it is the desire to relate to others in an unhindered and undistorted, or natural, fashion." [11] In short, most communes differ from the larger society in that they stress the importance of the group over the individual. This means that members of the commune almost always pool their material resources, that individual desires are subordinate to the needs of the group, and that considerable emphasis is placed on joint decision making by all members of the commune.

There are, of course, several ways to classify communes according to type. For example, Gardner suggests that "of the many ways that modern communes might be divided into categories, there are basically just two types that matter most." [12] The first of these categories includes communes that are anarchistic, libertarian, and unstructured (e.g., almost all of the hippie communes that had their heyday in the late 1960s and early 1970s). The second category includes the communes that are religiously oriented and are disciplined, authoritarian, and hierarchically structured. Examples of communes that fall into this category, to a greater or lesser degree, are the Bruderhof and Hutterian communes as well as some of the communes that are an outgrowth of the recent Jesus movement and the renewed interest in Eastern religions such as Zen Buddhism.

Kanter has also developed a way of classifying communes according to type. Specifically, Kanter distinguishes between retreatist communes and service communes.[13] Basically, the members of retreatist communes seek to escape the pressures of the larger society and to establish family-like relationships among themselves: retreatist communes tend to be

10 Redekop, "Communal Groups," p. 143.
11 Ibid.
12 Gardner, "Dropping into Utopia," p. 44.
13 Kanter, *Commitment and Community*, pp. 165–212.

"small, dissolvable, structureless communes of five to thirty people." As such, "they may provide welcome interludes from the pressures of society. Such groups may be increasing in importance as the modern version of the extended family." [14] As we shall see later, retreatist communes usually do not survive for very long, mainly because they do not develop effective mechanisms of social control and because they do not gain the full commitment of their members.

Service communes have a very different purpose from retreatist communes. The latter offer their members escape from the larger society, whereas the former see their goal as that of serving a specific target population. One such commune is Koinonia, an interracial commune near Americus, Georgia, whose members seek to live a Christian life, to bring an end to segregation, and to introduce local farmers to improved methods of farming.[15] Likewise, one might include Synanon, a purposeful community devoted to the rehabilitation of narcotics addicts, in the category of service communes. Service communes may tend to have a longer life expectancy than retreatist communes, partly because they do have a specific mission or task to perform.

There are some problems associated with the distinction that Kanter draws between retreatist and service communes. Among other things, many religious communes do not seem to fit into either category. For example, members of the Bruderhof have, in a sense, retreated from the larger society so that they can serve God and live a Christian life. However, the Bruderhof communes do not fit Kanter's description of retreatist communes, nor do they have much in common with, say, a small, hippie commune located in the New Mexico desert. Rather, the Bruderhof communes are highly structured organizations that elicit the total commitment of their members. They are also characterized by highly developed mechanisms of social control, and their members are "deeply concerned with world problems and totally committed to bringing about radical social change." [16] On the other hand, the Bruderhof communes are not, in the strictest sense of the word, service communes: They do not seek to serve a specific target population such as poor farmers or narcotic addicts.

Communes: Some Shared Characteristics

We suggested earlier that communes are ventures in group living. To a greater or lesser degree, most communes emphasize the importance of

[14] Ibid., pp. 189–90.
[15] Ibid., p. 192.
[16] Zablocki, *The Joyful Community*, p. 27.

the group over the individual. Because of their group-oriented nature, communes tend to take on several other characteristics, such as the following [17]:

1. Most communes are "communistic" in the sense that the private ownership of goods or property is frowned on or forbidden. One reason for this may be that the private ownership of goods creates distinctions among people and therefore alienates individuals from one another. Indeed, Redekop hypothesizes that "the more the intentional community [commune] stresses the destruction of the walls of alienation, the more complete will be the common ownership and use of resources." [18]

2. Even though communes tend to be group oriented, they are concerned with the growth and development of the individual. There are communes today that purposefully seek to relieve people of their drug dependency or sexual hang-ups. Likewise, many religious communes have a deep belief in the perfectability of humankind.[19] Among the Bruderhof, for example, one must be completely stripped of personal ego before one can fully serve God: "A woman with an exceptionally beautiful voice was in the habit of bursting into song while sitting alone out of doors or at work. The community made her stop this in order to chastise her ego." [20] Finally, even many of the hippie-retreatist communes have the goal of helping individuals overcome their hang-ups or to get more in tune with themselves, their fellow human beings, and nature.

3. We live in a highly competitive society that stresses the importance of *individual* success and achievement. As has already been indicated, most communes reject this value system: "the individual exists for the group and not vice versa." [21] It is interesting to speculate about why this is the case. Three reasons come to mind. First, a heavy emphasis on the individual could be highly dysfunctional for the commune. Many communes exist in a hostile natural or social environment, and it is essential that individuals "give their all" to the group if it is to survive. Second, it is possible that many people who join communes, especially retreatist communes, are people who find it difficult to function in a highly competitive society. Finally, there is the matter of ideology. One of the core beliefs of the commune movement is that people can achieve perfection only by subjugating themselves to the group.[22]

---

[17] The following discussion draws heavily on the work of Calvin Redekop. See Redekop, "Communal Groups," pp. 143–46.

[18] Ibid., p. 143.

[19] See Kanter, *Commitment and Community*, pp. 33–39.

[20] Zablocki, *The Joyful Community*, p. 250.

[21] Redekop, "Communal Groups," p. 145.

[22] The belief in the perfectability of human beings is a strong and recurrent theme in the commune movement. See Kephart, *Extraordinary Groups*, pp. 285–86.

4. Most communes develop decision-making processes that are quite different from those that characterize the larger society. Specifically, the stricture against individual achievement that characterizes most communes makes it unlikely that a great deal of decision-making power will be placed in the hands of a few individuals: The height of individual success and achievement is to have power over other individuals. It is therefore not at all uncommon to find that "a form of consensus making is the tendency in most intentional communities [communes], where each person is supposed to be 'heard out' before any action ensues." [23] As we shall see in a moment, some of the most serious problems that communes encounter arise when the members of the commune cannot reach a decision that is agreeable to all.

Communes: Some Shared Problems

Regardless of their type, all communes seem to have certain shared problems. The degree to which a commune successfully copes with such problems undoubtedly has a lot to do with how long it survives.

Sustaining Commitment. Communes often demand much of their members. At the physical level, life in the commune may be extremely demanding. There is usually hard work to be done, and sometimes food is in short supply. The summers may be long and hot; the winters cold and bleak. At the emotional level, it is by no means easy for people to abandon their selfish wishes and desires in favor of group unity. It is difficult for most of us to leave our individualistic, competitive, status-seeking ways behind.

Hence one of the most difficult problems facing communes is that of obtaining and sustaining the commitment of their members. We shall explore the concept of commitment in more detail.

Commitment has been most thoroughly analyzed by Rosabeth Moss Kanter. Basically, Kanter tells us that "commitment refers to the willingness of people to do what will help maintain the group because it provides what they need." [24] She goes on to explain, "Commitment links self-interest to social requirements. A person is committed to a relationship or to a group to the extent that he sees it as expressing or fulfilling some fundamental part of himself; he is committed to the degree that he can no longer meet his needs elsewhere." [25] New members of a commune do not necessarily have this high level of commitment. Rather,

[23] Redekop, "Communal Groups," p. 145.
[24] Kanter, *Commitment and Community*, pp. 33–39.
[25] Ibid., p. 66.

successful communes develop specific mechanisms by which they engender commitment among their members.

According to Kanter, there are six different ways by which successful communes have engendered commitment among their members. These are listed in Table 3-1. Not all communes, of course, use all six of these commitment-gaining mechanisms. For a specific example of a commune that has been successful in inspiring commitment among its members we can turn once more to the Bruderhof. Basically, the key to creating and sustaining commitment in the Bruderhof lies in a socialization process that makes the individual completely dependent on the larger collectivity, or commune, for a sense of worth: "The entire socialization process of the Bruderhof is geared to produce in the individual feelings of his own selfishness, worthlessness, and inadequacy. The collective self is an absolute good. The individual self is an absolute evil." [26] In this regard, it should be noted that the Bruderhof has a tremendous advantage over retreatist communes. Most retreatist communes are formed by adults who have not been socialized to accept the norms and values of communal living. On the other hand, Bruderhof children are socialized to accept the norms and values of their commune almost from the day they are born. This probably explains why the Bruderhof has been in existence for many, many years whereas most retreatist communes have a life expectancy of only one or two years.

The analysis of commitment mechanisms in communes helps us understand why some communes persist for centuries whereas others have a very short life span. It also sheds light on some of the problems facing contemporary villages, cities, and metropolitan areas. Specifically, it appears that most modern communities, whether large or small, have failed to develop a strong sense of commitment among their residents. It would, of course, be naive to suggest that the high rates of crime, delinquency, mental illness, and so on, that plague our communities today are entirely due to the fact that the interests of the community are not linked to the interests of its residents. However, most successful units of organization are characterized by a sense of loyalty and commitment among their members. A successful university, for example, is undoubtedly one in which the faculty trusts the administration and vice versa; a successful government is one that is led by a person who captures the admiration and loyalty of the public. There are probably very few modern American communities where more than a tiny fraction of the residents feel a strong sense of commitment to the community, its institutions, and its leaders. This may well be one reason why modern communities are experiencing such turmoil. It may also help to explain why many com-

[26] Zablocki, *The Joyful Community,* p. 158.

TABLE 3-1. Commitment Mechanisms Utilized in Successful Communes

	Description	Examples
Sacrifice	People have to give up certain things as a condition of membership in the commune. When people sacrifice in order to become members of a group, they are particularly likely to remain loyal to that group.	Abstinence from the use of alcohol, tobacco, coffee, etc. Abstinence from sexual relations; renunciation of worldly goods and vows of poverty.
Investment	People must give their time, money, and effort to the commune, and they are not entitled to be reimbursed if they renounce their membership. They therefore have a stake in the success of the commune.	Transfer of all of the recruit's money and property to the commune.
Renunciation	People must relinquish relationships that might weaken their loyalty to the commune itself. People will be committed to the commune to the extent that it is their sole source of emotional satisfaction.	Discouragement of contacts with persons outside the commune, of two-person intimacy, as in monogamous marriage, and of close ties between parents and their offspring.
Communion	People are helped to develop a strong sense of unity with the larger group. They are committed to the commune to the degree that they feel a strong sense of "we-ness" with other members of the commune.	Communion engendered by the communal sharing of property and work assignments and by submergence of the individual in a continuous round of group activities.
Mortification	People are provided with a new identity that is based on their membership in the commune. They will be committed to the commune to the extent that they are able to overcome their feelings of self-pride, self-importance, and vanity.	Mortification through socialization and sanctioning processes that stress the "sin of pride," the wrongness of being too independent and self-sufficient, and so on.
Transcendence	People endow the group with great power, meaning, and significance. They are committed to the extent that they submit to the greater power of the commune.	Transcendence engendered by leaders and groups that inspire awe in their members; elaborate routines, a strong ideology, and a body of traditions.

Adapted from Rosabeth Moss Kanter, *Commitment and Community: Communes and Utopias in Sociological Perspective* (Cambridge, Mass.: Harvard University Press, 1972), pp. 75–125.

67

munities are virtually immobilized when it comes to launching a meaningful attack on the problems that they face.

Order and Control. Many communes, and particularly retreatist communes, strive to be leaderless and unstructured.[27] At least two reasons for this come to mind. First, many people who are attracted to communal living are seeking escape from a society that they see as rigid and repressive. Thus Melville tells us that most communes are deliberate experiments "in erasing boundaries and eliminating rules."[28] Second, as has already been suggested, most communes have the goal of establishing complete equality among their members.[29] To elevate someone to a position of leadership would conflict with this equalitarian ideal.

It is at this point that communes encounter a fundamental dilemma. In order for any social group to persist, order must be established and maintained and there must be ways to deal with people whose behavior represents a threat to the group. Hence those communes that persist do develop some sort of leadership structure, they develop rules, and they develop means of enforcing these rules. In so doing, however, they sacrifice some of their equalitarian ideals.

A variety of leadership and control mechanisms have been developed in successful communes. Generally speaking, in most communes the right to exercise leadership and punish the wayward member is vested in the entire group rather than in specific individuals. In many communes, for example, decisions are made through a consensus-reaching process. By this we mean that the adult members of the commune express their opinions, air their doubts, and eventually arrive at a joint decision concerning the matter at hand. Some of the greatest crises faced by communes arise when consensus on an issue cannot be reached, and some of the most rewarding moments in communal living come when a decision is reached that satisfies everyone.[30] Powers of social control are also frequently invested in the group rather than in specific individuals. One method of social control commonly found in communes is mutual criticism in which the group discusses and criticizes the behavior of each individual, particularly as it relates to the goals and purposes of the group as a whole.[31]

---

[27] See Melville, *Communes in the Counter Culture,* pp. 126–30.

[28] Ibid., p. 126.

[29] One writer maintains that communes have been rather successful in establishing full sexual and genderal equality between their male and female members. See Conover, "An Analysis of Communes and Intentional Communities with Particular Attention to Sexual and Genderal Relations," pp. 453–62.

[30] Redekop, "Communal Groups," p. 146.

[31] Kanter, *Commitment and Community,* p. 37.

Relationships with the Larger Society. Some of the most difficult problems faced by communes lie in their relationships with the larger society. Among other things, commune members are often the target of hostility emanating from their "straight" neighbors. In some cases, the commune is seen by the surrounding society as a hotbed of drugs, sexual deviancy, and unusual child-rearing practices. In other cases, commune members are thought to be communists, radicals, or religious fanatics. Sometimes this hostility turns into outright harassment or even violence. Another great threat to communes is hordes of curious visitors.[32] Sometimes the motives of these visitors are aboveboard: They may wish to try living in a commune themselves for a few days, weeks, or months. Sometimes, however, the visitors are no more than curiosity seekers who come to the commune in hopes of obtaining drugs or sexual thrills. In any event, hordes of visitors can put a severe strain on a commune's resources and on the relationships among the members.

The Future of Communes

Probably no more than a fraction of the total U.S. population will ever live in communes. Among other things, in order to be successful, communes usually must be kept small, and they demand much of their members; most Americans are unwilling to make the sacrifices that successful attempts at communal living entail. Nonetheless, Americans are experimenters and a few of them will continue to experiment with communal living arrangements. In some cases, these people will find a viable alternative to living in a highly competitive, success-oriented society. Virtually every writer on communes sees them as one means by which the alienation and isolation that supposedly characterize modern society can be escaped.

☐ NEW COMMUNITIES

The purpose of this chapter is to explore some of the different forms that purposeful communities can take. We are not attempting to argue that communes, new communities, and total institutions have a great deal in common with one another. In fact, in many ways communes and new communities are polar opposites. Communes, for example, are usually extremely simple and provide their members with little more than the bare necessities for survival. On the other hand, new communities are fully planned, and they provide their residents with a full range of

---

[32] See Melville, *Communes in the Counter Culture*, p. 142.

69

facilities and services.[33] Indeed, the idea behind the construction of new communities is to provide adequate housing for a variety of different people and to provide community members with jobs, cultural and recreational opportunities, and so on. However, there is at least one thing that communes and new communities do have in common: Their purpose is to provide people with an environment that is significantly different from and better than the environment in which most Americans currently live.

The Concept of New Communities

In 1898 Ebenezer Howard of Great Britain published an influential book entitled *Tomorrow: A Peaceful Path to Real Reform*.[34] In his book Howard proposed that entirely new communities called "garden cities" be built from the ground up. These garden cities would have all of the features that would make for a good community. The community would be built around a central park, which, in turn, would be surrounded by houses and gardens. The location of commercial and industrial establishments as well as of schools, churches, and cultural centers would be carefully planned so as to make the community as aesthetically appealing and functional as possible.[35] Finally, these garden cities would be surrounded by a green belt of fields and forests. In Palen's words, "the green belt not only provided a way for the residents to enjoy nature: it also effectively was to prevent the city from growing beyond its planned limit of 30,000 inhabitants." [36] The green belt was to be owned by the community itself and could not be encroached on.

Howard had high hopes for his garden cities. He believed that garden cities would "lead society on to a higher destiny than it has ever yet ventured to hope for." [37] Garden cities would presumably do this by combining the advantages of town life with the advantages of country living. As Howard himself puts it:

[33] See Robert W. Marans and Robert B. Zehner, "Social Planning and Research in New Communities," in Gideon Golany and Daniel Walden (eds.), *The Contemporary New Communities Movement in the United States* (Urbana: University of Illinois Press, 1974), pp. 98–100.

[34] Howard's book was later reissued under the title *Garden Cities of Tomorrow*. See Ebenezer Howard, *Garden Cities of Tomorrow* (London: Faber and Faber, 1945).

[35] For a more in-depth description of "garden cities" see Frederick J. Osborn, *Green-Belt Cities* (New York: Schocken, 1969), esp. pp. 56–95.

[36] J. John Palen, *The Urban World* (New York: McGraw-Hill Book Company, 1975), p. 297.

[37] Howard, *Garden Cities of Tomorrow*, p. 128.

> There are in reality not only, as is so constantly assumed, two alternatives —town life and country life—but a third alternative in which all of the advantages of the most energetic and active town life, with all the beauty and delight of the country, may be secured in perfect combination.[38]

This statement has a familiar ring to it. It sounds much like the promotional literature distributed today by the builders of privately financed new communities in the United States.

In 1902 Howard established a garden city about 30 miles north of London. In 1920 he began work on a second garden city. Apparently these garden cities were at best moderately successful: they did provide their residents with a pleasant place to live but they were also plagued by financial difficulties. In addition, they were never able to provide jobs for all their residents who were in need of employment. The construction of new communities in Great Britain probably would have not proceeded further had it not been for the fact that in 1946 the British government launched an active new towns program. As of 1971, twenty-eight new communities had been constructed in Great Britain that, all told, housed 1,667,000 people.[39] One of Great Britain's motives for building new towns has been to disperse the huge population in and around London.

New Communities in the United States

New communities in the United States have had, until recently, a rather stormy history. During the 1930s the federal government constructed three green belt cities, these being Greenbelt, Maryland, Green Hills, Ohio, and Greendale, Wisconsin.[40] The reason for building these communities was to create jobs. The green belt cities also provided good housing and the other amenities of community living for moderate-income people. After World War II the private housing industry pressured Congress to get the government out of the business of building new communities. Now the green belts surrounding the three green belt cities have been converted to other uses. The three green belt communities are now barely distinguishable from other unplanned communities.

Today the development of new communities in the United States is

---

[38] Ibid., pp. 45–46.
[39] Palen, *The Urban World,* p. 300.
[40] For further discussion see Paul K. Conklin, *Tomorrow a New World: The New Deal Community Program* (Ithaca, N.Y.: Cornell University Press, 1959); Arthur Hillman, *Community Organization and Planning* (New York: Macmillan Publishing Co., Inc., 1950), esp. pp. 111–20.

carried out under private auspices. As of the late 1960s there were purportedly about sixty-four new communities completed or substantially completed in the United States.[41] Two of the best known of these are Reston, Virginia, and Columbia, Maryland. Apparently both Reston and Columbia have at least some of the characteristics that new communities should have if they are to be successful.[42]

First, if new communities are to be successful, they must be integrated along the lines of race and social class. Little is to be gained by building new communities populated exclusively by affluent white Americans. Rather, it is hoped by some that new communities can "provide an avenue of upward mobility for those who are beginning to escape the cycle of poverty, despair, and crime."[43] Indeed, the Urban Growth and New Community Development Act, passed in 1970, specifically requires that the developers of new communities provide housing that moderate- and low-income families can afford (see later). It also requires that the developers of new communities comply with laws and executive orders pertaining to equal rights in regard to jobs, housing, and the use of community facilities.

Second, new communities should provide jobs for many of their residents. The new communities are not intended to be simply bedroom communities whose residents go elsewhere during the day to find work. Data reported by Underhill suggest that the new communities that have qualified for assistance under the Urban Growth and New Community Development Act have been rather successful in this regard. With a total population of 800,513, these communities have created a total of 197,689 jobs.[44]

Finally, a new community must, of course, provide a full range of services and facilities for its residents. This includes shopping facilities, schools, churches, medical facilities, and recreational facilities. In sum, new communities must offer essentially the same services and facilities that are to be found in unplanned communities of comparable size. Apparently, Columbia, Maryland, has done well in this regard. In reference to Columbia, Ficker and Graves tell us "although it is a bit early to say with certainty, it does appear that the goal of building an 'ideal' city for 100,000 people will be met in an orderly and satisfying manner."[45]

[41] Palen, *The Urban World*, p. 305.
[42] For a discussion of what new communities should achieve see Jack A. Underhill, "New Communities Planning Process and National Growth Policy," in Golany and Walden, *The Contemporary New Communities Movement in the United States*, pp. 44–51.
[43] Ibid., p. 48.
[44] Ibid., p. 58.
[45] Victor B. Ficker and Herbert S. Graves (eds.), *Social Science and Urban Crisis: Introductory Readings* (New York: Macmillan Publishing Co., Inc., 1971).

The Future of New Communities

Some experts do not foresee much of a future for new communities in the United States. Anthony Downs, for example, is extremely critical of new communities on the grounds that they are extraordinarily costly.[46] It is true that a huge investment must be made by the developer many years before the new community starts yielding a profit: The community has to be essentially completed before people start moving in and businesses and industries open their doors. Likewise, some of the facilities that the developer must provide such as roads, parks, and an aesthetically pleasing environment cannot be provided on a profit-making basis. The developer must pay for them and hope to recover money through the sale of homes, land, and so on. This brings us to the question of whether private developers will be willing to invest their money and effort in constructing new communities. The answer will depend on what steps the federal government takes in regard to new communities and on whether those new communities now in operation or nearing completion prove to be financially successful.

During the next few years we shall probably not see the wholesale development of new communities in the United States. Nonetheless, new communities deserve careful attention and analysis. First, they represent an alternative to unplanned urban sprawl. Today our cities and metropolitan regions are growing in a topsy-turvy fashion. A subdivision is constructed here, a shopping center there, and so on. The result is that huge tracts of valuable land are squandered. New communities, on the other hand, are compact and orderly. As a matter of public policy, it might be wise to encourage the development of new communities around large metropolitan areas as an alternative to further urban sprawl. Second, new communities can be used to demonstrate innovations in community life that can perhaps be transferred to existing cities.[47] To some extent, new communities have already demonstrated that the members of different races and classes can live together without major problems. Likewise, the new communities now in existence have demonstrated that with careful planning job and revenue-producing industries and businesses can be attracted to centers of population.

The future of new communities in the United States hinges a great deal on the stance that the federal government takes toward them. Congress took a big step forward when it passed the Urban Growth and New Community Development Act in 1970. Among other things this

---

[46] See Anthony Downs, *Urban Problems and Prospects* (Chicago: Rand McNally & Company, 1970), esp. pp. 12–14.

[47] See Robert C. Weaver, "New Communities," in Ficker and Graves, *Social Science and Urban Crisis*, p. 77.

act (1) insures loans that are made by either public or private developers for the purpose of building new communities, (2) makes federal grants available to help pay the costs entailed in planning new communities, (3) makes federal loans available to cover the interest payments that developers have to pay on the money they borrow, and (4) makes grants available to existing units of local government to help them provide essential public services in the new communities.[48] For those who see much of promise in new communities, this piece of legislation represents a step in the right direction.

At the same time, the federal government has not yet made a total commitment to the development of new communities. The development of new communities is still largely left to private enterprise. It is doubtful that private enterprise will venture wholeheartedly into the business of developing new communities because the costs are formidable and many years pass before they yield a profit. It is regrettable that federal, state, and local governments do not have a deeper interest in new communities, for they "represent a major attempt to relate population, organization, technology, and environment in a way that produces a livable urban ecology." [49]

☐ TOTAL INSTITUTIONS

Sometimes society perceives the behavior of specific individuals as so threatening that they are restrained, at least for a while, in a prison or mental hospital. In yet other cases, the individual desires to go through a process of socialization and resocialization that is so complete that it can only be accomplished in institutions such as monasteries and convents. Finally, there are people who because of their age, a sickness, or the lack of parents have to be placed in such places as "homes" and hospitals. In a classic paper, Erving Goffman has assigned the term *total institutions* to these units of organization.[50]

It must be stressed that total institutions are not communities, at least in the narrowest sense of the term. Nonetheless, it is appropriate to consider total institutions in this chapter. First, total institutions, like communes and new communities, are started for a specific purpose. It may be to reform criminals, rehabilitate the mentally ill, provide humane care for old people, or whatever. Second, total institutions, again like com-

[48] Palen, *The Urban World*, p. 308.
[49] Ibid., p. 309.
[50] See Erving Goffman, "Characteristics of Total Institutions," in Maurice R. Stein, Arthur J. Vidich, and David Manning White, *Identity and Anxiety: Survival of the Person in Mass Society* (New York: The Free Press, 1960), pp. 449–79.

munes and new communities, provide alternative living arrangements for their residents. These residents may, of course, be called inmates, patients, novitiates, or whatever, depending on the type of total institution that we are discussing.

Similarities in Total Institutions

Goffman has made much of the similarities among total institutions. One thing that almost all total institutions have in common is that they seek to bring about significant change in their residents; the prison seeks to convert the inmate from a criminal to a law-abiding citizen, the mental hospital seeks to change the behavior of its patients, and the convent encourages the religious and spiritual growth of its members. Even a good nursing home seeks to improve the physical and mental health of its clients. Indeed, one reason that we have total institutions is so that the behavior or spiritual, mental, or physical health of some members of society can be altered—sometimes dramatically. For this reason, Goffman has called total institutions "the forcing houses for changing persons." [51]

It would be well to remember once more that the purpose of this chapter is not necessarily to identify commonalities among communes, new communities, and total institutions. It is interesting to note, however, that some communes also attempt to bring about significant change in their members. This is true of religious communes such as the Bruderhof, and it is true of some of the communes that strive to help their members develop their full potentials.

Total institutions vary in the degree to which they are successful in bringing about change in their members. For example, rates of recidivism are high among ex-convicts.[52] Similarly low rates of success have been reported for residential treatment centers for narcotic addicts.[53] On the other hand, institutions such as convents and well-staffed hospitals may well be more successful in achieving their goal of change. It is tempting to offer the hypothesis that the more people undergo the total institution's "treatment program" on a voluntary basis, the more successful the total institution will be in changing them.

Because they share the goal of changing persons, Goffman maintains

[51] Erving Goffman, *Asylums* (Chicago: Aldine Publishing Company, 1961), p. 12.
[52] See Daniel Glaser, "How Many Prisoners Return," in Leon Radinowicz and Marvin E. Wolfgang (eds.), *Crime and Justice,* Vol. III, *The Criminal in Confinement* (New York: Basic Books, 1971); Edwin H. Sutherland and Donald R. Cressey, *Criminology,* 9th ed. (Philadelphia: J. B. Lippincott Company, 1974), esp. pp. 517, 608.
[53] For example, see U.S. Department of Health, Education, and Welfare, *Narcotic Drug Addiction,* Public Health Service Publication No. 1021 (Washington, D.C.: U.S. Government Printing Office, 1965), p. 11.

that all total institutions share certain structural characteristics. We cannot discuss all the features that such institutions as prisons, mental hospitals, and convents have in common. However, three of the most important ones are as follows.

First, Goffman maintains that almost all total institutions purposefully isolate their residents from the larger society. Thus prisoners are rarely if ever allowed to leave the prison prior to parole, and only a small number of hospitalized mental patients are given "town passes" that allow them to leave the hospital grounds. As Goffman puts it, the "encompassing or total character [of total institutions] is often built right into the physical plant: locked doors, high walls, barbed wire, cliffs and water, open terrain, and so forth." [54] Within their own walls total institutions do provide their residents with the minimal necessities of life. This is one reason why Goffman uses the term *total institution* to refer to these units of organization.

Second, Goffman maintains that within all total institutions there is a basic split between the staff and the residents.[55] Antagonism and hostility between the two groups are not uncommon, and communication between the two groups is often kept at a minimum. One reason for this is that the staff has the goal of bringing about change in the residents of the institution. Very often the residents do not understand or accept the idea that there is need for change in their behavior, attitudes, or values. As a result, they deeply resent the staff as well as the larger society that the staff represents.

Finally, Goffman maintains that a central feature of total institutions is that they rely on force to change the person: total institutions are "forcing houses for changing persons." In prisons, for example, convicts are forced to follow a daily regimen that is intended to contribute to their reformation. In mental hospitals patients may be forced to undergo a treatment program (e.g., electroshock or psychotherapy) for their own good even if they would prefer not to have treatment. Even in institutions such as convents, orphanages, and TB sanatoriums, the residents may be given little choice but to carry out certain activities that presumably will change them for the better.

Total Institutions: Is the Concept Useful?

Until recently, the use of the term *total institution* to refer to a wide variety of institutions was not seriously questioned. Instead, it was assumed that prisons, mental hospitals, orphanages, convents, and so on,

[54] Goffman, "Characteristics of Total Institutions," p. 450.
[55] Ibid., 452.

had enough in common that they could be analyzed using the same conceptual framework. However, recent research has suggested that Goffman's use of the concept of total institution may be too broad. For example, Hillery has shown that convents lack many of the features that presumably characterize total institutions. In the convents studied by Hillery, a major "staff-inmate" split was not to be found, the novitiates could leave the convent if they desired, and the "staff" of the convent made little use of force in attempting to achieve goals.[56] To a greater or lesser degree these same traits are probably missing in other entities that Goffman calls total institutions, including orphanages, homes for the aged, boarding schools, and hospitals for the physically disabled. Goffman's concept of total institutions seems to fit best those institutions whose residents are (1) recruited on an involuntary basis and (2) restrained from leaving the institution. In short, Goffman's analysis fits prisons and mental hospitals better than it fits convents and boarding schools. It seems to fit such institutions as TB sanatoriums, army barracks, orphanages, and homes for the aged only moderately well. It is true that the residents of such institutions may be forbidden to leave the institution at will. Beyond this, at most there may be a moderate split between the staff and the residents; and force, in the strictest sense of the word, is not a central feature of these institutions.

Nonetheless, there are at least two reasons why it is important for the student of community to analyze total institutions. First, the existence of total institutions reminds us that millions on millions of Americans do not live in villages, cities, and metropolitan areas. Rather, they live in institutions that provide them with at least the minimal necessities of life. Second, in many cases total institutions are designed to deal with people who cannot function in the larger society: they represent society's way of dealing with these people. With exceptions (such as convents) people are placed in total institutions because we think they represent a threat to society or because they are too old, sick, immature, or disabled to function without intensive care and supervision.

☐ SUMMARY

Most Americans live in villages, cities, and metropolitan areas. However, a few people have chosen to live in communes, and a small fraction of the population lives in new communities. Finally, several million Americans live in what Goffman has called *total institutions*.

[56] George A. Hillery, Jr., "The Convent: Community, Prison, or Task Force?" *Journal for the Scientific Study of Religion*, 8 (Spring, 1969), esp. 143–47.

The differences among communes, new communities, and total institutions are much greater than their similarities. However, communes, new communities, and total institutions do have one thing in common: *they have been established with a purpose in mind*. It is for this reason that we have coined the term *purposeful communities* to refer to them.

Communes differ greatly from one another both in their size and in their purpose. Nonetheless, they do have some shared characteristics. Among other things, they stress the importance of the group over the individual, and they are "communistic" in the sense that all resources belong to the group as a whole and not to specific individuals. In order to be successful, a commune must engender commitment among its members; that is, its members must be willing to make great sacrifices if the commune is to remain viable. Likewise, communes must develop some sort of leadership structure, they must develop rules, and they must develop means of enforcing the rules. In so doing, however, they fall short of their goal of being unstructured and totally egalitarian. For some people communes represent an alternative to living in a highly competitive, success-oriented society.

New communities are fully planned, and they seek to provide their residents with a full range of facilities and services. In the United States the development of new communities is carried out under private auspices. If new communities are to be successful, they must be integrated along the lines of class and race, they must provide jobs for their residents, and they must provide a full range of services and facilities. Some experts doubt that new communities have much of a future because of the extremely high costs involved in building them. Nonetheless, they represent an alternative to continued unplanned urban sprawl. They can also be used to test and demonstrate innovations in community life that can perhaps be transferred to existing cities.

The term *total institution* is a broad one that encompasses a variety of different organizations including prisons, mental hospitals, orphanages, homes for the aged, convents, boarding schools, and hospitals for the physically disabled. Total institutions, regardless of their purpose, do have several things in common. Almost all total institutions seek to bring about significant change in their residents, and many total institutions purposefully isolate their residents from the larger society. Goffman argues that there is usually a "staff-inmate" split in total institutions and that one of the central features of total institutions is that they rely on force to change the person. It appears that Goffman's use of the term *total institution* is too broad. His concept of total institution fits best those institutions whose residents (1) are recruited on an involuntary basis and (2) are restrained from leaving.

BIBLIOGRAPHY

Allen, Irving Lewis. "New Towns and the Suburban Ideology: Selling the American Dream," *Sociological Symposium*, **12** (Fall, 1974), 16–38.

Conover, Patrick W. "An Analysis of Communes and Intentional Communities with Particular Attention to Sexual and Genderal Relations," *The Family Coordinator*, **24** (October, 1975), 453–64.

Fava, Sylvia F. "Blacks in American New Towns: Problems and Prospects," *Sociological Symposium*, **12** (Fall, 1974), 110–26.

Gardner, Hugh. "Dropping into Utopia," *Human Behavior*, **7** (March 1978), 43–47.

Goffman, Erving. *Asylums*. Chicago: Aldine Publishing Company, 1961.

Golany, Gideon, and Daniel Walden (eds.). *The Contemporary New Communities Movement in the United States*. Urbana: University of Illinois Press, 1974.

Hillery, George A., Jr. "The Convent: Community, Prison, or Task Force?" *Journal for the Scientific Study of Religion*, **8** (Spring, 1969), 140–51.

Holloway, Mark. *Heavens on Earth: Utopian Communities in America: 1680–1880*, 2nd rev. ed. New York: Dover, 1966.

Howard, Ebenezer. *Garden Cities of Tomorrow*, London: Faber and Faber, 1945.

Kanter, Rosabeth Moss. *Commitment and Community: Communes and Utopias in Sociological Perspective*. Cambridge, Mass.: Harvard University Press, 1972.

Kephart, William M. *Extraordinary Groups: The Sociology of Unconventional Life-Styles*. New York: St. Martin's Press, 1976.

McGuire, Chester C. "Operational Problems of New Communities," *Journal of Sociology and Social Welfare*, **3** (November, 1975), 136–40.

Melville, Keith. *Communes in the Counter Culture: Origins, Theories, Styles of Life*. New York: William Morrow & Company, 1972.

Nordhoff, Charles. *The Communistic Societies of the United States*. New York: Hillery House, 1960.

Osborn, Frederick J. *Green-Belt Cities*. New York: Schocken, 1969.

Palen, J. John. *The Urban World*. New York: McGraw-Hill Book Company, 1975, esp. pp. 295–310.

Redekop, Calvin. "Communal Groups: Inside or Outside the Community," in Jack Kinton (ed.), *The American Community: Creation & Revival*. Aurora, Ill.: Social Science and Sociological Resources, 1975, 135–58.

Smookler, Helene V. "Administration Hara-Kiri: Implementation of the Urban Growth and New Community Development Act," *The Annals of the American Academy of Political and Social Science*, **422** (November, 1975), 129–40.

Susskind, Lawrence. "Planning for New Towns: The Gap Between Theory and Practice," *Sociological Inquiry*, **43** (1973), 3–4, 291–310.

Weaver, Robert C. "New Communities," in Victor B. Ficker and Herbert S. Graves (eds.), *Social Science and Urban Crisis: Introductory Readings*. New York: Macmillan Publishing Co., Inc., 1971.

Zablocki, Benjamin. *The Joyful Community*. Baltimore: Penguin Books, 1971.

PART II

Theories of Community

A vast body of literature has emerged pertaining to communities. This literature is so widely scattered throughout textbooks, monographs, scientific journals, and even popular magazines that it is, for practical purposes, inaccessible to all but the most serious student of community life. To search it out requires months, if not years, of effort.

Hence in the next six chapters of this text an attempt is made to explore some of the significant literature on community structure and process. To be more specific, in Chapter 4 the reader's attention is drawn to theories of human ecology. There are several different schools of human ecology, but all have one thing in common: they seek to explain the physical layout and growth dynamics of cities. Indeed, theories of human ecology shed light on the spatial organization of cities and are based on the assumption that the distribution of demographic, social, and economic phenomena within the city follows regular, recurrent, and predictable patterns. In Chapter 5 we turn our attention to constructed type theories of community. In actuality, constructed types are rather complex entities, and their characteristics cannot be specified at the present time. It should be noted, however, that many theorists have made use of constructed types in their efforts to analyze community structure and change. Perhaps the most famous of these theorists was Ferdinand Tonnies, whose *Gemeinschaft und Gesellschaft* laid the foundation for the further development of the constructed type approach to community analysis. Among the other theorists who have worked within the constructed type tradition and whom we shall consider in Chapter 5 are Robert Redfield, Robert MacIver, Carle Zimmerman, Gideon Sjoberg, Roland L. Warren, and George A. Hillery, Jr. Chapter 6 of this text differs from its companion chapters in that it borrows theoretical systems from general sociology and explores their relevance to community analysis. In particular, this chapter deals with functionalism and social system theory. In the present writer's thinking, the chief contribution that social system theory makes to community analysis is that it gives meaning to the term *community structure* and clarifies the way in which various components of the community, such as its groups and institutions, are interrelated. Functionalism supplements this by reminding us that any social system is a complex, multifaceted whole and there are human and social needs that must be met if a community is to persist through time. In Chapter 7 theories of community conflict are examined. Among other things, we look at what various writers have had to say about the origins of community conflict, about the course of community conflict, and about how community conflicts can be resolved. Another approach to community analysis is explored in Chapter 8. In this chapter we use community action theory to examine patterns of action at the local level and as a tool that helps us understand the role of power and leadership in community affairs. Finally, in Chapter 9 we consider community change and development. Today, many communities are changing at an extremely rapid rate, and unless these change processes are understood, we cannot claim to have a full understanding of the modern community.

To the best of the writer's knowledge, this sixfold classification of types of community theory encompasses the dominant sociological approaches to community analysis. It is true, of course, that a great deal of literature on the community does not fit into this scheme. It should be noted, however, that the focus of this text is on the *community as a whole* rather than on the groups and institutions typically found *within* the community. It is in this respect that the present text differs from many of the other textbooks on community life.

CHAPTER 4

□□□□□□□□
□
□
□
□
□
□
□
□
□
□

Human Ecology

The city has always been a source of fascination and wonder. To some it has been a place to fear and detest, a seat of corruption and decay, whereas others have regarded it as the center of all progress. One of the most penetrating analyses of the city, however, has come not from the many philosophers, poets, and reformers who have loudly praised or condemned it but from a small group of social scientists called human ecologists. It is from human ecology that some of the most elaborate and most controversial theories of community have been derived.

There is of course more than one approach to human ecology. Certainly the blueprint for human ecology set forth by Robert E. Park is significantly different than that developed by Walter Firey some years later. However, all those working within the ecological tradition that is discussed in this chapter seem to agree that the *foremost goal of human ecology is to explain the spatial organization and growth dynamics of urban communities.* Furthermore, it is almost essential that human ecologists work on the assumption that the growth and resulting layout of the city, its population, and its institutions follow regular, recurrent patterns. Hence it becomes the task of human ecologists to discover basic patterns of city growth and to explain why cities tend to take on characteristic spatial configurations.

Human Ecology: Another Omnibus Term

The definition of human ecology just offered is quite narrow and specific, which for some readers could be a source of confusion. In its broadest sense, the term *ecology* refers to the adjustment of populations to their environment. Indeed, as early as 1873 the word *ecology* was used to refer to biological studies of the adjustment of plants and animals to their environment. More recently, scholars interested in the study of such diverse issues as environmental pollution, resource depletion, and overpopulation have referred to themselves as ecologists. This is entirely appropriate because all of these issues, in one way or another, deal with the adjustment of human beings to their environment. Nonetheless, in this chapter we are strictly concerned with what might be called urban ecology, that is, the spatial organization and growth dynamics of urban communities.[1] There is a rich body of literature on the spatial organization of cities and metropolitan areas that simply cannot be ignored.

The Importance of Human Ecology

In the pages that follow, we shall be looking at a number of theories and research findings pertaining to the spatial organization of cities. Some of these theories are rather complex. To fully comprehend them, the reader will have to pause, think, and analyze. It is therefore perfectly legitimate to raise the question: Why bother? Why is it important to study, in some detail, the spatial organization of cities?

A picture of the spatial organization of cities can contribute to our efforts to improve urban life. For example, suppose that there is a need to organize several neighborhood improvement associations within a large urban slum. The improvement associations are unlikely to be successful if the geographic area that they are concerned about includes several ethnic groups who are afraid and distrustful of one another. On the other hand, the improvement associations may be quite successful if they include people who share a common culture and who share common concerns. The point is, of course, that ecological analysis can be used to locate what might be called "natural communities," that is, small areas within the huge urban milieu where people do share a common culture and common concerns.

More importantly, however, we can get a good deal of insight into people's behavior by knowing something about the territorial milieu in which they function. For example, Gerald D. Suttles has introduced the concept of the defended neighborhood. Basically, defended neighborhoods are areas within the city whose residents feel safe and secure.[2] Quite frequently, the residents of a defended neighborhood belong to the

---

[1] For two works that approach human ecology from a much broader perspective see Paul R. Ehrlich, Anne E. Ehrlich, and John P. Holdren, *Human Ecology: Problems and Solutions* (San Francisco: W. H. Freeman and Company, 1973); Michael Micklin (ed.), *Population, Environment, and Social Organization: Current Issues in Human Ecology* (Hinsdale, Ill.: The Dryden Press, 1973).

[2] See Gerald D. Suttles, *The Social Construction of Communities* (Chicago: University of Chicago Press, 1972), 54–55.

same ethnic group and, above all, they know and trust each other. In fact, sometimes urbanites are reluctant to leave their own neighborhood and enter into an adjoining neighborhood. If they do so, they encounter people who seem to constitute a real or potential threat to them. As a matter of fact, in some large cities it may well be dangerous for a black person to venture into a nearby white neighborhood, or vice versa.

The residents of a defended neighborhood also try to protect their neighborhood from encroachment by outsiders. Indeed, Suttles defines a defended neighborhood as a "residential group which seals itself off through the efforts of delinquent gangs, by restrictive covenents, by sharp boundaries, or by a forbidding reputation." [3] Again, the residents' motives in doing so are at least partly to protect themselves from people whom they fear, distrust, or regard as undesirable.

Our brief discussion of defended neighborhoods suggests that territorial considerations do, to some extent, influence our behavior. Again, the point is that human ecology focuses on the spatial structure of cities. When we learn something about the spatial structure of cities we also learn something about people's behavior and motivations.

Finally, human ecologists have never confined themselves to simply describing the spatial organization of cities. Rather, they have advanced a variety of propositions that help us understand the processes operating in cities that lead to segregation, the ghettoization of minority groups, and so on. Likewise, they have given us a great deal of insight into the life-styles of the many, many different racial, ethnic, and status groups found within large urban areas.

☐ HISTORICAL DEVELOPMENT

Even though the term *human ecology* dates back only to 1921, writings that might be classified as ecological in nature go back as far as the early years of the nineteenth century.[4] Indeed, although the term was coined by Robert Park it is impossible, chronologically speaking, to identify the first human ecologist. Some possibilities, however, are M. de Guarry de Champnouf, who as early as 1825 investigated the spatial distribution of criminal acts in France,[5] and Charles Booth, whose classic studies of London and its people contain many of the insights later re-

---

[3] Ibid., p. 21.

[4] For a review of some of these studies see Yale Levin and Alfred Lindesmith, "English Ecology and Criminology of the Past Century," *Journal of Criminal Law and Criminology*, 27 (March, 1937), 801–16.

[5] See M. C. Elmer, "Century-Old Ecological Studies in France," *The American Journal of Sociology*, 39 (July, 1933), 63–70.

discovered and explored by the Chicago ecologists.[6] Nor can the social morphological approach developed by Emile Durkheim and Maurice Halbwachs be ignored.[7] It also focused on the spatial distribution of social phenomena and on the interrelationships of population, technology, and the environment.

Nonetheless, it was Robert Park and his colleagues at the University of Chicago during the 1920s and 1930s who gave human ecology its major impetus. They gave human ecology its theories and many of its methods, and history seems to dictate that Robert Park be declared the father of modern human ecology. Park coined the term, provided the basic assumptions for a theory of human ecology, and, most importantly, stimulated other outstanding scholars to seek a thorough understanding of the city. Furthermore, the truly significant contributions of Park and his associates were not erased when classical ecology was brought under severe criticism during the late 1930s. Perhaps the greatest tribute paid to Robert Park and his University of Chicago colleagues is that many of those who questioned the validity of classical ecology later developed their own theories of urban spatial organization.

☐ CLASSICAL ECOLOGY

We shall now examine some of the major theories of human ecology. In so doing, we shall follow the lead of George A. Theodorson, who has suggested that there are four different approaches to ecological analysis [8]: classical ecology, neo-orthodox ecology, sociocultural ecology, and social area analysis. We shall begin with the classical school of human ecology because it precedes the other approaches in time and because the other approaches attempt either to refine classical ecology or to provide an alternative explanation of urban spatial organization.

Basic Assumptions

One of the fundamental assumptions made by Robert E. Park and his associates was that human society consists of two levels of organization,

[6] Charles Booth, *Life and Labour of the People in London* (London: Macmillan Company, Limited, 1902), Vols. 1–8.

[7] Thus Schnore tells us that "whether we examine earlier or more recent versions of human ecology, Durkheim's stamp is clearly imprinted." See Leo F. Schnore, "Social Morphology and Human Ecology," *American Journal of Sociology*, 63 (May, 1958), 631. For a brief review of the social morphological approach see Maurice Halbwachs, *Population and Society: Introduction to Social Morphology*, trans. by Otis Dudley Duncan and Harold W. Pfautz (New York: The Free Press, 1960), pp. 7–21.

[8] See George A. Theodorson (ed.), *Studies in Human Ecology* (New York: Harper & Row, 1961).

the biotic and the social.[9] The biotic level is not unique to human beings but is found wherever living things share a common habitat. Perhaps the most important feature of the biotic level is that it is characterized by close-knit patterns of interdependence among its cohabitants and is therefore essentially communal in character. Because this level of organization is common to all forms of life, one of Robert Park's basic aims was to determine the applicability of principles of plant and animal ecology to the study of human communities. In contrast, the social level exists only among human beings and involves relationships that only people are capable of creating and sustaining. Because the dichotomy between the biotic (communal) and social levels of organization is of central importance to classical ecology, it must be examined in more detail.

The biotic or communal level is not a product of deliberate and rational activities. Rather, its organizational pattern is automatically determined as numerous individuals congregate in a limited territory, such as within the boundaries of a city. Hence the forces giving the community its shape and structure are impersonal and subsocial, a product of natural distributive processes of which people are normally not aware. Furthermore, the classical ecologists assume that relationships at the biotic level are symbiotic, that is, they consist of impersonal patterns of coexistence and interdependence. Although the inhabitants of a human community are not always aware of it, they are dependent on each other in much the same way that the plants or animals found in any given area are dependent on each other for their survival. Finally, and most importantly, the classical ecologists maintain that the patterns of organization that typify the biotic level result from certain impersonal processes of competition. Thus James A. Quinn points out that

> Park, Burgess, and McKenzie . . . emphasize the importance of impersonal, continuous, universal "competition" among living organisms, which in the long run selects and distributes the populations and institutions of an area. This impersonal interaction "without social contact" results, so they say, in a basic underlying areal structure that serves as a foundation on which the consensus aspects of social structure arise.[10]

Because the concept of competition is of central importance in classical ecological theory, it will be considered in more detail later.

In contrast to the biotic level of organization, the social level consists of a network of interpersonal relationships. Its hallmarks are con-

---

[9] For example, see Robert E. Park, "Human Ecology," *The American Journal of Sociology*, 42 (July, 1936), 1–15.
[10] James A. Quinn, *Human Ecology* (Englewood Cliffs, N.J.: Prentice-Hall, Inc., 1950), p. 297.

sensus and communication. Thus Park frequently pointed out that community life always has its impersonal, competitive (i.e., biotic) aspects, but that "men and women are bound together by affections and common purposes; they do cherish traditions, ambitions, and ideals that are not all their own. . . ." [11] The fact that people do have these ties of sentiment and common purpose gives rise to social organization.

Park has occasionally been criticized on the grounds that he overlooked the fact that human relationships do involve consensus and communication. Although this criticism may apply to some of his followers, it is not applicable to Park himself. As a matter of fact, some of his most penetrating insights dealt with the role of communication and consensus in social organization.[12] Nonetheless, Park did regard the fundamental task of human ecology to be that of exploring and explaining the biotic or communal level of organization. He, along with his followers, maintained that consensus and communication grow out of people's struggle for existence on an impersonal level. It is this struggle for existence that determines patterns of urban spatial organization.

The Central Role of Competition

We have already suggested that the classical ecologists saw competition as the central factor that determines the spatial organization of the city. This competition arises because the amount of land that it is feasible for a city to occupy is limited and must be allocated to many different groups and institutions. At the same time, all these groups and institutions must be accommodated simply because they are dependent on another: both business and industry may desire the same land, but neither wishes to see the other destroyed. This is what the term *symbiosis* implies and is why the classical ecologists speak of competitive cooperation rather than of a type of competition that borders on conflict. In short, urban spatial organization does not result from the attempt of one group or institution to eliminate other groups or institutions. Rather, it results from the fact that each group or institution tries to find a niche in the community that it can profitably occupy. The community could not persist through time if the majority of its groups and institutions were not eventually accommodated.

To be more specific, competition centering around the use of land

[11] Robert Ezra Park, *Human Communities* (New York: The Free Press, 1952), p. 180. This citation originally appeared in an article entitled "Sociology, Community, and Society," in Wilson Gee (ed.), *Research Methods in the Social Sciences* (New York: Macmillan Publishing Co., Inc., 1929).
[12] For example, see Robert E. Park, "Reflections on Communication and Culture," *American Journal of Sociology*, 44 (September, 1938), 187–205.

and competition for residential sites are the two main forces that determine the spatial organization of cities. The first, competition centering around the use of land, arises out of the fact that various groups and institutions have preferred locations in terms of the city as a whole. Sometimes these overlap and conflict. As a result, the question continually arises as to whether a given piece of land shall be used for commercial, industrial, institutional, or residential purposes. Presumably, this problem is resolved through the process of competition, with the economically most powerful groups and institutions being the winners. Because commercial and industrial interests usually have the most power in the competitive struggle, they control the vital land near the center of the city and/or at the intersection of main transportation routes. Other groups and institutions must then find convenient locations on the land that remains available. This is known as the *principle of dominance* in classical ecological theory.

In addition to the allocation of land to various commercial, industrial, and institutional interests, land must be distributed to various residential groups. Because of this, the classical ecologists maintain that urban spatial organization is also influenced by competition among various socioeconomic, racial, and ethnic groups for residential sites. Presumably, the wealthiest people get the choicest land, and other residential groups get what remains. Because the most preferred residential locations are often near the outskirts of the city, a gradient is established with the wealthiest persons living some distance away from the center of the city whereas the poorest and most disadvantaged live on what little land is available for residential purposes within the already crowded centers of business and industry. Other groups compete for the land between these two extremes.

In a recently published book, Brian J. L. Berry and John D. Kasarda shed additional light on the factors determining where different families reside within a city or metropolitan area.[13] These determinants of residential location are shown in Table 4-1. First, income influences where a family resides. People who earn $40,000 a year will most likely buy or rent in a different part of the city than people who make $4,000 a year. Second, the stage that families have reached in their life cycle influences where they buy or rent. Newly marrieds often live in an apartment complex, families with children often seek needed space in a single-family suburban dwelling unit, and it is becoming increasingly common for older people to sell the family home and move into condominiums or apartment complexes whose residents are approximately their same

[13] See Brian J. L. Berry and John D. Kasarda, *Contemporary Urban Ecology* (New York: Macmillan Publishing Co., Inc., 1977), pp. 126–31.

TABLE 4-1. Determinants of Housing Choice

Individual Characteristics		Housing Characteristics
Income	↔	Price
Stage in life cycle	↔	Type of home
Life-style preferences	↔	Neighbors, type of community institutions
Attitude toward journey to work	↔	Location with respect to the job

Source: Brian J. L. Berry and John D. Kasarda, *Contemporary Urban Ecology* (New York: Macmillan Publishing Co., Inc., 1977), p. 126.

age. A third factor that often influences where people buy or rent is their life-style preference. One couple may enjoy living near the center of the city where theaters, nightclubs, and museums are nearby, whereas another couple may prefer to live in a suburban area where there is room for a private swimming pool and where recreation is defined in terms of sunbathing, having barbecues with the neighbors, and so on. Finally, the location of one's place of employment influences where one buys or rents. Prosperous people can afford to live farther from their place of employment than poor people.

It must be stressed that Berry and Kasarda's analysis does not contradict the classical ecologist's contention that competition is the main determinant of where people buy or rent living quarters. Affluent people can buy or rent the type of home they want in the location that they want it. Poor people, on the other hand, have to take what they can get in crowded slums and ghettos.

The Ecological Processes

The classical ecologists therefore view competition as a master process affecting the spatial organization of the city. However, there are other processes that come into play, partly as a concomitant of competition and partly as independent forces impinging on city growth and organization. These ecological processes are centralization, concentration, segregation, invasion, and succession and were first delineated by Roderick D. McKenzie.[14]

The first of these, centralization, refers to the tendency for selected institutions and services to cluster near the city's focal points of transportation and communication. As the city gains in population and evolves a high division of labor, relatively specialized commercial interests seek

[14] See R. D. McKenzie, "The Scope of Human Ecology," *Publications of the American Sociological Society,* **20** (1926), 141–54.

locations in the central business district. The chief reason for this is that these specialized shops and services must be accessible to large numbers of persons. A department store that handles only expensive, high-quality merchandise or an exclusive health food store must be exposed to a large market if it is to realize a profit because the percentage of the population that uses these services is small. In brief, the central business district represents that one point of greatest average convenience for all persons who might utilize the facility or service in question. Similarly, McKenzie argued that with the passage of time the central business district comes to dominate not only the city but also the surrounding hinterland with its villages and small towns.[15] The small-town grocery is gradually absorbed by the huge chain store with its centralized offices and distribution facilities, and the small-town bank disappears as its functions are absorbed by its more powerful urban competitors. Thus centralization is a twofold process that involves both the expansion and proliferation of services offered in the central city and the increasing dominance of the central city over its hinterland.

Competition has a key role to play in this process. Arnold Rose, for example, points out that "merchants specializing in a certain product —such as wholesale clothing or used cars—may find it expedient and profitable to settle near one another so that customers can 'shop around.' "[16] Hence, although two department stores are in competition for the consumer's dollar, they may nonetheless benefit by being located in proximity to one another. Being so located means that a large number of potential customers are attracted to the area and that these customers can compare and choose among the goods offered by the department stores. This is a prime example of what classical ecologists mean by competitive cooperation. Likewise, the tendency for businesses located in the hinterland to lose their independence reflects, in a real sense, the operation of competition. The small-town grocery or bank simply lacks the capital and population base that allows it to meet the challenge posed by commercial interests located within the city.

The classical ecologists recognized that there are limits to the amount of centralization that can occur. Competition for land within the central city causes an increase in land values to a point at which further expansion is economically infeasible. Furthermore, the central city can become so congested that businesspeople and shoppers alike find it extremely costly, in both time and patience, to visit it regularly. Thus a considerable amount of decentralization may eventually occur. Indeed, one of the

---

[15] Ibid., p. 150.
[16] Arnold M. Rose, *Sociology: The Study of Human Relations,* 2nd rev. ed. (New York: Alfred A. Knopf, 1965), p. 521.

fundamental facts of urban life today is the increasing tendency for stores, professional offices, industries, and entertainment facilities to seek suburban locations. The result is that suburban areas often assume many of the same characteristics and go through many of the same processes that were originally manifested in the central city. They become little cities in themselves.

The second subprocess, concentration, has been conceptualized in two distinctly different ways by classical ecologists. First, it has occasionally been used to refer to the tendency for some parts of the city to become extremely congested and overcrowded while other parts remain sparsely populated. As a concept developed by McKenzie, however, concentration refers to the tendency for the population of urban areas to increase as a result of migration from outlying regions. During recent years, for example, metropolitan areas have grown at the expense of small towns and villages. Concentration has been the core process underlying urbanization in the United States and in many other countries.

This tendency toward population concentration in urban centers can also be attributed to competition. As McKenzie explains it, "the degree of concentration attained by any locality is . . . a measure of its resources and location advantages as compared to those of its competitors." [17] To be more specific, the relative size of markets, availability of raw materials, and number of jobs available determine the extent to which competing urban centers can draw persons into their orbit. At the same time, heavy migration into an urban area increases the amount of competition that occurs within its boundaries, and especially for residential sites. Drastic overcrowding such as in New York's Harlem is, to a great extent, the result of continuous and heavy in-migration from rural areas and from the southern states. Competition among these newcomers for housing has forced rental prices up to a level equal to or greater than those found in the more desirable sections of the city.

The third major ecological subprocess identified by McKenzie is segregation. This refers to the tendency for various groups and institutions to locate in separate and distinct parts of the city. Segregation helps to account for the fact that some parts of the city are characterized by upper-class housing, a minority group population, certain types of industry, or whatever. Presumably, the process of segregation manifests itself in about the same way in all large, rapidly growing cities, and thus certain patterns of segregation become almost universal.

There are several things that must be noted about the concept of segregation as it is employed in classical ecological theory. First, it refers only to the tendency for similar ecological units to cluster in proximity to

[17] McKenzie, "The Scope of Human Ecology," p. 147.

one another. The classical ecologists say little about the type of segregation that arises from racial prejudice and discrimination. Second, like the other ecological processes, segregation refers both to an ongoing process of change and to the end product of this change.[18] To be more specific, the classical ecologists concerned themselves not only with the fact that various parts of the city are characterized by different patterns of land use but also with the reasons why this is the case. Why do cities have black belts, better residential areas, wholesale districts, and areas where vice runs rampant? Finally, the classical ecologists maintained that segregation is the primary factor leading to the emergence of natural areas. Because segregation brings together people who are racially, economically, or socially homogeneous, they tend also to share common interests, life-styles, and needs. Because the concept of natural areas is an important one in classical ecological theory, more will be said about it in later parts of this chapter.

That competition is the chief sorting and selecting mechanism in this process of segregation is entirely clear. The wealthy become isolated from the poor because of their greater ability to command and control choice residential sites. On the other hand, certain minority groups are unable to compete at all and must therefore take up residence in the least desirable sections of the city. Likewise, it has already been indicated that centralization leads to a certain amount of ecological segregation as specialized shops and service facilities outbid all other interests for locations in the central city. One ecologist has suggested that the processes of centralization and segregation can proceed so far that even within retail shopping districts one finds "shoe stores in one or two adjacent blocks; men's and women's clothing stores in another sector; and florists and other units combined in still other locations." [19]

The fourth and fifth ecological subprocesses identified by McKenzie are invasion and succession. These two concepts draw one's attention to the fact that the spatial organization of the city is constantly in a state of flux. Various pieces of land are constantly changing hands and areas once devoted to one type of activity are given over to new ones.

To be more specific, invasion refers to a situation in which one group or institution encroaches on the territory held by another group or institution. More often than not, the involved territories are adjacent to one another, but this does not have to be the case. For example, invasion occurs when the central business district begins expanding into immediately adjacent areas, but it also occurs when commercial estab-

[18] See Quinn, *Human Ecology*, p. 353.
[19] Amos H. Hawley, *Human Ecology* (New York: The Ronald Press, 1950), pp. 279–80.

lishments begin appearing in suburban residential areas. Likewise, a particular population group (e.g., blacks, Puerto Ricans, or Mexican-Americans) may begin moving into an area adjacent to where they originally resided, or they may begin filtering into a far-removed suburb. In short, invasion can be traced to either (1) outward growth and expansion from the original territory or (2) permanent movement from one territory to another.

The classical ecologists have used the term *succession* in more than one way. As defined by McKenzie, however, succession refers to a completed process of invasion, that is, the complete conversion of an area from one use to another. Succession would therefore occur when an area that was formerly residential becomes totally commercial, or when a residential area that was formerly restricted to whites becomes inhabited by nonwhites alone. This means that succession is a temporal as well as a territorial phenomenon. It entails the replacement of old population groups by new ones and the appearance of new and different institutional types in a given area. This may require years of continuous and steady change.

The Concentric Zone Hypothesis

The ecologists were firmly convinced that these processes, and especially competition, are operative in every large city. Because of this, they hypothesized that as the city grows it tends to assume certain clearly delineated patterns of spatial organization. It was the classical ecologists who developed the concentric zone hypothesis. According to Ernest Burgess, who originally suggested this hypothesis, the city tends to become divided up into five distinct zones (see Figure 4-1). These zones, and the forces that supposedly lead to their emergence, are as follows:

1. Zone I consists of the central business district and is found in every city of moderate to large size. According to Burgess, it is where "we expect to find the department stores, the skyscraper office buildings, the railroad stations, the great hotels, the theaters, the art museum, and the city hall." [20] This area inevitably becomes the hub of economic, political, and cultural activities for the city and its hinterland. Needless to say, the central business district is a product of centralization and, on occasion, becomes the victim of decentralization. It will be recalled, however, that centralization itself is partly attributable to competition among various commercial interests for favorable locations and numerous customers.

[20] Ernest W. Burgess, "The Growth of the City: An Introduction to a Research Project," in Robert E. Park, Ernest W. Burgess, and R. D. McKenzie (eds.), *The City* (Chicago: University of Chicago Press, 1925), p. 52.

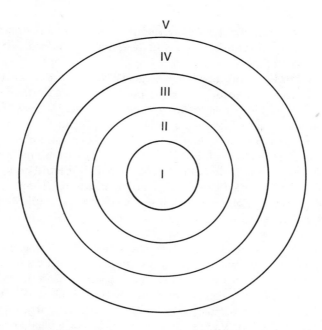

Zone I   Central Business District. Large department stores, skyscrapers, large hotels, theaters, and so on.

Zone II Zone of Transition. Slum housing, skid-row hotels and drinking establishments, industry, and so on.

Zone III Zone of Independent Workingmen's Homes. Modest homes, interspersed with an occasional school, park, corner grocery, and so on.

Zone IV Zone of Better Residences. Single-family dwellings, apartment houses, and bright-light areas.

Zone V Commuters' Zone. Suburban residential areas, satellite cities, and so on.

FIGURE 4-1. The concentric zone pattern. *[Adapted from R. E. Park, E. W. Burgess, and Roderick D. McKenzie,* The City *(Chicago: University of Chicago Press, 1925), p. 55.]*

2. Zone II is aptly called the zone of transition. As such, it forms a circle around the central business district. Within it are usually found the city's slum districts, immigrant colonies, part of the "black belt," centers of crime and vice, and roominghouse districts, as well as some light industry. The individuals who live in this zone often have only one thing in common. They are the losers in the competitive struggle through which different parts of the city are allocated to various groups and institutions. This may be because they have rejected the competitive

struggle itself (criminals, hobos, or derelicts) or because they have not been given the opportunity to compete (black Americans and other minority group members).

Two basic forces lead to the emergence of the zone of transition. First, this zone is allocated to those people and institutions who are unable to occupy land in any other part of the city. They frequently cannot bear the costs of living farther from the central city, or, if they can, land may not be made available to them. For example, because of prejudice and their disadvantaged economic condition, many minority groups are given no choice but to occupy the dilapidated, rundown sections of the city. Likewise, houses of prostitution, cheap hotels, and skid-row drinking establishments would never draw a sufficient number of customers in a middle-class suburban shopping center and undoubtedly would not be permitted in such areas.

The dilapidation that characterizes the zone of transition is not, however, directly attributable to the types of people and institutions that occupy it. Rather, it can be traced to the fact that this zone is the chief target of invasion by the central business district. Indeed, the term *zone of transition* implies that this part of the city is constantly in a state of invasion and succession. The process involved is made clear by Walter C. Reckless:

> The improved property in these mobile, decaying neighborhoods that are in direct line of business expansion is allowed to run down, to deteriorate, for upkeep generally results in a total loss to the owner, since business only ordinarily demands the site. These deteriorated dwellings of the slum, because of their undesirability, can command but very low rents. It is unavoidable that the poor and vicious classes share the same locality in the city's junk heap.[21]

Reckless's last sentence once more underscores the fact that the classical ecologists consider urban spatial organization to be the result of uncontrolled, impersonal processes.

3. The third zone delineated by Burgess, that of independent workingmen's homes, is chiefly residential in character. As such, this zone is "inhabited predominately by factory and shop workers,"[22] whose homes are smaller, older, and of frame construction. Burgess also suggests that quite often the inhabitants of zone III moved there from the zone of transition. They are, in effect, people who have escaped from the slums.

[21] Walter C. Reckless, "The Distribution of Commercialized Vice in the City: A Sociological Analysis," *Publications of the American Sociological Society,* **20** (1926), 175.
[22] Burgess, "The Growth of the City," p. 56.

At the same time, these persons, or their sons and daughters, frequently aspire to residence in zone IV with its restricted residential areas, its apartment house regions, and its "bright light" districts.

Burgess does not discuss the forces that lead to the emergence of the zone of independent workingmen's homes. However, once again it appears that competition has a key role to play. The inhabitants of this zone have acquired the means to escape from the slum but still lack the ability to compete for residential sites in the "best" sections of the city.

4. The fourth ring is called the zone of better residences. The standard housing type found in this area is the single family dwelling unit, but Burgess indicated that in Chicago zone IV was becoming increasingly characterized by apartment houses and residential hotels.[23] In any event, it is in this section of the city that one finds the homes of small business-people, professional people, clerks and salesmen, and other members of the native-born middle class.[24] However, zone IV is not devoted exclusively to residential uses. It is also an area where local shopping centers or "satellite loops" appear. It is common to find commercialized areas within this zone that contain banks, supermarkets, drug stores, and restaurants. In addition, Burgess suggests that zone IV may have its clusters of motion picture theaters, cabarets, and smart hotels. Burgess refers to these entertainment centers located within the zone of better residences as "bright light" areas.

5. The commuter's zone is the final one delineated by Burgess. The inner side of this zone is bounded by the zone of better residences, but its outer periphery may be quite amorphous. Within the commuter's zone are found a variety of small hamlets, towns, and suburban areas that are not legally integrated with the central city but are nonetheless dependent on it for goods, services, and jobs. These satellite communities are "in the main, dormitory suburbs, because the majority of men residing there spend the day at work in the Loop (central business district), returning only for the night."[25] At the same time, the characteristics of these satellite communities are varied: they range all the way from quiet, upper-class "bungalow" districts to gaudy entertainment centers. With the appearance of these satellite communities, the city has indeed become metropolitan in character.

Many of the same processes that account for the emergence of zones I, II, and III help to account for zones IV and V. The latter zones are also a product of competition, for in them dwell the winners in the

[23] See E. W. Burgess, "Urban Areas," in T. V. Smith and L. D. White (eds.), *Chicago: An Experiment in Social Science Research* (Chicago: University of Chicago Press, 1929), p. 116.
[24] Ibid., p. 116.
[25] Ibid., p. 117.

competitive struggle for land. The fact that the desirable land near the outskirts of the city is controlled by middle- and upper-class groups explains why less advantaged members of the urban population are frequently crowded into slums and ghettos. No other locations are made available to them. Furthermore, the recent suburbanization of American cities can be traced to the combined effects of decentralization, segregation, invasion, and succession. Suburbs are a product of continuous and rapid decentralization and are among the most homogeneous, "segregated" areas found in the modern city.

Before we leave the concentric zone hypothesis, a few concluding observations are in order. First, the present writer has followed Burgess's own description of the city and its spatial organization as closely as possible. This is because the focus of this book is on *theories of community* rather than on *the community itself*. If Ernest Burgess were alive today, he might well revise his hypothesis in order to take into account recent developments in urban spatial organization. Second, it must be stressed that Burgess saw the formation of concentric zones as an ongoing process. He points out, for example, that under conditions of rapid population growth the city constantly expands outward in such a way that what was once a part of zone II becomes a part of zone I. Finally, the concentric zone hypothesis has been criticized because there are many factors that can interfere with the emergence of perfect concentric circles. Burgess apparently anticipated these criticisms: "neither Chicago nor any other city fits perfectly into this ideal scheme. Complications are introduced by the lake front, the Chicago River, railroad lines, historical factors in the location of industry, the relative degree of the resistance of communities to invasion, etc." [26] Whether the concentric zone hypothesis itself has any validity is a different question. It will be considered in later parts of this chapter.

Although the concentric zone hypothesis has consistently received the most attention, there have been other theories of urban spatial organization. One of these is Homer Hoyt's sector theory.[27] Basically, Hoyt maintains that cities tend to become divided into a number of sectors that radiate out from the central business district (see Figure 4-2). Some of these sectors are devoted to residential use; others are devoted to industrial and related uses. The residential sectors may, in turn, display a pattern wherein the poorest districts are located near the central business district whereas the best residential areas are found near the periphery of the city. Hoyt argues that this pattern results from

[26] Burgess, "The Growth of the City," pp. 51–52.
[27] See Homer Hoyt, *The Structure and Growth of Residential Neighborhoods in American Cities* (Washington, D.C.: U.S. Government Printing Office, 1939), Chapter 6.

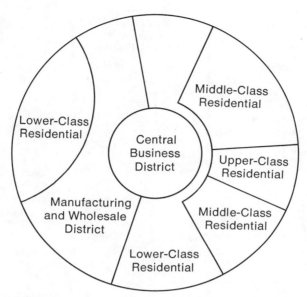

FIGURE 4-2. The sector theory of urban spatial organization. *[Adapted from Chauncey D. Harris and Edward L. Ullman, "The Nature of Cities,"* Annals of the American Academy of Political and Social Science, **242** *(November, 1945), 12.]*

the tendency for different groups and institutions to expand along the major transportation routes leading from the central city to the periphery: Residential areas expand along one route, industrial establishments along another, and so forth.

Another well-known theory of urban spatial organization is Harris and Ullman's multiple-nuclei theory.[28] Harris and Ullman argue that the city has not one but several nuclei or centers (see Figure 4-3). Each of these centers is devoted to different activities. Thus one nucleus may be devoted exclusively to wholesaling, another to governmental functions, and yet a third to financial activities. Harris and Ullman have developed four principles that supposedly account for the emergence of these separate nuclei:

1. Certain groups and institutions demand specialized facilities if they are to flourish. Heavy industry, for example, requires large acreages whereas the retail business district must be located so as to be conveniently accessible to the majority of the city's population.

2. Certain groups and institutions benefit from being located in proximity to one another. Large retail establishments, for example,

[28] See C. D. Harris and L. Ullman, "The Nature of Cities," *The Annals of the American Academy of Political and Social Science,* **242** (November, 1945), 7–17.

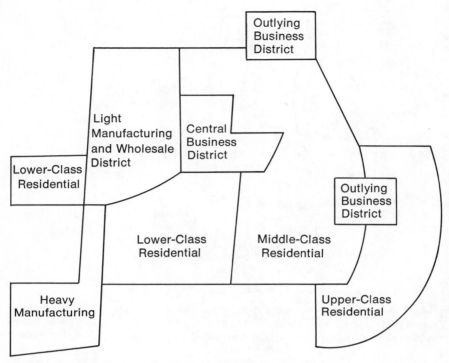

FIGURE 4-3. The multiple-nuclei pattern of urban spatial organization. *[Adapted from Chauncey D. Harris and Edward L. Ullman, "The Nature of Cities," Annals of the American Academy of Political and Social Science, **242** (November, 1945), 12.]*

benefit from being located in the same general part of the city. This brings a large number of potential customers to the area. These customers can compare and evaluate the price and quality of the goods offered by the different establishments.

3. Certain unlike groups and institutions find it disagreeable and disadvantageous to be located in proximity to one another. It is, for example, more pleasant to have as one's next-door neighbor a person of similar background and values than it is to have a large, noisy industrial plant as one's next-door "neighbor."

4. Finally, the inability to pay high rents forces some groups and institutions to cluster together. In most cities there is a limited amount of land that can be obtained at relatively low cost. This land is often taken up by lower-quality housing developments, bulk wholesaling or storage facilities, and other groups and institutions that need large amounts of land at a low price.

Natural Areas

If the classical ecologists had concluded their analysis of the city with the concentric zone hypothesis, they would have been guilty of gross oversimplification. Even though it is reasonable to hypothesize that the city is divided into a series of concentric zones and that each zone is homogeneous in comparison to the others, it is also reasonable to suggest that the various zones themselves display a considerable diversity of people and institutions. The zone of transition, for example, supposedly contains a black belt, immigrant colonies, centers of crime and vice, a skid row, a rooming house district, and areas of light industry. Because of this, the classical ecologists developed their final major concept, that of natural areas.

The concept of natural area has several different dimensions. From a geographic point of view, it refers to the smallest meaningful territorial unit found within the city. Because of features of the landscape (rivers, hills, and so on) and man-made barriers such as railroads, highways, and parks, the city becomes divided into a number of small, semi-isolated areas. Sometimes this isolation is rather complete, as is the case when a modern freeway splits one formerly well-integrated neighborhood into two completely distinct ones. This simple illustration also suggests why the resulting areas are said to be natural, that is, "they are the unplanned, natural product of the city's growth." [29]

Of more importance is the fact that each natural area tends to become segregated in terms of the type of people and institutions found within its boundaries. In short, natural areas are homogeneous units found within the heterogeneous urban milieu. There are several ways by which this segregation might be explained, but once again the classical ecologists relied on the competitive struggle for land as their key explanatory variable: wealthy, powerful groups gain control of the most desirable natural areas whereas weak, disadvantaged groups and institutions find their niche in less desirable areas. Furthermore, because of the homogeneous character of each natural area, these small units of urban spatial organization tend to become culturally distinct from one another. Robert Park, for example, tells us that "every natural area has, or tends to have, its own peculiar traditions, customs, conventions, standards of decency and propriety, and, if not a language of its own, at least a universe of discourse, which is appreciably different for each local community." [30]

---

[29] Harvey W. Zorbaugh, "The Natural Areas of the City," *Publications of the American Sociological Society*, **20** (1926), 191.
[30] Park, *Human Communities*, p. 201.

Thus when someone refers to Chinatown or Skid Row we think not only of a district that can be plotted on a map but also of a section of the city that has its own unique social and cultural patterns.

The concept of natural area was central to classical ecological theory. For one thing, the assumption that the city is divided into a number of natural areas rounds out the picture that the classical ecologists painted of urban spatial organization. In essence, they suggested that the city is a complex mosaic of zones and subareas, each of which represents a "pocket" into which the heterogeneous urban population is sorted and segregated. Furthermore, the classical ecologists made brilliant use of natural areas in their research. Among other things, they were able to show that different natural areas become characterized by high or low crime rates, by varying degrees of family disorganization, and by different types of mental illness.[31] Indeed, the research conducted by the Chicago ecologists was fully as important as their contributions to ecological theory. Finally, one of the Chicago ecologists, Harvey W. Zorbaugh, made it clear that the existence of natural areas has numerous implications in terms of efficient administration of city government. Put most simply, Zorbaugh suggested that far too often the city's political units cut across and ignore the boundaries of natural areas and that, because of this, our desire to make political units meaningful to their inhabitants is frustrated. This problem is well illustrated by a community council that "set out to make a community of a section of the city including a colony of 6,000 Persians, a belt of some 4,000 Negroes, a colony of 1,000 Greeks, a rooming house population of 25,000, 'Towertown' —Chicago's Greenwich Village—and Chicago's much vaunted 'Gold Coast.'"[32] The utter futility of attempting to bring such a diversity of people together into one "community" of interest and association is obvious.

During recent years, discussion of natural areas has pretty much dropped out of the literature on human ecology. Nonetheless, the idea that cities are divided into small, homogeneous subareas is still very much alive. For example, what Gerald Suttles refers to as defended neighborhoods are closely akin to natural areas (see earlier). Among other things, defended neighborhoods have territorial boundaries and their residents usually share a common ethnicity. Presumably, the residents of each defended neighborhood also share a distinctive set of

[31] An excellent summary of some of these studies is contained in Maurice R. Stein, *The Eclipse of Community: An Interpretation of American Community Studies* (Princeton, N.J.: Princeton University Press, 1960), pp. 34–46.
[32] Zorbaugh, "The Natural Areas of the City," p. 194.

cultural traits that differentiate them from the residents of other defended neighborhoods.[33]

The Growing Tide of Criticism

During the 1920s and the early 1930s the Chicago ecologists worked feverishly to develop their conceptual scheme. By 1935 their work was essentially complete, at least in its main outlines. Human ecology had reached the stage in its development at which it included the dichotomy between biotic and social levels of organization, the concentric zone hypothesis, and the concept of natural area. Furthermore, the assumption that competition is the key variable influencing urban spatial organization had been taken for granted. However, classical ecology barely reached this stage when it came in for a period of rather severe and devastating criticism. The critics of classical ecology not only questioned its validity as a theoretical system but also raised questions about some of the empirical findings reported by the Chicago ecologists.

As a system of theory, classical ecology was attacked on several grounds. About the most serious of these attacks centered around the dichotomy that was drawn between the biotic and social levels of organization. A particularly vocal critic in this regard was Milla A. Alihan, who argued that the classical ecologists were themselves unable to make the distinction between biotic and social levels a meaningful one: Although they focused on spatially distributed phenomena, they were eventually forced to rely on social and cultural variables to explain their observations.[34] Similarly, Warner E. Gettys argued that the concept of "biotic level" in classical ecological theory was symbolic of a form of biological and geographic determinism:

> In spite of statements in the literature to the contrary, there is considerable evidence that the ecologists held to a theory of biological and/or geographic determinism in human affairs. In other words, men and their institutions are represented as being spatially, temporally and

[33] During recent years there have been a number of ethnographic studies of "natural areas." For example, see Ulf Hannerz, *Soulside: Inquiries into Ghetto Culture* (New York: Columbia University Press, 1969); Elliot Liebow, *Tally's Corner: A Study of Negro Streetcorner Men* (Boston: Little, Brown and Company, 1967); James G. Spradley, *You Owe Yourself a Drunk: An Ethnography of Urban Nomads* (Boston: Little, Brown and Company, 1970); Carol B. Stack, *All Our Kin: Strategies for Survival in a Black Community* (New York: Harper & Row, 1974).

[34] See Milla A. Alihan, *Social Ecology: A Critical Analysis* (New York: Cooper Square Publishers, 1964), pp. 81–84. This volume was originally published in 1938 by Columbia University Press.

occupationally distributed by the operation of forces either inherent in the biological nature of man or existing external to man in the so-called "natural world." [35]

Finally, August B. Hollingshead strongly and convincingly argued that sociocultural systems influence every facet of human affairs, including those of an ecological nature. Among other things, cultural norms and values dictate that personal cooperative relationships will have a role to play in determining the spatial organization of communities.[36]

In addition to these basic criticisms, the emphasis that the classical ecologists put on competition as the key variable determining urban spatial organization was attacked. Alihan, for example, seriously questioned the validity of designating competition as "the primary, the universal, and the fundamental process" determining the physical layout of the city.[37] Could not some other process, such as cooperation, conflict, or assimilation, be arbitrarily chosen as an explanatory variable and a theory of human ecology built on this base? This, of course, would be a meaningless question if we could demonstrate that competition is the key process influencing the spatial organization of the city. The problem in doing this, however, is indicated by Amos Hawley:

> A related problem exists with regard to the observability of the operation of competition. The specific sequence of changes by which a homogeneous aggregate is converted into a differentiated and interdependent population has not been described in detail. Consequently it is almost impossible to indicate what to look for in order to see competition in action. This situation is not improved by pointing out that the process is a type of interaction, that is, a process of mutual internal modification. Ecologists, unfortunately, lack the technique for the observation of internal phenomena. Defined in terms of competitive interaction, ecology amounts to little more than the contemplation of a concept.[38]

Thus the entire theoretical system developed by the classical ecologists represented but one approach to the explanation of ecological phenomena. Furthermore, their key explanatory variable, competition, had the disadvantage that it did not lend itself to direct observation and empirical

[35] Warner E. Gettys, "Human Ecology and Social Theory," *Social Forces*, 18 (May, 1940), 470.
[36] A. B. Hollingshead, "A Re-examination of Ecological Theory," *Sociology and Social Research*, 31 (January–February, 1947), 194–204.
[37] Alihan, *Social Ecology*, p. 91.
[38] Amos H. Hawley, "Ecology and Human Ecology," *Social Forces*, 22 (May, 1944), 401.

verification. Classical ecological theory was at best an untested, post hoc interpretation of urban growth dynamics.

Many of the hypotheses put forth by the classical ecologists were also questioned on empirical grounds. The classical ecologists did use Chicago as their research arena, but they maintained that the same ecological processes were operative in all large and growing cities. Presumably, all such cities would be characterized by five concentric zones and be divided into natural areas. As might be expected, this hypothesis was soon put to empirical test.

One of the earliest of these tests was conducted in 1938 by Maurice R. Davie. After carefully identifying twenty-two "natural or distinctive areas" within New Haven, Connecticut, and collecting a considerable amount of data on each of these, Davie arbitrarily divided a map of the city into a series of concentric zones. The resulting analysis revealed that distance from the center of the city apparently had no influence on the distribution of social, economic, and ecological phenomena. As a result, Davie had to conclude that "the hypothesis of the concentric zone pattern . . . clearly does not apply to New Haven." [39] Among other things, Davie found that the wealthiest and poorest sections of the city were practically equidistant from the central business district and therefore within the same zone. However, Davie did uncover one ecological pattern, that low-grade housing is found near centers of transportation and industry. Yet another study, conducted by Walter Firey, found that the city of Boston definitely did not conform to the concentric zone pattern (see later).[40] Paul K. Hatt has seriously questioned whether natural areas are basic units of urban organization. In research conducted in Seattle, Hatt found that (1) not all parts of the city are divided into natural areas and (2) the number and type of natural areas found within a city depend exclusively on the methods used in delineating them. Because of this, Hatt concluded that natural areas are not real entities but that the concept itself might be useful for research purposes.[41] Finally, since as early as 1934 ecological studies have been conducted in countries other than the United States.[42] These studies reveal that in some parts

[39] Maurice R. Davie, "The Pattern of Urban Growth," in George F. Murdock (ed.), *Studies in the Science of Society* (New Haven: Yale University Press, 1937), p. 159.
[40] See Walter Firey, *Land Use in Central Boston* (Cambridge, Mass.: Harvard University Press, 1947).
[41] Paul K. Hatt, "The Concept of Natural Area," *American Sociological Review,* 11 (August, 1946), 423–27.
[42] For a sampling of these studies see Asael T. Hansen, "The Ecology of a Latin American City," in E. B. Reuter (ed.), *Race and Culture Contacts* (New York: McGraw-Hill Book Company, 1934), pp. 124–42; Theodore Caplow, "The Social Ecology of Guatemala City," *Social Forces,* 28 (December, 1949), 113–35; Theodore Caplow, "Urban Structure in France," *American Sociological Review,* 17 (October,

of the world the ecological organization of cities is quite similar to that described by the Chicago ecologists but that in other places, such as Latin America, urban spatial organization differs radically.

☐ NEO-ORTHODOX ECOLOGY

By the mid-1940s classical ecology had been subjected to rather severe criticism. However, even though one particular brand of human ecology had been almost utterly destroyed, interest in the study of ecological phenomena persisted.

The first major innovation in ecological theory was pioneered by two men, James A. Quinn and Amos H. Hawley, and is often referred to as neo-orthodox ecology. As the name suggests, the neo-orthodox ecologists were in basic sympathy with the goals and purposes of the classical ecologists. They sought to correct the deficiencies in classical ecological theory rather than to replace it with some other theoretical scheme. Nonetheless, both Quinn and Hawley disagreed with the classical ecologists on several important issues. First, they thought that human ecologists should study more than the spatial distribution of social phenomena. This was certainly one of their tasks, but there were also other things that ecologists should investigate. Second, both men were suspicious of elevating competition to the status of a key explanatory variable. Both men recognized that the forces that influence the spatial organization of cities are extremely complex and involve many elements *in addition to* competition. Finally, both Quinn and Hawley objected to the rigid distinction that the classical ecologists made between the biotic and social levels of organization and maintained instead that all human relationships, including those of an ecological nature, are influenced by culture. At the same time, neither man treated culture as a basic concept in ecological theory. They still thought that the ecological structure of cities was the result of impersonal and largely subsocial forces.

James A. Quinn

Although Quinn and Hawley agreed on the points just described, there are some fundamental differences between the theories that they put forth. Quinn viewed human ecology as a branch of sociology that in-

1952), 544–49; Erdmann Deane Beynon, "The Morphology of the Cities of the Alfold," *Geographical Review*, 27 (April, 1937), 328–29; Fernando Penalosa, "Ecological Organization of the Transitional City: Some Mexican Evidence," *Social Forces*, 46 (December, 1967), 221–29.

vestigates one facet of human interaction. However, the type of interaction that ecologists study is considerably different from the type studied by the general sociologist. Quinn summarizes the differences between social and ecological interaction as follows:

> Ecological interaction occurs upon different levels from those of truly social interaction. Human social interaction involves consensus, exchange of meaning through symbolic communication, and imaginative playing of the roles of others. Ecological interaction, in contrast, involves only an indirect, impersonal form of mutual modification by which each living man influences others by increasing or decreasing the supplies of environmental factors upon which the others depend.[43]

It is this process of ecological interaction that gives the modern community its basic spatial and functional structure. Quinn assumes that the way in which scarce environmental factors, such as land and jobs, are allocated to various ecological units is the chief force determining urban spatial organization. It should be noted, however, that ecological interaction is not always synonymous with competition. The allocation of land, resources, and jobs can also involve cooperation and mutual aid.

Even though the study of ecological interaction is very important to Quinn, it is, in the final analysis, only a means by which we can gain understanding of ecological structure. Basically, the concept of ecological structure refers to two different but interrelated phenomena. First, it encompasses the division of labor found at the community level. The division of labor is properly a part of ecological study simply because it involves impersonal, subsocial relationships and represents one facet of people's adjustment to the environment. Second, ecological structure includes the spatial organization of the community. Unlike the classical ecologists, Quinn apparently subscribes to no one theory of urban spatial organization. Instead, he argues that the spatial organization of cities depends on patterns of ecological interaction that are, to some extent, unique to each community. This does not mean, however, that there are no principles that govern urban growth dynamics. Rather, Quinn hypothesizes that four basic factors determine the location of ecological units within a community:

1. Minimum Cost. Quinn's first hypothesis is that ecological units tend to distribute themselves throughout a given area so as to minimize the cost of adjusting to other ecological units and to the environment. One can assume, for example, that when other conditions are equal, heavy

[43] James A. Quinn, "Human Ecology and Interactional Ecology," *American Sociological Review*, **5** (October, 1940), 722.

industries will locate where the costs of transporting labor, raw materials, and the finished product are kept to a minimum. It should be noted, however, that Quinn includes within the concept of "cost" not only expenditures of time, money, and energy but also various noneconomic factors. Thus he points out that the prestige value of an area must be taken into account in calculating the costs or rewards attached to any given location. In any event, it is Quinn's opinion that "the hypothesis of maximum satisfaction at minimum cost affords a general guiding principle to the interpretation of the spatial patterning of areas." [44]

2. Minimum Ecological Distance. The hypothesis of minimum ecological distance is simply an extension of the hypothesis of minimum costs. According to this hypothesis, ecological units distribute themselves throughout an area so as to minimize the total ecological distance between them and the other ecological and social units on which they depend. This helps to explain why industries tend to locate in proximity to one another: they utilize each other's products. Likewise, schools and churches normally locate near the residential areas that they serve.

3. Median Location. The hypothesis of median location states that "the most efficient location for any ecological unit is at the median (weighted) of all units which are to be transported to and from it." [45] Included among these units are "the environmental resources which it (the original unit) utilizes, the other units on which it depends, and the other units that it serves." [46] The reader will note, of course, that this hypothesis is simply a restatement, in different terms, of the hypotheses of minimum ecological distance and minimum ecological cost.

4. Intensiveness of Utilization. The hypothesis of intensiveness of utilization takes into account the fact that two or more ecological units may have a common median and therefore desire the same site. In situations of this type, Quinn argues, "that ecological unit tends to occupy the common median which can utilize it most intensively." [47] If two ecological units are in competition for the same location, presumably the unit that serves the most persons and realizes the most profit from occupying the sought-after location will gain control of it.

In summary, Quinn maintains that considerations of cost and distance determine patterns of spatial organization at the community level. His

[44] Quinn, *Human Ecology,* p. 285.
[45] James A. Quinn, "Discussion of Hollingshead's 'Community Research: Development and Present Condition,'" *American Sociological Review,* 13 (April, 1948), 148.
[46] Quinn, *Human Ecology,* p. 286.
[47] Ibid., p. 288.

is therefore an economic interpretation of ecological structure: the spatial organization of communities results from the tendency for ecological units to minimize their costs and maximize their satisfactions by occupying that one point in space which represents the most efficacious location vis-à-vis other ecological units.[48] This, of course, is the chief point on which Quinn's theory may be criticized. It is assumed that the typical community is organized in a highly rational and efficient manner with respect to the movement of both goods and people. The rationality and efficiency are supposedly the product of impersonal and subsocial forces.

Amos H. Hawley

Of the human ecologists, Amos H. Hawley takes the broadest view of the field, its scope and its purposes. Evidence of this comes when, in defining human ecology, Hawley states that

> ecology is concerned with the elemental problem of how growing, multiplying beings maintain themselves in a constantly changing but ever restricted environment. . . . The subject of ecological inquiry then is the community, the form and development of which are studied with particular reference to the limiting and supporting factors in the environment. . . . It attempts to determine the nature of community structure in general, the type of communities that appear in different habitats, and the specific sequence of change in community development.[49]

Because human ecology has as its primary task the analysis of community structure, it is important that we understand the meaning that Hawley assigns to this term. Basically, Hawley considers community structure to consist of those mechanisms by which a population organizes itself for survival in a particular habitat. Among the most important of these mechanisms is a division of labor appropriate to the needs and characteristics of the community in question. Because of this, Hawley considers his analysis of urban service institutions to be within the scope of human ecology.[50] In this study he examines the correlation between the size and composition of different urban populations and the number of commercial institutions found within the area that they inhabit.

Like Quinn, Hawley does not consider the fundamental task of human

---

[48] According to Quinn, there are three different kinds of ecological units: (1) single living organisms, (2) a group that produces or consumes as a unit, and (3) any specialized function, such as a store or factory, that occupies a spatial position of its own. See ibid., p. 280.

[49] Hawley, "Ecology and Human Ecology," p. 403.

[50] See Amos H. Hawley, "An Ecological Study of Urban Service Institutions," *American Sociological Review*, 6 (October, 1941), 629–39.

ecology to be that of analyzing the spatial distribution of social phenomena. However, he does argue that there is a general tendency for all communities to display a series of zones that are roughly concentric but never perfectly homogeneous. Furthermore, he maintains that instead of having a single center the modern community has its central business district plus a series of subcenters. The ecological units that occupy these centers are those least able to withstand the friction of space, that is, the cost and time involved in locating at more distant points. The units with a maximum need for accessibility are the ones that become most centralized.

☐ SOCIOCULTURAL ECOLOGY

Neo-orthodox ecology has its merits as an explanation of the spatial organization of American cities. In a society that places great emphasis on economic gain, considerations of cost and profit do influence the location of many ecological units. Nonetheless, the neo-orthodox ecologists make two assumptions that can be questioned. The first is that space —more particularly, distance—is simply a given to which people must adjust. No recognition is accorded the fact that, regardless of how it is measured, the distance between two points is itself a matter of cultural definition. In some cultures five miles may appear to be a great distance whereas in other cultures something located five miles away may be defined as nearby. Second, the neo-orthodox ecologists also assume that ecological units always seek that location where their costs, largely defined in economic terms, are kept to a minimum. However, there is much reason to think that economic rationality is not the only factor that influences urban spatial organization.

Because of the difficulties inherent in these two assumptions, yet another approach to ecological theory has been developed. This approach, known as sociocultural ecology, views social and cultural variables as the chief factors influencing the spatial organization of cities. The leading proponent of this approach is Walter Firey, whose study, *Land Use in Central Boston*, has become a classic.[51] According to Firey, there are two basic forces that determine urban spatial organization. First, he does not deny that "rational adaption," or the minimization of costs and the maximization of satisfactions, influences the location of ecological units. However, he does argue that rational adaption is itself a culturally defined and culturally relative concept. To illustrate, Firey suggests that the retail business district as found in the modern American city is the out-

[51] Firey, *Land Use in Central Boston.*

growth of a particular value configuration that emphasizes the constant acquisition of material goods. Purchasing entails a considerable expenditure of time, and, "what is more important, it involves a rational comparison of price and quality at different markets." [52] Hence it is "rational" for selected retail outlets to cluster near the center of the city. This makes them readily accessible to individual shoppers and allows them to compare the quality and price of goods offered by the different stores. Presumably, "rational adaption" would entail something quite different in a culture that does not place a premium on the acquisition of material goods.

Second, Firey argues that sentiment and symbolism have an impact on urban spatial organization. That this may be the case seems to be amply documented by Firey's extensive analysis of the ecological structure of Boston.[53] For example, one of Boston's most fashionable residential areas, Beacon Hill, has preserved its identity and character despite its proximity to the central business district and despite the fact that the land could be used in much more profitable ways. The reason for this is that Beacon Hill has been consistently viewed by its residents as a center of profound cultural and historical significance. Thus numerous attempts to convert it to more "rational" uses have been effectively thwarted. The Boston Commons, a large plot of land located in the center of the city, provides another illustration of the role of sentiment and symbolism in determining the ecological structure of the city. There are many different ways in which the retention of the Commons is uneconomical in terms of commercial values, but again all attempts to convert it to more "rational" uses have been frustrated. The Commons symbolizes many individual and collective traditions to the residents of Boston and has, in effect, become a sacred object to them. Intangible forces such as these are the ones that, according to Firey, determine the spatial organization of the city.

Another interesting example of the role of sociocultural variables in influencing urban spatial organization can be observed in Salt Lake City and some of Utah's other urban communities. Visitors to these cities, if they are the least observant, will immediately notice that the streets run due north and south and east and west, that most of these streets are exceptionally wide, and that barns and farm equipment sheds are frequently found on residential sites well within the city limits. In fact, it becomes apparent that the larger cities of Utah are not the product of the same forces that gave shape and form to our large eastern cities. Rather, they are the result of careful, consistent planning.

[52] Ibid., p. 256.
[53] For a brief summary of Firey's findings see his "Sentiment and Symbolism as Ecological Variables," *American Sociological Review,* 10 (April, 1945), 140–48.

In order to explain the somewhat unique pattern of spatial organization found in Utah cities, it is necessary to examine both the environmental conditions under which these communities were settled and the value configurations of the people who settled them. When these communities were founded (circa 1848 to 1860), the environment was untamed, which virtually dictated that all settlers, including farmers, locate their homes in proximity to one another, that is, within what later became the city limits. Among other things, this was the only feasible method of gaining protection against the Indian tribes who inhabited the area and who were purportedly somewhat hostile on occasions. More importantly, it fostered the close, intimate cooperation required to make the arid undeveloped land productive and livable.

An even more significant influence on the spatial organization of Utah cities was the belief in millennialism that is a part of the Mormon religion. According to the doctrines of the Church of Jesus Christ of Latter-Day Saints (Mormon), North America has been chosen to be the scene of gathering in the last days and, furthermore, the specific site of this gathering is to be the Salt Lake Basin. As a result, it has always been a dominant passion of the Mormons to build a perfect city as a "dwelling place of the Savior and those human beings freed from selfishness, greed, and vanity and thus perfected after the order of their tradition." [54] Among the specifications for this utopian city were that all streets should be eight rods wide and oriented toward the four points of the compass, that the city should be exactly one mile square, and that each block within the city should contain ten acres and be divided into twenty half-acre residential sites. This was not only a master plan of utopian dimensions; it also became a plan of action that was at least partially carried out.

Our examples from Boston and Salt Lake City are sufficient to illustrate the sociocultural approach to the analysis of ecological phenomena. In effect, the sociocultural ecologists argue that the spatial organization of cities is almost wholly determined by various social and cultural forces, including value configurations, spatially referred sentiments, and traditions that are held in high esteem. This approach has a tremendous appeal among social scientists who regard culture as a concept of extremely high explanatory power. However, one crucial implication of the sociocultural approach must be pointed out. If the social and cultural forces that influence urban spatial organization are at least partly unique to each city, then each community should have its unique patterns of spatial organization. Whether students of human ecology are willing to abandon the

[54] Albert L. Seeman, "Communities in the Salt Lake Basin," *Economic Geography.* **14** (July, 1938), 306.

search for uniformities in urban spatial organization is open to question.

☐ SOCIAL AREA ANALYSIS

Social area analysis represents yet another approach to the study of ecological phenomena.[55] However, social area analysis differs from the other approaches to human ecology in that it does not advance a full-blown theory of urban spatial organization. Rather, the proponents of social area analysis are concerned only with patterns of differentiation and stratification as they are manifested in urban areas. In brief, social area analysis is essentially a research technique by which we can study the spatial distribution of different population groupings that are typically found in urban settings.

To be more specific, social area analysis is used to identify urban census tracts whose populations are similar in terms of three key variables. The three variables, originally delineated by Eshref Shevky and Marilyn Williams, are social rank, urbanization, and segregation.[56] The first, social rank, is essentially a measure of the socioeconomic status of the population that inhabits the census tract in question and utilizes census data relating to occupation and education. The second, urbanization, is reflective of the degree of "familialism" present in the census tract. This variable is measured by the use of census data relating to fertility differentials, differentials in the number of women in the labor force, and differentials in the number of single-family detached dwelling units. Finally, the third variable, segregation, is indicative of significant differentials in the composition of census tract populations and requires the use of census data relating to racial and ethnic composition, and to nativity.[57] Some time ago Wendell Bell suggested that much could be gained by way of clarification if the term *economic status* were substituted for *social rank*, *family status* for *urbanization*, and *ethnic status* for *segregation*.[58]

[55] Social area analysis was first discussed in Eshref Shevky and Marilyn Williams, *The Social Areas of Los Angeles: Analysis and Typology* (Berkeley: University of California Press, 1949). The basic theory and computational procedures used in social area analysis were elaborated on in Eshref Shevky and Wendell Bell, *Social Area Analysis: Theory, Illustrative Application and Computational Procedures* (Stanford, Calif.: Stanford University Press, 1955).
[56] Ibid., esp. pp. 33–57.
[57] These variables are described in greater detail in Shevky and Bell, *Social Area Analysis*, pp. 17–18.
[58] Wendell Bell, "The Utility of the Shevky Typology for the Design of Urban Subarea Field Studies," *Journal of Social Psychology*, 47 (February, 1958), 72.

113

These three variables supposedly reflect fundamental and meaningful distinctions among the different population groupings found in American society.[59] Certainly in the large American city distinctions are made between white- and blue-collar groups, family- and non-family-oriented groups, and native-born whites and the members of various minority groups. Furthermore, there is often a strong correlation between these factors and the values that people hold, their life chances, and their modes of living. Hence a social area simply consists of one or more census tracts that display a unique configuration of these traits as measured by the indices of social rank, urbanization, and segregation.

From the standpoint of human ecology, several valuable things may be achieved through the use of social area analysis. First, social area analysis potentially constitutes a powerful tool by which to ascertain whether there are predictable, recurrent patterns in urban spatial organization. By identifying social areas within several different cities and then comparing them, any generalizations that can be made about the spatial distribution of social phenomena within urban settings should become immediately apparent. This can be done without incurring the expense of conducting field surveys or personally observing the cities in question. Second, social area analysis represents an excellent method for studying ecological change as it occurs between two or more consecutive census dates. This simply requires that the social areas within a city be identified with data taken from the different censuses and the results compared. Have the populations of some census tracts changed enough to qualify them for inclusion in different social areas? Have new social areas emerged? What seems to be the overall pattern of change? Third, social area analysis can be utilized in a similar way to compare the spatial organization of different cities at one point in time. Among other things, this may reveal regional differences in urban ecological structure and lead to the identification of certain types of cities about which it is safe to make ecological generalizations. Finally, social area analysis represents an excellent way of selecting urban subareas for more intensive study.[60] Indeed, Shevky and Bell tell us that

[59] It is important to note that the proponents of social area analysis see the city as a reflection of the society in which it is found. Thus Shevky and Williams tell us that "every city is a product of its time and can only be understood in terms of the society in which it comes into being." Shevky and Williams, *The Social Areas of Los Angeles*, p. 2. It should also be noted that the differentials measured by the indices of social rank, urbanization, and segregation are of relatively recent origin: they have come in the wake of rapid industrialization and the continuing trend toward heterogeneity in the racial and ethnic composition of American society.

[60] For example, see Bell, "The Utility of the Shevky Typology for the Design of Urban Sub-area Field Studies," pp. 71–83.

The concepts of "natural area" and "subculture" are not unrelated to our concept "social area" for we view a social area as containing persons with similar social positions in the larger society. The social area, however, is not bounded by the geographical frame of reference as is the natural area, nor by implications concerning the degree of interaction between persons in the local community as is the subculture. We do claim, however, that the social area generally contains persons having the same level of living, the same way of life, and the same ethnic background; and we hypothesize that persons living in a particular type of social area would systematically differ with respect to characteristic attitudes and behaviors from persons living in another type of social area.[61]

If this is the case, social area analysis represents an excellent tool by which urban sociologists can identify those parts of the city that they wish to study in greater detail.

The proponents of social area analysis have a great deal of faith in their methodological approach. This is made clear by Shevky and Bell's statement that "we feel that the application of this typology to census and comparable data available for American cities will allow the beginning of the systematic accumulation of knowledge about the social organization, especially the stratification and differentiation, of American urban populations." [62] The faith that Shevky and Bell have in social area analysis seems to be at least partially justified. Thus it appears that the three variables of social rank, urbanization, and segregation (or some modification thereof) do help to account for much of the variation among census tracts in terms of other variables on which census data are collected.[63]

☐ SUMMARY

It has been several decades since human ecology had its inception at the University of Chicago. Since that time the human ecologists have not developed a single, coherent theoretical system. Rather, human ecology has developed in a variety of different directions, and several different

[61] Shevky and Bell, Social Area Analysis, p. 20.
[62] Ibid., p. 2.
[63] A number of studies have been completed that use factor analysis to investigate the intercorrelations of social rank, urbanization, and segregation and a variety of other social phenomena that vary from tract and tract. Because of the highly technical nature of this material, it will not be considered in this text. The reader who wishes to pursue "factorial ecology" further should consult the excellent bibliography provided by Janet L. Abu-Lughod in her "Testing the Theory of Social Area Analysis," American Sociological Review, 34 (April, 1969), 210–12.

explanations of ecological phenomena have been advanced. However, the human ecologists have agreed that their fundamental task is to explain the spatial organization and growth dynamics of urban communities. This is a goal that Park, Burgess, Quinn, Hawley, Firey, and most other ecologists have held in common.

Needless to say, the success of this undertaking depends entirely on whether there are basic similarities in the spatial organization of different cities. If this is the case, then the common patterns should be identified and adequate explanations for them put forth. However, the literature reviewed in this chapter suggests that the search for predictable, recurrent patterns in urban spatial organization has not been so successful as one might hope. Although there are undoubtedly a few broad similarities in the spatial organization of cities, every city is apparently somewhat unique in this regard. If this is the case, then the very basis on which human ecology rests is brought into question.

Even if we eventually find predictable, recurrent patterns of urban spatial organization, the significance of such findings can be questioned. There are many important facets of community life that exist quite independently of its spatial dimension. Indeed, the most significant thing about the community would seem to be that this is where people meet other people. As a result, we are able to satisfy our biological, social, and emotional needs. Thus the greatest need in community study today is for a continued probing of the sociological dimensions of community life and of the strictly human problems that have arisen as a concomitant of urbanization. This is not to suggest that people who seek to ameliorate urban problems cannot benefit from the knowledge and insights gathered by human ecologists. In fact, it can be argued that the physical environment within which individuals find themselves does have an influence on their attitudes, behavior, and outlook on life. Time and again we find that rates of reported mental illness, crime, delinquency, and so on are highest in those areas of the city that are deteriorated. Nonetheless, it must be remembered that the reasons for this are social, psychological, and economic. The physical environment is no more than a setting in which these problems occur.

This is not a direct criticism of the human ecologists, who have been among the most productive, thought-provoking social scientists the United States has produced. However, the ultimate value of human ecology itself must still be determined. Ample opportunity for doing this will exist as the city increasingly becomes the focus of intensive research. In any event, the human ecologists must be given credit for suggesting an approach to the study of urban communities that remains challenging and of high potential significance. There is nothing faulty or picayune about the problems that the human ecologists have outlined for themselves.

There is no way to know whether interest in human ecology will persist and, if so, in what directions the field might develop. However, there are a few things worth noting. First, it is still worthwhile to search for generalizations concerning the spatial organization of cities, but apparently these must be carefully qualified and of rather limited scope. Even though broad, all-inclusive formulations such as the concentric zone hypothesis are apparently not feasible, there may still be some recurrent features in the spatial organization of American cities. Second, it seems apparent that the successful ecological theory of the future will be one that makes use of the insights contributed by sociologists, anthropologists, historians, and other social scientists. One must agree with Firey that urban spatial organization is the product of human relationships and social values rather than of subsocial and impersonal forces. Finally, a successful theory of human ecology will be one that is both change oriented and future oriented. Today most large communities are in a continuous state of flux and change. The value of any theory that fails to take this fact into account can be seriously questioned.

BIBLIOGRAPHY

Abbott, Walter F. "Moscow in 1897 as a Preindustrial City: A Test of the Inverse Burgess Zonal Hypothesis," *American Sociological Review*, **39** (August, 1974), 542–50.

Abu-Lughod, Janet L. "Testing the Theory of Social Area Analysis," *American Sociological Review*, **34** (April, 1969), 198–212.

Aldrich, Howard. "Ecological Succession in Racially Changing Neighborhoods: A Review of the Literature," *Urban Affairs Quarterly*, **10** (March, 1975), 327–48.

———, and Albert J. Reiss, Jr. "Continuities in the Study of Ecological Succession: Changes in the Race Composition of Neighborhoods and Their Businesses," *American Journal of Sociology*, **81** (January, 1976), 846–66.

Alihan, Milla A. *Social Ecology: A Critical Analysis.* New York: Columbia University Press, 1938.

Anderson, Theodore R., and Janice A. Egeland. "Spatial Aspects of Social Area Analysis," *American Sociological Review*, **26** (June, 1961), 392–98.

Bell, Wendell, "The Utility of the Shevky Typology for the Design of Urban Sub-area Field Studies," *Journal of Social Psychology*, **47** (February, 1958), 71–83.

Berry, Brian J. L., and John D. Kasarda, *Contemporary Urban Ecology.* New York: Macmillan Publishing Co., Inc., 1977.

———, and Philip H. Rees. "The Factorial Ecology of Calcutta," *American Journal of Sociology*, **74** (March, 1969), 445–91.

Briggs, Ronald, and Dennis Conway. "The Evolution of Urban Ecological Structure: Theory and a Case Study, Port of Spain, Trinidad," *Social Science Quarterly*, **55** (March, 1975), 871–88.

Burgess, Ernest W. "The Growth of the City: An Introduction to a Research Project," in Robert E. Park, Ernest W. Burgess, and R. D. McKenzie (eds.), *The City*. Chicago: University of Chicago Press, 1925.

———. "Urban Areas," in T. V. Smith and L. D. White (eds.), *Chicago: An Experiment in Social Science Research*. Chicago: University of Chicago Press, 1929.

Caplow, Theodore. "The Social Ecology of Guatamala City," *Social Forces*, **28** (December, 1949), 113–35.

Davie, Maurice R. "The Pattern of Urban Growth," in George P. Murdock (ed.), *Studies in the Science of Society*. New Haven: Yale University Press, 1937.

DeFlour, Lois B. "Ecological Variables in the Cross-Cultural Study of Delinquency," *Social Forces*, **45** (June, 1967), 556–70.

Elmer, M. C. "Century-Old Ecological Studies in France," *American Journal of Sociology*, **39** (July, 1933), 63–70.

Firey, Walter. *Land Use in Central Boston*. Cambridge, Mass.: Harvard University Press, 1947.

———. "Sentiment and Symbolism as Ecological Variables," *American Sociological Review*, **10** (April, 1945), 140–48.

Gettys, Warner E. "Human Ecology and Social Theory," *Social Forces*, **18** (May, 1940), 469–76.

Guest, Avery M. "Ecological Succession in the Puget Sound Region," *Journal of Urban History*, **3** (February, 1977), 181–210.

Hansen, Asael T. "The Ecology of a Latin American City," in E. B. Reuter (ed.), *Race and Culture Contacts*. New York: McGraw-Hill Book Company, 1934.

Harris, Chauncey D., and Edward L. Ullman. "The Nature of Cities," *The Annals of the American Academy of Political and Social Science*, **242** (November, 1945), 7–17.

Hatt, Paul. "The Concept of Natural Area," *American Sociological Review*, **11** (August, 1946), 423–27.

Hawley, Amos H. "Ecology and Human Ecology," *Social Forces*, **22** (May, 1944), 398–405.

———. *Human Ecology*. New York: The Ronald Press, 1950.

Hollingshead, A. B. "A Re-examination of Ecological Theory," *Sociology and Social Research*, **31** (January–February, 1947), 194–204.

Hoyt, Homer. *The Structure and Growth of Residential Neighborhoods in American Cities*. Washington, D.C.: U.S. Government Printing Office, 1939.

Levin, Yale, and Alfred Lindesmith. "English Ecology and Criminology of the Past Century," *Journal of Criminal Law and Criminology*, **27** (March, 1937), 801–16.

McKenzie, R. D. "The Scope of Human Ecology," *Publications of the American Sociological Society*, **20** (1926), 141–54.

Michaels, James W. "On the Relation Between Human Ecology and Behavioral Social Psychology," *Social Forces*, **52** (March, 1974), 313–21.

Michelson, William H. *Man and His Urban Environment: A Sociological Approach.* Reading, Mass.: Addison-Wesley Publishing Company, 1976, esp. pp. 3–32.

Park, Robert E. "Human Ecology," *American Journal of Sociology,* 42 (July, 1936), 1–15.

Peñalosa, Fernando. "Ecological Organization of the Transitional City: Some Mexican Evidence," *Social Forces,* 46 (December, 1967), 221–29.

Quinn, James A. *Human Ecology.* Englewood Cliffs, N.J.: Prentice-Hall, Inc., 1960.

————. "Human Ecology and Interactional Ecology," *American Sociological Review,* 5 (October, 1940), 713–22.

Reckless, Walter C. "The Distribution of Commercialized Vice in the City: A Sociological Analysis," *Publications of the American Sociological Society,* 20 (1926), 164–76.

Seeman, Albert L. "Communities in the Salt Lake Basin," *Economic Geography,* 14 (July, 1938), 300–8.

Shevky, Eshref, and Wendell Bell. *Social Area Analysis.* Stanford, Calif.: Stanford University Press, 1955.

————, and Marilyn Williams. *The Social Areas of Los Angeles: Analysis and Typology.* Berkeley: University of California Press, 1955.

Suttles, Gerald D. *The Social Construction of Communities.* Chicago: University of Chicago Press, 1972.

Sweetser, Frank L. "Factorial Ecology: Helsinki, 1960," *Demography,* 2 (1965), 372–85.

Theodorson, George A. (ed.). *Studies in Human Ecology.* New York: Harper & Row, 1961.

Zorbaugh, Harvey W. "The Natural Areas of the City," *Publications of the American Sociological Society,* 20 (1926), 188–97.

CHAPTER 5

□ □ □ □ □ □ □ □ □
□
□
□
□
□
□
□
□
□

Constructed Types and Community Theory

Sociologists have made extensive use of ideal types and constructed types.[1] Among the most famous of these have been Emile Durkheim's analysis of organic and mechanical solidarity, Max Weber's modes of action orientation, Charles Horton Cooley's concept of the primary group, and the pattern variables as delineated by Talcott Parsons.[2] Likewise, the process of type construction has been very popular in the study of human communities. It is to some of the constructed type theories of community that we must now turn.

□ CONSTRUCTED TYPES

The Nature of Constructed Types

Although the process of type construction is used with regularity by the sociologist, there are few statements in the literature concerning the nature and purposes of constructed types. As a matter of fact, most texts on social research make no reference to constructed types, and many

---

[1] Technically, there is a difference between an ideal type and a constructed type. A constructed type is derived directly from empirical data whereas an ideal type is better thought of as a "mental construct" that is less closely linked to empirical data, specific case studies, or whatever. See Gideon Sjoberg, *The Preindustrial City: Past and Present* (New York: The Free Press, 1960), esp. p. 21. To avoid unnecessary confusion, however, throughout this chapter we shall use the term *constructed type* even though some of the theories we shall examine might be considered by some scholars to be ideal rather than constructed types.

[2] John C. McKinney and Charles P. Loomis, "The Typological Tradition," in Joseph S. Roucek (ed.), *Contemporary Sociology* (New York: The Philosophical Library, Inc., 1958), pp. 557–71.

sociologists routinely engage in type construction without realizing it. Nonetheless, it is easy to specify the nature of a constructed type. A constructed type is basically a simplified and sometimes purposely exaggerated model of the personality, social, or cultural system being examined by the investigator. In type construction the investigator ignores the welter of details that characterize the phenomena being examined and focuses on those variables that are most significant in describing the system in question. For example, even a small rural community is a very complex form of organization. However, sociologists who use type construction as their basic methodological tool might conclude that in its purest form the rural community is characterized by a completely homogeneous population, by the dominance of the family over all other institutions, and by social relationships of a primary nature.

It is important to note that constructed types are not a figment of the investigator's imagination. Rather, a good constructed type is always based on an intimate familiarity with empirical cases and can be derived only after careful, prolonged research on the phenomenon under consideration. To put the case differently, an adequate but simplified model of a personality, social, or cultural system cannot be advanced until the investigator is thoroughly acquainted with the many variables that characterize the system. At the same time, a constructed type is never a verbatim description of the system being studied. The reasons for this are twofold. First, by its very nature a constructed type is a simplified model of reality so that only the *key* variables are included. This is what makes a constructed type an extremely valuable tool in sociological analysis. Second, almost all constructed types are based on an examination of more than one case. In type construction the peculiarities of individual cases are ignored and the focus is on the variables common to all manifestations of whatever is being studied. Howard Becker makes this point clear when, in discussing "typical" revolutions, he says that "the constructed type is merely a tool. Hence when the methodologically sophisticated sociologist talks about a type of revolution, his hearers can be very sure that it will never correspond exactly to an empirical instance, to any 'real' situation." [3]

Finally, the typologist often concerns him- or herself not only with the system being studied but also with its polar opposite. In short, constructed types frequently are used to delineate the outermost limits of a rural-urban, sacred-secular, or some other important continuum. As will be seen later, this practice can immeasurably enhance both the theoretical relevance and the pragmatic utility of the original constructed type. How-

---

[3] Howard Becker, *Through Values to Social Interpretation: Essays on Social Context, Actions, Types, and Prospects* (Durham, N.C.: Duke University Press, 1950), p. 107.

ever, the delineation of the polar opposite is not an essential step in type construction. Contrary to what some students may conclude, Cooley did not offer a model of the secondary group as a polar opposite for his primary group, and some things that sociologists study simply do not have meaningful opposites. What, for example, is the polar opposite, the other extreme, of revolution?

The Utility of Constructed Types

In his discussion of type construction, John McKinney makes it clear that typological procedures have an important role to play in theory construction and in the conduct of empirical research.[4] In the analysis of communities, for example, it appears that there are four ways in which constructed types are especially helpful. First, a good constructed type should shed light on the nature of various communities if they were ever encountered in pure form. Thus, although all modern communities are probably a complex mixture of rural and urban patterns, by the use of type construction it is possible to identify and single out those variables that are unique and peculiar to rural communities. In effect, the sociological connotations of rurality can be sharpened and refined. The same would be true in a model of the urban community, the secular society, the inner-directed personality, the capitalistic system, or whatever. Second, type construction can be a powerful tool in the derivation of much-needed generalizations about communities. It hardly needs to be pointed out, for example, that each community is unique and has its own distinctive constellation of traits and patterns. Nonetheless, in type construction the theorist ignores the idiosyncratic features of the communities being studied and focuses only on their shared traits. By doing so, it is possible to offer generalizations that apply to all communities falling within a particular class (e.g., rural communities). Third, constructed types, especially when they represent the outer limits of a continuum, can be extremely useful in drawing comparisons between two or more communities. Quite frequently, the question arises as to whether one community is more rural or more urban than another. This question and others like it can easily be answered by assessing the degree to which the communities in question deviate from the pure types that represent the polar ends of a rural-urban continuum. Finally, constructed types are often helpful in the study of social change and in making predictions about the path of development that a changing community may follow. A good polar typology of rural and urban communities, for example,

[4] John C. McKinney, *Constructive Typology and Social Theory* (New York: Appleton-Century-Crofts, 1966).

should yield insight into the process of urbanization and indicate the traits that a community takes on as it becomes increasingly urban.

An Illustrative Polar Type

The significance and utility of constructed types can best be conveyed by a highly simplified example. For this purpose, Figure 5-1 has been

Community A	Community B
(Rural Community)	(Urban Community)
Homogeneity of Action	Heterogeneity of Action
Familistic Organization of Activities	Nonfamilistic Organization of Activities
Action Guided by Tradition	Action Guided by Rationality

FIGURE 5-1. Patterns of action in rural and urban communities: an illustrative polar typology.

prepared. In this figure a crude polar typology has been developed that indicates differences in patterns of human action between rural and urban communities. This typology is based on the assumption that patterns of human action in rural communities differ in very basic ways from those in urban communities. Likewise, the degree of deviation of two fictitious communities from the "pure" type has been indicated. Although this typology is a product of armchair analysis, it does illustrate the uses to which constructed types may be put.

1. The typology helps us to understand how human activity might be patterned in both rural and urban communities if either were found in their purest form. For example, if a small, completely isolated community could be found, all of its members might well be engaged in highly similar activities. Virtually *all* able-bodied adult males might spend winter, spring, summer, and fall in caring for the fields and livestock, whereas *all* adult females might devote their entire efforts to rearing children and running the household. Likewise, in the same community virtually all activities might be carried on in conjunction with other family members. In short, all work, recreation, worship, and education would involve interaction with kin rather than with nonrelated individuals. Finally, in our fictitious rural community, all human activity might well be guided by tradition. On the other hand, if the concept of *urban* is pushed to its logical limits, it would denote a type of community in which no two people engage in the same activities or play identical roles, in which most activity occurs in nonfamilial groups, and in which human action is

guided by norms of rationality and expediency. It should be noted that there are probably few communities that fit either of these models exactly. Nonetheless, it is the prerogative of typologists to exaggerate in order to give meaning and utility to their concepts.

2. If the polar types suggested in Figure 5–1 were based on empirical research they would constitute a set of generalizations relating to patterns of human action in rural as opposed to urban communities. If the peculiar and idiosyncratic features of individual rural communities were ignored and the common features of many rural communities focused on, it might well be concluded that the activities of rural dwellers are homogeneous, that rural people do engage in a disproportionate amount of action involving other members of their family, and that the activities of rural people are to some extent dictated by tradition.

3. Assuming that the profiles for communities A and B actually represent their relative positions on a rural-urban continuum, then there is no question but that community A is more rural than community B. In short, a typology provides us with a means by which two or more communities can be classified and systematically compared. Before the typology can be used in this way, however, we would have to collect and analyze a considerable amount of data pertaining to the two communities.

4. Assuming once more that the typology is valid, it is possible to predict some of the more significant changes that will occur as both communities undergo further urbanization. For example, if community A begins to grow in size and complexity, then the activities in which community members engage will become more heterogeneous, the family will less often be the context in which human activities occur, and human action will increasingly be guided by norms of rationality and expediency.

☐ FERDINAND TONNIES

The typological tradition is an extremely old one. Pitirim Sorokin points out, for example, that Confucius, Plato, Aristotle, St. Augustine, and Ibn Khaldun all authored constructed types.[5] For our purposes, however, the German scholar Ferdinand Tonnies (1855–1936) can be considered the father of the typological tradition in sociology. First published in 1887, his famous *Gemeinschaft und Gesellschaft* was a predecessor to the works of Durkheim, Becker, Redfield, and the many other scholars who have developed type construction into a highly useful tool for the analysis of

---

[5] See Pitirim A. Sorokin, "Forward," in Ferdinand Tonnies, *Community and Society*, ed. by Charles F. Loomis (New York: Harper Torchbook Edition, 1963), p. vii.

social systems. Hence, even though a brief review of the theory set forth by Tonnies poses a significant challenge for both reader and writer, the concepts of *Gemeinschaft* and *Gesellschaft* simply cannot be ignored.

Tonnies was not directly interested in the analysis of territorial communities. Rather, he sought to identify fundamental types of social relationships that develop among human beings [6] and to specify how these relationships change through time. Nonetheless, it is important for the student of territorial communities to have some understanding of the basic elements that compose Tonnies's scheme. Among other things, Tonnies has had a profound influence on those who have used typological procedures in their attempt to understand territorial communities. Most of the writers who are considered in later sections of this chapter explicitly recognize this influence. Furthermore, much of what Tonnies says is reflective of differences between rural and urban communities. Above all, Tonnies sheds a great deal of light on the changes that are occurring in human societies as they undergo the processes of industrialization and urbanization.

Before we explore the theoretical scheme set forth by Tonnies, a warning is in order. Tonnies's theory is amazingly complex and multifaceted, and defies simple interpretation. In order to follow it, one must be somewhat knowledgeable in sociology, psychology, philosophy, economics, and jurisprudence and also have the ability to see the forest for the trees. So there is really only one satisfactory way to gain insight into the thinking of Ferdinand Tonnies—by reading *Gemeinschaft und Gesellschaft*.[7]

The Types of Will

At the very heart of Tonnies's theory is the assumption that all social relationships are willed, that is, they exist only because individuals want them to exist. However, the reasons why individuals wish to associate with each other vary from person to person and from situation to situation. In some cases, people associate with each other because they attach intrinsic significance to their relationships; in other cases, individuals form relationships with each other for the sole purpose of pursuing a tangible goal. According to Tonnies, the first type of relationship has its basis in natural will whereas the second type of relationship has its basis in rational will.

Because the concepts of natural will and rational will are of central importance in understanding the concepts of *Gemeinschaft* and *Gesell-*

---

[6] See Talcott Parsons, *The Structure of Social Action* (New York: Free Press, 1949), pp. 686–94.

[7] One of the most convenient editions is that cited in footnote 5.

schaft, they must be explored in more detail. Although the first, natural will, has many different dimensions, its key components are understanding and unity. In a relationship resting on natural will each individual fully understands the other and takes a direct interest in the other's welfare. Furthermore, a unity of goals, values, and beliefs that rests on sentiment and the memory of common traditions and experiences is achieved. All of this adds up to one thing: the relationship that springs from natural will becomes an end in itself rather than a means to some other end. The prototype of such a relationship is, of course, the family wherein each member is valued for his or her own sake, but Tonnies also maintains that natural will is dominant in the thinking of peasants, artisans, women, and young people.

Rational will, on the other hand, entails the careful weighing of various means to a desired end. When two merchants deal with each other, for example, they have a definite end or purpose in mind and each one carefully plans and plots so that they might achieve their goals. Thus the individual driven by rational will is concerned chiefly with his or her future well-being and bases his or her actions on deliberation and discrimination. Although Tonnies implies that there is a subtle distinction between deliberation and discrimination, both concepts refer to the individual's ability to choose means and ends carefully and wisely. According to Tonnies, rational will, based as it is on deliberation and reasoning, is dominant in the thinking of businesspeople, aged persons, scientists, and the educated classes. It may also be characteristic of many urbanites.

Gemeinschaft and Gesellschaft

Hence Tonnies assumes that social relationships may rest on two bases: on understanding, unity, and sentiment (i.e., natural will) or on the desire to reach some specific end (i.e., rational will). Once this is understood, then the two basic types of relationships delineated by Tonnies, *Gemeinschaft* and *Gesellschaft*, can be elaborated on.

There are many different features of the *Gemeinschaft*-like relationship. Among other things, McKinney and Loomis maintain that relationships of this type are characterized by aid and helpfulness, mutual interdependence, reciprocal and binding sentiment, diffuse or blanket obligations, and authority based on age, wisdom, and benevolent force.[8] Furthermore, persons enmeshed in the *Gemeinschaft*-like relationship share sacred traditions and a spirit of brotherhood that grows out of bonds of blood, common locality, or common mind. Tonnies expresses this point clearly:

[8] See McKinney and Loomis, "The Typological Tradition," p. 558.

The Gemeinschaft of blood, denoting unity of being, is developed and differentiated into Gemeinschaft of locality, which is based on a common habitat. A further differentiation leads to a Gemeinschaft of mind, which implies only co-operation and co-ordinated action for a common goal. Gemeinschaft of locality may be conceived as a community of physical life, just as Gemeinschaft of mind expresses the community of mental life. In conjunction with the others, this last type of Gemeinschaft represents the truly human and supreme forms of community.[9]

The specific organizational forms in which Gemeinschaft-like relationships are manifested will be considered in more detail later.

In distinct contrast to this type of relationship is the Gesellschaft-like relationship, in which the participating individuals are separated rather than united, and individualism reaches its zenith. The individual rarely takes action on behalf of the Gesellschaft itself. Rather, all actions are taken in light of their potential benefit for the individual. Because of this, the relationships that emerge between members of the Gesellschaft are contractual and functionally specific, and frequently involve the exchange of goods, money, or credit and obligations. Tonnies puts the case well when he says that in Gesellschaft-like relationships "nobody wants to grant and produce anything for another individual . . . if it be not in exchange for a gift or labor equivalent that he considers at least equal to what he has given." [10] Because of this, the Gesellschaft is supposedly characterized by a continual state of tension. Open conflict between its members is avoided only through the media of convention, legislation, and public opinion.

At this point it might be well to remember that Tonnies was interested in the analysis of two fundamentally different types of social relationships: he also used his concepts of Gemeinschaft and Gesellschaft to shed light on how human societies are changing through time. However, the concepts that he developed can also be used to study various forms of social organization. Perhaps the best example of a truly Gemeinschaft-like relationship is the family, especially the relationship that develops between a mother and her children. This type of relationship rests almost entirely on sentiment and understanding (i.e., natural will) and is devoid of the desire for tangible gain. Other forms of organization that involve Gemeinschaft-like relationships are neighborhoods, villages, and towns. According to Tonnies, the town represents the most complex form of Gemeinschaft-like relationship and "both village and town retain many of the characteristics of the family; the village retains more,

---

[9] Tonnies, *Community and Society*, p. 42.
[10] Ibid., p. 65.

the town less." [11] In contrast to these *Gemeinschaft*-like organizations, the city, the national capital, and the metropolis are typically *Gesellschaft*-like organizations. In these communal types money and capital reign supreme, and the emphasis is on the production of goods, profit, and knowledge in a rational and efficient manner. In the city and metropolis, the mentality of the capitalist and businessperson prevails.

The Types of Law

During the era when Tonnies wrote *Gemeinschaft und Gesellschaft*, there was much interest in law and the forms it assumes. Much of this interest was stimulated by Sir Henry Maine, whose book *Ancient Law* was first published in 1861. Basically, Maine argued that in primitive societies "all the members of the family, except its head, are in a condition best described as *status:* they have no power to acquire property, or to bequeath it, or to enter into contracts in relation to it." [12] On the other hand, in modern complex societies social relations are regulated by means of *contract;* that is, the person is free to enter into legally binding agreements with individuals other than the members of his or her family. Hence Maine suggested that "the movement of the progressive societies has hitherto been a movement from status to contract." [13]

Tonnies's thinking about law and social control appears to have been heavily influenced by Sir Henry Maine.[14] Specifically, Tonnies argued that social control in the *Gemeinschaft*-like organization is based on folkways, mores, and customs that, from the standpoint of members of the *Gemeinschaft*, possess eternal truth and never lose their binding force. Above all, the law of the *Gemeinschaft* involves the control of the whole over its parts, and the interests of the family, village, or town always come before those of the individual. On the other hand, the form of law typical of the *Gesellschaft* is more rational and scientific, and exists independently of superstition, faith, and tradition. As such, law represents a rational agreement among members of the *Gesellschaft*, and its only purpose is to uphold the rights, duties, and obligations of these members. In short, law in a *Gesellschaft*-like organization is simply another form of contract. The members of the *Gesellschaft* abide by the law because it is to their benefit to do so.

[11] Ibid., p. 227.
[12] J. H. Morgan, "Introduction" in Sir Henry J. S. Maine, *Ancient Law* (London: J. M. Dent & Sons, 1917), p. viii.
[13] Ibid., p. 100.
[14] Similarly, Maine's influence is clearly evident in the works of Emile Durkheim. See Emile Durkheim, *The Division of Labor in Society*, trans. by George Simpson (New York: Macmillan Publishing Co., Inc., 1933).

Concluding Remarks

Before we leave Tonnies and the concepts of *Gemeinschaft* and *Gesellschaft*, a few concluding remarks are in order. First, Tonnies viewed his work as an exercise in the articulation of ideal types that rarely, if ever, appear in the real world. In commenting on the concepts of rational and natural will, for example, Tonnies points out that

> Between these two extremes all real volition takes place. The consideration that most volition and action resembles or is inclined toward either one or the other makes it possible to establish the concepts of natural will and rational will, which concepts are rightly applied only in this sense. I call them normal concepts. What they represent are ideal types, and they serve as standards by which reality may be recognized and described.[15]

The last sentence in this statement is of particular interest because it suggests that Tonnies regarded his ideal types as merely tools by which empirical phenomena may be classified and understood.

Second, we have already implied that Tonnies conceived of his theoretical system as a dynamic one. More than anything else, he presents a theory of social and cultural change. On various occasions, for example, Tonnies points out that, as time passes, *Gesellschaft*-like relationships replace those that are *Gemeinschaft*-like, and that natural will continually yields to the triumph of rational will. To be more specific, Tonnies offers what is, in essence, an economic interpretation of social and cultural change. He maintains that with the emergence of capitalism and the concomitant desire for monetary gain, the values and ideologies associated with *Gemeinschaft* fade away and are replaced by values associated with trade and commerce. Thus "the merchants or capitalists . . . are the natural masters and rulers of the Gesellschaft." [16] It is they who stimulate the shift from a *Gemeinschaft*-dominated society to one dominated by *Gesellschaft*-like relationships.

Just how Tonnies evaluated this basic change in the nature of social relationships is open to question. On the one hand, Loomis correctly points out that "Tonnies continually reminded his readers that the process of change through which the individual who was controlled by natural or integral will in his Gemeinschaft was 'freed' and became the subject of rational will was 'healthy' and 'normal.' Although critics accuse him of recommending Gemeinschaft as good and condemning Gesellschaft as bad, he disclaimed any such intention." [17] At the same time, Tonnies

---

[15] Tonnies, *Community and Society*, p. 248.
[16] Ibid., p. 83.
[17] Ibid., p. 3.

seems to betray a preference for *Gemeinschaft*-like relationships and a belief that *Gesellschaft*-like relationships are superficial and even unnatural. This preference is most clearly indicated when, in citing the political scientist Bluntschli, Tonnies states that

> Whenever urban culture blossoms and bears fruit, Gesellschaft appears as its indispensable organ. The rural people know little of it. On the other hand, all praise of rural life has pointed out that the Gemeinschaft among people is stronger there and more alive; is it the lasting and genuine form of living together. In contrast to Gemeinschaft, Gesellschaft is transitory and superficial. Accordingly Gemeinschaft should be understood as a living organism, Gesellschaft as a mechanical aggregate and artifact.[18]

It is interesting to note that Tonnies's attitude toward *Gemeinschaft*, to the extent that it is reflected in this passage, is very similar to that of many Americans as they look back with nostalgia on "the good old days" when the United States was no more than a collection of rural villages and towns.

Be this as it may, Tonnies echoes a theme that we have already encountered in Chapter 2 of this book. This is the idea that as communities or other units of social organization become larger and more complex, fundamental changes occur in the nature of human relationships. Among other things, people may tend to become more reserved, they may become more individualistic, and they may oftentimes view each other as means to an end. The fact that so many theorists have arrived at this same conclusion (even though they state it in different ways) suggests that analyses such as Tonnies's have some validity and explanatory power. Yet things must be kept in perspective. Even though urbanites may experience *Gesellschaft*-like relationships more often than ruralites, the urbanite nonetheless enters into many relationships that are marked by mutual aid and helpfulness, unity, genuine concern for other persons, and so on. In sum, even in the largest of metropolitan areas, *Gemeinschaft*-like relationships have not completely disappeared.

COMMUNAL TYPES: MAJOR AMERICAN CONTRIBUTIONS

Following the publication of *Gemeinschaft und Gesellschaft*, the use of type construction as a basic methodological tool in the social sciences became rather popular. Needless to say, many of the best-known constructed types, including those of Max Weber, Emile Durkheim, and Howard Becker, have only an indirect bearing on the analysis of terri-

[18] Ibid., p. 35.

torial communities. Hence they are not considered by the present writer. However, three constructed type theories of community that cannot be ignored are those developed by Robert M. MacIver, Carle C. Zimmerman, and Robert Redfield.

Robert M. MacIver

The wisdom of including Robert M. MacIver's concepts of communal and associational relations in a discussion of typological theories of community might be questioned. For one thing, the distinction that MacIver draws between communal and associational relations is not expressed in a highly formalized typology. Rather, the two concepts simply point to two fundamentally different types of relationships that can develop among human beings. Of more importance, however, is the fact that MacIver used the term *community* in a somewhat different way from the way it is used in this book. MacIver's concept of community is much more inclusive than that of the present author's. Nonetheless, the two concepts that he has developed are meaningful ones and are applicable to the analysis of territorial communities.

The distinction that MacIver draws between communities and associations is simple. He begins with the assumption that all social relationships are an outgrowth of the common interests that prevail among people: many of the goals that human beings pursue can be realized only by working together, and as a result, human beings affiliate with each other because it is to their interest to do so. This brings us to MacIver's basic definition of the term *community*. Thus when persons unite together to pursue "not this or that particular interest, but the basic conditions of a common life, we call that group a community. The mark of a community is that one's life may be lived within it, that all one's social relationships may be found within it." [19] In brief, it is within a community that an individual can satisfy all of his or her physical, psychological, social, and economic needs. As such, a community may encompass a territorial area as small as a household or as large as a nation.

In contrast to the all-encompassing nature of communal relations are those of an associational nature. According to MacIver, an association consists of persons united together to pursue some particular interest or interests. Therefore, the difference between communities and associations is entirely clear, that is, "a community is a focus of social life, the common living of social beings; an association is an organization of

---

[19] Robert M. MacIver, *Society: A Textbook of Sociology* (New York: Farrer & Rinehart, Inc., 1937), p. 9.

social life, definitely established for the pursuit of one or more common interests. An association is partial, a community is integral." [20] More specifically, associations are a part of community structure itself and may be of a "political, economic, religious, educational, scientific, artistic, literary, recreative, philanthropic, and (or) professional nature." [21]

Carle C. Zimmerman

The theory developed by Carle C. Zimmerman centers around his concepts of "localistic" and "cosmopolitan" communities. In reality, this theoretical scheme contains little that is new, and, as a matter of fact, Zimmerman readily acknowledges that his concepts closely parallel Tonnies's concepts of *Gemeinschaft* and *Gesellschaft*.[22] Nonetheless, Zimmerman's scheme is of interest because it was one of the first constructed types that dealt directly and specifically with territorial communities, that is, with communities that have a "relatively definite and compact geographic base." [23] Furthermore, Zimmerman is the first theorist whom we have considered in this chapter whose conceptual scheme is based on empirical research. At one time his book was as valuable for its insightful case studies of various communities as it was for its theoretical framework.[24] Nonetheless, Zimmerman constantly maintains that the concepts of "localism" and "cosmopolitanism" are themselves ideal types and should be so regarded.

The Typology. The distinction between localistic and cosmopolitan communities is rather simple.[25] Conditions found in the localistic community dictate, among other things, that the individual enjoys strong, viable ties with his or her family and community and that the interests of both groups come before those of the individual. In fact, the bonds between individuals and their community become so strong that they think of their community as "my group." [26] Furthermore, in the localistic community almost all associational ties are of a face-to-face nature and there

[20] Robert M. MacIver, *Community: A Sociological Study* (New York: Macmillan Publishing Co., Inc., 1931), p. 24.
[21] Ibid.
[22] See Carle C. Zimmerman, *The Changing Community* (New York: Harper & Row, 1938), esp. pp. 80–84.
[23] Ibid., p. 15.
[24] It should be stressed that only one facet of Zimmerman's theory of community is presented in this chapter. The student with a deep interest in community theory would be well advised to read *The Changing Community* in its entirety.
[25] "The Distinctive Traits of Localism and Cosmopolitanism" are summarized in *The Changing Community*, pp. 107–10. The present discussion closely follows Zimmerman's.
[26] Ibid., p. 107.

is much overlapping of group memberships. Thus "Masons are also Odd Fellows; Eastern Star women belong to the Culture Club; family members participate in the same groups, etc." [27] Needless to say, the associational structure of the localistic community is rather simple and unspecialized, and the number of such associations is limited.

The localistic community is both secluded and isolated.[28] Its members place a strong emphasis on neighborliness and friendliness and consciously seek to meet one another's needs. Because of this, Zimmerman argues that the localistic community tends to encourage the development of healthy, stable personalities in its members, that relatives take direct responsibility for the sick and the poor, and that police officers "show considerable pride in the fact that they prevent crime rather than punish it." [29] Likewise, the orientations that members of the localistic community have toward materialism, government, and social change are much different from those of the modern city dweller. According to Zimmerman, the localite is mainly concerned with the nonmaterial pleasures of life, tends to mistrust "big" government, and is generally fearful and suspicious of change. The attitude of the localite toward change is often summed up in such statements as "Change is usually for the worse" and "We might be better off the way we are." [30]

The traits that characterize the cosmopolitan community are the opposite of those that typify the localistic community. To be more specific, the term *cosmopolitan* applies to communities in which (1) there is a general emphasis on individuals and their ability to realize their essentially selfish desires; (2) there is little neighborliness or friendliness; (3) time-honored traditions and customs are shunned or even abandoned; (4) great emphasis is placed on the pursuit of wealth and material goods; and (5) isolation and seclusion from the larger society are typical of days gone past. In the cosmopolitan community there is little fear of strong, centralized government and the typical cosmopolitanite has a very positive attitude toward social change. This attitude is sometimes reflected in such statements as "Let's get on with it" and "We can't be worse off than we are now." [31]

Concluding Remarks. It should be remembered that Zimmerman's typology grows out of research that he conducted between 1905 and 1929

[27] Ibid.
[28] It should be noted that the number of communities in the United States that are both "secluded and isolated" has been greatly diminished with the development of mass communications and good transportation facilities.
[29] Zimmerman, *The Changing Community*, p. 108.
[30] Ibid.
[31] Ibid., p. 110.

and that American community life has changed dramatically since that time. Among other things, the localistic community is quickly disappearing from the American scene. This accounts for the fact that Zimmerman's typology sounds old-fashioned. This should not, however, be construed as a criticism of Zimmerman or his work. He recognized that the localistic community with all of its purported virtues would gradually disappear and that the cosmopolitan community would become the order of the day.[32]

Be this as it may, the distinction that Zimmerman drew between localistic and cosmopolitan communities has influenced the thinking of other sociologists. For example, Robert K. Merton has drawn a distinction between localistic and cosmopolitan influentials (see Chapter 8).[33] Indeed, this is one of the fascinating things about the typological tradition in sociology: by studying various constructed types, we can see clearly how our knowledge pertaining to the structure and dynamics of human societies develops and accumulates. Thus, Zimmerman built on the work of Ferdinand Tonnies, Merton drew his concepts of localistic and cosmopolitan from Zimmerman, and so on. Furthermore, the fact that both community theorists and general sociologists keep developing concepts that closely parallel the concepts of *Gemeinschaft* and *Gesellschaft*, localistic and cosmopolitan, or whatever, strongly suggests that these dichotomies are meaningful and significant. For instance, the distinction we drew between moral communities and mass societies in Chapter 1 has much in common with *Gemeinschaft* and *Gesellschaft*, localistic and cosmopolitan, and the other constructed types examined in this chapter.

☐ ROBERT REDFIELD: THE FOLK-URBAN CONTINUUM

Some of the most penetrating analyses of community life have come from those anthropologists who examine the lifeways of people who dwell in the more remote, isolated regions of the world. Especially to be singled out in this respect is the late Robert Redfield. Not only did Redfield provide students of the community with a wealth of colorful and well-documented case material relevant to life in rural Mexico, but he also made brilliant use of theory, and especially type construction, in organizing and interpreting these materials.[34]

[32] Zimmerman clearly had doubts about the desirability of this trend. See esp. ibid., pp. 652–53.

[33] See Robert K. Merton, *Social Theory and Social Structure*, rev. and enlarged ed. (New York: The Free Press, 1957), pp. 387–420.

[34] In addition to the specific materials discussed in this chapter, some of Redfield's major works are *Tepoztlan: A Mexican Village* (Chicago: University of Illinois Press,

Redfield readily acknowledges the inspiration that he drew from Tonnies and other typologists. From a methodological standpoint, however, Redfield's work represents a major step forward. In particular, Maine, Tonnies, Zimmerman, and most of the other typologists who preceded Redfield simply identified clusters of traits that they believed to be associated with different types of communities and societies: they also suggested that more and more of the traits associated with the *Gesellschaft* "pole" would manifest themselves as communities and societies become larger and more complex. On the other hand, Redfield clearly specified the precise changes that he thought would occur as communities undergo the transition from folk (rural) to urban.[35] One reason why Redfield was able to do this was that his typology is based on data collected by himself and others. Indeed, Redfield is the first theorist we have considered in this chapter whose work approaches the ideal in terms of scientific endeavor. He alternates between the articulation of theory and the examination of data that potentially support the theory. Because of this we cannot fully understand Redfield's folk-urban typology until we examine briefly the four communities he studied.

Four Communities: A Thumbnail Sketch

The four communities Redfield studied were all located on the Yucatan Peninsula. This body of land juts northward and eastward from the lower portion of Mexico and is divided into the Mexican states of Yucatan and Campeche, and the territory of Quintana Roo.[36] Redfield tells us that when he conducted his studies during the early 1930s the Yucatan Peninsula was both physically and politically isolated from the rest of Mexico and, above all, retained a distinctive regional culture.[37] Furthermore, there were communities on the peninsula that represented the extremes of primitive and modern, folk and urban.

To be more specific, one of the communities Redfield studied, Merida, was of interest because it was the only major urban center in the entire

.1930); *The Little Community* (Chicago: University of Chicago Press, 1955); *Peasant Society and Culture* (Chicago: University of Chicago Press, 1956); *The Primitive World and Its Transformations* (Ithaca, N.Y.: Cornell University Press, 1953). See also Robert Redfield and Alfonso Villa, *Chan Kom: A Maya Village* (Washington, D.C.: Carnegie Institution of Washington Pub. 448, 1934).

[35] This does not mean that Redfield lacked interest in the outer limits of his continuum. Perhaps the nearest he comes to articulating these outer limits is in his article "The Folk Society," *The American Journal of Sociology,* **52** (January, 1947), 293–308.

[36] For Redfield's own description of the Yucatan Peninsula see *The Folk Culture of Yucatan* (Chicago: University of Chicago Press, 1941), esp. pp. 1–18.

[37] Ibid., p. 2.

region.[38] As of 1930, the city had a population that was both large (96,660 inhabitants) and heterogeneous. Redfield reports that a wide variety of occupations were represented in the city, as were several different racial and ethnic groups, three major linguistic groups (Spanish, Maya, and English), and people of all social classes and income levels. Furthermore, Merida was by no means isolated. Because it was the capital of the state of Yucatan and the largest city in the region, its population was highly mobile and it exercised a great deal of influence over the economic, political, and cultural affairs of the entire peninsula. At the same time, it was closely integrated with and exposed to influences originating in other parts of Mexico and the world.

In distinct contrast to Merida was the tribal village of Tusik, tucked far away from the mainstream of Yucatan society. Located in central Quintana Roo, it was one of the nine settlements within the territory claimed by the X-Cacal subtribe of Maya Indians. As such, it represented the epitome of the folklike community. As of the 1930s the village had a population of 106 persons,[39] almost all of whom were of Mayan blood and background. Furthermore, the people of Tusik were homogeneous in regard to their occupations. The only adult male who was completely freed from agricultural pursuits was the community's priestly leader, and specialization was almost unknown in Tusik, except for one man who occasionally repaired guns and sewing machines. Although Redfield does not specifically mention the activities of Tusik women, it is safe to assume that they too were limited to the traditional tasks of maintaining the household and caring for the young.

In addition to its homogeneity, Tusik was extremely isolated. Members of the community harbored feelings of suspicion and hostility toward their more urbane neighbors and toward the Mexican government, and hence avoided communication and contact with outsiders. As a result, Tusik had neither school teachers nor representatives of larger governmental units, and the Tusik native rarely ventured into larger towns and cities. About the only contact community members had with outsiders was with traveling merchants who stayed in Tusik for only as long as was required to conduct business. The isolation of Tusik and its sister communities is expressed by Redfield as follows:

> Tusik hides itself in the bush; none of the nine villages are built on the roads that connect Santa Cruz del Brava with Valladolid and Peto, and the paths that lead to Tusik are deliberately concealed. The advent of a visitor is a cause for alarm, and the news of the appearance of a stranger

---

[38] The following description of Merida, and of the other three communities, is summarized from ibid., pp. 19–57.
[39] Ibid., p. 51.

within the territory of the group is an occasion to send out a party to reconnoiter.[40]

This strongly suggests that Tusik's success in maintaining its social and cultural isolation was partly due to its geographic and physical isolation. The other two communities, Chan Kom and Dzitas, represented intermediate points along a continuum that began with the folk community of Tusik and ended with the thoroughly urbanized community of Merida. The first, Chan Kom, resembled Tusik in many important respects. Its population was small (250 inhabitants as of 1930), everyone was dependent on agriculture, and the vast majority of people were of Mayan blood and background. However, Chan Kom differed from Tusik in one important respect: its people did not place any value on isolation. Rather, they sought to become incorporated into the larger Yucatan society and to take on many of the ways of the city. Partly because of this, Chan Kom had a "reputation in Yucatan for industry, determination, and ambition." [41] The final community, Dzitas (population 1200) represented yet another stage in the transition from folk to urban. Because it was located at the junction of a major railway and was a seat of local government, Dzitas was far from isolated. Furthermore, although Dzitas lacked the heterogeneity of Merida, its population was composed of various racial and social groups. Although most of the men of Dzitas were agriculturalists, a number of them had other occupations including a district judge, a variety of merchants, and numerous artisans.[42] Redfield says of Dzitas that "it lies on the frontier between the urban and rural ways of life." [43]

These are the four communities on which Redfield based his folk-urban typology. When these communities are arranged in proper order (Tusik, Chan Kom, Dzitas, and Merida), a natural continuum exists from the isolated, homogeneous tribal village to the mobile, heterogeneous city. Redfield uses isolation-mobility and homogeneity-heterogeneity as the key independent variables in his typology.

The Folk-Urban Continuum

It will be recalled that Redfield sought to analyze the changes that occur in communities as they evolve from folk to urban rather than to describe the outer limits of his continuum. He maintains that three basic changes occur as a community becomes more urbanized:

[40] Ibid., pp. 52–53.
[41] Ibid., p. 50.
[42] Ibid., p. 38.
[43] Ibid., p. 43.

1. The community undergoes a process of *cultural disorganization*. By this Redfield means simply that the roles and norms that guide human action become more complex, multifaceted, and at times inconsistent. Cultural disorganization involves four basic elements.[44] First, much of the unity that was once characteristic of the community's culture is lost. All of the members of the Tusik and Chan Kom communities, for example, subscribed to one organized body of beliefs, values, and ideas, whereas in the larger communities there were numerous subcultures built around ethnic, religious, and class differences. Second, cultural disorganization implies that a wide variety of cultural alternatives are open to the individual and that relatively few behavioral patterns are normatively defined. Because cultural disorganization is typical of the city, the urbanite has to make many more choices than the ruralite, and the likelihood that his or her neighbors will follow the same course of action is slight. For example, Redfield points out that in the villages there is only one acceptable way to cope with illness, whereas in Merida many ways exist. Thus "if a conservatively thinking native of Chan Kom falls ill and does not soon recover, he calls the shaman-priest. A Meridiano of the working class in similar circumstances may call an herbalist, buy a patent medicine, see a spiritualist, or visit a doctor." [45] Third, Redfield suggests that the path from cultural organization to disorganization entails a decrease in the amount of interdependence of the various elements of the culture. In Tusik different facets of the local culture are so interrelated that one cannot, for example, understand the beliefs, values, and practices associated with illness without also understanding those associated with agriculture and the supernatural. In Merida this is not the case. One's occupational successes or failures have little to do with one's religious strengths or shortcomings, nor is illness interpreted as evidence of impiety. Finally, Redfield argues that cultural disorganization often entails conflict and inconsistency among various cultural standards. In the folk village every cultural aspect harmonizes with every other, whereas in the urban community the individual faces behavior expectations that are inconsistent.

2. Another major change that occurs as communities evolve from folk to urban is that they become more *secularized*. Thus Redfield suggests that almost all activities in the folk communities are imbued with religious connotations, whereas in the more urbanized communities most human action is guided by considerations of expediency and rationality. It must be stressed, however, that Redfield does not equate the concept of *sacred* with formalized religion.[46] Rather, the term *sacred* implies only

[44] For a more complete discussion of cultural disorganization see ibid., pp. 346–52.
[45] Ibid., pp .11–12.
[46] Ibid., p. 354.

that "there is reluctance, emotionally supported, to call the thing rationally or practically into question." [47] Hence the shift from sacred to secular is well illustrated by the fact that in the fields of Chan Kom and other folklike communities the growing of maize is surrounded by a host of inviolable religious connotations and beliefs. Once the crop is taken to market, however, the rule "show the man how to get a better price, and he will follow the suggestion" applies.[48]

3. The final basic change that accompanies the transition from folk to urban involves the degree to which *individualism* becomes a hallmark of human behavior. In the villages of Yucatan all of one's actions have implications for one's family and community, and hence these become extremely powerful reference groups. One plans his or her activities with their welfare in mind. On the other hand, in the more urbanized communities the welfare of one's family and community does not depend so much on one's actions. As a result, individuals are given more leeway to do what they want to do and be what they want to be. In the city the practice of one's occupation becomes less a matter of obligation to family and community and more a matter of individual choice. Likewise, the right of individuals to hold land and use it for their own benefit becomes recognized, and the selection of a marital partner becomes a matter of individual discretion.[49]

The Folk-Urban Continuum: Summary and Criticisms

Summary. In Figure 5-2 a schematic drawing of Redfield's folk-urban continuum is presented. This figure helps to summarize the preceding discussion and to make the differences between folk and urban communities readily apparent. In essence, a folk community in its purest form is characterized by a highly homogeneous population that is both vicinally and socially isolated. As a consequence, its culture displays a considerable amount of organization (all of its parts are woven together in a consistent whole), emphasis is placed on the sacred nature of things and activities, and members of the community are collectivistic in orientation. On the other hand, the urban community is characterized by cultural disorganization, secularity, and individualism. These three characteristics can, of course, be attributed to the heterogeneity of urban populations and to the high rates of mobility found within cities and between them and other places.

[47] Ibid., p. 353.
[48] Ibid., p. 354.
[49] Ibid., p. 355.

	Folk	Urban
Independent Variables	Homogeneity _____	Heterogeneity
	Isolation _____	Mobility
Dependent Variables	Organization of Culture _____	Disorganization of Culture
	Scared _____	Secular
	Collectivistic _____	Individualistic

FIGURE 5-2. The folk-urban continuum.

Criticisms. Even though Redfield's folk-urban continuum is highly regarded by many anthropologists and sociologists, it has also been the target of criticism and controversy. The best-known critic of Redfield's work is anthropologist Oscar Lewis, who has also studied community life in rural Mexico. Lewis has aimed numerous criticisms at the folk-urban continuum and at Robert Redfield.[50] However, three of his criticisms seem to be especially important. First, he points out that communities may change but that this change may have nothing to do with the movement from folk to urban.[51] For example, the introduction of a new method of farming into a small rural community may change that community dramatically, but the community may remain as rural, or folklike, as it ever was. Lewis's second criticism of Redfield's typology is a bit more complex: he suggests that Redfield erred in treating the variables that make up the folk-urban continuum as *inter*dependent variables.[52] Thus Redfield assumes that as a community becomes more heterogeneous and less isolated, it will automatically experience more cultural disorganization. It will also become more secular and individualistic. However, Lewis suggests that these variables can and sometimes do vary independently of one another, i.e., a community may become more heterogeneous but

[50] See Oscar Lewis, *Life in a Mexican Village: Tepoztlan Restudied* (Urbana: University of Illinois Press, 1963), esp. pp. 427–48; Oscar Lewis, "Tepoztlan Restudied: A Critique of the Folk-Urban Conceptualization of Social Change," *Rural Sociology*, 18 (June, 1953), 121–34.
[51] Ibid., pp. 432–33.
[52] Ibid., p. 433.

this might not be accompanied by an increase in secularity and individualism. For example, in his study of Tepoztlan, a village that Redfield had studied some seventeen years earlier,[53] Lewis found that there had not been a decrease in the stability of family life even though the community had increasingly been exposed to urban influences.[54] This is contradictory to what one would expect if Redfield's thinking were entirely accurate. Finally, Lewis suggests that the folk-urban continuum obscures important differences between societies and therefore can be misleading.[55] For example, the Blackfoot Indians display two traits that are normally thought to be associated with urbanism—they are highly competitive and individualistic—but their culture is much more folklike than urbanlike.

What, then, can we conclude about the folk-urban continuum? Lewis's criticisms of Redfield's work are well taken, but, at the same time, Redfield's continuum does seem to have a measure of validity. Redfield convincingly demonstrated that the communities of Tusik, Chan Kom, Dzitas, and Merida represent points along the folk-urban continuum. The folk-urban continuum also proved helpful to Redfield in his efforts to understand religious, economic, familial, and governmental activities in the four communities. Perhaps about the best that we can do is to agree with Horace Miner, who concludes that the folk-urban continuum is helpful and important but that it is also in need of clarification, refinement, and the addition of important variables overlooked by Redfield.[56]

☐ SOME RECENT INNOVATIONS

During recent years the use of type construction in the analysis of communities has been overshadowed by the development of newer theoretical approaches. Nonetheless, the typological approach to community analysis is still used with effectiveness by several sociologists, including Gideon Sjoberg, George A. Hillery, Jr., and Roland L. Warren. Hence we shall conclude this chapter by examining recent innovations in constructed type theories of community.

Before we examine the substantive contributions of Sjoberg, Hillery, and Warren something must be said about their methodological orientations. All three theorists, and especially Sjoberg and Hillery, link their theoretical schemes closely to empirical data. Indeed, Sjoberg and Hillery

---

[53] See Redfield, *Tepoztlan: A Mexican Village.*
[54] Lewis, *Life in a Mexican Village*, p. 436.
[55] Ibid., pp. 433–34.
[56] See Horace Miner, "The Folk-Urban Continuum," *American Sociological Review*, 17 (October, 1952), 537.

use type construction as a tool by which they can derive generalizations from case studies and documents relating to specific communal forms. Because of this, both theorists deny that their concepts are ideal types in the usual sense of the term. Rather, Hillery refers to his models of the *vill* and the *total institution* as empirical abstractions for the simple reason that all elements in the models are derived directly from an examination of actual community studies.[57] Presumably, there is nothing hypothetical about his work. Likewise, Sjoberg makes a distinction between ideal types and constructed types and maintains that his work falls into the latter category. According to him, a constructed type conforms much more closely to empirical reality than does an ideal type.[58] Furthermore, Sjoberg, Hillery, and Warren are all dedicated to the clarification of fuzzy concepts. One of Hillery's foremost goals is to bring some order to the chaos surrounding the term *community*, whereas Sjoberg forces the reader to recognize that the "preindustrial city" is something quite different from the city as it is found in modern, industrialized societies. Similarly, Warren argues that we must focus more clearly on the ties between the local community and the larger society. We can no longer look at communities as though they are "independent islands, cut off from interaction with their geographical regions and with the larger culture." [59]

Gideon Sjoberg

After analyzing a wealth of literature pertaining to cities in various cultural settings, Gideon Sjoberg became disillusioned with urban sociologists who base their generalizations about cities on observations drawn from modern, industrialized societies. In fact, he argues that there is a pressing need for comparative analysis in the study of cities. Furthermore, he advances the thesis that there are two distinctively different types of cities—the industrial and the preindustrial—and that the differences between them can be traced to differences in the level of their technological development.[60] We shall look more closely at the influence of technological factors on the structure of cities in a moment. Before so doing, however, we need to examine some of the most important features of the preindustrial city itself.

Sjoberg uses typological procedures to distinguish between the in-

[57] See George A. Hillery, Jr., "Villages, Cities, and Total Institutions," *American Sociological Review*, **28** (October, 1963), 780.
[58] Sjoberg, *The Preindustrial City*, p. 21.
[59] Roland L. Warren, "Toward a Typology of Extra-community Controls Limiting Local Community Autonomy," *Social Forces*, **34** (May, 1956), 338.
[60] Sjoberg, *The Preindustrial City*, esp. p. 7.

dustrial and the preindustrial city.[61] His description of the preindustrial city and of the ways in which it differs from the industrial city is elaborate and impossible to describe in a short sketch. However, a few of the more striking features of the preindustrial city can be described under the headings of ecological, economic, and social organization.[62]

In regard to ecological organization, Sjoberg successfully demonstrates that the preindustrial city displays patterns of spatial organization considerably different from those found in cities in the industrial world.[63] Four basic differences seem to stand out. First, the preindustrial city tends to be centered around edifices devoted to governmental and religious activities rather than around a "commercialized core" as is the case in the industrialized city. This is because commercial activities are not highly developed in preindustrial societies and are considered subordinate to activities of a governmental and religious nature. Second, in many preindustrial cities the spatial distribution of social classes is approximately the opposite of that found in the modern American city. The elitist upper class clusters around the city center whereas the lower classes live on the outskirts of the city.[64] Third, there is usually a rigid segregation of persons in accordance with ethnic, occupational, and other differences. Most preindustrial cities have ethnic and/or religious ghettos, and entire streets may be devoted to particular occupations and crafts.[65] Finally, even though spatial segregation is found in the preindustrial city, there is little specialization in terms of land use. The same plot of land is frequently used as one's home, workplace, and commercial establishment, and public edifices may be used for worship, education, trade, and recreation.[66]

The preindustrial city also differs from the industrial city in its economic organization. One major difference lies in the lack of industrialization in the preindustrial city. This is because preindustrial societies lack an advanced technological base that utilizes inanimate sources of energy and power. As a result, the preindustrial city displays a low division of

[61] Needless to say, preindustrial cities are quickly disappearing from the world scene. However, they are still found throughout India and the Middle East, as well as in parts of Latin America, Central Asia, Africa, and even Europe.

[62] This is the scheme used by Sjoberg in one of his earlier discussions of the preindustrial city. See Gideon Sjoberg, "The Preindustrial City," *The American Journal of Sociology*, **60** (March, 1955), 438–45.

[63] For a more complete discussion see Sjoberg, *The Preindustrial City*, esp. pp. 91–103.

[64] See also Walter F. Abbott, "Moscow in 1897 as a Preindustrial City: A Test of the Inverse Burgess Zonal Hypothesis," *American Sociological Review*, **39** (August, 1974), 542–50.

[65] Sjoberg, *The Preindustrial City*, p. 101.

[66] Ibid., pp. 102–3.

labor in comparison to that found in urban-industrial societies, and one individual often has complete responsibility for the production and marketing of a particular item. Put differently, assemblyline production is simply nonexistent in the preindustrial city. This does not mean, however, that occupational specialization is absent. The preindustrial city does have its glassmakers, goldsmiths, carpenters, merchants, teachers, and so forth. Many of these are organized into guilds that have numerous functions, including the minimization of competition and the recruitment and training of new members of the profession.[67]

Finally, the preindustrial city displays a number of interesting features in terms of its social organization. Two of these are of particular importance. First, kinship bonds are very strong, and, contrary to the statements of many urban sociologists, the extended family system is held in much higher esteem than is the small nuclear family. As Sjoberg puts it:

> The preindustrial urbanite functions within a family system and subordinates himself to it. One consequence is that, typically, marriages are arranged by families, not by individuals. The large extended family, with numerous relatives residing in a single "household"—i.e., one that is a functioning social unit—is the ideal toward which all urbanites strive, though a sizable, closely knit family is generally attainable only by the upper class. Economic circumstances prevent the urban poor and the peasantry alike from maintaining large households; for them the famille souche is more normal.[68]

One reason why the extended family system is popular in preindustrial cities is that it is a source of safety and security for its members. The preindustrial city lacks welfare agencies and financial programs to aid the old, the sick, and the disabled. Hence people are dependent on their kinfolk during times of crisis.[69] These kinfolk can respond more quickly and efficiently to the individual's needs if they live under the same roof or in close proximity to one another. It should also be noted that in some preindustrial cities one or two extended families may almost totally dominate the community's economic, political, religious, and other institutions.[70]

Second, Sjoberg found that the preindustrial city tends to have a two-class system of stratification that consists of a small group of literate, upper-class leaders ("the elite") and a much larger group of lower-class and outcast persons; a middle class of any significant size does not exist. This again is in distinct contrast to industrial cities. Findings of this type

[67] For further elaboration see ibid., pp. 190–96.
[68] Ibid., p. 324.
[69] Ibid., pp. 159–60.
[70] Ibid., p. 161.

led Sjoberg to doubt the universality of generalizations concerning city life that are based exclusively on studies conducted in industrialized societies.

It must be stressed that Sjoberg explains these and many other differences between the preindustrial and the industrial city in terms of differences in their technological base. In contrast to the modern city, the preindustrial city is totally dependent on animate sources of energy, that is, energy supplied by human beings and animals. This explains many of the features of the preindustrial city. For example, the lack of modern transportation and communication facilities means that the outskirts of the city have little appeal to anyone, especially to the elite. As a result, the upper classes cluster around the center of the city whereas the lowest classes are forced to inhabit the least accessible section of the city, i.e., the part farthest from the center of activities. Similarly, the state of technological development that characterizes the preindustrial city helps to explain the existence of a rigid two-class system of stratification. A preindustrial city is complex enough to require a group of leaders and coordinators, but, according to Sjoberg, the system of production still does not yield sufficient surpluses, including food, to support a large group of leisured or semileisured individuals.[71] Other ways in which the relatively simple technological base found in preindustrial cities influences their ecological, economic, and social organization could be cited, but perhaps we have made our point.[72]

Sjoberg also suggests that, with the continued spread of modern technology and industrialization throughout the world, the preindustrial city will gradually disappear. He tells us, for example, that "the heyday of the preindustrial city is past. A few cities of this type persist in almost pure form, but in the face of industrialization they are fast relinquishing their special characteristics."[73] If it is true that the disappearance of the preindustrial city is inevitable, then we would have to agree with Sjoberg that "the dissolution before our very eyes of a city-type that has existed for fifty-five centuries or more is deserving of our attention."[74]

George A. Hillery, Jr.

Like many other conceptual and theoretical schemes, George A. Hillery's has unfolded over time. Beginning with his attempt to give

[71] Ibid., p. 441.
[72] In all fairness it must be pointed out that Sjoberg is not a technological determinist. He recognizes that other factors influence urban development and that technology itself is, to some extent, a product of urbanization. See ibid., esp. pp. 13–18 and 67–77.
[73] Ibid., p. 335.
[74] Ibid., p. 335.

added meaning and precision to the term *community*, Hillery has since developed his methodological approach into an effective tool for constructing nonmathematical models of various units of social organization, including communities. The key to understanding Hillery's work is to understand his methodology.

Hillery uses case studies as his chief source of data. In reference to those studies Hillery points out that they "are in reality sources of data, sources which have greater value if they are taken in concert than if examined singly." [75] In order to tap these data systematically, he "inventories" the various case studies and notes those traits that are typical of all villages, cities, total institutions, or whatever else he might be studying. [76] These traits are then articulated into a "model" that emphasizes those traits common to every example of the object that is being studied (i.e., villages, cities, total institutions, or whatever). One question is always foremost in Hillery's mind, i.e., "what traits do all villages [or other types of organization] have, and which do they lack?" [77]

The Vill. The value of this approach can be conveyed by examining Hillery's concept of the vill. In his *Communal Organizations*, [78] Hillery focuses on villages and cities as organizational types and compares them to prisons and mental institutions. Hillery's sources of data for this study are case studies of ten folk villages, five cities, two prisons, and three mental hospitals. The villages, cities, and mental hospitals are located in different parts of the world so that the typology developed has cross-cultural applicability. Each case study is systematically compared with all the others in terms of nineteen different traits. We need not list and discuss these traits. It will suffice to say that they are elements that Hillery found, to a greater or lesser degree, characteristic of all ten folk villages. [79]

Basically, Hillery reports that the villages and cities are rather similar to one another in regard to the nineteen traits, as are the prisons and mental institutions. At the same time, the two sets of organizations differ rather sharply from each other. The folk villages and cities have much in common with each other but little in common with prisons and mental hospitals. It therefore follows that these two sets of organizations should be referred to by different names. Hillery suggests that we use the term

---

[75] George A. Hillery, Jr., "The Folk Village: A Comparative Analysis," *Rural Sociology,* 26 (December, 1961), 337.

[76] For a more detailed discussion of Hillery's methodology see ibid., pp. 34–42. See also George A. Hillery, Jr., *Communal Organizations: A Study of Local Societies* (Chicago: University of Chicago Press, 1968), pp. 11–25.

[77] Hillery, "The Folk Village," p. 341.

[78] See footnote 76.

[79] For an enumeration and description of these traits see Hillery, *Communal Organizations,* Table 2.

total institution as originally coined by Erving Goffman to refer to prisons, mental hospitals, and similar organizations. In an earlier article, he also proposed that we use the term *vill* to refer to "folk villages and cities and *to nothing else.*" [80] The reason for adopting the latter term is to avoid the confusion that currently surrounds the word *community.*

In elaborating further on his model of villages and cities, Hillery maintains that the elements of space, cooperation, and family are of central importance in differentiating vills from other organizational types. He also maintains that these three elements help to integrate and establish order among the remaining components of the model. The way in which this integration and order are achieved can be shown by means of an example. Thus Hillery tells us that in the folk village the family "is the basic economic, stratification, and socialization unit and the basis on which government, religion, and recreation operate." [81] Similar statements apply to space and cooperation and their relationship to other traits of which the model is composed. At the same time, Hillery does not maintain that a small isolated folk village is, for all practical purposes, identical to a large city. The chief difference between these two types of vill is that the family is the key unifying element in the folk village whereas contractual cooperation is the key unifying force in the city. Nonetheless, villages and cities do array themselves along the same continua. The differences between them are a matter of degree. Hence the same definition can apply to both folk villages and cities, i.e., "the vill is a localized system integrated by means of families and cooperation." [82] This definition does not fit the total institution. These organizations are, in a sense, localized. However, they are not organized around the family, and cooperation among members is not one of their essential properties.

Communal Organizations. Hillery's model of the vill represents an important contribution to the literature on community. In the final analysis, however, the distinction that he makes between communal and formal organizations and his typology of human groups may prove even more useful.[83] The value of this typology lies in the fact that it helps us (1) to explore the relationship between vills and other communitylike organizations such as families, neighborhoods, and nations and (2) to distinguish communitylike organizations from formal organizations such as governmental units, service organizations (e.g., hospitals), and business concerns. The basic difference between formal organizations and communal organizations is, according to Hillery, very simple: the formal organiza-

[80] Hillery, "Villages, Cities, and Total Institutions," p. 782.
[81] Ibid., p. 781.
[82] Hillery, *Communal Organizations,* p. 65.
[83] See ibid., pp. 145–52.

tion has one or more specific goals that it seeks to attain.[84] On the other hand, the term *communal organization* "refers to a system of institutions formed by people who live together. The system has no specific goal. The reasons for living together are often no more than that of being born in the locality (for all communal organizations occupy a particular territory)."[85]

The relationship between communal organizations and vills becomes apparent once the two concepts are understood. The term *vill* is a very specific one that refers only to villages and cities. On the other hand, the concept of communal organization is much broader and applies not only to villages and cities but also to families, neighborhoods, nations, and other units of social organization that have no specific goal and that occupy a particular territory. Thus the correspondence between the concept of communal organization and the concept of community as it is used in the present book is not direct. Rather, there is a close correspondence between what Hillery calls a vill and what the present writer calls a community.

Roland L. Warren

One criticism that can be leveled at many students of community life is that they largely ignore the fact that most communities are a part of a larger society and culture. All too often, sociologists seem to work on the assumption that communities are isolated, self-sufficient units of organization. Needless to say, nothing could be farther from the truth. The modern community is profoundly influenced by events that occur and decisions that are made in other communities and at the extra-community (or societal) level. In the United States, for example, it sometimes appears that "communities are simply points of geographical contact of criss-crossing networks of different organizations like the Presbyterian Church, the Grange, Rotary International, Standard Oil Company of New Jersey, Atlantic & Pacific, and so forth."[86] This fact forces us to consider whether there is any value in studying the community as a *discrete, distinct* unit of social organization. Should we not simply study the community as a place where extralocal organizations

[84] It should be noted that Hillery uses Talcott Parsons's definition of a "specific goal," i.e., "following Parsons we may describe a specific goal as having at least three characteristics: (1) the product of the goal is identifiable, such as automobiles, academic degrees, etc; (2) the product can be used by another system—that is, the output of one system is an input for another system; and (3) the output is amenable to a contract, it can be bought and sold." See ibid., p. 147.
[85] Hillery, *Communal Organizations*, pp. 185–86.
[86] Warren, "Toward a Typology of Extra-community Controls Limiting Local Community Autonomy," p. 338.

converge because of their dependence on one another and because of their need to be accessible to a population that will "consume" the goods and services they offer?

An answer to this question is implied in the concept of *community autonomy* as it has been developed by Roland L. Warren.[87] Basically, Warren's concept of community autonomy reminds us that communities can be arrayed along a continuum in terms of the degree to which they have control over events and activities that occur within their boundaries. Some communities enjoy a high degree of autonomy whereas others do not. Likewise, the concept of community autonomy applies to institutions and organizations that are found within a community. Some community-based institutions and organizations are almost completely autonomous in their operations whereas others are subject to a great deal of extra-community control. Thus the Baptist church is often cited as an organization whose operations are almost totally controlled by members of the local congregation. On the other hand, the operation of the local branch of Bell Telephone Company may be entirely controlled by decision makers who have never visited the host community. Communities, as well as the institutions and organizations found within them, can presumably be classified in terms of the degree to which they have retained or lost their autonomy. The student of community life would do well to bear this fact in mind when he or she studies the community, especially as it exists in the modern, urban world.

Warren's discussion of community autonomy is closely related to his discussion of the community's horizontal and vertical axes. Put very simply, the term *horizontal axis* refers to the interrelationships of various institutions and organizations that are found within the community. As examples we might cite the relationships among local welfare agencies, among local churches, and so forth. In contrast, the community's *vertical axis* consists of "the relationship of the individual to a local interest group and of that local interest group to a regional, state, or national organization." [88] It is tempting, of course, to suggest that as the vertical axis becomes increasingly strong, there is a decrease in local autonomy. This, however, does not necessarily have to be the case. Rather, the variables of community autonomy and the strength or weakness of a community's horizontal axis may be only minimally related.[89] For example, a com-

---

[87] Ibid., esp. p. 339.

[88] Roland L. Warren, "Toward a Reformulation of Community Theory," *Human Organization,* **10** (Summer, 1956), 8.

[89] The author is indebted to Professor Larry M. Landis for drawing this to his attention. In the first edition of this book it was maintained that "as the vertical axis becomes increasingly strong and well-developed, there is a decrease in local autonomy." This statement now seems to at best be only partially accurate.

munity might well retain almost complete control over its religious, educational, and welfare institutions at the very same time that new business firms, controlled by outside corporations, are locating branch offices, stores, or factories in the community.

☐ SUMMARY

There are several "tests" that can be used to evaluate the merits of a theoretical system. The theories developed by Tonnies, MacIver, Zimmerman, Redfield, Sjoberg, Hillery, and Warren meet some of these tests well. Among other things, each theorist has made his purposes clear, and the degree to which each has built on the work of his predecessors is impressive. Nevertheless, two questions require further exploration. First, do the theories we have considered in this chapter represent *significant* contributions to the literature on communities? Our answer to this question can be positive only if the theories shed light on community structure and process. Second, the question of adequacy must also be raised. Do the theoretical systems considered in this chapter represent valid analyses of the phenomena under scrutiny?

The first question, that of significance, can be approached from several different directions. Certainly the significance of the constructed type approach itself can hardly be questioned. To the extent that the core properties of different types of communities can be isolated, a step forward has been made. The theorists considered in this chapter have made progress in this direction, especially in identifying some of the characteristics of rural and urban communities. At the same time, the typologists are still a long way from agreeing on the specific variables that best differentiate between these two community types. This can be attributed partly to the fact that no two of them have focused on communities in the same historical and cultural setting. Tonnies, for example, based his analysis on an intimate knowledge of medieval and nineteenth-century European society, Zimmerman focused on American communities as they were found during the first three decades of the twentieth century, and Redfield examined communities in a relatively under-developed region.

There is, of course, a potential hazard associated with some of the constructed type theories of community. They may lead us to overexaggerate and overestimate the differences between rural and urban communities, particularly as they are found in the modern, western world. With the development of modern means of transportation and communication, communities both large and small have been increasingly drawn into one all-encompassing orbit. The assumption that communities represent "sub-

151

societies" and "little cultures," which was made explicitly by Redfield and Zimmerman and implicitly by some of the other typologists, no longer holds. Rather, the differences between rural and urban communities have been reduced to a minimum. This is why Warren's work is important. In essence, Warren seems to be telling us that the small American community simply cannot be described as socially and vicinally isolated, nor does it have a culture distinct from that of the larger society. The basic features of American society, such as its materialistic orientation and emphasis on individualism, have penetrated into all communities. Under these conditions, any attempt to identify fundamentally different types of communities may be quite misleading unless the typologist is very careful to keep things in perspective.

The question of how adequate these theories are in terms of their explanatory power is something quite different. Certainly our review of constructed type theories of community indicates a growing tendency to view empirical observation as an integral part of type construction. Thus Tonnies's scheme is only loosely integrated with empirical data and, as a result, must be thought of as an exercise in the derivation of concepts. With increasing precision, however, Zimmerman, Redfield, Sjoberg, Hillery, and Warren provide concrete evidence suggesting that their typologies are valid. After reading Sjoberg's work, for example, one can hardly doubt that there are fundamental and basic differences between preindustrial cities and cities as they are found in the industrial world.

Up to this point, we have said relatively little about the typologies developed by MacIver, Sjoberg, and Hillery. This is because these theorists have had different purposes than Tonnies, Zimmerman, and Redfield. In the main, MacIver, Sjoberg, and Hillery have been concerned with conceptual clarification and with adding increased precision to our knowledge of communities. With the exception of Hillery, they have not attempted to construct polar typologies. MacIver, for example, simply draws a logical distinction between communities and associations, a distinction that seems both valid and significant. Likewise, the significance of Sjoberg's work is clear. The fact that urban sociologists have focused most of their attention on communities as they exist in highly industrialized societies has meant that many of our theories of the city have been limited in both scope and applicability. With the publication of the *Preindustrial City* a new dimension was added to our knowledge of the urban community. Finally, Hillery has made an outstanding contribution to the literature on communities by bringing the term *community* itself under close scrutiny. On the basis of Hillery's work, one can only conclude that this word, with its many shades of meaning, is virtually useless for purposes of scientific communication. Even more important, however, are Hillery's methodological innovations. It is the present writer's conviction that one of the most important tasks that faces sociology today is to take stock of what is *already* known. This is precisely what Hillery does when he uses case studies as sources of data.

BIBLIOGRAPHY

Cahnman, Werner J. "Tonnies and Social Change," *Social Forces,* **47** (December, 1968), 136–44.

Heberle, Rudolf. "The Sociology of Ferdinand Tonnies," *American Sociological Review,* 2 (February, 1937), 9–25.

Hillery, George A., Jr. *Communal Organizations: A Study of Local Societies.* Chicago: University of Chicago Press, 1968.

———. "The Folk Village: A Comparative Analysis," *Rural Sociology,* **26** (December, 1961), 337–53.

———. "Villages, Cities, and Total Institutions," *American Sociological Review,* **28** (October, 1963), 779–91.

Jonassen, Christen T. "Community Typology," in Marvin B. Sussman (ed.), *Community Structure and Analysis.* New York: Thomas Y. Crowell Company, 1959.

Lewis, Oscar. *Life in a Mexican Village: Tepoztlan Restudied.* Urbana: University of Illinois Press, 1963.

MacIver, Robert M. *Community: A Sociological Study.* New York: Macmillan Publishing Co., Inc., 1931.

Maine, Sir Henry J. S. *Ancient Law.* London: J. M. Dent & Sons, 1917.

McKinney, John C. "Constructive Typology and Social Research," in John T. Doby et al., *An Introduction to Social Research.* Harrisburg, Pa.: Stackpole Company, 1954.

———. *Constructive Typology and Social Theory.* New York: Appleton-Century-Crofts, 1966.

———, and Charles P. Loomis. "The Typological Tradition," in Joseph S. Roucek (ed.), *Contemporary Sociology.* New York: The Philosophical Library, Inc., 1958.

Miner, Horace. "The Folk-Urban Continuum," *American Sociological Review,* **17** (October, 1952), 529–37.

Redfield, Robert. *The Folk Culture of Yucatan.* Chicago: University of Chicago Press, 1941.

———. "The Folk Society," *American Journal of Sociology,* **52** (January, 1947), 293–308.

Sjoberg, Gideon. "The Preindustrial City," *American Journal of Sociology,* **60** (March, 1955), 438–45.

———. *The Preindustrial City: Past and Present.* New York: The Free Press, 1960.

Tonnies, Ferdinand. *Community and Society,* edited by Charles P. Loomis. New York: Harper & Row, 1963.

Warren, Roland L. "Toward a Typology of Extra-community Controls Limiting Community Autonomy," *Social Forces*, 34 (May, 1956), 338–41.

Wirth, Louis. "The Sociology of Ferdinand Tonnies," *American Journal of Sociology*, 32 (November, 1926), 412–22.

Zimmerman, Carle C. *The Changing Community*. New York: Harper & Row, 1938.

CHAPTER 6

□ □ □ □ □ □ □ □ □
□
□
□
□
□
□
□
□
□

Social System Theory, Functionalism, and Community

Social system theory and structural-functionalism have emerged as major types of sociological theory. Interestingly enough, sociologists have been relatively slow in applying these theoretical approaches to the analysis of territorial communities.[1] As a result, our understanding of the community has suffered. Thus, rather than focusing on theories of community per se, in this chapter we examine the community in terms of concepts and theoretical systems borrowed from general sociology. Furthermore, the relationships between social system theory and structural-functionalism are explored. Although the social system approach is "neither synonymous nor coextensive with structural-functionalism," [2] the two theoretical systems are complementary. One's understanding of the community can be enhanced by bringing both approaches to bear on its analysis.

---

[1] Two notable exceptions are the textbooks by Sanders and Warren. See Irwin T. Sanders, *The Community*, 3rd ed. (New York: The Ronald Press, 1975), esp. Part III; Roland L. Warren, *The Community in America*, 2nd ed. (Chicago: Rand McNally & Company, 1972). See also Frederick L. Bates and Lloyd Bacon, "The Community as a Social System," *Social Forces*, 50 (March, 1972), 371–79; John E. Bebout and Harry C. Bredmeier, "American Cities as Social Systems," *American Institute of Planners Journal*, 29 (May, 1963), 64–76. Finally, one of the leading social system theorists of recent times, Talcott Parsons, makes reference to territorial communities in many of his works. Perhaps his most insightful analysis of territorial communities from a social system perspective is contained in a chapter entitled "The Principal Structures of Community," which appears in his *Structure and Process in Modern Societies* (New York: The Free Press, 1960), pp. 250–79.
[2] Joseph H. Monane, *The Sociology of Human Systems* (New York: Appleton-Century-Crofts, 1967), p. 11.

☐ THE COMMUNITY AS A SOCIAL SYSTEM

The term *social system* has been defined in many different ways. For our purposes, however, a social system might be thought of as a *highly organized set of socially significant relationships between two or more persons or groups.* Seemingly, this statement fits every unit of organization that can be analyzed as a social system, including a family, a municipal government, a religious institution, or a community. To this definition we might add the qualification that the relationship must endure through time. This would exclude fleeting, temporary relationships between two or more people from social system analysis. However, the phrase *endure through time* creates problems, and by pointing out that the relationship must be "highly organized" and "socially meaningful" we accomplish the same purpose. Everyone has fleeting relationships with salespeople, casual acquaintances, and so forth, but these relationships lack the highly organized quality that social systems possess. Likewise, they are not socially significant in the sense that they are the "bricks" on which society is built.

The reader who is well versed in social system theory will immediately object that interaction is not mentioned in our definition. That interaction is of central importance in social system theory is evidenced when Loomis states that the "social system is composed of the patterned interaction of members." [3] This is a difficult idea to grasp, however, and the place of interaction in social system theory must be explored in great detail. It will suffice for now to point out that the terms *social system* and *interaction* are not necessarily synonymous, as Loomis's definition implies. Rather, interaction of its members is one of several properties that a social system possesses.

Community Structure

One of the most significant contributions of social system theory is that it sheds light on the ways in which communities are structured and organized. In short, the community can be viewed as a system, the component parts of which are statuses and roles, groups and institutions. Furthermore, these components (or subsystems) are closely articulated with one another: roles and statuses are combined with other roles and statuses to form groups, groups are combined with other groups to form

[3] Charles P. Loomis, *Social Systems: Essays on Their Persistence and Change* (Princeton, N.J.: D. Van Nostrand Company, Inc., 1960), p. 4. Similarly, Homans tells us that "the activities, *interactions,* and sentiments of the group members . . . constitute what we shall call the social system." See George C. Homans, *The Human Group* (New York: Harcourt Brace Jovanovich, Inc., 1950), p. 87. Italics added.

institutions, and, finally, institutions are combined with other institutions to give rise to communities.

Status and Roles. Sociologists often view statuses and roles as the basic building blocks of social organization. Indeed, the term *statuses* refers to the individual positions of which any social group, regardless of its size, is composed. The typical four-person nuclear family, for example, may be built around the statuses of husband and wife, mother and father, son and daughter, and brother and sister. This means that statuses are the most elementary units of social organization. Likewise, the term *role* refers to the manner in which individuals behave as they occupy statuses that have been assigned to them. Needless to say, people are free to decide for themselves what patterns of behavior are appropriate to some of the statuses they occupy. At the same time, they may occupy other statuses that do not allow them a great deal of freedom in defining their role. The role behavior appropriate to their status may be rigorously defined for them by the larger group, community, or society.

Groups. It should be apparent that one's statuses and roles cannot exist in isolation. For instance, a man cannot have the status of father unless he has a child (another status), nor can he play the role of husband unless he has a wife. Hence statuses become combined with other statuses and roles with other roles to give rise to groups. Groups constitute the second layer of organization that is found within a community.

There are several types of groups, not all of which are amenable to social system analysis. In his excellent introductory textbook, for example, Robert Bierstedt classifies groups according to a fourfold scheme that includes the statistical group, the societal group, the social group, and the associational group.[4] The term *statistical group* refers to such aggregates as all persons who voted for a particular political candidate, all persons who watch the same television program, all persons who purchase "Brand X," ad infinitum. The members of these "groups" do not interact with each other and hence do not form a social system. Much the same thing can be said about societal groups, e.g., all persons of the same sex, race, or occupation. The members of this type of group may have a "consciousness of kind," but this does not inevitably mean that they interact with each other. On the other hand, it is appropriate to view Bierstedt's social and associational groups as social systems. The social group is characterized by consciousness of kind and interaction and includes such diverse units of organization as kinship groups, cliques,

---

[4] Robert Bierstedt, *The Social Order: An Introduction to Sociology*, 2nd ed. (New York: McGraw-Hill Book Company, 1963), pp. 293–300.

friendship groups, and children's play groups. The members of an associational group also interact with one another, and, in addition, the associational group has a formal structure.[5] By this we mean that the associational group is organized on a hierarchical basis and has leaders and followers, presidents and secretaries, full and associate members. Many groups of this type are found in a modern community. Bierstedt includes within this category such entities as a college or university, the community chest, the United States Steel Corporation, the Missouri Synod of the Lutheran Church, and the United States government, to cite a few of his examples.[6]

It should also be pointed out that some sociologists, the most notable of whom is E. T. Hiller, have viewed the community as a social group.[7] Thus, to Bierstedt's fourfold classification of groups, Hiller might add a fifth category, the "community-group." [8] Hiller argues that all groups (with the exception, of course, of statistical and societal groups) have four basic properties. First, all social groups have a body of members. In the case of a community, we would call this body of members a population. Second, Hiller maintains that all social groups have certain tests of admission or membership. Again, in the case of the community a person who takes up residence in the community, locates employment, and so on, would undoubtedly be identified as a community member. On the other hand, a hobo who wanders through the community and sleeps one night on a local park bench would not be considered a member of the "community-group." Third, the members of any social group either adopt or are assigned one or more social roles. At the community level, for instance, some people (e.g., mothers and teachers) play a key role in socializing the young, others assume a primary role in the production of goods and services, and so on. Finally, Hiller points out that all social groups develop norms that help to regulate the relationships among the members of the group. This again is as true of the community as it is of any other social group. In Hiller's thinking, about the only thing that distinguishes communities from other types of social groups is that communities have a territorial dimension. Albert J. Reiss, in commenting on Hiller's work, suggests that a "community system [or group] differs from other systems [or groups] in that locality is a datum in the integration of the system." [9]

---

[5] Ibid., p. 297.
[6] Ibid.
[7] E. T. Hiller, "The Community as a Social Group," *American Sociological Review,* 6 (April, 1941), 189–202.
[8] Ibid., p. 191.
[9] Albert J. Reiss, "The Sociological Study of Communities," *Rural Sociology,* 24 (June, 1959), 127.

The suggestion that communities should be viewed as one of several types of social groups has its merits. A major task of sociologists is to look for similarities among what at first appear to be dissimilar units of organization. Hence, when it is profitable to do so, sociologists should not shy away from analyzing the community in exactly the same way that they analyze any other group. At the same time, in analyzing community structure per se, it appears more profitable to stick to the fundamental thesis of this chapter, that is, roles and statuses are combined with other roles and statuses to form groups, groups are combined with other groups to form institutions, and institutions are combined with other institutions to give rise to communities.

Institutions. We have already inferred that just as statuses and roles are the units of which groups are composed, so groups become the basic units out of which social institutions are formed. To be more specific, many of the groups found at the community level cannot exist in isolation from other groups that have complementary goals, functions, and purposes. For example, the local police department would be rather ineffective if it failed to receive the support and cooperation of the mayor's office, the city council, and the fire department. Because of the interrelatedness of these groups, they are often analyzed as component parts of the same social system (i.e., the government system). The specific groups included in this system (the police department, mayor's office, etc.) are referred to as subsystems.

It is with some hesitancy that the present writer calls this the institutional level of communal organization. The term *institution* is rather ambiguous and has taken on many different shades of meaning. Nonetheless, most sociologists agree that all institutions share at least one essential property: they perform certain crucial functions that must be performed if the community (or society) is to persist through time. In order for an institution to carry out these functions, however, it must have an organizational structure. In the modern American community, for example, the function of governing is carried out by the governmental subsystem and the function of educating is carried out by the school subsystem. This is not to argue that the institutional structure of communities is the same in all societies. More will be said about this point when we consider the concept of *functional alternative.*

The Community. Our final task is to examine the structural features of the community itself. From the preceding discussion, the reader can anticipate what we shall say. In short, a community is a system of systems or, more precisely, a system whose component parts are its various social institutions. Although the number of distinct institutional systems found at the community level varies from society to society, the most important ones found within the typical American community are the governmental, economic, educational, religious, and familial subsystems. Each of these can be broken down into a wide variety of social and/or associational groups. These, in turn, can be analyzed in terms of their component statuses and roles.

Although this approach to the analysis of community structure has its merits, it can also lead to serious misconceptions. First, the reader might well conclude that every group is totally integrated into the larger community through the media of institutions. This is not the case. Although most groups are subunits of larger institutions, such entities as play groups, friendship groups, and delinquent gangs are not. This suggests that a distinction must be made between those groups that are and those that are not a part of community structure itself. Second, the reader might mistakenly assume that the community possesses an extremely high degree of integration and conclude that all subsystems are closely articulated with all other subsystems. Again, this is not always the case. There are groups or institutions within every social system that operate with a high degree of autonomy and independence.

Interaction in Social Systems

There is interaction both within and among social systems. In fact, we indicated previously that a social system is essentially a network of interaction, although this point was not elaborated on in any great detail. Thus the nature of interaction and its place in social system theory must now be considered.

In relatively simple groups, the term *interaction* implies that the actions of one person call for reciprocal action on the part of other persons.[10] In the police department cited previously, for example, the chief may issue an order to one of his officers. This officer will obviously respond to the order, although we cannot always predict the nature of his response. Among other things, he may agree immediately to carry out the order, or he may ask for further clarification (e.g., "Where did the accident occur?"). The important thing to note is that the officer's response, in turn, affects the subsequent responses of the police chief. Hence interaction is a mutually adjustive, dynamic process in which person A responds to person B and person B responds to person A for as long as the parties are in contact. It is in this sense that a small, uncomplicated social system can be viewed as a network of interaction.

[10] For a more detailed discussion of the concept of interaction see Homans, *The Human Group,* pp. 35–37.

Unfortunately, the concept of interaction is more difficult to apply to a complex system such as the community. The individuals who belong to a social system of this size do not interact with all other members of the system. Rather, face-to-face interaction is manifested *within* the subsystems of which the community is composed. Because of this, the social system theorist sometimes analyzes the relationships among social systems in terms of systemic linkage. As defined by Loomis, this term refers to "a process whereby one or more elements of at least two social systems is articulated in such a manner that the two systems in some ways and on some occasions may be viewed as a single unit." [11] In essence, the concept of systemic linkage means that interaction occurs not only between individuals but also between groups and other groups, between groups and institutions, and even between two or more institutions.

The linkages that develop among the subsystems of which a community is composed have much in common with face-to-face interactive relationships. For example, one can imagine a community in which an ecumenical council is formed to investigate the treatment of poor people by the local police department. It might well be found that police practices leave much to be desired. When this fact becomes known, members of the police department may react by attacking the ecumenical council, its leaders, and their motives. As a result, the basic goal of the ecumenical council may well be diverted from improving the police department to defending its own position. The similarities between this chain of successive responses and the interaction that occurred in the police chief–officer relationship are clear.

Hence a considerable amount of interrelatedness and linkage develops among the social systems of which a community is composed. Unfortunately, the specific mechanisms by which systemic linkage is achieved have not been clearly specified by social system theorists. Nonetheless, there are several possibilities, including the following:

1. Units from within different systems may merge and, in so doing, give rise to a new system. It is in this way that the ecumenical council may have been formed: small groups from several different churches could have been drawn together to become the component parts of the council. Once in existence, however, the ecumenical council would represent a new subsystem within the community's religious system. Furthermore, the fact that various churches become linked together by councils of this type may strengthen the linkage among them on other fronts. In many cases, for example, there may be an increase in good will among their members and greater cooperation and understanding between their pastors.

[11] Loomis, *Social Systems*, p. 32.

2. Leading members of the linked systems may interact on behalf of their respective systems. For example, delegates of the ecumenical council could directly confront the police chief, and vice versa. In confrontations of this type, the "delegates" normally act on behalf of their respective subsystems rather than for their own advantage as individuals.

3. A significant development at the community level during recent years has been the emergence of social systems that have the explicit purpose of coordinating relationships among other systems. Examples are community welfare councils that provide coordinative services for various welfare agencies and the chamber of commerce that attempts to link together and coordinate the activities of business establishments. Similarly, our fictitious ecumenical council may have been created as a means of furthering cooperation among local churches, especially in regard to helping the poor.

4. Finally, the interaction between two or more social systems can transpire in a very indirect manner. Among other things, messages can be carried between the systems by the press, radio, or television. A short announcement in the local newspaper that the ecumenical council has found police procedures to be unsatisfactory may, for example, set off a whole series of responses and adjustments in the latter system.

Another method of studying interaction at the community level is in terms of the inputs and outputs that flow between its various subsystems.[12] As Roland Warren puts it, every subsystem in the community "will receive inputs of various types from other units in the locality: inputs which are a deliberate part of its operating needs, inadvertent inputs from the adaptive adjustments made by other local units, inputs involving the attitudes and behavior of those it employs or with whom it deals."[13] This classification of types of inputs, in the present writer's thinking, contributes much to our understanding of the relationships that can develop between two or more social systems. A local school system, for example, receives all of these inputs. In order for it to operate, it must receive funds from its supporting agency, that is, local government. Likewise, the school is also affected by changes and adjustments that occur in other systems, especially within the governmental subsystem. For instance, the latter system may be forced to greatly reduce its budget, with the inadvertent consequence that school programs must be curtailed. Finally, the school system is profoundly influenced by the atti-

---

[12] For an interesting example of this approach see Talcott Parsons, "General Theory in Sociology," in Robert K. Merton, Leonard Broom, and Leonard S. Cottrell, Jr. (eds.), *Sociology Today: Problems and Prospects* (New York: Basic Books, Inc., 1959), esp. pp. 16–29.
[13] Warren, *The Community in America*, pp. 294–95.

tudes and behavior of the persons with whom it deals. This includes the attitudes and behavior of the teachers it hires, the students it serves, and the public that supports it.

Yet another way of viewing the inputs and outputs that flow between social systems is presented in an article by John E. Bebout and Harry C. Bredmeier.[14] According to Bebout and Bredmeier, there are essentially four ways by which social system A can get what it needs from other social systems. First, it can sometimes rely on *coercion*. Coercion implies that system A is so powerful that it can narrow some other system's choices to the point that the latter system must comply with the demands made by system A. Second, system A can use *bargaining* as a means of obtaining the desired input. Bebout and Bredmeier use the term *bargaining* in its usual sense, and thus we need not elaborate on what it, as a means of obtaining a desired input, entails. The third way by which social systems obtain needed inputs is through *legal-bureaucratic mechanisms*. If system A receives inputs through legal-bureaucratic mechanisms, this implies that it is a member of a larger system and receives the input because it has a right to receive it and because the larger system "has a duty to hand it over." [15] For example, most governments have a duty to supply individual citizens with certain services (police protection, fire protection, etc.) on demand. Finally, system A sometimes obtains needed inputs from other social systems through *identification or solidarity mechanisms*. Bebout and Bredmeier tell us that "what we have in mind here is the mechanism which causes you to give your children, parents, wives, husbands, or friends, what they want from you, and causes you to accept their outputs. You do so because you 'identify' with them, in the sense of seeing and feeling them as extensions of yourself; so that to have them indicate their needs to you is tantamount to your desire to satisfy them." [16]

Bebout and Bredmeier use this conceptual scheme to analyze the precarious position in which one type of social system, the central city, finds itself today. They tell us that "most central cities must at present bargain with other units in their regions for the residents and industry they need; and their bargaining power is so weak as to threaten their viability unless aid from state and federal governments is supplied." [17] Bebout and Bredmeier seriously question whether the cities' bargaining power vis-à-vis other units (e.g., suburban communities) can ever be improved to the point that they can once more be self-supporting. Assuming that they can, however, a threefold effort will be required—land renewal, trans-

[14] See Bebout and Bredmeier, "American Cities as Social Systems," pp. 64–76.
[15] Ibid., p. 66.
[16] Ibid.
[17] Ibid., p. 64.

portation renewal, and human development.[18] In the meantime, other social systems, such as suburban communities and the state and federal government, must take responsibility for helping central cities to cope with the many crises that they face. It might be noted in passing that the poor bargaining position central cities find themselves in today illustrates a basic principle of social system theory: *if a social system is to receive the inputs it requires, then it must also contribute to the other systems on which it is dependent.* Otherwise, it is unable to bargain for the input it needs and must either wither away or rely on other social systems to voluntarily supply it with the required inputs.

Interrelatedness in Social Systems

It should be apparent that there is a high degree of interrelatedness of the various units that compose a social system. The nature of the ties that develop among social systems was briefly touched on in our discussion of systemic linkage. However, we must also look at the external and internal patterns that all social systems possess and examine the concept of equilibrium as it has been developed by social system theorists.

External and Internal Patterns. To George C. Homans must go the credit for developing the concepts of external and internal pattern. Homans explains these concepts by stating that "We shall not go far wrong if, for the moment, we think of the external system [or pattern] as group behavior that enables the group to survive in its environment and think of the internal system [or pattern] as group behavior that is an expression of the sentiments towards one another developed by the members of the group in the course of their life together." [19] To put the case differently, the external pattern consists of all the relationships that develop between one social system and another, whereas the internal pattern consists of the relationships that members of a social system have with each other. It should be pointed out that whether the relationship between two or more systems is "external" or "internal" depends on the perspective of the observer. For example, the relationships that a local department of public welfare has with the local police department are a part of that welfare department's external pattern. On the other hand, the ties between the welfare department and the police department are part of the same internal pattern when viewed from the perspective of the larger governmental system of which both units are subsystems.

A closely related distinction is that which social system theorists draw

[18] Ibid., p. 68.
[19] Homans, *The Human Group*, p. 110.

between instrumental and expressive activities.[20] Whereas the concepts of internal and external pattern refer to structural relationships within and among systems, the instrumental-expressive dichotomy focuses on the activities carried on by social system members. Thus on some occasions the members of a social system must direct their activities toward obtaining those things that the system needs in order to persist through time: School officials must appeal to the local government for funds, must enlist the cooperation of parents, and otherwise must engage in "instrumental" activities. At other times, the focus must be on the needs of system members themselves. Among other things, approval and reward must be distributed to system members and potential conflicts among these members must be smoothed over.

Do these dichotomies, especially those relating to external and internal patterns, apply to the community itself? Clearly, the answer to this question depends on one's perspective. For example, local government is present as a social system in most communities. By focusing on the external and internal patterns of this particular system we can gain insight into the nature of community structure itself. However, the dangers of applying these concepts to the community as a whole are somewhat greater. Certainly we can refer to the ties among subsystems within a community as that community's internal pattern; that is, a community's internal pattern consists of numerous relationships that exist among the groups and institutions of which it is composed. Similarly, we might refer to the community's ties with other communities as its external pattern. However, the present writer agrees wholeheartedly with Roland Warren that it is not the community as a whole that is related to other communities. Rather, the relationships that do exist are between subsystems within one community and those in another. As Warren puts it:

> Most models of the community's relation to a larger region consider communities as units, relating them in their entirety to other communities in the region. Whether or not this type of analysis was adequate for preindustrial communities, it offers little help in analyzing contemporary American communities. . . . Putting this another way, the important contemporary link between the community and the outside world is not an undifferentiated link between the community as such and other communities of the surrounding region, but rather it is the link between the highly differentiated parts of the community and their respective extracommunity systems.[21]

[20] See in particular Talcott Parsons, *The Social System* (New York: The Free Press, 1951), esp. pp. 48–49.
[21] Warren, *The Community in America*, p. 242.

In order to give substance to this important but subtle distinction, Warren differentiates between the community's vertical and horizontal patterns. The vertical pattern of a community includes "the structural and functional relations of its various social units and subsystems to extracommunity systems" whereas its horizontal pattern is found in the "structural and functional relations of its various social units and systems to each other." [22]

Interstitial Groups. Bates and Bacon have shed yet further light on the interrelatedness within a complex social system such as the community.[23] Like other social system theorists, they recognize that the community consists of a wide, wide variety of different groups. Some examples are families, wholesale and retail outlets, schools, and trade unions. Bates and Bacon use the term *elemental group* to refer to these units of organization. However, they go one step further and suggest that these groups are linked together by *interstitial groups.* An interstitial group is simply a group that is formed when the members of two or more elemental groups come together to exchange goods or services. A good example is the relationship between a grocery store clerk and a housewife. In this case, the housewife is acting as a representative of her family whereas the grocery store clerk is acting as a representative of the store. Even though relationships within interstitial groups may be quite fleeting, they may be repeated hundreds of times each day, i.e., the grocery store clerk may interact with hundreds of different customers.

Bates and Bacon's analysis is interesting in that it suggests that the interrelations of the various subsystems that compose the community are often of a competitive or conflictive rather than a cooperative nature:

> A housewife who goes to the grocery store to buy food for her family is performing a function for that family. This function is best performed when she succeeds in securing the highest quality and amount of food for the lowest cost. On the other side, the grocer is performing a function for the grocery store and performs best when he sells the lowest quality and amount of food for the highest price.[24]

This same statement could apply to virtually any customer-salesperson relationship. It could also apply to the relationship that develops, say, between a representative of a teachers' organization and a representative of the school board. In the latter case, the representative of the teachers'

[22] Ibid., pp. 161–62.
[23] See Bates and Bacon, "The Community as a Social System," pp. 371–79.
[24] Ibid., p. 374.

organization may be trying to secure the highest possible wages for the elemental group that he or she represents (all other teachers in the school system) whereas the representative of the school board is trying to keep teachers' salaries to a minimum. The importance of noting that relationships within interstitial groups are often of a competitive or conflictive nature cannot be overemphasized. Social system theorists have been vigorously criticized for ignoring the high levels of conflict that are often found within social systems.[25]

Contradictory Functional Requirements and Structural Freewheeling

As the preceding discussion indicates, it is widely agreed that a considerable amount of interrelatedness, interaction, and cooperation exists among the various subsystems of which the community is composed. At the same time, there are dangers in overemphasizing the degree of integration and interrelatedness that exists within complex social systems such as the community. Because of this, Gideon Sjoberg has introduced the concept of *contradictory functional requirements*. By this he means that the requirements or "needs" of one subsystem may conflict with the requirements or "needs" of another subsystem. For example, during World War II, when there was a severe manpower shortage, it became essential to recruit women into the labor force. A requirement of this type, however, could conflict with the need to have an adult in the home to care for and nurture children. Sjoberg puts it well when he says that "within the . . . city [community, etc.], various structural arrangements may be at odds with one another: some strains in fact appear to be intrinsic to the system." [26]

In a similar vein, George A. Hillery, Jr. has introduced the concept of *structural freewheeling*.[27] This concept draws our attention to the fact that complex systems such as the community are not so tightly integrated that it is impossible for one subsystem to get out of balance with other subsystems. For example, local government may become so complex and bulky that it eats up tax dollars that are needed to support the city's independent school district, hospital district, or whatever. It may literally take years before reequilibrium is established between local government and the other subsystems.

[25] For example, see Ralf Dahrendorf, "Out of Utopia: Toward a Reorientation of Sociological Analysis," *American Journal of Sociology*, 64 (September, 1958), 115–27.
[26] Gideon Sjoberg, *The Preindustrial City: Past and Present* (New York: The Free Press, 1960), p. 13.
[27] See George A. Hillery, Jr., *Communal Organizations: A Study of Local Societies* (Chicago: University of Chicago Press, 1968), esp. pp. 69–72.

Equilibrium

Equilibrium is another major concept in social system theory. In fact, this concept is of such central importance to social system theory that one of Talcott Parsons's definitions of "social system" is basically a definition of equilibrium. He tells us that a social system consists of "two or more units, $x_1, x_2, \ldots, x_n$, related such that a change in state of x_1 will be followed by change in the remaining $x_i, \ldots, x_n$, which is in turn followed by a change in the state of x_i etc." [28] This statement is very similar to the definitions of equilibrium offered by other writers, especially George C. Homans and Kingsley Davis.[29]

To be more specific, social system theorists maintain that the various components of a social system must be closely integrated with one another. Without this integration, the system itself could not meet the needs of its members. This integration is guaranteed by the tendency for subsystems to move continually toward a state of equilibrium. To paraphrase Parsons, the concept of equilibrium implies that when one unit of a social system undergoes change, then other units in the system also change. As a result, functional relationships among the units are maintained.

The nature of equilibrium as it is manifested at the community level can be illustrated by returning to our example of the interplay between the schools and governmental spending programs. Assuming that the governmental system does reduce the amount of money it allocates to the school subsystem, local school officials may be forced to eliminate supervised recreation programs. If the demand for recreational programs is great enough, however, there may be an increase in the number of recreational programs offered under commercial auspices. To state the case differently, the community may absorb changes in one of its subsystems (the school) through the mechanism of change in other subsystems.

The merits and deficiencies of social system theory will be considered at a later point in this chapter. Here we must note that the concept of equilibrium has been vigorously criticized.[30] The gist of these criticisms is that the concept of equilibrium represents an overmechanized view of social organization. It cannot always be assumed that the components of a social system are so closely interrelated that a change in one com-

[28] Morris Zelditch, "Note on the Analysis of Equilibrium Systems," in Talcott Parsons and Robert F. Bales, *Family, Socialization and Interaction Process* (New York: The Free Press, 1955), p. 402.

[29] See Homans, *The Human Group*, esp. pp. 303–4; Kingsley Davis, *Human Society* (New York: Macmillan Publishing Co., Inc., 1948), pp. 633–36.

[30] For example, see Walter Buckley, *Sociology and Modern Systems Theory* (Englewood Cliffs, N.J.: Prentice-Hall, Inc., 1967), esp. pp. 23–31.

ponent dictates a change in the other components. For example, sometimes trade and vocational schools are notoriously slow in changing their curricula to accommodate changes in the economic system and particularly in the job market. As a result, sometimes people are carefully trained for jobs that do not exist. Unfortunately, the reciprocal relationships between social systems and the units of which they are composed are much more complex than is implied by the concept of equilibrium.

Boundary Maintenance

We have purposely emphasized the interrelatedness that develops within and among social systems. However, every social system must also encourage a sense of cohesiveness and loyalty among its members. Because of this, social systems develop boundaries, and their members engage in various boundary-maintaining activities.[31] We are given a clue to the nature of boundary maintenance by Loomis: "this is the process whereby the identity of the social system is preserved and the characteristic interaction pattern maintained." [32] Furthermore, he suggests that both boundary maintenance and systemic linkage are essential properties of a social system, that is, "without boundary maintenance, social groups would be indistinguishable among a mass of individuals and interaction would be haphazard; without systemic linkage an unthinkable parochialism would deny to groups any form of contact outside their own boundaries." [33]

A social system may possess three different types of boundaries. First, most social systems have *psychological boundaries*. By this we mean that some individuals are accepted as members of the system and enjoy the psychological rewards of acceptance, whereas others are not. An example of this is often seen in oldtimer-newcomer relationships, especially in a small community.[34] On occasions, oldtimers may appear to be suspicious

[31] For a discussion that sheds much light on the boundary-maintaining activities of two groups, the Old Order Amish and the Hutterian Brethren, see Russell E. Lewis, "Controlled Acculturation Revisited: An Examination of Differential Acculturation and Assimilation between the Hutterian Brethren and the Old Order Amish," *International Review of Modern Sociology*, 6 (Spring, 1976), 75–83. The two groups are especially interesting in that they are, to a greater or lesser extent, receptive to technological innovation, particularly in the realm of agriculture, but nonetheless clearly seek to maintain spatial, psychological, and social boundaries between themselves and the larger society.
[32] Loomis, *Social Systems*, p. 31.
[33] Ibid., p. 33.
[34] See Edith E. Graber, "Newcomers and Oldtimers: Growth and Change in a Mountain Community," *Rural Sociology*, 39 (Winter, 1974), 504–13; David L. Birch, "From Suburb to Urban Place," *The Annals of the American Academy of Political and Social Science*, 422 (November, 1975), 25–35.

of new persons who migrate into their community and reluctant to accept these new persons as fellow community members. When this occurs, the newcomer may complain that the "natives" are unfriendly, uppity, or whatever. It might be hypothesized that under these conditions newcomers will not identify with the community until they sense that the oldtimers accept them. Second, most social systems are characterized by a variety of *social boundaries*. Most communities, for example, are crisscrossed with boundaries between various socioeconomic, racial, and ethnic groups. Finally, a few social systems have *physical or geographic boundaries*. Most communities, for instance, have legal boundaries beyond which their influence does not extend. Quite often these boundaries are of limited significance. They exist only on maps or in the minds of a few interested persons, and have little meaning for the average citizen.

☐ FUNCTIONALISM AND COMMUNITY ANALYSIS

Throughout our discussion of social system theory, we have emphasized the organizational and structural features of the community. Among other things, it was suggested that the community is a constellation of interrelated groups and institutions and that this interrelatedness is due to the fact that all social systems have both internal and external patterns. It is only because of this interrelatedness that the community can be subjected to social system analysis.

Social system theory is often supplemented by functionalism, another basic type of modern sociological theory. Although social system theory and functionalism are closely related, there are differences between the two approaches. The social system theorist focuses on units of social organization and on their structural relationships. Thus the concept of external pattern tells us only that social systems are interrelated. It does not tell us why these relationships exist or what they entail. Functionalism, on the other hand, examines these relationships in terms of their content and consequences. In examining religion, for example, the functionalist is interested in why religious organizations are found in virtually all communities, what contributions the religious system makes to the total community system, and what the consequences for the community would be if the religious system disintegrated.

The Functional Approach

The term *function* is a central one in the theoretical system under consideration; it is also a term that has numerous connotations and therefore gives rise to confusion.[35] Yet there have been clear statements of its meaning. One such statement is that offered in the form of a biological analogy by A. R. Radcliffe-Brown, a pioneer in the analysis of primitive societies:

> If we consider any recurrent part of the life process, such as respiration, digestion, etc., *its function is the part it plays in, the contribution it makes to, the life of the organism as a whole.* As the terms are here being used a cell or an organ has an activity and that activity has a *function.* It is true that we commonly speak of the secretion of gastric fluid as a "function" of the stomach. As the words are used here we should say that this is an "activity" of the stomach, *the function of which* is to change proteins of food into a form in which these are absorbed and distributed by the blood to the tissues.[36]

Hence when we use the term *function* in sociology we mean the contribution that a unit of social organization makes to the larger system of which it is a part. For example, one of the functions of the family is to socialize the young so that they can take their place in society. Likewise, one of the functions of government is to restrain persons who, by their actions, threaten social order.

In addition to using the word *function* in several different ways, sociologists have at times failed to clearly specify the purposes of functional theory. However, functional theory seems to serve two basic purposes. First, functionalism gives the sociologist some insight into the "functional requisites" of social life, that is, the functions that must be performed if a social system is to persist through time. To cite an example, the members of a society must reproduce if that society is to exist for any length of time. Second, functionalism reveals what consequences, if any, a unit of social organization has for other units and for the total system. Thus one of the consequences of marriage and the family is that the population is reproduced, and one of the consequences of government is that a modicum of social control is assured.

It is apparent that these two purposes of functional theory are, in the final analysis, almost identical. The functionalist assumes that *most* of the components of a social system perform certain activities that must be performed if the system is to persist through time. The task of the functionalist is to determine what these activities are and which subsystems are responsible for them.

[35] For a discussion of some of the uses to which the word *function* has been put see Robert K. Merton, *Social Theory and Social Structure*, rev. ed. (New York: The Free Press, 1957), pp. 20–23.
[36] A. R. Radcliffe-Brown, "On the Concept of Function in Social Science," *American Anthropologist*, 37 (July–Sept., 1935), 359. Italics added.

Before we examine some of the basic concepts used in functional analysis, two cautions are in order. First, we must avoid falling prey to what Robert Merton calls the *postulate of universal functionalism*. As Merton explains it, "this postulate holds that all standardized social or cultural forms have positive functions." [37] He further quotes Bronislaw Malinowski, a leading anthropologist of the functionalist school, as saying that "the functional view of culture *insists* therefore upon the principle that in *every type of civilization, every custom, material object, idea and belief fulfills some vital function. . . .*" [38] Today most sociologists and anthropologists recognize that this is simply not the case. There can be components of a social system that perform no major functions for the system as a whole, and it is even possible that some of these components hinder other subsystems in the performance of their functions. Second, Malinowski's statement makes it clear that functionalism is not limited to the analysis of social systems. One can also study values and beliefs, ideals and material objects in terms of their functions. When pursued to its limits, the functional analysis of a system as complex as the community can become extremely detailed and elaborate.

Basic Concepts

A few of the basic concepts used in functional analysis have been alluded to in the preceding discussion. In order to round out our understanding of functionalism as a theoretical system, there are several other terms that must be considered.

The first of these is the concept of functional requisite. This concept dovetails with one of the major purposes of functionalism—to determine what functions must be performed if a social system is to persist through time. As has already been suggested, one of the major assumptions made by functionalists is that all social systems have certain "needs" that must be met if the system is to persist through time. These needs are referred to as functional requisites of the system. [39]

Although the concept of functional requisite is a useful one, it can also be misleading. This is partly because social systems do not literally have "needs" in the sense that individuals do. Although it is acceptable, for purposes of communication, to say that a system has needs, it should be realized that all we are really saying is that there are certain condi-

---

[37] Merton, *Social Theory and Social Structure,* p. 30.

[38] Ibid., p. 30. Merton's reference is to B. Malinowski, "Anthropology," *Encyclopaedia Britannica,* 1st suppl. vol. (New York, 1926), p. 132. Italics in original.

[39] One of the most thorough discussions of functional requisites is contained in Marion J. Levy, Jr., *The Structure of Society* (Princeton, N.J.: Princeton University Press, 1952), esp. pp. 71–76 and 149–97.

tions that must be met if a social system is to maintain its viability. Furthermore, the concept of functional requisite increases the likelihood that the functionalist will offer explanations of a teleological nature, that is, explanations that account for the existence of a unit of social organization in terms of its purpose. For instance, the statement that "religion is found in a particular society because it contributes to the survival of that society" is both teleological and scientifically unacceptable. It may be true that religion is one of the functional requisites of society. Yet the question of why and how religion becomes a part of a particular society can be answered only through historical research.

A more serious difficulty inherent in the concept of functional requisite is that it suggests the *postulate of indispensability*. By this we mean that functionalists sometimes tend to regard all components of a social system as absolutely essential to its survival and persistence.[40] In the study of communities, the greatest danger posed by this postulate is that it can lead to the conclusion that all communities *must* have discrete governmental, economic, educational, and religious subsystems. Although it is safe to assume that the functions performed by these systems must, in one way or another, be performed in all communities, this does not necessarily mean that every community has discrete systems that correspond to these functions.

This brings us to another major concept used by functionalists, that is, the concept of *functional alternative*. This concept simply draws our attention to the fact that the same functional requisite may be met in a variety of ways. We have, for example, pointed out that one of the major functions of government in modern society is to punish those individuals who persistently violate the norms. In many primitive societies, this same function is carried out by the family. A governmental system as Americans know it may be nonexistent.[41]

The final concepts central to functional theory are those of *manifest function* and *latent function*. The former term refers to the obvious, visible consequences and contributions of a social unit (group, institution, and so on), whereas the latter term refers to the "unintended and unrecognized consequences" of the unit.[42] Thus the manifest function of a religious organization is to bring the individual into unity with the supernatural and to provide means by which proper respect may be paid to higher beings. These functions of religion are recognized by everyone and are used as glib explanations for the existence of religious systems. On the other hand, it may only be the functionalist who recognizes that the religious system serves to reinforce communal and societal norms and

[40] For further discussion see Merton, *Social Theory and Social Structure,* pp. 32–36.
[41] A description of one such society is contained in Davis, *Human Society,* pp. 481–85.
[42] Merton, *Social Theory and Social Structure,* p. 62.

to give persons a sense of security and well-being. The latter are latent functions of religion. More will be said about them later.

Functionalism and the Modern Community

Functionalism has not been tailormade for the student of community life. As a matter of fact, functionalists have had little to say about modern communities. Nonetheless, there is every reason to think that functional analysis will help us in the study of such entities. It is true that the institutions found in mass society are organized on a national basis. However, the behavior that leads to the performance of functions occurs at the local level: a mass society exists in and through the communities of which it is composed. Furthermore, there are certain conditions that must be met if a community is to survive as a viable, ongoing social system. Communities, like societies, have their functional requisites.

Needless to say, a full-fledged functional analysis of any community would be tedious indeed. Because of this, the following analysis has been simplified and abbreviated. In the first place, our analysis is limited to the modern community. No attempt is made to analyze the primitive community or to shed light on the suburb, rural neighborhood, or whatever. Second, because the central theme of this chapter has been that the community is a network of interrelated social systems, our analysis has been further limited by examining only the functional consequences of these systems. Although students of the community disagree on many things, they do agree that the most important subsystems found at the community level are those concerned with governmental, economic, educational, religious, and familial activities.

Government. Local government is one of the most complex subsystems found in the American community.[43] Not only does the web of local government encompass a host of special districts (e.g., school districts, sewerage districts, port authorities), but also municipal government itself may have dozens of branches and subunits. Included among these are such entities as the police department, the welfare department, the fire department, and the parks and recreation department. One of the virtues of social system theory is that it provides a framework for analyzing the ways in which these many units are interrelated.

We can classify the functions of local government in a variety of ways.

---

[43] For a brief discussion of some of the complexities of American local government see Committee for Economic Development, *Modernizing Local Government to Secure a Balanced Federalism* (New York: Committee for Economic Development, 1966), pp. 20–33.

For example, a list of every unit of local government could be compiled and its functions identified. Thus the function of the welfare department is to provide welfare services, the fire department fights fires, and so forth. However, this classificatory scheme would be needlessly long and detailed, and of little relevance to the sociologist.

We need then to find a simplified, relevant classification of the functions of local government. Even if we confine our attention to the national level, there seem to be only two functions of government on which sociologists agree. First, there is widespread agreement that government has the ultimate responsibility for social control.[44] This responsibility belongs to local government as well as to state and national government. Local government can, through its police department, courts, and other regulatory agencies, forcefully restrain people who do not voluntarily obey the laws. The high rates of crime and delinquency typical of many communities suggest that this function must be carried out if the community is to persist through time: It is a functional requisite of community life.

The other major function that most sociologists attribute to government is to oversee a society's relationships with other societies. However, to argue that local government has this function would be absurd. The governments of modern communities do not wage war, nor do they enter into treaties with other communities or societies. About the best that can be said is that local government represents one of the vertical links between the local community and government at the state and national level. The importance of this linkage cannot be ignored. Whether or not a community receives its share of assistance from state and federal agencies depends partly on local political officials.

This gives us some clues as to the functions of local government. There are, however, two other functions of local government that most sociologists seem to overlook. One is the provision of public facilities and services. During recent years all governments, especially those at the local level, have been forced to assume increased responsibility for furnishing roads, parks, sewage treatment plants, garbage collection services, and a variety of other facilities and services. Likewise, one of the most important developments during recent years has been the proliferation of social services provided by local government. The term *social services* should be construed broadly enough to include not only welfare services but also health services, recreational programs, and programs for the educationally disadvantaged. Whether the provision of these services should be viewed as an essential function of local government depends on a variety of things. Certainly most of the facilities and

[44] See Davis, *Human Society*, pp. 486–88, and Bierstedt, *The Social Order*, pp. 505–6.

services mentioned are essential if the city or metropolitan area is to survive in the twentieth century.[45]

Economics. In modern societies the economics system is organized on a national rather than a communal basis. Indeed, no modern community produces every good and service that its members use. Nonetheless, it is legitimate to talk about economic systems at the community level. These systems encompass many and diverse units of social organization, including wholesale and retail outlets, banks and loan companies, factories, and labor unions.

Although production is organized on a national basis, there is one major function that local economic systems must perform. They must provide the mechanisms and means by which goods and services can be procured by the individual. It is in local communities that people find jobs, earn money, and make the majority of their purchases. This is one reason why human beings live together in communities and why they will always do so. Hence the provision of jobs, goods, and services by local businesses and industries must be thought of as one of the functional requisites of community life. If business and industry become unable to do this, outmigration and consequent depopulation occur.

Education. Some readers of this book will object because we consider education to be a distinct community subsystem. It is true, of course, that most schools are supported by local government or, if not, by a religious body or private foundation. Nonetheless, it is more accurate to consider local schools as a distinct subsystem at the community level, partly because they enjoy a great deal of autonomy from their sponsoring agencies. Furthermore, there has been a tremendous increase in the number of functions that schools are expected to perform. Today, the school system is an active, functionally important part of virtually all modern communities.

Although the educational subsystem has many functions, one stands out above all others in importance: The school, along with the family, has a key role in socializing the young. If a community is to persist through time, it must develop human potentials, transmit cultural norms and values, and impart formal knowledge and skills. In a relatively simple society, the family can accomplish these tasks on its own. In a modern

---

[45] For a discussion of some of the major problems faced by and of some of the changes occurring in metropolitan government see Joseph F. Zimmerman, "The Metropolitan Area Problem," *The Annals of the American Academy of Political and Social Science,* **416** (November, 1974), 133–47.

society, however, parents simply do not have the knowledge and skill, insight and experience required to teach their children everything that they must know in order to become self-sufficient adults. As a result, a wide variety of educational systems have been created to assist in the complex and absolutely essential task of socializing the young. It is entirely possible that the extensive process of socialization through which the American child goes, involving as it does both family and school, is one of the most thorough ever devised.

In addition to its responsibilities as an agency of socialization, the school system performs many other functions. For example, some school systems play a part in the creation of new knowledge and values, are active participants in community recreation programs, and keep young persons out of the labor force. The last is an excellent example of what the functionalist means by a latent function. It is an unanticipated consequence of the emphasis we place on school attendance.

Religion. There is no area in which functionalism has been more influential than in the study of religion.[46] Basically, functionalists see religion as a "societal necessity" and attribute two essential functions to it. First, they maintain that religion contributes to the system of which it is a part by encouraging people to adhere to norms and values that are "functional" for that system. Specifically, the injunctions against stealing, murder, adultery, and other transgressions promoted by most religious bodies not only are important as religious precepts but also must be obeyed by the majority of community members if the community is to persist through time. Second, most functionalists argue that religion helps people to develop and maintain a healthy, stable personality. This it purportedly does by providing an "explanation" of the inexplicable (e.g., the premature death of a beloved spouse) and by promising the individual a more exalted status at some future time. It is true, of course, that the world is one in which sorrow, failure, and gross inequalities are a reality. To the extent that religion can explain these uncomfortable realities, it contributes directly to personality integration and indirectly to the stability of the community itself.

Although this theory may fit the facts in simple, homogeneous societies, its applicability to the modern community is more problematic. Among other things, there have been several instances in which religion has not

---

[46] For a brief account of the influence of functionalism on sociological and anthropological theories of religion see J. Milton Yinger, *Sociology Looks at Religion* (New York: Macmillan Publishing Co., Inc., 1963), pp. 121–28. One of the best explanations of the functional theory of religion is contained in Davis, *Human Society*, pp. 518–35.

been an integrative force in community life. Rather, it has led to conflict among community members.[47] This conflict often arises when religious organizations champion norms and values that are at odds with those championed by other groups. One need only consider the controversies that surround birth control programs, abortion, and liquor by the drink legislation. Likewise, some of the functional theories of religion do not allow for the fact that not all members of a modern community participate in the religious subsystem. Yet there is no solid evidence to suggest that these persons spurn basic norms and values or suffer from personality disintegration more frequently than persons who participate in formalized religious activities.

Because of these facts, the value of functional theory as an explanation of religious phenomena within the modern community is questionable. About the most that can be said is that religion *may help some people* develop and maintain healthy personalities and *may encourage some people* to observe basic social norms and values. Obviously, this statement cannot be extended to everyone for the simple reason that religion is not an integral part of everyone's life.

Family. It is extremely difficult to analyze the family as a structural component of the modern community. To be more specific, in communities where the nuclear family predominates, there is no such thing as *the* family subsystem in the sense that there is a governmental subsystem, a religious subsystem, or an educational subsystem. Rather, families have their structural embodiment in a multitude of small groups.[48] Each of these can be analyzed as subsystems of the larger community, but they do not become interrelated with each other in such a way as to form a discrete system.

Nonetheless, the family is a social institution. Those small groups we refer to as families perform functions that must be performed if the community is to maintain itself. In the first place, the family retains its age-old responsibility for reproduction. Although human beings can be reproduced outside the framework of marriage, there are no societies that

[47] For a description of two such cases see Gus Turbeville, "Religious Schism in the Methodist Church: A Sociological Analysis of the Pine Grove Case," *Rural Sociology,* 14 (March, 1949), 29–39; Kenneth W. Underwood, *Protestant and Catholic: Religious and Social Interaction in an Industrial Community* (Boston: The Beacon Press, 1957).
[48] The situation is, of course, considerably different in those preliterate and pre-industrial societies in which the extended family system is popular, especially among the upper-class elite. In some cases, one household may have hundreds of members and the extended family may perform almost all of the functions that are performed by the governmental, economic, educational, religious, and recreational subsystems in industrial societies. For an excellent discussion see Gideon Sjoberg, *The Preindustrial City*, pp. 145–79.

sanction this practice. One reason for this is that the presence of an adult male helps to assure that the child's needs will be fully met. Second, the family has an important role to play in socialization. Among other things, the family has almost total responsibility for children when they are young and when the vast bulk of socialization occurs.[49] Finally, the fact that the family is a primary group seems to dictate that it will retain its functional importance. Americans today live in a world where secondary groups predominate and where the individual is subjected to a considerable amount of insecurity, instability, and frustration. The family, however, is one of the few remaining groups within which individuals can potentially meet their needs for affection, security, and emotional support. Because these needs must be met in one way or another, the family may become increasingly important as human societies become increasingly urbanized.

☐ SUMMARY

Social system theory and functionalism have often been criticized on the grounds that they are unduly complicated and difficult to grasp. This is neither a fair nor a valid criticism. Some of the theorists we have considered in this chapter, especially Kingsley Davis and Robert K. Merton, are elegant and articulate spokesmen for their theoretical systems. Furthermore, even though some writers do succeed in making social system theory and functionalism appear hopelessly complex, it is the present writer's contention that, in reality, both theoretical systems are relatively simple. This simplicity can be best conveyed by briefly summarizing the basic principles of social system theory and functionalism as they apply to modern communities.

1. The community is a social system, the major subsystems of which are the institutions of government, economy, education, religion, and family. Each of these subsystems, in turn, is composed of a variety of social and/or associational groups. Finally, statuses are the basic building blocks out of which these groups are structured. The individual becomes a part of these groups, and hence a member of larger social systems, by playing the roles attached to these statuses.

2. There is a high degree of interrelatedness among the members of a given system and between one system and another. The concept of internal pattern refers to the relationships that develop within a system, whereas the concept of external pattern refers to the relationships that develop between one system and another. In studying the community,

---

[49] For further discussion of the family's strategic importance in socialization see Davis, *Human Society*, pp. 405–7.

it is helpful to supplement these concepts with Warren's concepts of horizontal and vertical pattern. A community's horizontal pattern includes the ties that develop among its various subsystems, whereas the vertical pattern encompasses the ties that exist between these subsystems and extracommunity systems.

3. There is a tendency for all social systems, including the community, to move toward a state of equilibrium. This means that a change in one component of the system stimulates changes in other components. The result is adjustment, coordination, and integration among the various parts of a social system.

4. Even though there is much interrelatedness among the units of which a social system is composed, each subsystem still must establish itself as a discrete entity and command the loyalty of its members. Thus the members of every social system consciously or unconsciously engage in various boundary-maintaining activities. As a result, social systems may have psychological, social, and/or geographic boundaries.

5. Some of the basic concepts that are central to functionalism serve to enrich and give substance to social system theory. The functional approach is based on the dual assumption that (a) certain activities must be carried out if a social system is to persist through time and (b) *most* units of social organization "contribute" to the system of which they are a part. These contributions make it possible for the larger system to persist through time.

The fact that social system theory and functionalism are relatively simple does not mean that they are above criticism. In reality, both theoretical systems have been the target of abundant criticism, and any attempt to summarize all the objections raised against them would require that we add another chapter to this book.[50] However, many of the objections center around the contention that social system theory and functionalism represent overly mechanistic views of social organization. It is a fact that social system theorists and functionalists do tend to view a social system as a series of neatly articulated, well-coordinated parts that satisfy the "needs" (i.e., functional requisites) of the system and its members. Clearly, this is not always the case. There can be a considerable amount of conflict among the units of a system. Furthermore, there is no guarantee that the members of any given subsystem will act in such a way as to assure that the subsystem does make positive contributions to the larger social system.

[50] For a sampling of some of this criticism see Dorothy Gregg and Elgin Williams, "The Dismal Science of Functionalism," *American Anthropologist*, **50** (Oct.–Dec., 1948), 594–611; Wayne Hield, "The Study of Change in Social Science," *British Journal of Sociology*, **5** (March, 1954), 1–10; David Lockwood, "Some Remarks on the 'Social System,'" *British Journal of Sociology*, **7** (June, 1956), 234–46.

The criticisms leveled at social system theory and functionalism should not blind us to the merits of these approaches. Thus social system theory has given us many helpful clues as to how communities and other social systems are structured and organized (see preceding items 1 and 2). Likewise, social system theory provides sociologists with concepts, tools, and propositions that they can use in the analysis of diverse units of social organization. Social system theory has been found helpful in the study of small groups, industrial and political bureaucracies, and entire societies as well as in the study of communities. Finally, both social system theory and functionalism force sociologists to raise questions that, in the final analysis, are the meat and substance of their discipline. Kingsley Davis, for example, argues that functional theory leads us to ask such questions as

> What features of social organization or behavior appear in all or nearly all societies? Why are these features so nearly universal while others are more variable? What particular features characterize each type of society, and how do they mesh together in the operation of that type? [51]

Questions of this type must also be asked by the student of community life. Until they are answered, our understanding of villages, cities, and metropolitan areas will be limited.

BIBLIOGRAPHY

Adams, Bert N. *Kinship in an Urban Setting.* Chicago: Markham Publishing Company, 1968.

Bates, Frederick L., and Lloyd Bacon. "The Community as a Social System," *Social Forces,* **50** (March, 1972), 371–79.

Bebout, John E., and Harry C. Bredmeier. "American Cities as Social Systems," *Journal of the American Institute of Planners,* **29** (May, 1963), 64–76.

Committee for Economic Development. *Modernizing Local Government to Secure a Balanced Federalism.* New York: Committee on Economic Development, 1966.

Crain, Robert L., and Donald B. Rosenthal. "Community Status as a Dimension of Local Decision-Making," *American Sociological Review,* **32** (December, 1967), 970–84.

Herriott, Robert E., and Nancy Hoyt St. John. *Social Class and the Urban School: The Impact of Pupil Background on Teachers and Principals.* New York: John Wiley & Sons, Inc., 1966.

Hiller, E. T. "The Community as a Social Group," *American Sociological Review,* **6** (April, 1941), 189–202.

[51] Kingsley Davis, "The Myth of Functional Analysis as a Special Method in Sociology and Anthropology," *American Sociological Review,* 24 (December, 1959), 762.

Homans, George C. *The Human Group*. New York: Harcourt Brace Jovanovich, Inc., 1950.

Lewis, Gordon F. "Sociological Study of Communities: Is There Still a Role for Microcosmic Analysis?" *Journal of the Community Development Society*, **5** (Spring, 1974), 10–18.

Loomis, Charles P. *Social Systems: Essays on Their Persistence and Change*. Princeton, N.J.: D. Van Nostrand Company, Inc., 1960.

Monane, Joseph H. *A Sociology of Human Systems*. New York: Appleton-Century-Crofts, 1967.

Munters, Q. J. "Some Remarks on the Opening up of Rural Social Systems," *Sociologia Ruralis*, **15** (1975), 1–2, 34–45.

Parsons, Talcott. *The Social System*. New York: The Free Press, 1951.

———. *Structure and Process in Modern Societies*. New York: The Free Press, 1960, esp. pp. 250–79.

Turbeville, Gus. "Religious Schism in the Methodist Church: A Sociological Analysis of the Pine Grove Case," *Rural Sociology*, **14** (March, 1949), 29–39.

Underwood, Kenneth W. *Protestant and Catholic: Religious and Social Interaction in an Industrial Community*. Boston: The Beacon Press, 1957.

Warren, Roland L. *The Community in America*, 2nd ed. Chicago: Rand McNally & Company, 1972, esp. Chapter V.

———. "Toward a Reformation of Community Theory," *Human Organization*, **15** (Summer, 1956), 8–11.

CHAPTER 7

□ □ □ □ □ □ □ □
□
□
□
□
□
□
□
□
□

Community Conflict

In the course of their history, most communities occasionally become embroiled in conflict and controversy. Conflict may be limited to verbal exchanges between two or more parties, or it may become violent and bloody. An endless variety of issues may give rise to community conflict. During recent years, some of the most bitter conflicts at the community level in America have centered around strained race relations.

In this chapter we shall look at community conflict. As in previous chapters, an attempt will be made to integrate the findings and insights of several different theorists and researchers who have concerned themselves with conflict. This will be especially difficult because the literature on conflict is so diverse. Before we begin looking at theories of community conflict, however, perhaps we should examine the sources of conflict.

□ THE SOURCES OF CONFLICT

Conflict can spring from at least three different sources.[1] First, conflict may arise when two or more individuals or groups seek contradictory goals. For example, the black citizens of a community may seek complete equality whereas the white citizens may seek to keep these blacks in a subordinate position and to retain the major share of money, power, and prestige for themselves. Situations such as this may lead to verbal hostility, continuous strife between the two groups, or violence.

Second, conflict may arise when different groups pursue the same goal

---

[1] See Arline McCord and William McCord, *Urban Social Conflict* (St. Louis: C. V. Mosby, 1977), p. 5.

by contradictory means. For example, within the black movement some groups such as the NAACP have sought to bring about change through legal and political channels whereas other groups have advocated the use of more militant means. In situations of this type, the "radical organizations [often] accuse more moderate organizations of 'selling out the movement' while moderate organizations accuse the radicals of creating a bad image for the movement and its supporters, thereby arousing public hostility and bringing on repression." [2] Conflicts of this type probably do not engender a great deal of violence. However, they can give rise to a great deal of bickering and intergroup and interpersonal hostility.

Finally, conflict almost inevitably arises when "two individuals or groups pursue the same goals, but only one party can win." [3] As a concrete example, in a Kentucky community conflict almost arose over the location of a new medical arts building. The mayor and local businesspeople urged that the new facility be built near the central business district. This presumably would bring potential customers downtown. On the other hand, local doctors favored building the new facility adjacent to the community hospital located several blocks from the central business district. In this case both groups had the same goal, that is, to construct a new medical arts building. However, only one of the groups could win, because it would have been infeasible to build two medical arts buildings. Similar types of conflict-producing situations can develop on an intercommunity level, such as when two or more communities fight over the location of a proposed new consolidated high school. In any event, conflicts in which one of the parties is destined to be the "winner" and the other the "loser" may become particularly bitter.

It must be stressed that conflict always involves interaction between two or more individuals or groups.[4] Here a distinction must be drawn between conflict and hostility. Thus, if nobody had actively opposed black people in their efforts to achieve full equality, one could not say that the black movement gave rise to conflict. However, even if the black movement had not given rise to conflict, a high degree of hostility could have been engendered. This hostility might have manifested itself in statements such as "Those black people always get their way" or "Black people think the world owes them a living." In other words, "hostile attitudes are predispositions to engage in conflict behavior." [5] Conflict

2 John R. Howard, *The Cutting Edge: Social Movements and Social Change in America* (Philadelphia: J. B. Lippincott, 1974).
3 McCord and McCord, *Urban Social Conflict,* p. 5.
4 See Lewis A. Coser, *The Functions of Social Conflict* (New York: The Free Press, 1956), p. 37.
5 Ibid.

itself, however, always entails two or more individuals or groups taking action in regard to one another.

☐ TYPES OF CONFLICT

There have been several attempts to differentiate among types of conflict. For instance, Gamson draws a distinction between conventional community conflict and rancorous community conflict (see later), and Coser draws a distinction between realistic and nonrealistic conflict.[6]

One especially perceptive classification of types of conflict has been offered by John R. Howard,[7] who distinguishes four different types of conflict. The first is what he calls *substantive conflict*. This centers around the question of who is to control valued and scarce resources such as wealth and good jobs. For example, if black people get more and more good jobs there may be fewer good jobs for the white majority. This type of conflict may be particularly strident. A second type of conflict that Howard identifies is *conflict over symbolic issues*. An example here might be the refusal of people of certain religious faiths to pay allegiance to the national flag, much to the annoyance of other community members. According to Howard, conflict over symbolic issues is not usually very intense because if the "deviant" group does win, few tangible losses accrue to the dominant group.[8] A third type of conflict identified by Howard involves the *conflict of ideologies*. Dominant groups almost always develop a set of ideologies or rationalizations to justify their superior position. For example, sexist ideologies exist in our society that picture women as passive, dependent, and emotional. When the woman's movement began challenging these stereotypes considerable controversy and conflict arose. The fourth type of conflict that Howard identifies is *cultural conflict*. This arises when a segment of the population advocates the adoption of new life-styles. For instance, the increasing use of marijuana among young people in the early 1970s was seen by many older people as a very serious problem.[9] In some cases, intense conflict developed at the community level over the issue of marijuana use by the young. More generally, "'the repudiation of a middle-class life-style by many youths was seen as perverse. Life-style was made an issue, par-

[6] Ibid, pp. 48–55.
[7] See Howard, *The Cutting Edge*, pp. 3–4.
[8] Ibid, p. 4.
[9] See Dennis E. Poplin, *Social Problems* (Glenview, Ill.: Scott, Foresman and Company, 1978), esp. pp. 123–24.

ticularly by the youth movement, and became a source of severe conflict." [10]

☐ COMMUNITY CONFLICT: THEORIES AND RESEARCH FINDINGS

We must now turn our attention to theories and research findings pertaining to community conflict. Specifically, we shall examine what a number of social scientists have had to say about conflict. However, two things should be noted. First, some of the people whom we shall discuss have not been interested in *community* conflict per se. We will therefore have to attempt to apply their findings to the community. Second, we cannot completely review the work of the people discussed herein. To do so would be a very lengthy undertaking. So we shall be selective and dwell on the most significant points made by each author.

Karl Marx

One of the most influential theories pertaining to conflict is that developed by Karl Marx (1818–1883). Basically, "Marxist theory is the most comprehensive explanation of the conflicts created by the advent of urbanization and industrialization." [11]

Marx argued that urbanization and industrialization had helped to create two distinct social classes.[12] The first of these classes, the bourgeoisie, owned and controlled the means of production. As a result, landless laborers (the proletariat) were completely dependent on them for jobs. Hence wages could be kept extremely low, and the bourgeoisie reaped a large profit. Wages were supposedly kept even lower by keeping the supply of unused labor large.

However, Marx thought that this type of economic system is inherently unstable. Among other things, the proletariat is subjected to such degrading conditions that it becomes unified and develops class consciousness. Marx predicted that eventually the proletariat would overthrow the bourgeoisie and a classless society would emerge. This would be a society in which "each individual would be his own boss, contribute according to his abilities, and receive according to his needs." [13]

Marxian theory has been used to analyze some types of community

---

[10] Howard, *The Cutting Edge,* p. 4.
[11] McCord and McCord, *Urban Social Conflict,* p. 54.
[12] See Karl Marx, *Capital* (Chicago: Encyclopaedia Britannica, 1955).
[13] McCord and McCord, *Urban Social Conflict,* p. 57.

conflict such as racial conflict. For example, Oliver Cox put forth an essentially Marxian argument: "Race prejudice . . . is a social attitude propagated among the public by an exploiting class for the purpose of stigmatizing some group as inferior so that the exploitation of either the group itself or its resources may both be justified." [14] It should be noted, however, that there are other explanations for the existence of racial prejudice. Thus a variety of psychological theories have been developed to explain prejudice,[15] and it is quite likely that we acquire our racial prejudices in the same way that we acquire our knowledge of any other pattern of culture, that is, through the socialization process. Further, it is clear that the race riots that rocked our large cities in the mid-1960s were not stimulated by a desire to overthrow the ruling white class and to create a classless society. Rather, they had their roots in the frustrations felt by black Americans who wished to participate more fully *in the system*.[16]

Simmel and Coser

Georg Simmel was a German social theorist who was born in 1858 and who died in 1918. Lewis Coser is an American sociologist who published his major work on conflict in 1956. Yet it is entirely appropriate to consider the contributions of these two men together. With the possible exception of Karl Marx, Georg Simmel has probably contributed more to our understanding of conflict than anyone else. It was Lewis Coser, however, who showed American sociologists the significance of Simmel's work.

The heart of Simmel's, and later Coser's, argument is that conflict can be functional for a unit of social organization: [17] Conflict is not necessarily bad, nor is it necessarily something to be avoided. Among other things, Simmel and Coser argue that conflict with an outgroup can serve to solidify the ingroup. Coser puts it succinctly: "conflict with another group leads to the mobilization of the energies of group members and hence to increased cohesion of the group." [18]

[14] Oliver C. Cox, *Caste, Class, and Race* (Garden City, N.Y.: Doubleday, 1948), p. 393.

[15] For example, see T. W. Adorno, Else Frenkel-Brunswik, D. J. Levinson, and R. N. Sanford, *The Authoritarian Personality* (New York: Harper & Row, 1950); John Dollard et el., *Frustration and Aggression* (New Haven: Yale University Press, 1939).

[16] See National Advisory Commission on Civil Disorders, *Report of the National Advisory Commission on Civil Disorders* (Washington, D.C.: U.S. Government Printing Office, 1968), esp. Part II.

[17] See especially Georg Simmel, *Conflict & the Web of Group Affiliations*, trans. by Kurt H. Wolff and Reinhard Bendix (New York: The Free Press, 1955), pp. 14–16.

[18] Coser, *The Functions of Social Conflict*, p. 95.

The hypothesis that conflict with an outgroup can produce ingroup cohesiveness is confirmed by our everyday experiences. One thinks immediately, for example, of a big brother "sticking up" for his little sister when she is confronted with an adversary outside the family. Likewise, there are undoubtedly cases in which communities have drawn together and gotten their hackles up to resist encroachment by an outside force such as the federal government. Certainly this happens on a national level when a country is threatened by war.

In addition to demonstrating that conflict with another group can strengthen the solidarity and cohesion of the ingroup, Simmel and Coser advance a variety of other significant propositions concerning conflict and its impact on units of social organization. They suggest, for example, that multiple conflicts may have less impact on a unit of social organization than one major conflict.[19] Thus the average citizen may harbor some resentment toward the police, he or she may have some disagreements with the mayor, and his or her church may occasionally come into conflict with bookstore owners who sell pornography. Yet in other situations the interests of these groups converge, such as when the citizen who has a gripe against the police receives much needed assistance from an officer. Communities of this type—communities that are characterized by multiple conflicts—are likely to be more cohesive and less threatened by disintegration than communities that are divided into two warring camps.

Simmel and Coser also advance an interesting proposition concerning the resolution of conflict. Following the lead of Simmel, Coser suggests that conflicts cannot be resolved until the relative power of each group is known.[20] To put it in simple terms, if group A wants more of something that group B has a lot of, group A may be willing and eager to attack group B. However, if group A enters into conflict with group B and discovers that the latter group possesses much more power and can easily win the conflict, then group A will probably cease attacking group B and the conflict will subside.

Finally, Simmel advanced a proposition that appears again and again in the literature on conflict. Specifically, he maintained that urbanization leads to increased levels of conflict.[21] As societies become more urbanized, the conditions that are conducive to strife and conflict are increasingly present.

---

[19] Ibid., esp. pp. 76–80.
[20] Ibid., pp., 133–37.
[21] See *The Sociology of Georg Simmel*, trans. and ed. by Kurt H. Wolff (New York: The Free Press, 1950), esp. pp. 409–24.

James S. Coleman

Marx, Simmel, and Coser all advanced general propositions about conflict that, to a greater or lesser degree, apply to communities. Likewise, during the 1940s and 1950s numerous case studies of community conflict were published.[22] However, it was James S. Coleman who drew together a great deal of the information that we have on community conflict and who constructed a comprehensive account of community controversy. Coleman's basic thesis is best captured in his statement that "the most striking fact about the development and growth of community controversy is the similarity they exhibit despite underlying sources and different kinds of precipitating events."[23]

We must stress that Coleman's monograph on community conflict is extremely elaborate and, on occasions, complex: we cannot possibly discuss every proposition that Coleman advances. Nonetheless, we can explore what he has to say about (1) the sources of community conflict, (2) the dynamics of community conflict, (3) the effects of conflict on community structure, and (4) the resolution of community conflict.

Sources of Community Conflict. According to Coleman, there are three basic sources of community conflict.[24] First, conflict can arise over *economic* issues. For instance, more than one community has experienced conflict over a school bond election or the rezoning of a piece of land from residential to more profitable commercial uses. Second, conflict can arise over issues involving *power* or *authority*. One of the most famous case studies of community conflict focused on the ouster of a school superintendent who had incurred the wrath of powerful individuals in the community,[25] and several communities have been thrown into bitter conflict centering around the control of local government.[26] Finally, community conflict can arise from *differences over cultural values and beliefs.* For example, school desegregation controversies arise because our attitudes toward black people conflict with our belief in equality

---

[22] For example, see David Hurlburd, *This Happened in Pasadena* (New York: Macmillan Publishing Co., Inc., 1950); James Rorty, "Thirty Days that Shook Norwalk," *Commentary,* 17 (April, 1954), 330–36; Robert Shaplen, "Scarsdale's Battle of the Books," *Commentary,* 10 (December, 1950), 530–40; Theodore H. White, "The Battle of Athens, Tennessee," *Harper's,* 194 (January, 1947), 54–61.
[23] James S. Coleman, *Community Conflict* (New York: The Free Press, 1957), p. 9.
[24] Ibid., pp. 5–6.
[25] See Hurlburd, *This Happened in Pasadena.*
[26] The city manager plan in particular has given rise to considerable controversy in many communities. This may be because local lay leaders see the city manager as a threat to their power.

of opportunity and because of the willingness of blacks to fight for their rights.

In addition to these three sources of conflict, Coleman recognizes that conflict can easily be generated from hostilities that exist between different groups in the community. In other words, there may be deep-rooted antagonisms in the community that cause people to take sides quickly and to say "I'm against it because he's for it." [27] In communities of this type about any issue—economic, political, or whatever—may give rise to intense controversy.

Dynamics of Community Conflict. Coleman sheds a great deal of light on the dynamics of community conflict. In particular, he helps us understand how conflict gets started, how it is sustained, and how it is resolved. Three important propositions about the dynamics of community conflict that Coleman advances are as follows: [28]

1. There is a tendency for community conflict to move from specific issues to general issues. For example, conflicts between citizens and local governmental officials often begin with very specific issues (e.g., the failure of the sanitation department to pick up the garbage on time) but soon end up as attacks on the integrity of local officials themselves. Likewise, in Scarsdale, New York, critics of the school system "began by attacking books in the school library; soon they focused on the whole educational philosophy." [29] A number of other examples of the tendency for community conflicts to move from specific to general issues could be cited.

It must be stressed, however, that not all instances of community conflict show this tendency to move from specific to general. Seemingly, the movement from specific to general is most likely to occur when there are deep-seated antagonisms in the community that require only a spark to set them off. If the community is basically cohesive and does not have a history of conflict, the movement from specific to general is less likely to occur.

2. Once community conflict is under way, there is a tendency for new and different issues to emerge. For example, the opponents of an increase in school taxes may soon add to this issue questions concerning educational philosophy, the competency of the school administration, and so on.

Coleman suggests that there are two reasons why diversification and proliferation of issues occur.[30] First, once a conflict starts, the doors are

[27] Coleman, *Community Conflict*, p. 6.
[28] Ibid., pp. 10–11.
[29] Ibid., p. 10.
[30] Ibid.

opened for injecting new issues into the controversy. In other words, people may be reluctant to raise an issue out of the blue but not at all reluctant to raise a new issue when conflict is already a fact of life. We see this operating in arguments between spouses: once an argument has started over balancing the family budget, additional bones of contention may be brought into the argument such as whether the wife should work or not, whether the family should buy a home, and so on. Coleman suggests that this same phenomenon occurs at the community level. In his words, "in a sense the stable relation suppresses topics which might upset it. But once the stability of the relation is upset, the suppressed topics can come to the surface uninhibitedly." [31]

However, in many cases new issues do not just inadvertently creep into the conflict. Rather, they are purposefully introduced into the conflict by the antagonists. Among other things, the introduction of new issues into a controversy can broaden the base of support for the antagonists.[32] For instance, many citizens may not object to a small increase in their school taxes. However, they might quickly jump on the antischool administration bandwagon if it is suggested to them that the school is failing to teach children to read and write, that the school principal is immoral, or whatever.

3. Finally, there is a tendency for conflicts at the community level to move from disagreement over specific issues to direct antagonism toward opponents. Again, this principle can best be illustrated on an interpersonal level. It often happens, for example, that what starts out as a disagreement with one's boss about one's salary ends up as a general dislike of the boss: pretty soon he or she appears to be "all bad." Likewise, at the community level a dispute over fluoridating water supplies [33] can soon engender dislike of city officials themselves. When this occurs the conflict may continue for years even though the original issue has long since been resolved.

Conflict and Social Organization. As a community becomes embroiled in conflict, definite changes occur in its social organization. Among other things, there is a polarization of social relations as people begin to associate more and more with individuals and organizations favoring

[31] Ibid.

[32] This clearly happened in a dispute over refuse collection in Grand Rapids, Michigan. See Russell E. Lewis, "The Role of Cultural Beliefs in Community Decision-Making: A Case Study" (Paper presented to the North Central Sociological Association, Louisville, Kentucky, May, 1976).

[33] A few years ago the issue of fluoridating water supplies gave rise to heated controversy in literally hundreds of American communities. For an in-depth analysis of fluoridation controversies see Robert L. Crain, Elihu Katz, and Donald B. Rosenthal, *The Politics of Community Conflict* (Indianapolis: Bobbs-Merrill, 1969).

their point of view and less and less with those who oppose it. Similarly, new leaders emerge to spearhead the dispute. Coleman tells us that usually these people have not been leaders in the past.[34] Established community leaders may feel too many cross-pressures and have too much to lose by becoming deeply embroiled in the controversy. Furthermore, "the new leaders . . . are seldom moderates: the situation itself calls for extremists." [35] Finally, as the conflict intensifies there are changes in communication patterns within the community. Formal means of communication (newspapers, radio stations, etc.) become less able to tell people as much as they want to know about the conflict because they are restrained from reporting gossip, rumor, slanderous accounts of people's behavior, and so on. Yet in the heat of controversy people seem to have an insatiable need to hear these things about their opponents. Hence there is increasing use of word-of-mouth communication as the conflict proceeds.

The Control and Resolution of Conflict. Coleman does not dwell at length on the control and resolution of community conflict. Nonetheless, he does suggest that the response of community leaders and community organizations can have a great bearing on the outcome of a controversy.[36] If responsible community leaders and organizations take a strong and united stand against the dissident group or groups, the conflict is often quickly brought under control. An example of this can be found in the Scarsdale, New York, school controversy already cited. It will be recalled that in this incident a group of self-appointed critics launched an attack on the school's policies on books contained in its library. However, as soon as the attack became known, eighty-one influential people in the community drew up a statement of support for the school board and its policies—a statement that was printed on the front page of the local newspaper.[37] The public quickly rallied around the school board, and the conflict was squelched.

The initial reaction of local authorities can also intensify conflict. For example, more than one race riot has gotten out of control because the police themselves displayed an antagonistic attitude toward blacks and did not take action to quell the riot in its early stages. In other words, the police have occasionally created a permissive atmosphere that permits riots to blossom.[38]

[34] Coleman, *Community Conflict*, p. 12.
[35] Ibid.
[36] Ibid., pp. 19–20.
[37] Ibid., p. 20.
[38] Ibid.

192

William A. Gamson

The literature on community conflict that we have reviewed so far has been of a theoretical nature. Gamson's work, however, is based on an empirical study of conflict as it manifested itself in eighteen different communities.[39]

Basically, Gamson attempts to isolate the variables differentiating between the communities that have experienced *conventional* conflicts and those that have experienced *rancorous* conflicts. Gamson explains the difference between these two types of conflict as follows:

> In *conventional conflicts*, established means of political expression are used to influence the outcome of issues. Opponents regard each other as mistaken or as pursuing different but legitimate goals, but not as representatives of evil forces. Such tactics as threats of punishment, personal vilification, and deliberate, conscious deceptions are not involved. In contrast to conventional conflicts, *rancorous conflicts* are characterized by the belief that norms about the waging of political conflict in American communities have been violated. In such conflicts, actions occur which produce a shared belief that tactics used to influence the outcome are "dirty," "underhanded," "vicious," and so forth.[40]

Basically, Gamson hypothesizes that three variables differentiate between communities that experience conventional conflict and those that experience rancorous conflict. The first of these variables is *conduciveness,* a term that refers "to the extent to which structural characteristics of the community permit or encourage rancorous conflicts." [41] The second variable is *strain.* This term refers to the extent to which the structural characteristics of the community generate discontent or dissatisfaction among community members. Finally, the third variable that supposedly differentiates between the two types of community is *integration.* This term "refers to the extent to which structural characteristics [of the community] prevent or inhibit rancorous conflict." [42] The way in which Gamson measures these three variables will become evident as we discuss his findings.

Gamson's findings can be summarized rather briefly. First, he found that rancorous conflict is associated with political instability. As Gamson puts it, "only one of the nine conventional towns is undergoing political

[39] William A. Gamson, "Rancorous Conflict in Community Politics," *American Sociological Review,* 31 (February, 1966), 71–81.
[40] Ibid., p. 71. Italics in original.
[41] Ibid.
[42] Ibid.

change while two-thirds of the rancorous towns are undergoing such change." [43] Second, Gamson did not find a relationship between two of his measures of conduciveness—participative political structure and the presence of solidary groups—and the presence or absence of rancorous conflict.[44] Apparently communities that encourage citizen participation in government and that have a variety of clearly defined minority groups are no more or less likely to be characterized by rancorous conflict than those that do not. Finally, Gamson found that "the average degree of acquaintance among opponents is substantially lower in rancorous than in conventional towns." [45] The degree of acquaintanceship between opponents is one of Gamson's measures of integration.

What Gamson's research suggests is that bitter, vitriolic conflict is most likely to occur in communities that are politically unstable and in which the opponents in the conflict are not well acquainted. Furthermore, Gamson suggests that rancorous conflict is not necessarily bad for a community. Rather, he found that "many of the conventional communities are rather dull and stagnant, while some of the rancorous ones are among the most vital." [46]

Anthony Oberschall

Anthony Oberschall does not focus specifically on community conflict in his book on social conflict and social movements. Nonetheless, he gives us some insights into conflict that are applicable to the community.

Following Coser, Oberschall suggests that conflicts over principles are likely to be fought harder than conflicts for personal gain.[47] In an election campaign, for example, the opponents may fight vigorously to win the race, but when the election is over all semblance of conflict between the two parties usually subsides. In some cases, the loser may even pledge his or her support to the winner. On the other hand, conflicts over principles such as praying in school or educational philosophies do not resolve themselves so easily. One reason for this is that the leaders in this type of conflict are representing the interests of a larger group. Indeed,

[43] Ibid., p. 78.
[44] A participative political structure is one in which political leaders permit or encourage widespread citizen participation in the political process. By *solidary groups*, Gamson means such entities as racial, ethnic, and religious minority groups (e.g., Jews). According to Gamson, "clearly identifiable solidary groups are conducive to rancorous conflict because they provide readily identifiable targets for hostility." See ibid., p. 73.
[45] Ibid., p. 79.
[46] Ibid., p. 81.
[47] See Anthony Oberschall, *Social Conflict and Social Movements* (Englewood Cliffs, N.J.: Prentice-Hall, Inc., 1973), p. 50.

Coser recognizes that "conflicts in which the participants feel that they are merely the representatives of collectivities and groups, fighting not for self but for ideals of the group they represent, are likely to be more radical and merciless than those that are fought for personal reasons." [48]

Another reason why conflicts over principles are difficult to resolve is that they frequently do not lend themselves to compromise. Thus, in a battle centering around school integration, either the pro- or anti-integration forces will win. The other side is destined to lose completely, and there is no way that the losing side can feel that it gained anything. On the other hand, in conflicts waged for personal gain people can often reap concessions from the opponent. At the end of an election, for example, the loser may be offered a good job in the newly elected administration. In short, something is gained by everyone and the conflict subsides.

Conflict situations similar to the ones described in the previous paragraph have been analyzed in terms of zero-sum and non-zero-sum games. [49] In a non-zero-sum game both sides can gain something and the parties to the conflict will bargain and negotiate to keep their losses at a minimum. On the other hand, in zero-sum games no compromises are possible and the interests of the conflicting parties are diametrically opposed. In situations of this type the conflict is likely to be particularly intense and heated because one of the parties is destined to go down in total defeat.

Oberschall also suggests that "conflicts that are delayed usually appear in aggravated form later and, consequently, are more difficult to regulate." [50] One reason for this is that between the time that the grievance arises and the actual conflict erupts, hostilities grow and grow. In addition, both parties have time to muster all their resources for the conflict; for example, they can recruit new members to their side, build up their supply of armaments, or whatever. This, of course, means that potential community conflicts can best be resolved if they are dealt with as soon as the issue in contention arises.

McCord and McCord

Arline McCord and William McCord present strong and convincing evidence that there is a link between urbanization and conflict. Among

[48] Coser, *The Functions of Social Conflict*, p. 118.
[49] See Oberschall, *Social Conflict and Social Movements*, pp. 52–54. For a more detailed account of game theory as it pertains to human conflict see Anatol Rapoport, "Game Theory and Human Conflict," in Elton McNeil (ed.), *The Nature of Human Conflict* (Englewood Cliffs, N.J.: Prentice-Hall, Inc., 1965), pp. 196–225.
[50] Ibid., p. 71.

other things, there is an intensification of conflict in urban areas and "totally new arenas for conflict are opened." [51] Indeed, most of the major issues of our time, such as the conflict over women's rights, had their origin in urban areas. In addition, in urban areas new ways of resolving conflict are invented.[52] For example, the modern police force, which plays such a major role in regulating some types of conflict today, is a "relatively modern invention of the more stable citizens of London who feared for their lives in the midst of urban chaos." [53]

The McCords suggest that much conflict has its roots in the gap that so often exists between people's expectations and the realities of the situation in urban areas.[54] For example, the women's rights movement was partially triggered by women who realized that they were not being given equal opportunities to compete for the jobs, money, power, and status that urban areas have to offer. Likewise, newcomers to the city often find their hopes dashed. Rather than being granted a share of the opportunities that the city has to offer, they may instead find themselves unemployed and confined to rundown, decayed ghettos. This creates frustration and despair that can easily turn into violent conflict.

☐ SUMMARY

We have now reviewed some of the significant literature pertaining to community conflict. We must now comb through this literature once more in a search for more general principles relating to community conflict.

The work of Simmel, Coser, and Gamson suggests that conflict is not inevitably bad for a community. Conflict can create increased cohesion within the conflicting groups themselves. Likewise, communities that do occasionally become embroiled in controversy may be more dynamic and viable than those in which little or no conflict occurs.

Community conflict seems to follow certain predictable patterns. There is a tendency for community conflicts to move from specific issues to general issues, and, once the conflict is under way, there is a tendency for new and different issues to emerge. Similarly, there is a tendency for conflicts at the community level to move from disagreement over specific issues to antagonism toward opponents. Definite changes occur in the social organization of communities as they become embroiled in controversy. There is a polarization of social relations in the community, new leaders emerge, and formal means of communication (newspapers,

[51] McCord and McCord, *Urban Social Conflict*, p. 45.
[52] Ibid., p. 46.
[53] Ibid., p. 52.
[54] Ibid., pp. 181–82.

radio stations, etc.) become less important as vehicles for conveying information to the public.

It is widely thought that there is a link between urbanization and increased levels of conflict. This link was recognized by Simmel and Coser and elaborated on by the McCords. There are many reasons why urbanization may give rise to increased levels of conflict, including the fact that there are many, many things for people to fight about in urban areas. In addition, much urban conflict has its roots in the gap that frequently exists between people's expectations and the realities of the situation. This gap can create frustation and despair that can easily erupt into violent conflict.

Most of the writers considered in this chapter have had something to say about the resolution of conflict. Coser suggests that conflicts cannot be resolved until the relative power of the conflicting parties is known. Likewise, Coleman suggests that the response of influential community leaders and community organizations can have a great bearing on the outcome of a controversy. If these leaders and organizations take a strong and united stand against the dissident group, the conflict is often quickly brought under control. Oberschall suggests that conflicts over principles may be harder to resolve than conflicts that are fought for purely personal gain. In addition, conflicts in which there will be a clear-cut winner and in which no compromise is possible may be more difficult to resolve than conflicts in which both parties can gain something.

BIBLIOGRAPHY

Coleman, James S. *Community Conflict*. New York: The Free Press, 1957.

Coser, Lewis A. *The Functions of Social Conflict*. New York: The Free Press, 1956.

Crain, Robert L., Elihu Katz, and Donald B. Rosenthal. *The Politics of Community Conflict*. Indianapolis: Bobbs-Merrill, 1969.

Dennis, Philip A. "The Uses of Inter-village Feuding," *Anthropological Quarterly*, 49 (July, 1976), 174–84.

Gamson, William A. "Rancorous Conflict in Community Politics," *American Sociological Review*, 31 (February, 1966), 71–81.

Hollos, Marida. "Conflict and Social Change in a Norwegian Mountain Community," *Anthropological Quarterly*, 49 (October, 1976), 239–57.

Kaul, Mohan L. "Block Clubs and Social Action: A Case Study of Community Conflict," *Journal of Sociology and Social Welfare*, 3 (March, 1976), 437–50.

Maier, Henry W. "Conflict in Metropolitan Areas," *The Annals of the American Academy of Political and Social Science*, 416 (November, 1974), 148–57.

McCord, Arline, and William McCord. *Urban Social Conflict*. St. Louis: C. V. Mosby, 1977.

National Advisory Commission on Civil Disorders. *Report of the National Advisory Commission on Civil Disorders.* Washington, D.C.: U.S. Government Printing Office, 1968.

Simmel, Georg. *Conflict & the Web of Group Affiliations,* trans. by Kurt H. Wolff and Reinhard Bendix. New York: The Free Press, 1955.

Turk, Herman. "The Policy Outputs and Conflicts of Large Communities from an Interorganizational Viewpoint," *Sociological Focus,* 8 (April, 1975), 111–23.

CHAPTER 8

□□□□□□□□□
         □
         □
         □
         □

Community Action and Community Leadership

□
□
□
□
□
□

Social system theory and functionalism provide the basic tools for a rather comprehensive analysis of community structure. These theoretical systems force us to focus our attention on the units of which the community is composed and on the relationships that develop among these units. However, during recent years there has been a growing interest in viewing the community from a more dynamic, "on-the-scene" perspective.[1] Could we not gain much by using human action itself as a unit of analysis? Would not our understanding of community life be greatly enhanced by focusing on local residents as they attempt to solve the problems that inevitably arise when people live in proximity to each other? Should we not examine patterns of leadership and decision making at the local level? Several students of the community have offered affirmative answers to these questions. Hence it is to theories of community action and community leadership that we now turn.

□ COMMUNITY ACTION THEORY

One of the central problems in community action theory is to delineate the universe of community actions. Human beings are constantly acting: they work and play, get married and rear children, wage war and make

---

[1] For example, see Norton E. Long, "The Local Community as an Ecology of Games," in Roland L. Warren, (ed.), *New Perspectives on the American Community: A Book of Readings* (Chicago: Rand McNally Company, 1977), pp. 58–72; Kenneth P. Wilkinson, "The Community as a Social Field," *Social Forces,* 48 (March, 1970), 311–22; Kenneth P. Wilkinson, "A Behavioral Approach to Measurement and Analysis of Community Field Structure," *Rural Sociology,* 9 (Summer, 1974), 247–55. See also the references to Kaufman, Sutton, Sutton and Kolaja, and Wilkinson cited later.

peace, write books and burn them, seek solitude and fervently enter into group activities. Not all of these activities are related to community living, nor are they of interest to the student of community life. Because of this the first task the community action theorist must face is that of determining what activities should be classified as communal in nature and how communal activities can be distinguished from noncommunal ones.

Communal Phenomena

At the heart of community action theory is a rather narrow and circumscribed but nonetheless useful concept of communal phenomena. The mere fact that an event or activity occurs in a specific locality does not mean that it is an integral part of community life. Rather, some events and activities that occur in a given locality do have a direct bearing on community life; other events and activities do not. Harold F. Kaufman makes this point clear: "in the search for a more precise definition of community there is not only the question of differentiating localities as to their size and complexity, but within any given locality there is the problem of *distinguishing community phenomena* from those which might be considered noncommunity." [2]

To be more specific, Kaufman and other community action theorists view the community as but one of several interactional fields that exist in circumscribed, inhabited territories. Again, as Kaufman explains it, "the community field is not a Mother Hubbard which contains a number of other fields, but rather is to be seen as only one of the several interactional units in a local society." [3] From this it follows that the average citizen participates in the community field during only some of his or her waking hours. Sometimes he or she acts as a community member and participates in community-relevant activities, but on other occasions he or she acts as a family member and engages in activities of family relevance, as an employee and engages in activities of an economic nature, and so forth.

From this it follows that the key to a successful theory of community action is to find criteria by which events and activities of communal relevance can be distinguished from those that are not relevant. How does one decide which actions are properly included within the community field? What does the sociologist focus on in studying community action? Indeed, what is the so-called universe of community actions?

There have been several attempts to answer questions of this type and to make the concept of community action operational. Among the most

[2] Harold F. Kaufman, "Toward an Interactional Conception of Community," *Social Forces*, 38 (October, 1959), 9. Italics added.
[3] Ibid., p. 10.

successful of these attempts is that made by Willis A. Sutton, Jr., and Jiri Kolaja.[4] According to Sutton and Kolaja, a sharp distinction cannot be drawn between events and activities that are properly included in the universe of community actions and those that are not. Rather, they maintain that locality-centered events and activities should be studied in terms of the degree of "communityness" they possess. Needless to say, "communityness" is a rather complex variable and has several components. These include (1) the degree to which the event or activity is locality related, (2) the degree to which the persons who are involved in or influenced by the event or activity are identified with the locality, and (3) the extent to which local people participate in the activity.[5]

Sutton and Kolaja discuss these components at length and offer several suggestions as to how they might be made operational.[6] They make one thing totally clear: the task of distinguishing between activities and events that are a part of the universe of community actions and those that are not is a difficult one. Nonetheless, because this chapter is built around a discussion of community action, the following guidelines for identifying events and activities that are of interest to the student of community life is offered. (In developing these guidelines the present writer has leaned heavily on the work of Sutton and Kolaja.)

1. An activity or event is a part of the universe of community actions to the extent that the participants intend to solve some problem related to the locality where they live. There are of course a number of problems with which local citizens may concern themselves. Examples would be raising money to repair city streets, setting the school budget for the year, coordinating the services offered by health and welfare agencies, and bringing racial tensions under control.

2. An activity or event is a part of the universe of community actions when most of the persons who are involved in or influenced by the action are members of the local community. If the persons who are involved in or influenced by the event or activity are outsiders, then the event or activity would not, in most cases, be a part of the universe of community actions. Furthermore, an event or activity is more likely to belong within the universe of community actions when the participants in the action episode enact roles that are relevant to the entire community. Presumably, an event or activity that involves the mayor, school board, or representa-

---

[4] See Willis A. Sutton, Jr., and Jiri Kolaja, "Elements of Community Action," *Social Forces*, 38 (May, 1960), 325–31; Willis A. Sutton, Jr., and Jiri Kolaja, "The Concept of Community," *Rural Sociology*, 25 (June, 1960), 197–203.

[5] Sutton and Kolaja, "Elements of Community Action," pp. 325–31. This is one of two approaches that Sutton and Kolaja have developed for measuring degrees of "communityness." Their other approach is discussed in Sutton and Kolaja, "The Concept of Community," esp. p. 200.

[6] Sutton and Kolaja, "Elements of Community Action," pp. 325–29.

tives of broad-based community associations (chamber of commerce, the ecumenical council, the PTA, etc.) would be more a part of the universe of community action than would an event or activity that involves only the members of a *particular* religious denomination, labor union, business firm, or whatever.

3. An activity or event is most likely to be a part of the universe of community actions when a large number of community members participate in it. On the other hand, the number of participants in the event or activity does not matter if these participants come from elsewhere and exert no influence on local affairs.

Morris Freilich has also developed an operational definition of community that could be of use to community action theorists.[7] He maintains that human settlements (e.g., villages, cities, and metropolitan areas) are composed of a variety of different centers (see Figure 8-1). Some examples of such centers are churches, bars, certain restaurants, and the post office. Further, he maintains that certain people interact at these centers on a regular, recurrent, and frequent basis. These people, in turn, disperse information to other members of the "community"[8]

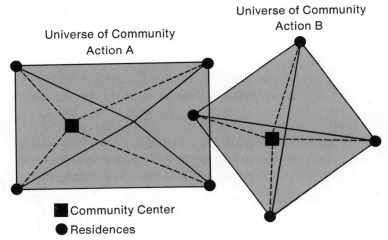

Universe of Community Action A

Universe of Community Action B

■ Community Center

● Residences

FIGURE 8-1. Universe of Community Actions A and B. *Adapted from Morris Freilich, "Toward an Operational Definition of Community," Rural Sociology,* **28** *(June, 1963), 124.*

[7] See Morris Freilich, "Toward an Operational Definition of Community," *Rural Sociology,* **28** (June, 1963), 117–27.

[8] It should be pointed out that Freilich uses the term *community* in a different way than it is used in this book. To his way of thinking, a city, for example, would be made up of a variety of different communities. There is a close correspondence among Freilich's concept of community, the human ecologist's concept of natural area, and Gerald Suttles's concept of the defended neighborhood.

and a local-interaction culture develops.[9] From the standpoint of community action theory, it could be argued that each of these centers and the people who are directly or indirectly tied to them represent a distinct universe of community action.

Types of Community Action

We have suggested that a great deal of effort has been spent in developing criteria by which the universe of community actions can be delineated. Unfortunately, much less time and effort have been devoted to a systematic analysis of the *specific types of activities and events* that fall within this universe. What kinds of activities and events are properly included within the universe of community actions? How might these activities and events be classified? Some light can be shed on these questions by analyzing locality-related activities and events in terms of whether they are spontaneous, routinized, or planned.

Spontaneous Community Action. During the late 1960s and early 1970s a number of American cities were rocked by events and activities that were apparently spontaneous, unanticipated, and unorganized. Among the examples that might be cited were the race riots that occurred with disturbing frequency, some of the student demonstrations that disrupted not only college campuses but also the surrounding community, and mob reactions to unpopular governmental policies. Subject to more positive evaluation on the part of most citizens are the spontaneous efforts of individuals and groups to render assistance when disaster strikes a community.[10]

Events and activities of this type are of interest to the student of community action, although the degree to which they are a part of the universe of community actions varies from case to case. Thus riots and similar breakdowns of civil order are clearly a part of the universe of community actions: they apparently feed on frustrations generated within

---

[9] In explaining what he means by a local-interaction culture, Freilich tells us that in a "community" composed of two or more ethnic groups, "each ethnic group would have its own version of a traditional culture, as a member of a family of similar ethnic groups in various parts of the world. In addition, all the ethnic groups would jointly share a community culture, or what I will hereafter refer to as a *local-interaction culture*." Ibid., p. 122. Italics in original.

[10] A growing body of literature has emerged that relates to the influence of disaster on the community and on human behavior. See William H. Form and Sigmund Nosow, *Community in Disaster* (New York: Harper & Row, 1958); George W. Baker and Dwight W. Chapman, *Man and Society in Disaster* (New York: Basic Books, Inc., 1962; Allen Barton, *Communities in Disaster: A Sociological Analysis of Collective Stress Situations* (Garden City, N.Y.: Doubleday, 1969).

the local community and, contrary to popular opinion, represent the efforts of local residents to cope with their problems. In its carefully documented analysis, for example, the 1967 National Advisory Commission on Civil Disorders points out that

> Rioters are not only more likely than the noninvolved to have been born in the region in which the riot occurred, but they are also more likely to have been long-term residents of the city in which the disturbance took place. The Detroit survey data indicates that 59.4 percent of the self-reported rioters, but only 34.6 percent of the noninvolved, were born in Detroit. The comparable figures in the Newark survey were 53.5 percent and 22.5 percent.[11]

In addition, the Advisory Commission reports that

> Outsiders who temporarily entered the city during the riot might have left before the surveys were conducted and therefore may be underestimated in the survey data. However, the arrest data which is contemporaneous with the riot, suggest that few outsiders were involved: 90 percent of those arrested resided in the riot city, 7 percent lived in the same state, and only 1 percent were from outside the state. Our interviews in 20 cities corroborate these conclusions.[12]

These findings strongly suggest that the riots and civil disorders that occurred in Chicago, Newark, Detroit, Los Angeles, and a host of other cities belong within the universe of community action, at least in the sense that they represent collective responses to problems and frustrations encountered by community members. At the same time, one can envision sporadic acts of violence that are stimulated by people whose goal is to put pressure on a specific individual, a specific corporation, the federal government, or whatever. One thinks immediately, for example, of the kidnapping of Patricia Hearst by the Symbionese Liberation Army.[13] One of the goals of the Symbionese Liberation Army was to force Patricia Hearst's wealthy father to finance a massive food giveaway program. An event of this type would possess a much lower degree of "communityness" than the events described by the National Advisory Commission. Among other things, events and activities of this type are

---

[11] National Advisory Commission on Civil Disorders, *Report of the National Advisory Commission on Civil Disorders* (Washington, D.C.: U.S. Government Printing Office, 1968), p. 74.

[12] Ibid., pp. 74–75.

[13] For an in-depth account of the Hearst case see Marilyn Baker with Sally Brompton, *Exclusive! The Inside Story of Patricia Hearst and the SLA* (New York: Macmillan Publishing Co., Inc., 1974).

not intended to solve a community problem, and very few, if any, local community members participate in them.

Routinized Community Actions. The universe of community actions also encompasses a variety of events and activities that occur on a routinized basis. In this context the term *routinized* must be defined in such a way that it includes any event or activity that is a normal, recurrent part of community life. Thus it is entirely possible to imagine a community where there are more riots than charity drives. Nonetheless, a charity drive that is held on an annual basis would be an example of routinized community action; a riot would not. Among other examples of routinized community action that might be cited would be the periodic meetings and deliberations of local governing bodies, annual parades, fairs, and other "social" events, as well as a host of other events and activities that happen on a recurrent basis. Some of these events and activities are of profound significance for the community and its members. Because of their routinized character, however, they often remain unanalyzed by community action theorists.[14]

Initiated Community Action. For one reason or another, community action theorists have focused much of their attention on what might be referred to as initiated community action. Activities and events of this type, in contrast to those delineated previously, have as their main purpose the initiation of change at the community level through the mechanism of orderly group processes. Hence initiated community action can be viewed as an episode in the life of the community: a group comes into being, action is taken to bring about a desired change, and the group disbands or undertakes some other project. Some of these episodes may require only a few days for their completion; others may require a much greater period of time.

Although sociologists have generated a wealth of literature pertaining to initiated community action, the characteristics of this type of action have not always been clearly spelled out. However, initiated community

---

[14] It would be of considerable interest to know how many routinized activities and events occur in a typical community and how these are distributed by institutional type, i.e., how many are executed by the local government, by the local school system, by local churches, and so forth. Unfortunately, we simply do not have data that provide full and accurate answers to questions of this type. However, some of the research conducted by Willis A. Sutton, Jr., is suggestive of what might be found. See Sutton, "Toward a Universe of Community Actions," pp. 48–59. We should note that Sutton does not make a distinction between routinized and other types of community action. However, it is probably safe to assume that most of the actions observed by Sutton were of a routinized nature, i.e., they were a normal part of life in the community that he studied.

action appears to have several characteristics, including (1) an emphasis on problem solving or achieving a concrete goal, (2) the participation of local citizens in the episode, and (3) a democratic or semidemocratic orientation. Each of these characteristics must be elaborated on.

1. Initiated community action represents one method by which change in some facet of the community can be brought about. Therefore, a major characteristic of initiated community action is that emphasis is usually placed on solving a problem or reaching some tangible, well-defined goal. The purpose of a community action episode may be to raise money for the United Fund, change attitudes toward mental illness,[15] or establish a community health council and improve local health facilities.[16] We must stress, however, that initiated community action can also be used to preserve the status quo. Persons whose interests are threatened may use initiated community action to prevent minority groups from gaining access to adequate housing, to block the expansion of services offered by local government, or whatever.

2. A second major characteristic of initiated community action is that most of the participants in the action episode are members of the local community. The one exception might be a professional person who is sent in by an outside sponsoring agency to help community members carry out a successful community action program. Moreover, the local participants usually have not been professionally trained to fulfill their roles in the action program. Sometimes these people participate in the action program because they feel that it is worthwhile or because they stand to gain if the program is successful: they receive no financial remuneration. In other cases, the participants in the action program receive a wage from the sponsoring agency (e.g., the federal government). Funded community action programs have the dual advantage that they create jobs and at the same time they *may* help to ameliorate community problems.

The fact that some local citizens participate in community action programs without receiving compensation does not mean that their motives are always pure. In fact, many people are openly suspicious of com-

---

[15] For a description of a community action project of this type see Elaine Cumming and John Cumming, *Closed Ranks: An Experiment in Mental Health Education* (Cambridge, Mass.: Harvard University Press, 1957).

[16] There are numerous accounts of community action projects of this type. See especially Floyd Hunter et al., *Community Organization: Action and Inaction* (Chapel Hill: University of North Carolina Press, 1956); Solon T. Kimball and Marion Pearsall, *The Talladega Story: A Study in Community Process* (University: University of Alabama Press, 1954); Christopher Sower et al., *Community Involvement: The Webs and Informal Ties That Make for Action* (New York: The Free Press, 1957).

munity action programs and of the individuals who become involved in them. For example, Kimball and Pearsall report that the citizens of Talladega, Alabama, seem to have a rather skeptical attitude toward proposals to broaden streets, extend sewers, fluoridate water supplies, and so forth:

> When action is proposed for the problems just mentioned, there is a traditional way of first responding to them. Talladegans always look behind proposals of citizens which call for public action to see what self-interest is being served. Thus, when an Ed Hyde wanted North Street widened, others suggested that he was motivated by the desire to have traffic flow past his hotel on that street. Similarly, it was implied that none of the city commissioners could benefit directly from extending sewerage to West End so they made no effort to meet the majority interest shown for this facility. When the dentists pushed for fluoridation of water, rumors were started which implied that the dentists would profit. Examples could be multiplied many times.[17]

It is undoubtedly true that on occasion the participants in community action programs are motivated by a desire for economic, political, or personal gain. This does not mean, however, that community action programs are undesirable or that they do not have a role to play in improving community life. The widening of a road may have economic rewards for an Ed Hyde, but it may also mean prosperity for other members of the community.

3. Many community action theorists also agree that the ideal community action program is one that has a democratic orientation. Specifically, community action programs should be free from control by vested interest groups, and the participation of all interested, conscientious citizens should be welcomed. Likewise, one of the fundamental characteristics of the ideal community action program is that all members of the action group, and not just a leader, should be involved in setting goals, planning for action, and carrying the project through to completion. This is a feature of community action programs that must be borne in mind by professional persons whose job it is to assist local citizens in reaching their goals through initiated community action. The role of these persons is to educate and facilitate rather than to choose, plan, and carry out the action program.[18]

[17] Kimball and Pearsall, *The Talladega Story*, pp. 191–92.
[18] For discussions of the role of professional consultants in community action and community development see Otto G. Hoiberg, "Contributions of the Social Scientist to Community Development," in Marvin B. Sussman (ed.), *Community Structure and Analysis* (New York: Thomas Y. Crowell Company, 1959), pp. 129–43; Paul W. Inbody, "The Role of the Change Agent in Community Development," *Free Inquiry,*

Needless to say, many community action programs do not conform to this rather idealistic model. In actuality, many community action programs are controlled by vested interest groups, and some people are purposefully discouraged from participating in the program. Among other things, they may not be willing to play by the rules of the game, they may be seen as members of the "enemy" camp, or they may belong to an unpopular minority group. Similarly, many community action programs do require a strong leader who can organize the action episode and who can get things done.[19]

It should be noted that several community action theorists have attempted to map the stages through which episodes of initiated community action pass as they move from initiation to completion. Although action episodes consist of a complex series of intertwined events, it nevertheless seems reasonable, for purposes of analysis, to break this flow of events down into a few basic stages or clusters of activity. It is to a consideration of these stages that we now turn.

Table 8-1 compares the stages through which community action episodes pass as they have been identified by several different sociologists. This table to some extent represents an oversimplification of the schemes developed by these theorists. Green and Mayo, for example, posit a series of substages within each of the four basic stages that they identify. Likewise, there is only a rough correspondence among the four schemes that are considered in Table 8-1. This is partly the result of the fact that each scheme sheds light on slightly different aspects of the total action process: Holland and his associates focus on the mechanics of community action episodes, Kaufman as well as Green and Mayo delineate the specific steps that are required to carry a project through to successful completion, and Warren focuses on the emergence and operation of action systems. Nonetheless, there is enough similarity in the four schemes that Table 8-1 can be used to describe briefly the stages through which community action episodes pass.

These stages can be summarized rather easily. Episodes of initiated community action begin when at least a few people become aware of a

---

1 (1972), 19–36; Austin Bennett, "Professional Staff Members' Contributions to Community Development," *Journal of the Community Development Society,* **4** (Spring, 1973), 58–68.

19 For a series of studies suggesting that different types of community power structure are associated with different types of successful community action programs see Amos H. Hawley, "Community Power and Urban Renewal Success," *American Journal of Sociology,* **68** (January, 1963), 422–31; Richard A. Smith, "Community Power and Decision Making: A Replication and Extension of Hawley," *American Sociological Review,* **41** (August, 1976), 691–705; James R. Lincoln, "Power and Mobilization in the Urban Community: Reconsidering the Ecological Approach," *American Sociological Review,* **41** (February, 1976), 1–15.

Table 8-1. Stages in Community Action Episodes

	Holland et al.*	Kaufman †	Green and Mayo ‡	Warren §
Stage 1	Convergence of interest	Rise of interest	Initiation of action	Initial systemic environment
Stage 2	Establishment of an initiating set	Organization and maintenance of sponsorship	Goal definition and planning for achievement	Inception of the action system
Stage 3	Legitimation and sponsorship	Goal setting and the determination of specific means for their realization	Implementation of plans	Expansion of the action system
Stage 4	Establishment of an execution set	Gaining and maintenance of participation	Goal achievement consequences	Operation of the expanded action system
Stage 5	Fulfillment of "charter" (i.e., goal)	Carrying out of the activities that represent goal achievement		Transformation of the action system

* John B. Holland, Kenneth E. Tiedke, and Paul R. Miller, "A Theoretical Model for Health Action," *Rural Sociology*, **22** (June, 1957), 149–55.
† Harold F. Kaufman, "Toward an Interactional Conception of Community," *Social Forces*, **38** (October, 1959), 9–17.
‡ James Green and Selz C. Mayo, "A Framework for Research in the Actions of Community Groups," *Social Forces*, **31** (May, 1953), 320–27.
§ Roland L. Warren, *The Community in America*, 2nd ed. (Chicago: Rand McNally & Company, 1973), pp. 315–20.

problem and express an interest in working toward its solution (stage 1). This interest may arise in discussions among neighbors or among the leaders of voluntary associations, and it may even be stimulated by an outside change agent, such as a community consultant employed by a university or governmental body. At this stage in the action episode only a few people are involved. However, if a community action project is to move beyond the discussion stage, a temporary action system must emerge which can "get the ball rolling" (stage 2). In the typical episode of community action this stage involves the formation of an "initiating set." The initiating set usually involves many of the same people who originally became aware of the problem. Among other things, the persons who participate in the initiating set must define the goals of the action episode and map out specific strategies by which these goals may be achieved. Once these things have been accomplished, the initiating set must establish its right to take action, i.e., it must enlist the cooperation of persons who, by virtue of their position in the community, can make or break the project (stage 3). There are essentially four groups that the initiating set must take into account, including "those whose approval gives sanction to the actions of the initiating set; those whose active sponsorship is essential for the mobilizing of community resources; those who remain neutral to the action; and those who may oppose the action." [20] Finally, a community action program of any consequence usually requires more than just the participation of members of the initiating set. Indeed, in most community action episodes the action system must be expanded in such a way that it includes actors who have not been previously involved (stage 4). These persons may be needed to carry out the project, and widespread public involvement is one way of gaining broad-based support for the action program.

Once the goals and purposes of the action episode are achieved (stage 5), two things may happen. First, the action system may be disbanded and its members may gradually lose contact with one another. However, in some cases the rewards of working together with other citizens to better the community are so great that the participants in the action episode desire to tackle other problems and pursue other goals. When this occurs we can be sure that the community action program has been worth the effort invested in it.

Initiated Community Action: Two Case Studies

So far, our discussion of initiated community action has been quite abstract. The characteristics of initiated community action have been

[20] Holland, Tiedke, and Miller, "A Theoretical Model for Health Action," p. 154.

discussed, and we have looked at the stages in community action episodes. We can increase our understanding of initiated community action further by briefly reviewing two case studies of specific community action episodes.

One of the most fascinating accounts of an episode of community action was presented in a classic article by Richard C. Fuller and Richard R. Myers.[21] Basically, Fuller and Myers argue that social (and community) problems have a natural history and that they go through three stages. The first of these stages is one in which growing numbers of people become aware of the problem (the awareness stage). In the second stage policies are formulated to deal with the problem (the policy determination stage). Finally, in the third stage action is taken to solve the problem (the reform stage).

The setting for Fuller and Myers's research was Detroit, Michigan, in the 1920s and 1930s. During this time trailer camps began springing up around the Detroit area. For the most part, these camps were occupied by poor factory workers and their families; many of these people were unemployed, and some were even unemployable. At first, however, the camps were small, and neither the public nor governmental officials expressed any concern about them. However, by the early and mid-1930s the size and number of these camps had increased significantly. Furthermore, they had become problem ridden. As Fuller and Myers put it,

> families averaged two to each trailer and accommodations were scarcely large enough for one; several of the camps had no toilet accommodations and there was little or no privacy in such matters; water supply was low and residents were often dependent on sources outside the camp; in winter, the heating accommodations were deficient, small gas stoves serving most trailers and others had no heating whatsoever; garbage disposal was indiscriminate and dumping on nearby vacant lots was the usual expedient.[22]

By this time homeowners residing near the camps, the Common Council, the police, and a number of other groups were saying that "Something ought to be done."[23] In short, the *awareness* stage had been reached.

As we indicated earlier, Fuller and Myers maintain that the second stage in community problem-solving episodes is the *policy determination* stage. In this stage people are "concerned primarily with 'what ought to be done' and people are proposing that 'this and that should be done'."[24]

[21] See Richard C. Fuller and Richard R. Myers, "The Natural History of a Social Problem," *American Sociological Review*, 6 (June, 1941), 320–28.
[22] Ibid., pp. 323–24.
[23] Ibid., p. 322.
[24] Ibid., p. 324.

In this stage of the action episode there may be a great deal of controversy as different interest groups express their version of how the problem should be solved. For example, homeowners who lived in areas immediately adjacent to the trailer camps had a very different version of what should be done than did the Mobile Home Owners' Association of America.

The third stage in community problem-solving episodes, according to Fuller and Myers, is the *reform* stage. As they put it, "this is the stage of action, both public and private" and the emphasis is on the fact that "this and that are being done." [25] Fuller and Myers published their research before the reform stage had fully run its course. However, by the time their article was published a law had been passed that restricted the camps to certain areas, the health and sanitation departments had established special rules for the trailer camps, and so on.

In a much more recent piece of research, Kenneth P. Wilkinson studied twenty-five different episodes of community action in two different communities.[26] The results of Wilkinson's research are reported in Table 8-2. It should be apparent that the stages or phases of community action episodes identified by Wilkinson are very similar to those delineated in Table 8-1, especially those identified by Harold Kaufman. Table 8-2 is particularly valuable, however, because it increases our understanding of some of the different things that take place as a community action program progresses from the initiation stage to the implementation stage. For example, in the initiation stage in community A two actors in two different action programs complained to formal authorities about a troublesome situation; in community B five actors in one program did the same thing.

☐ LEADERSHIP AND INVOLVEMENT

Any discussion of community action immediately brings to the forefront a wide variety of questions relating to community leadership and involvement. Who are the leaders in community activities and what are their characteristics? To what extent do community members become involved in local action episodes? Unfortunately, even though numerous investigators have focused on questions of this type, their research has yielded relatively little in the way of basic generalizations. This is partly because students of the community have used a variety of different research strate-

[25] Ibid., p. 326.
[26] Kenneth P. Wilkinson, "Phases and Roles in Community Action," *Rural Sociology,* 35 (March, 1970), 54–67.

Table 8-2. Number of Actors Performing Acts Classified by Phase, and Number of Programs in Which Acts Occurred, by Community

Phase and Act	Community A		Community B	
	Actors	Programs	Actors	Programs
Initiation	. . . . *number*			
Conceived of the need and discussed it privately with others, who then took action	3	3	7	7
Raised the issue with newspaper stories and editorials	0	0	1	5
Went before formal authorities to complain about a troublesome situation	2	2	5	1
First pointed out the need within a formal organization	6	5	4	3
Gathered information on the nature and extent of a local problem	5	4	2	2
Wrote letters to local residents pointing out a need	1	1	1	1
Took an individual action that forced the matter into public view	5	4	1	1
Organization of sponsorship				
Got a few people together privately and formed a new group	7	4	6	3
Called a public meeting or organized a new group	1	1	4	4
Made suggestions at a meeting in which a new group was organized	11	4	9	3
Urged an established group to take responsibility	6	6	3	3
Appointed a committee within an established group	5	4	3	4
Planned the structure of a new group to sponsor the action	9	5	14	8
Developed group structure after it was organized	18	9	3	2
Goal setting				
Participated in board meeting while long-range goals or policies were being planned	39	3	24	6
Collected data specifically for use in goal setting	5	3	5	6
Planned technical aspects of a facility or complex operation	10	7	7	5
Planned strategy for accomplishment of a specific goal	12	9	13	13

Table 8-2.—Continued

Phase and Act	Community A		Community B	
	Actors	Pro-grams	Actors	Pro-grams
Voted in government body meeting to resolve an issue	5	4	0	0
Personally suggested specific goals	0	0	5	5
Recruitment				
Spoke at civic clubs and public meetings	18	8	6	7
Made appeals and gave information through the mass media	20	19	6	8
Made other mass appeals, for example, letters or billboards	12	6	11	8
Appealed to individuals for money, support, or involvement	10	6	14	9
Asked local government for money or authorization	10	6	7	7
Sought money or authorization outside the community	16	7	14	8
Hired technical personnel for implementation	3	3	8	8
Implementation				
Provided money or materials	3	4	15	9
Gave technical or professional service	4	4	7	8
Directed construction or organization of a facility or event	9	5	2	2
Served as paid director of the continuous program of an agency after it was organized	16	6	9	8
Carried out the objectives of a program after it was organized	25	11	35	14

Source: Kenneth P. Wilkinson, "Phases and Roles in Community Action," *Rural Sociology*, **35** (March, 1970), 63–4.

gies in their study of community leadership and power—strategies that seem to yield different results.[27] It may also be partly because these investigators have not always distinguished among different types of community events and activities. Surely a different group of persons will

[27] See especially Linton C. Freeman, Thomas J. Fararo, Warner Bloomberg, Jr., and Morris H. Sunshine, "Locating Leaders in Local Communities: A Comparison of Some Alternative Approaches," *American Sociological Review*, **28** (October, 1963), 791–98.

normally be involved in events and activities of a spontaneous type than will be involved in activities and events of a routinized nature.

Types of Community Leadership

Apparently community leadership is not something that is firmly placed in the hands of a few individuals. Rather, leadership tends to become diffused throughout the community, with one person or group exercising leadership in one situation and another person or group exercising leadership in another situation. Indeed, in his study of New Haven, Connecticut, Robert A. Dahl tells us that "probably the most striking characteristic of influence in New Haven is the extent to which it is specialized; that is, individuals who are influential in one sector of public activity tend not to be influential in another sector."[28] Nonetheless, essentially three types of leaders may be identified at the local level. These three types of leaders and some of the more important facts about them are indicated in Table 8-3.

The first of these is the institutional leader. This person possesses the right to lead by virtue of the fact that he or she occupies a formal leadership position within the community. Included within this category are local political officials, such as the mayor and city council, as well as school principals, influential ministers, and labor union officials. Even though these persons are official leaders in the sense that they are elected or appointed, their right to lead is usually circumscribed. A mayor, for example, does not have the right to make and execute decisions relating to all aspects of community life. Rather, his or her right to lead is limited to the affairs of municipal government.[29] This does not mean of course that the mayor never has influence that goes beyond that officially delegated to him or her. In addition to being the mayor, he or she may also be a part of the community's informal but nonetheless influential "power elite." Essentially the same observation applies to ministers, school superintendents, labor union officials, and other institutional leaders. In any event, the right of institutional leaders to exert influence and to make decisions is confined almost exclusively to activities and events of a routinized nature. Although they may become involved in nonroutinized community events and activities, it is usually not among their officially prescribed duties to do so.

There has been a considerable amount of debate as to how much decision-making power local institutional leaders actually possess. This

[28] Robert A. Dahl, *Who Governs?* (New Haven: Yale University Press, 1961), p. 169.
[29] For a highly readable account of the mayor's role in exercising community leadership see Henry W. Mair, *Challenge to the Cities: An Approach to a Theory of Urban Leadership* (New York: Random House, Inc., 1966).

Table 8-3. Types of Community Leaders

Type	Basis for Leadership	Area of Authority	Examples
Institutional	Occupies a formal leadership position in the community and is elected or appointed to his or her post.	Confined to routinized community actions.	Mayor, city council, school principal, ministers, labor union officials, etc.
Grassroots	Has personal influence and the ability to get other people interested in a "cause."	Confined to community actions of a spontaneous and/or initiated nature.	Opponent of school desegregation, leader of campaign against water fluoridation, etc.
Power Elite	Has wealth, economic power, and/or personal influence.	Makes his or her influence felt in all areas of community action and decision making.	Wealthy businessperson, top-echelon employee of commercial, banking, or industrial firm.

debate has been spawned by contradictory findings from different communities. Thus several studies have indicated that in some communities institutional leaders are in fact the key decision makers.[30] On the other hand, an increasingly large body of research suggests that in many communities the formal leadership structure is very much influenced by a partially hidden "power elite."[31]

Another person who may make his or her influence felt at the local level is the grassroots leader.[32] This is the person who occasionally "pops" up from nowhere to assume leadership in some particular situation and then fades into the background, perhaps never to be heard from again. One example that can be cited is the local citizen who leads a crusade for or against school desegregation or who becomes the main opponent of a proposed water fluoridation program. Unfortunately, little is known about leaders of this type. However, Kornhauser has garnered some evidence suggesting that these persons are likely to oppose those programs and policies that are championed by the official leadership structure.[33] In any event, the opportunity to exercise leadership that these persons possess is confined almost exclusively to activities and events of a spontaneous or initiated nature. Community events and activities of a routinized nature are the province of institutional leaders.

More research has focused on the role of the "power elite" or "ruling elite" in making decisions and exercising leadership at the local level. This research has suggested that in many communities there is a small group of people who, because of their wealth or economic position,

[30] For example, see Dahl, *Who Governs?*; Charles Freeman and Selz C. Mayo, "Decision Makers in Rural Community Action," *Social Forces,* 35 (May, 1957), 319–22; Benjamin Walter, "Political Decision Making in Arcadia," in F. Stuart Chapin, Jr., and Shirley F. Weiss (eds.), *Urban Growth Dynamics* (New York: John Wiley & Sons, Inc., 1962), pp. 141–87; Aaron Wildavsky, *Leadership in a Small Town* (Totowa, N.J.: Bedminster Press, 1964).

[31] The number of studies that focus on the role of covert power elites in community leadership and decision making is legion. For a sampling of these studies see Robert S. Lynd and Helen M. Lynd, *Middletown* and *Middletown in Transition* (New York: Harcourt Brace Jovanovich, Inc., 1929 and 1937); Floyd Hunter, *Community Power Structure: A Study of Decision Makers* (Chapel Hill: University of North Carolina Press, 1953); Delbert C. Miller, "Industry and Community Power Structure: A Comparative Study of an American and an English City," *American Sociological Review,* 23 (February, 1958), 9–15; William V. D'Antonio et al., "Institutional and Occupational Representations in Eleven Community Influence Systems," *American Sociological Review,* 26 (June, 1961), 440–46.

[32] Perhaps a better designation for this person would be the *meteor,* a term that was apparently coined by Aaron Wildavsky. See his *Leadership in a Small Town,* p. 336.

[33] See William Kornhauser, "Power and Participation in the Local Community," *Health Education Monographs,* No. 6 (Oakland, Calif.: Society of Public Health Educators, 1959), 28–37.

largely determine the destiny of various community events and activities. One of the most thorough studies of such a power elite was that conducted by Floyd Hunter. In his study of the top forty leaders in a major southern city, Hunter found that over one half were top-echelon employees of commercial, banking and investment, or industrial firms and that only four were government employees.[34] Similarly, in his study of 218 different community action programs aimed at obtaining better community health facilities, Paul A. Miller reports that 34 per cent of the "most active" participants were self-employed businessmen; that 28 per cent were professionals, and that 16 per cent were employed executives or managers.[35] On the other hand, only 8.2 per cent were civil officials.[36] These findings strongly suggest that the top leaders identified by both Hunter and Miller possess all the characteristics usually attributed to the "covert power elite," i.e., they are leaders who "do not hold political offices or offices in associations, they are not recognized by the community at large as key decision makers, they are active in a wide range of decision areas, and they work together as a group rather than independently or in opposition."[37]

The hypothesis that most American communities fit this "ruling elite" model of community leadership and power has been seriously questioned. During recent years there has been much research suggesting that an alternative perspective is called for in conceptualizing the power structure of American communities. In commenting on the critics of the ruling elite model of community power, for example, Willis D. Hawley and Frederick M. Wirt tell us that

> This alternative perspective questions the existence of a single center of power, or a cohesive coalition of groups which wield power. Instead, the critics propose that there are usually (though not always) *multiple* centers of power, none of which is completely sovereign. In addition, these centers of power do not overlap or coalesce from issue-area to issue-area in any consistent way. In other words, *American cities are pluralistic.*[38]

Raymond Wolfinger adds further support to the pluralistic thesis in pointing out that the findings of Hunter and others who subscribe to a ruling elite model of community power may be a product of their meth-

[34] Hunter, *Community Power Structure,* Table 4.
[35] Paul A. Miller, "The Process of Decision Making Within the Context of Community Organization," *Rural Sociology,* 17 (June, 1952), 156.
[36] Ibid., Table 1.
[37] Charles M. Bonjean and David M. Olson, "Community Leadership: Directions of Research," *Administrative Science Quarterly,* 9 (December, 1964), 291.
[38] Willis D. Hawley and Frederick M. Wirt (eds.), *The Search for Community Power* (Englewood Cliffs, N.J.: Prentice-Hall, Inc., 1968), p. 89.

odological approach.[39] In attempting to identify local influentials, most of these studies have utilized the reputational approach to the analysis of community power. Those who use this approach simply ask informed people in the community to name those persons whom they believe to be most influential in community affairs. Those persons who are named most frequently are assumed to be a part of the ruling elite. However, there are difficulties inherent in this methodological approach. Among other things, one's informants may be familiar with the top leadership in only one area (schools, urban renewal, and so on) and the researcher's definition of *power* may be different from that of the informant.[40] Indeed, when we ask a person such questions as "Who is the 'biggest' man in town?" or "Who runs this town?" we may not get an accurate picture of who has the most influence on local affairs. Rather, we may in reality be getting answers to such questions as "Who gets the most publicity in local newspapers?" "Who is the richest person in town?" or "Who forms the 'uppercrust' of this community?" In short, the basic assumption underlying the reputational approach is that there is a correlation between the influence an individual reputedly has and the amount of influence he or she actually exerts. This assumption is rather shaky. Furthermore, those persons who serve as informants for the researcher usually tend to move in the same circles, to know the same people, and even to know each other. It is not surprising that there is agreement among them as to who constitute the most influential persons in the community.

The studies that we have discussed in the preceding pages, if not examined in concert, could lead the student to two distinctly different conclusions. First, one could conclude that every community has a covert power elite and that institutional leaders are merely pawns in the struggle for leadership at the local level. Second, one could adopt the opposite perspective, i.e., that in every community there is a pluralistic leadership structure: those who exercise leadership in relationship to one activity or event are not the same persons who exercise leadership in relationship to another activity or event. At the present time it would appear unwise to embrace fully either of these perspectives. About the only conclusion that can safely be drawn is that the nature of leadership structures varies from community to community. Some communities have a highly developed power elite; others do not. Bonjean and Olson are undoubtedly correct when they indicate that "apparently no single descriptive statement—not even a very general one—applies to community leadership in the United States today (unless the statement includes variability itself)." [41]

[39] Raymond E. Wolfinger, "Reputation and Reality in the Study of Community Power," *American Sociological Review,* **25** (October, 1960), 636–44.
[40] Ibid., p. 638.
[41] Bonjean and Olson, "Community Leadership: Directions of Research," p. 290.

Community Power and the Search for Knowledge

Literally hundreds of studies of community power and leadership have been conducted. Yet the findings of these studies are so inconsistent and contradictory that it is dangerous to make any generalizations concerning power and leadership at the local level. Indeed, these studies seem to tell us more about the nature of social science than about the nature of community power.

To be more specific, we have suggested already that the findings of social scientists are often influenced by their choice of research methods. This clearly appears to be the case in regard to studies of community power and leadership. For example, Curtis and Petras present evidence that sociologists tend to rely heavily on the reputational approach to the study of community power, and that the reputational approach almost automatically leads to the identification of a pyramidal (or elitist) type of power structure. On the other hand, political scientists tend to use other methods of studying community power and therefore arrive at different conclusions.[42] Curtis and Petras put it well when they say that the "researchers' theoretical perspectives, irrespective of discipline, tended to determine research procedures, and this in turn helped to determine findings."[43] Bell and Newby have arrived at the same conclusion.[44]

Findings of this type raise an extremely serious question: how many of our research endeavors would have yielded different findings if different research methods had been used? Certainly our research on community power structure suggests that we must always be aware that our perspectives (or biases?) influence the hypotheses that we seek to test. These hypotheses, in turn, influence the research methods that we use. Finally, our research methods may, to a great extent, influence our findings. If we had realized this years ago, we would not have hundreds on hundreds of studies of community power and leadership that seem to add up to very little. Likewise, we probably would not have "bibliographies of other bibliographies" pertaining to community power and leadership.[45]

Alternative Approaches

We have now identified three types of leaders who make their influence felt at the local level. Most communities have institutional leaders, grass-

---

[42] See James E. Curtis and John W. Petras, "Community Power, Power Studies, and the Sociology of Knowledge," *Human Organization*, 29 (Fall, 1970), 204–13.
[43] Ibid., p. 209
[44] See Colin Bell and Howard Newby, *Community Studies: An Introduction to the Sociology of the Local Community* (New York: Praeger Publishers, 1972), esp. p. 222.
[45] See John Walton, "Community Power and the Retreat from Politics: Full Circle after Twenty Years?" *Social Problems*, 23 (February, 1976), 292.

roots leaders, and "behind-the-scenes" leaders, although their number and degree of influence vary widely from community to community. We should note, however, that our classification of community leaders is but one among many and that the literature on community leadership is vast. Although we cannot hope to review all the typologies of community leadership that have been developed, there are three that merit our attention.

One of these is Robert K. Merton's classification of the *types of influentials* who make their impact felt at the community level.[46] Specifically, Merton distinguishes between the "local" influential and the "cosmopolitan" influential. Put most simply, the local influential confines his or her interests to the local community and "is preoccupied with local problems, to the virtual exclusion of the national and international scene."[47] Presumably, his or her advice would be sought in regard to local politics, the activities of local service clubs, and other events and activities of a strictly local nature. It should be noted that the local influential gets his or her influence by cultivating a wide number of acquaintanceships and by participating in an elaborate network of social relations. Indeed, Merton tells us that "influentials in this group act on the explicit assumption that they can be locally prominent and influential by lining up enough people who know them and are hence willing to help them as well as be helped by them."[48] Cosmopolitan leaders, on the other hand, are much more "worldly" in their attitudes and outlook. Although the cosmopolitan leader must show some interest in local affairs, he or she more often exercises influence over people's thinking on national and international issues. As such, the cosmopolitan leader claims the right to lead on the basis of prestige, skills, and knowledge. At the same time, he or she has little interest in becoming enmeshed in an elaborate network of social relationships. As Merton puts it, "it is the prestige of his previous achievements and previously acquired skills which make him eligible for a place in the local influence-structure."[49]

There is another important fact about localistic and cosmopolitan influentials. Merton maintains that the influence the cosmopolitan influential wields is likely to be monomorphic, whereas the influence wielded by the local influential tends to be polymorphic.[50] By this Merton means simply that the cosmopolitan's ability to exert influence is often limited to a

[46] See Robert K. Merton, *Social Theory and Social Structure*, rev. and enlarged ed. (New York: The Free Press, 1957), pp. 387–420. It must be stressed that Merton's typology is not the product of armchair theorizing. Rather, it grew out of research that was conducted in "Rovere," a town of 11,000 persons located on the eastern seaboard.
[47] Ibid., p. 393.
[48] Ibid., p. 397.
[49] Ibid., p. 400.
[50] Ibid., pp. 413–15.

specific type of issue or event, whereas the localite may be able to exert influence in a variety of different situations. The cosmopolitan influential is, in effect, a *specialist;* the localite is a *generalist.* As a result, the cosmopolitan influential has influence in the realm of politics, fashion, *or* charitable activities. The local influential has influence in the area of politics, fashion, *and* charitable activities.

It should be apparent that Merton's typology carries on a grand tradition. He draws his terms, as well as some of his thinking, from Carle Zimmerman and, ultimately, from Ferdinand Tonnies. Likewise, the relationship between Merton's typology and Roland Warren's concepts of the horizontal and vertical axis should not be overlooked. Indeed, further research might well reveal that the local influential operates almost exclusively on the horizontal axis and has an integrative function within the community, whereas the cosmopolitan influential undoubtedly operates along the vertical axis and links the local community to the larger world.

Another typology of influentials of considerable interest to the student of community life is that developed by Nuttall, Scheuch, and Gordon.[51] The value of this typology lies in the fact that it sheds light on the dynamics of the decision-making process. The typology itself is shown in Figure 8-2. According to Nuttall and his associates, a person's ability to exert influence in a given situation depends on two factors: (1) whether the person actually has access to the appropriate resources and (2) whether other participants in the decision-making process believe that he or she possesses the appropriate resources. Among the resources that the

		Perceived Access to Resource	
		Yes	No
Actual Access to Resource	Yes	(A) Manifest Influence	(B) Potential Influence
	No	(C) Reputed Influence	(D) Without Influence

FIGURE 8-2. A typology of influentials. [*Source: Ronald L. Nuttall, Erwin K. Scheuch, and Chad Gordon, "On the Structure of Influence," in Terry N. Clark (ed.),* Community Structure and Decision-Making: Comparative Analyses *(San Francisco: Chandler Publishing Company, 1968), p. 351.]*

[51] See Ronald L. Nuttall, Erwin K. Scheuch, and Chad Gordon, "On the Structure of Influence," in Terry N. Clark (ed.), *Community Structure and Decision-Making: Comparative Analyses* (San Francisco: Chandler Publishing Company, 1968), especially pp. 352–64.

potential leader might possess would be the ability to reward persons who cooperate or to sanction those who do not. In the simplest case, the potential leader might be able to withhold from or deliver to another person a block of votes, depending on whether the other person "helps" the potential leader to reach his or her goals. Hence, in any episode of decision making, there are potentially four sets of actors: those with manifest influence, those with potential influence, those with reputed influence, and those with no influence. Once the decision has been made and the appropriate rewards or sanctions delivered, there may be of course a considerable reshuffling of actors in terms of their ability to exert influence. For example, the person with manifest influence may simply exhaust his or her resources and hence be left without influence when the next decision is made. Likewise, the person with potential influence, if he or she is wise and desires to do so, can often move into a position of manifest influence. On the other hand, those persons who have only reputed influence and those who have no influence at all are in a more precarious situation. Persons with reputed influence will try to avoid decision-making situations in which a "payoff" will be demanded from them. If it is discovered that they lack the ability to reward or sanction, their position will become that of persons without influence. Likewise, persons without influence have two choices open to them, i.e., they can attempt to gain resources or they can attempt to shift the issue or the mode of decision making to the point that they have resources to use. For example, if a certain building contractor cannot muster enough support among members of the city zoning commission to get a "ruling" in his favor, he may turn to the local mayor in the hopes that she will intervene on the contractor's behalf. In return for the mayor's help, the contractor may promise to deliver his employee's votes to the mayor during a forthcoming election.

Rather than attempting to classify types of leaders, Agger, Goldrich, and Swanson classify power structures themselves according to types.[52] They do this by cross-classifying two variables: (1) the degree to which the ideologies of local political leaders are compatible or conflicting and (2) the degree to which political power is distributed among local citizens. The result of cross-classifying these two variables is shown in Figure 8-3. In essence, there can be four types of power structure: the consensual mass, the consensual elite, the competitive mass, and the competitive elite. Basically, a power structure of the consensual mass type would correspond closely to the "democratic model" of community power, that is, key decision-making powers would rest in the hands of institutional leaders who are responsive to the suggestions, needs, and desires

[52] Robert E. Agger, Daniel Goldrich, and Bert E. Swanson, *The Rulers and the Ruled: Political Power and Impotence in American Communities* (New York: John Wiley & Sons, Inc., 1964), pp. 73–78.

| | | Distribution of Political Power Among Citizens | |
		Broad	Narrow
Political Leadership's Ideology	Convergent	Consensual Mass	Consensual Elite
	Divergent	Competitive Mass	Competitive Elite

FIGURE 8-3. Types of power structures. *[Source: Robert E. Agger, Daniel Goldrich, and Bert E. Swanson,* The Rulers and the Ruled: Political Power and Impotence in American Communities *(New York: John Wiley & Sons, Inc., 1964), p. 73.]*

of large numbers of local citizens. On the other hand, a power structure of the consensual elite variety would correspond to the "ruling elite" or "covert power elite" model that we have discussed previously. The other two types of power structure are a bit more difficult to visualize. Presumably, a power structure of the competitive elite variety would exist when the "elitist" leaders have become fragmented into two or more competing groups. Much the same would be true in regard to the competitive mass, except that more citizens would be involved. For example, the mayor might be exceptionally liberal whereas the city council might be dominated by a group of arch-conservatives. Presumably, large numbers of local citizens would align themselves with one or the other of these leadership factions.

Participation

It would be extremely interesting to know what percentage of the total population become involved in episodes of community action and what percentage occupy positions of leadership at the local level. Unfortunately, it is almost impossible to offer any ironclad generalizations concerning these questions. This is partly because adequate data relating to the extent of citizen participation in community action episodes are not available and partly because a number of contradictory statements have been made concerning the participation of Americans in community activities and associations. On the one hand, the idea has been propagated that Americans are pathological joiners. This idea can be traced back to a perceptive French observer of the American scene, Alexis de Tocqueville, who as early as the 1830s suggested that "in no country in the world has the principle of association been more successfully used or applied to a multitude of objects than in America." [53] On the other hand, one of the most common complaints voiced by community leaders is that

[53] Alexis de Tocqueville, *Democracy in America*, Vol. I (New York: Alfred A. Knopf, 1953), p. 191.

local citizens will not participate in community activities nor will they assume positions of leadership when they are given the opportunity to do so. The truth probably lies somewhere between these two extremes. For example, a 1974 survey of 1,484 respondents found that 36.2 per cent of them did not hold membership in any voluntary associations. On the other hand, 24.5 per cent of the respondents belonged to one voluntary association, 17.7 per cent belonged to two voluntary associations, and 21.7 per cent belonged to three or more voluntary associations.[54] These data hardly suggest that Americans are pathological joiners. At the same time, they certainly do not suggest that Americans are totally apathetic in regard to associational membership.

It is only in a very indirect manner that these data shed any light on the extent of citizen leadership and participation in community action episodes. They refer to associational memberships and not to participation in community activities. Nevertheless, on the basis of these data we might infer that citizen involvement in community action episodes is quite limited, a hypothesis that seems to be confirmed by the information that we do have at our disposal. Even in such emotion-packed episodes of community action as the 1967 riots in Detroit and Newark, our data indicate that approximately one half of those persons who might have become involved (48 to 53 per cent) remained aloof and noninvolved.[55] Likewise, the apparent apathy of American citizens in regard to community activities and events of a routinized nature, such as voting in local elections and participating in local government, has been noted many times. Harold Kaufman offers a realistic appraisal of the situation:

> The degree of involvement of a local population in the interactional community runs all the way from assuming a major role in policy making to no more than identification with the locality resulting from "residence and sustenance" activities. . . . It is likely that even in areas with the highest potential for community action, only a minority of the population is ever active at a given time.[56]

☐ SUMMARY

In this chapter we have reviewed some of the literature on community action, leadership, and involvement. The importance of this material lies

[54] See David Knoke and Randall Thomson, "Voluntary Association Membership Trends and the Family Life Cycle," *Social Forces*, **56** (September, 1977), esp. 54. Knoke and Thomson's data do not take church membership into account.
[55] National Advisory Commission on Civil Disorders, *Report of the National Advisory Commission on Civil Disorders*, p. 73.
[56] Kaufman, "Toward an Interactional Conception of Community," p. 11.

in the fact that it forces us to ask some rather significant questions about the dynamics of community life. It is important to understand decision-making processes as they occur at the community level and to know who makes those decisions that affect the entire community. Likewise, it is important to know something about the nature and types of community action and about the extent of citizen participation in episodes of community action.

It is hoped that this chapter has shed light on these matters. At the same time, it is clear that there are many unresolved problems in the study of community action, leadership, and involvement. For one thing, more adequate methods for delineating the universe of community actions must be developed. Until this is done, the concept of community championed by Harold F. Kaufman, Jiri Kolaja, Willis A. Sutton, Jr., and others will remain vague and ambiguous. Similarly, there is a real question whether it is worth pursuing further our studies of community power. It is possible that sociologists and political scientists have said about everything that can be said in response to the question "Who runs this community?" If sociologists and political scientists do continue to perform studies of community power, then they must refine their methodological approaches. At the present time, it appears that the findings of those who do research on community power and leadership are at least partly a product of their methodological approach. Specifically, the reputational approach yields different findings than does the issue area approach. Fortunately, technicalities of this type seem to work themselves out if the basic research problem is sound. Be this as it may, the students of community life whom we have considered in this chapter have raised important questions and developed some significant ideas, concepts, and hypotheses. Future researchers will benefit greatly from their successes and their failures.

BIBLIOGRAPHY

Agger, Robert E., Daniel Goldrich, and Bert E. Swanson. *The Rulers and the Ruled: Political Power and Impotence in American Communities.* New York: John Wiley & Sons, Inc., 1964.

Aiken, Michael, and Paul E. Mott. *The Structure of Community Power: An Anthology.* New York: Random House, Inc., 1970.

Barton, Allen. *Communities in Disaster: A Sociological Analysis of Collective Stress Situations.* Garden City, N.Y.: Doubleday, 1969.

Bell, Colin, and Howard Newby. *Community Studies: An Introduction to the Sociology of the Local Community.* New York: Praeger Publishers, 1972, esp. pp. 218–49.

Bonjean, Charles M., and David M. Olson. "Community Leadership: Directions of Research," *Administrative Science Quarterly*, 9 (December, 1964), 278–95.

Bruyn, Severyn T. *Communities in Action: Pattern and Process*. New Haven: College and University Press, Inc., 1963.

Clark, Terry N. (ed.). *Community Structure and Decision-Making: Comparative Analyses*. San Francisco: Chandler Publishing Company, 1968.

Conway, William J. "Economic Dominants and Community Power: A Reputational and Decisional Analysis," *The American Journal of Economics and Sociology*, 32 (July, 1973), 269–82.

Cumming, Elaine, and John Cumming. *Closed Ranks: An Experiment in Mental Health Education*. Cambridge, Mass.: Harvard University Press, 1957.

Curtis, James E., and John W. Petras. "Community Power, Power Studies, and the Sociology of Knowledge," *Human Organization*, 29 (Fall, 1970), 204–13.

Dahl, Robert A. *Who Governs?* New Haven: Yale University Press, 1961.

D'Antonio, William V., et al. "Institutional and Occupational Representation in Eleven Community Influence Systems," *American Sociological Review*, 26 (June, 1961), 440–46.

Form, William H., and Sigmund Nosow. *Community in Disaster*. New York: Harper & Row, 1958.

Freeman, Charles, and Selz C. Mayo. "Decision Makers in Rural Community Action," *Social Forces*, 35 (May, 1957), 319–22.

Freeman, Linton C., et al. "Locating Leaders in Local Communities: A Comparison of Some Alternative Approaches," *American Sociological Review*, 28 (October, 1963), 791–98.

Freilich, Morris. "Toward an Operational Definition of Community," *Rural Sociology*, 28 (June, 1963), 117–27.

Fuller, Richard C., and Richard R. Myers. "The Natural History of a Social Problem," *American Sociological Review*, 6 (June, 1941), 320–29.

Gilbert, Neil, Harry Specht, and Charlene Brown. "Demographic Correlates of Citizen Participation: An Analysis of Race, Community Size, and Citizen Influence," *The Social Service Review*, 48 (December, 1974), 517–30.

Green, James, and Selz Mayo. "A Framework for Research in the Actions of Community Groups," *Social Forces*, 31 (May, 1953), 320–27.

Hawley, Willis D., and Frederick M. Wirt (eds.). *The Search for Community Power*, Englewood Cliffs, N.J.: Prentice-Hall, Inc., 1968.

Holland, John B., Kenneth E. Tiedke, and Paul A. Miller. "A Theoretical Model for Health Action," *Rural Sociology*, 22 (June, 1957), 149–55.

Hunter, Floyd, et al. *Community Organization: Action and Inaction*. Chapel Hill: University of North Carolina Press, 1956.

———. *Community Power Structure: A Study of Decision Makers*. Chapel Hill: University of North Carolina Press, 1953.

Kaufman, Harold F. "Community Influentials: Power Figures or Leaders?" *Journal of the Community Development Society*, 6 (Spring, 1975), 71–87.

———. "Toward an Interactional Conception of Community," *Social Forces*, 38 (October, 1959), 9–17.

Kimball, Solon T., and Marion Pearsall. *The Talladega Story: A Study in Community Process.* University: University of Alabama Press, 1954.

Knoke, David, and Randall Thomson. "Voluntary Association Membership Trends and the Family Life Cycle," *Social Forces,* **56** (September, 1977), esp. 54.

Kornhauser, William. "Power and Participation in the Local Community," *Health Education Monographs,* No. 6 (Oakland, Calif.: Society of Public Health Educators, 1959), 28–37.

Long, Norton E. "The Local Community as an Ecology of Games," in Roland L. Warren, *New Perspectives of the American Community: A Book of Readings* (Chicago: Rand McNally & Company, 1977), pp. 58–72.

Lowry, Richie P. *Who's Running This Town?* New York: Harper & Row, 1965.

Magill, Robert S., and Terry N. Clark. "Community Power and Decision Making: Recent Research and Its Policy Implications," *The Social Service Review,* **49** (March, 1975), 33–45.

Mair, Henry W. *Challenge to the Cities: An Approach to a Theory of Urban Leadership.* New York: Random House, Inc., 1966.

McPhail, Clark. "Civil Disorder Participation: A Critical Examination of Recent Research," *American Sociological Review,* **36** (December, 1971), 1058–73.

Merton, Robert K. *Social Theory and Social Structure,* rev. and enlarged ed. New York: The Free Press, 1957, esp. pp. 387–420.

Miller, Delbert C. "Industry and Community Power Structure: A Comparative Study of an American and an English City," *American Sociological Review,* **23** (February, 1958), 8–15.

Miller, Paul A. "The Process of Decision Making Within the Context of Community Organization," *Rural Sociology,* **17** (June, 1952), 153–61.

Pieper, Hanns G., Nicholas A. Holt, and H. Max Miller. "Community Leaders and Followers," *The Southeastern Review,* **2** (Fall, 1974–75), 8–9, 31.

Ploch, Louis A. "Community Development in Action: A Case Study," *Journal of the Community Development Society,* **7** (Spring, 1976), 5–16.

Polsby, Nelson W. *Community Power and Political Theory.* New Haven: Yale University Press, 1963.

Smith, Richard A. "Community Power and Decision Making: A Replication and Extension of Hawley," *American Sociological Review,* **41** (August, 1976), 691–705.

Sower, Christopher, et al. *Community Involvement: The Webs and Informal Ties That Make for Action.* New York: The Free Press, 1957.

Sutton, Willis A., Jr. "Toward a Universe of Community Actions," *Sociological Inquiry,* **34** (Winter, 1964), 48–59.

———, and Jiri Kolaja. "The Concept of Community," *Rural Sociology,* **25** (June, 1960), 197–203.

———. "Elements of Community Action," *Social Forces,* **38** (May, 1960), 325–31.

Vogt, Evon Z., and Thomas F. O'Dea. "A Comparative Study of the Role of Values in Social Action in Two Southwestern Communities," *American Sociological Review,* **18** (December, 1953), 645–54.

Walter, Benjamin. "Political Decision Making in Arcadia," in F. Stuart Chapin, Jr., and Shirley F. Weiss (eds.), *Urban Growth Dynamics.* New York: John Wiley & Sons, Inc., 1962.

Walton, John. "'Community Power and the Retreat from Politics: Full Circle after Twenty Years?" *Social Problems,* **23** (February, 1976), 408–17.

Wildavsky, Aaron. *Leadership in a Small Town.* Totowa, N.J.: Bedminster Press, 1964.

Wilkinson, Kenneth P. "A Behavioral Approach to Measurement and Analysis of Community Field Structure," *Rural Sociology,* **39** (Summer, 1974), 247–55.

———. "The Community as a Social Field," *Social Forces,* **48** (March, 1970), 311–22.

———. "Phases and Roles in Community Action," *Rural Sociology,* **35** (March, 1970), 54–67.

Williams, Anne S. "Leadership Patterns in the Declining Rural Community," *Journal of the Community Development Society,* **6** (Fall, 1975), 98–106.

Wolfinger, Raymond E. "Reputation and Reality in the Study of Community Power," *American Sociological Review,* **25** (October, 1960), 636–44.

CHAPTER 9

□□□□□□□□□
□
□
□
□
□
□
□
□
□

Community Change and Community Problems

There are many unknowns in community study. However, two things may be said with absolute certainty. First, during recent years most communities have been undergoing continuous and rapid social change. These changes have entailed, among other things, modification in their demographic characteristics, ecological layout, economic structure, and organizational patterns. Second, most modern communities, like their ancient predecessors, have been plagued by a host of economic, demographic, ecological, and social problems. Included among these problems have been overcrowding, blight, poverty, and unrest in urban areas and depopulation and economic decline in many rural areas. Communities of all sizes share problems of crime and delinquency, mental illness, and racial conflict.

There is a two-way relationship between social change and social problems. On the one hand, social problems result from social change, especially when it is rapid and incessant. Robert Dentler, for example, reminds us that "vast social change produces vast social problems and these get magnified at the level of local communities." [1] Of more importance, however, is the fact that community problems can be solved only through yet further social change. Indeed, the word *solve* implies that conditions are changed to the extent that the problem disappears or subsides in importance. Thus a few of the problems that are faced by American communities will solve themselves with the passage of time. Most of them will be solved only through concerted, rational efforts to correct the problematic situation.

[1] Robert A. Dentler, *American Community Problems* (New York: McGraw-Hill Book Company, 1968), p. 94.

☐ TYPES OF COMMUNITY CHANGE

We have inferred that there are two types of community change. Thus one type of community change results from conscious efforts to modify one or more facets of community life. An example would be the efforts of a city planner to improve patterns of traffic flow in a congested city. The term *planned change* encompasses these types of activity. On the other hand, many of the changes that occur at the local level are not purposefully instigated. Sometimes people may indeed be the "victims" rather than the instigators of community change. We refer to the latter as *unplanned change*.

In distinguishing unplanned from planned community change, we are not suggesting that it is only the latter that results from human activity. Rather, we are suggesting that some types of change (i.e., planned) result from a deliberate effort to modify community life whereas other types of change are the unanticipated by-product of human activity and interaction. The only type of change that fits neither of these categories is the change caused by events beyond human control, such as natural disasters. All other types of change are a product of human activity, regardless of whether the activity is intended to bring about change or not.

This is not to deny that a two-way relationship sometimes exists between planned and unplanned change. We have already suggested that unplanned change frequently gives rise to problems that can be solved only through carefully executed programs of planned change. Likewise, planned change can be an independent variable that brings in its wake a wide array of changes not anticipated when the planned change was instigated. The construction of superhighways, for example, sometimes has an adverse impact on the economic prosperity of the small communities that are bypassed. However, it is not the goal of state highway departments to put small roadside establishments out of business.[2]

☐ UNPLANNED CHANGE AND THE MODERN AMERICAN COMMUNITY

Almost every observer of American community life has a favorite list of changes that have occurred at the local level.[3] Among those most fre-

[2] Similarly, decisions made by industries and large business firms can have a devastating impact on the economic prosperity of communities. For a fascinating case study see W. F. Cottrell, "Death by Dieselization: A Case Study in the Reaction to Technological Change," in Robert Mills French (ed.), *The Community: A Comparative Perspective* (Itasca, Ill.: F. E. Peacock Publishers, 1969), pp. 485–96.

[3] For example, see Irwin T. Sanders, *The Community: An Introduction to a Social*

quently mentioned are the growing impersonality and bureaucratization of community life, the growing complexity of the community as an ecological entity, and the continued spread of industrialization to virtually every village, city, and metropolitan area. However, if we were forced to identify the one change that has had a greater impact on American community life than all others it would have to be the continued spread of urbanization. One hundred years ago most Americans lived on farms or in small agricultural villages. Today the city or the metropolitan area is home for most Americans.

Urbanization and Urbanism

There is considerable confusion in the literature concerning the meaning of the terms *urbanization* and *urbanism.* Thus in discussing these two concepts an eminent sociologist, Robert Bierstedt, tells us that "it is instructive, but hardly encouraging, to note that distinguished books in the field of urban sociology use them in exactly opposite senses." [4]

In this book the term *urbanization* will be used to refer to two different processes. First, we shall use the term *urbanization* to refer to the clustering of population in large cities. This clustering can be brought about by an excess of births over deaths in cities, by migration from rural areas to the city, or by emigration from one country into the cities of another country (e.g., from Mexico to Los Angeles). Second, we shall also use the term *urbanization* to refer to the processes by which ruralities increasingly take on values, attitudes, and life-styles similar to those held by people in large cities. We shall have more to say about this type of urbanization in a minute.

The term *urbanism,* on the other hand, refers to the ways of thinking and acting that characterize people who live in large cities: "it is the human side of urbanization, the way of life of the city." [5] In Chapter 2 of this book we discussed in some detail the characteristics that seem to be associated with urbanism. Among other things, it was suggested that urbanism is characterized by anonymity, a reliance on secondary mechanisms of social control, heterogeneity, a high division of labor, and the ranking of individuals on the basis of overt symbols of status.

The process of urbanization does not necessarily bring urbanism in its

System, 3rd ed. (New York: The Ronald Press, 1975), pp. 244–46; Roland L. Warren, *The Community in America,* 2nd ed. (Chicago: Rand McNally & Company, 1972), pp. 53–94.

[4] Robert Bierstedt, *The Social Order,* 2nd ed. (New York: McGraw-Hill Book Company, 1963), p. 415.

[5] *Encyclopedia of Sociology* (Guilford, Conn.: The Dushkin Publishing Group, 1974), p. 300.

wake. Rather, even a very large city may be essentially "rural" in terms of the attitudes, values, and life-styles of its people. For example, J. John Palen has provided us with a revealing description of Addis Ababa, the capital of Ethiopia.[6] In 1973, the estimated population of Addis Ababa was 1,025,800. Yet the city has retained a distinctly rural culture, even though it is both the capital and the headquarters of the United Nations Economic Commission for Africa and the Organization of African Unity. Certainly Addis Ababa appears to be less "urban" in terms of the attitudes, values, and behavioral patterns of its people than a relatively small American city, such as Albany, New York (1970 population about 114,000).

In the remainder of this chapter we shall be concerned almost exclusively with the process of urbanization. Our first task will be to explain why urbanization has occurred. After that, we shall look at how some of the problems that seem to be associated with rapid urbanization might be ameliorated.

Urbanization in America. That urbanization has been the key change process that has occurred at the community level, at least in the United States, may be so clear as to require no further elaboration: the last one hundred years have marked the entrance of the United States into the urban world. Table 9-1 presents an overview of the extent to which the U.S. population has become urbanized since 1860; Figure 9-1 presents these same data in graph form. The meaning of these data is entirely clear. Today, in contrast to years gone past, the "statistically average" American is an urbanite who lives in a community that is both large and complex.

In Chapter 2 we pointed out that during the last few years small cities and areas that are technically classified as rural have been growing more rapidly than large metropolitan centers: in a sense there has been a "back to small towns" movement. However, there are two things that should be noted about "ex-metropolitanites." First, most of them are not moving to small, isolated rural communities. Rather, they are moving to smaller but diversified communities that are adjacent to large cities and metropolitan areas. Second, the bulk of these people are not going back to the old family farm. Walter J. Cartwright puts the case well when he suggests that we must examine "more closely the 27 percent of the population classified as rural in the 1970 census." Cartwright goes on to explain that

---

[6] See J. John Palen, *The Urban World* (New York: McGraw-Hill Book Company, 1975), pp. 377–81.

This figure includes many people who are *urban* in orientation and out-look. Lest it be assumed by students that this 27 percent consists mostly of farmers, it can be pointed out that less than 5 percent of the total population were employed in agriculture in 1970, when, incidentally, agriculture had become more productive than ever before. Who then makes up the 27 percent? In addition to farmers there are certain service workers such as operators of crossroads stores, automobile dealers, and farm equipment dealers. But there are also such *urban types* as artists' colonies, the operators of ski resorts, hunting and fishing lodges, seashore vacation resorts, and other recreational facilities intended for the *urban-ite* . . . a term paper could be based on this large *urban oriented* portion of the rural population.[7]

In sum, it seems highly unlikely that the "back to small towns" movement will halt or even slow down the urbanization of American society. In the present writer's opinion, it seems totally unreasonable to think that future textbooks on the community will contain sections or chapters on "the ruralization of American society."

The data cited in Table 9-1 refer only to the clustering of population in cities and metropolitan areas. However, we have already pointed out that "the term *urbanization* is sometimes used to denote much more than a population concentration. It denotes a process of urban culture dominance in the making."[8] This same idea is expressed by Nels Anderson:

> There is also the nonmigration aspect of urbanization; one can be ur-banized by going to the city, but urbanization can also come to him in a non-urban place. In this sense, urbanism is outward reaching. People may be urbanized without migrating to cities and without changing from agricultural to non-agricultural work.[9]

The type of urbanization to which Cole and Anderson refer has, to a great extent, swept the United States. Even though it may be a bit of an overgeneralization, J. John Palen basically puts the case well when he says that

> the cultural patterns of most of the supposedly rural areas of the United States are today clearly dominated by urban values, urban attitudes,

[7] Walter J. Cartwright, *Instructor's Manual to Accompany Dennis E. Poplin, Social Problems* (Glenview, Ill.: Scott, Foresman and Company, 1978), p. 6. Italics added.
[8] William E. Cole, *Urban Society* (Boston: Houghton Mifflin Company, 1958), p. 7. Italics in original.
[9] Nels Anderson, "The Urban Way of Life," *International Journal of Comparative Sociology,* 3 (September, 1962), 176–77.

Table 9-1. Percentage of the Total U.S. Population Living in Urban (over 2,500 population) and Rural (under 2,500) Places, 1860 to 1970

	Urban	Rural
1970	73.5	26.5
1960	69.9	30.1
1950 *	64.0	36.0
1940	56.5	43.5
1930	56.2	43.8
1920	51.2	48.8
1910	45.7	54.3
1900	39.7	60.3
1890	35.1	64.9
1880	28.2	71.8
1870	25.7	74.3
1860	19.8	80.2

* In 1950 the U.S. Bureau of Census modified its definition of urban. This accounts for 5 per cent of the increase between 1940 and 1950.
Source: U.S. Bureau of the Census, *Census of the Population: 1960*, Pt. I, *U.S. Summary* (Washington, D.C.: U.S. Government Printing Office, 1964), Table 3. Figures for 1970 taken from U.S. Bureau of the Census, *1970 Census of Population*, Vol. I, *Final Population Counts: U.S. Advanced Report* (Washington, D.C.: U.S. Government Printing Office, 1971), Table 2.

and urban life-styles. Rural dairy farmers, wheat growers, and cattlemen, with their professional lobbies and subsidies, are all part of a complex and highly integrated economic and social system which is essentially urban.[10]

This does not mean that predominantly rural cultures have completely disappeared from the American scene. They are still to be found in parts of the intermountain west, in Appalachia, in parts of the south and upper midwest, and so on.

Although urbanization seems to be the most important type of change affecting American community life today, the present writer is not blind to other types of community change. What one defines as significant in terms of social change depends a great deal on one's frame of reference. Thus a human ecologist might argue that the most significant change that has occurred in American communities since 1960 has been the increased

[10] Palen, *The Urban World*, pp. 7–8.

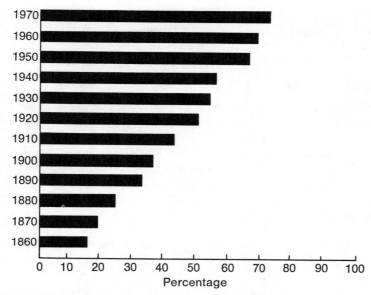

FIGURE 9-1. Percentage of total U.S. population living in urban places, 1860 to 1970. *[Source: U.S. Bureau of the Census,* Census of Population: 1960, *Pt. 1,* U.S. Summary *(Washington, D.C.: U.S. Government Printing Office, 1964), Table 3. Figures for 1970 taken from U.S. Bureau of the Census, 1970* Census of Population, *Vol. I,* Final Population Counts: U.S. Advanced Report *(Washington, D.C.: U. S. Government Printing Office, 1971), Table 2.]*

segregation of racial groups from one another,[11] but an industrial sociologist would maintain that industrialization is the most fundamental type of change occurring at the local level. However, it must be remembered that our interest lies in the community as a social system rather than in the groups of which it is composed or in the larger society of which it is a part. Seemingly, the increased segregation of racial groups from one another is properly studied by specialists in human ecology, whereas industrialization is properly studied by industrial sociologists and by economists. Furthermore, it might be noted that one type of change can be explained only by reference to another type of change.[12] Is it not safe to assume that urbanization itself has stimulated many of the changes that have occurred on the intracommunity level, including increased racial segregation? Likewise, can it not also be assumed that urbanization

[11] See Reynolds Farley and Karl E. Taeuber, "Population Trends and Residential Segregation Since 1960," *Science,* **159** (March 1, 1968), 653–56.
[12] Thus William F. Ogburn reminds us that "whenever a result occurs, something has varied." See his "How Technology Causes Social Change," in Francis R. Allen et al., *Technology and Social Change* (New York: Appleton-Century-Crofts, 1957), p. 12.

has been a by-product of various changes that have occurred at the societal level? One of these changes certainly has been the industrialization of American society.

Why Urbanization Has Occurred

If urbanization is in fact the most fundamental change affecting American community life, then our next task is to explain why it has occurred. It is widely agreed that the urbanization of American communities, as well as of communities throughout the world, has been stimulated by *the dual factors of improvement in agricultural technology and improvement in transportation and communication facilities.* The role these two factors have played in stimulating urbanization must be examined in greater detail.

Agricultural Technology. Several writers have observed that the emergence of cities and metropolitan areas had to await a revolution in agricultural productivity.[13] Throughout most of human history surplus agricultural commodities could not be produced in sufficient quantity to feed a large nonagricultural population. This meant that the majority of people had to work the soil. By March, 1968, however, 4.6 per cent of the total U.S. labor force (1.8 per cent of the total population) could produce enough to feed both the entire population of the United States and millions of people in other countries.[14] It is only under conditions similar to these that urbanization can occur.

Our increased ability to produce food and hence to support a large nonagricultural population can be traced to the dramatic modernization of agricultural technology that has occurred during recent years. In his analysis of the influence of technology on agriculture, for example, Delbert C. Miller points out that

> Through countless centuries, agriculture was carried on by hand labor, with only a few simple tools supplemented to a slight extent by animal power. The New England farmer of colonial times was dependent upon tools of the most primitive sort. His chief tools were the harrow, a spade, and a fork, all made of wood and clumsily constructed. Few could afford a plow, and a town often paid a bounty to anyone who would buy a

[13] See National Resources Committee, *Our Cities: Their Role in the National Economy* (Washington, D.C.: National Resources Committee, 1937), p. 29; Gideon Sjoberg, *The Preindustrial City: Past and Present* (New York: The Free Press, 1960), pp. 28–30.
[14] Calculated from U.S. Bureau of the Census, *Statistical Abstract of the United States: 1968* (Washington, D.C.: U.S. Government Printing Office, 1968), Tables 2 and 310.

plow and keep it in repair. One plow would be used to do the work for a large territory.[15]

Urbanization on a massive scale cannot occur when methods of farming are this primitive: most able-bodied people have to cultivate the soil. This means, in turn, that the population must be dispersed over the land and that only a small percentage of the population can cluster in cities. However, the nineteenth century ushered in an era of innovation in agricultural technology. Among the most significant breakthroughs were the mechanization of farm equipment, the improvement of plants and animals through selective breeding, and the development of scientific methods of insect control and soil replenishment.[16] Once these and related developments had occurred, the urbanization of America could also occur. Millions of people were released from agricultural endeavors and eventually found their way to the city.

At first, the statements contained in the preceding paragraph might appear to be contradicted by the great cities of the medieval era. What is often forgotten, however, is that these cities were very small by today's standards (see Table 9-2). Indeed, it has been suggested that Rome—by far the largest city of its time—probably had a population of no more than 350,000 in the first century A.D.[17] In other words, the "huge," "sprawling" cities of antiquity were neither huge nor sprawling. J. John Palen puts the point across when he says that "as late as the beginning of the nineteenth century, the produce of nine farms was still required to support one urban family. (Today each American farmer supports approximately forty-five other persons.)" [18]

This is not to deny, of course, that today large cities are located in countries where methods of farming are still extremely "crude" or "primi-

---

[15] Delbert C. Miller, "Impact of Technology on Agriculture," in Allen et al., *Technology and Social Change*, p. 327.

[16] For further discussion of these and related developments see ibid., pp. 326–35. Some of these developments have, of course, turned out to be a mixed blessing. For example, in some cases the use of pesticides such as DDT has led to the pollution of water supplies and has constituted a threat to the health (or even lives) of fish, birds, cattle, and even human beings. Similarly, agricultural technologies that are suited to one culture or one type of terrain may not be suited to another culture or type of terrain. Thus a huge John Deere tractor is of little use to a peasant farmer who tries to eke out enough to feed his family on one acre of mountainous, rocky land. For an insightful discussion along these same lines see John N. Andromedas and Russell E. Lewis, "Appropriate Technology, Energetics, and Draft Animals" (Paper presented to the Annual Meeting of the American Anthropological Association, Houston, Texas, 1977).

[17] William Petersen, *Population*, 3rd ed. (New York: Macmillan Publishing Co., Inc., 1975), p. 408.

[18] Palen, *The Urban World*, p. 33.

Table 9-2. Population Estimates of Some Large Medieval European Cities

City	Date of Estimate	Population
London	{1086 {1377	{18,000 {35,000
Milan	13th century	52,000
Naples	1278	27,000
Paris	1292	59,000
Padua	1320	41,000
Bruges	1340	25,000
Ghent	1356	60,000
Venice	1363	78,000
Bologna	1371	32,000
Florence	{1381 {1424	{55,000 {37,000
Nuremberg	1449	23,000
Bourges	1487	32,000
Genoa	early 16th century	38,000
Barcelona	1514	31,000
Rome	1526	55,000

Adapted from William Petersen, *Population*, 3rd ed. (New York: Macmillan Publishing Co., Inc., 1975), Table 11-1.

tive" by our standards. One thinks immediately, for example, of the huge cities of India. It is well to remember, however, that many of these cities, and the countries in which they are located, almost yearly face massive food shortages. They are cities, and societies, in which starvation runs rampant.

Industrialization and Urbanization. We have suggested that before people could cluster in cities to any great extent there had to be an increase in agricultural productivity. However, Gist and Fava have gone one step further and suggested that "the Agricultural Revolution made it possible for cities to exist and that the Industrial Revolution made it possible for cities to dominate the world." [19] In other words, without industrialization cities would have appeared and did so, but they probably could not have achieved the size of a modern-day Tokyo, New York, or London.

Basically, industrialization contributed to urbanization in at least two

[19] Noel P. Gist and Sylvia Fleis Fava, *Urban Society*, 6th ed. (New York: Thomas Y. Crowell Company, 1974), p. 27.

different ways. First, it created jobs: "to the factories in towns and cities
. . . flocked rural people, attracted not only by the novelty of city life
but also by the possibilities of greater economic rewards." [20] Second, the
industrial revolution helped to stimulate the revolution in agricultural
productivity that occurred in the nineteenth and twentieth centuries.
Major increases in agricultural productivity had to await the invention of
steam, electric, and gasoline engines as sources of power for agricultural
machinery and the development of applied chemistry, horticulture, and
agronomy. Likewise, a modern factory system was required before trac-
tors, harvesters, plows, and other tools could be produced in sufficient
quantity to meet the needs of modern agriculture.

Hence urbanization in the United States was the end result of a long,
complex chain of developments: the urbanization of American communities was stimulated by a revolution in agricultural technology, and
this revolution in agricultural technology was a part of the larger industrial revolution. It might be noted in passing that this account of
urbanization reflects the general approach to the explanation of social
and cultural change that was developed by William F. Ogburn.[21]
Basically, Ogburn argued that social and cultural changes, especially
those that involve a technological variable, occur in such a way that
change 1 stimulates change 2, change 2 stimulates change 3, and so on.
This, of course, is essentially what we have said about urbanization, i.e.,
the processes of urbanization that are sweeping the world today had their
roots in the industrial revolution.

Transportation and Communication. Our increased ability to produce
agricultural commodities helps to account for one facet of urbanization
in the United States, i.e., the growth of large cities. Nonetheless, our explanation of urbanization still suffers from two serious deficiencies. First,
other factors had to be combined with increases in agricultural productivity before the concentration of population in large cities became
possible. One of these factors was the development of efficient methods
of transportation.[22] Increased agricultural productivity is of little con-

[20] Ibid., p. 31.
[21] Ogburn, "How Technology Causes Social Change," in Allen et al., *Technology and
Social Change,* p. 20. The student who is particularly interested in technology and
its bearing on social and cultural change should become acquainted with Ogburn's
work. See especially his *Social Change* (New York: B. W. Huebsh, 1922). A 1950
edition of this work with a supplementary chapter has been published by the Viking
Press of New York. For a compilation of his more significant articles see William F.
Ogburn, *On Culture and Social Change,* edited and with an introduction by Otis
Dudley Duncan (Chicago: University of Chicago Press, 1964).
[22] An excellent discussion of the relationship between transportation and urban
development is contained in Harlan W. Gilmore, *Transportation and the Growth of*

241

sequence in hastening urbanization unless there are means by which agricultural products can be transported to the city.[23] Second, as it now stands our explanation of urbanization accounts only for the movement of people to cities. It does not tell us why rural people themselves have, in a real sense, become urbanized. In this connection it seems safe to suggest that the degree to which rural people become urbanized depends a great deal on the development of transportation and communications facilities; if transportation and communication facilities become highly developed, the differences between rural and urban people tend to disappear. In reality this is a simple generalization about a specific type of social change. It suggests that changes in the social and cultural patterns that characterize rural areas result from innovation in systems of transportation and communication.

There are numerous shreds of evidence that seem to support this generalization. Thus, in discussing the influence of the highway and, by implication, the automobile on rural life, Firey, Loomis, and Beegle suggest that

> Now more than ever before the farm family can participate in "the larger society" which is borne by metropolitan newspapers, urban recreational facilities, urban libraries and schools, and many other points of contact unknown to the nineteenth-century country dweller. Organizations and activities once the prerogative of the urbanite are now just as accessible to the ruralite. . . . Highways, in short, have made the rural population more cosmopolitan.[24]

Of even greater importance has been the development of motion pictures, radio, and television. With the emergence of these media of communication, the rural dweller has, in most cases, become a full participant in the urban society that now engulfs the United States. The era when the United States was characterized by two distinctly different societies, one rural and one urban, has almost passed.

Cities (New York: The Free Press, 1953). See also Avery M. Guest, "Ecological Succession in the Puget Sound Region," *Journal of Urban History,* 3 (February, 1977), 181–210.

[23] Thus Gilmore points out that "even if area A has sufficient surplus to support the population of area B, unless the transportation system can transport these goods, as far as B is concerned, the surplus of A does not effectively exist." Ibid., p. 137.

[24] Walter Firey, Charles J. Loomis, and J. Allan Beegle, "The Fusion of Urban and Rural," in *Highways in Our National Life: A Symposium,* ed. by Jean Labutut and Wheaton J. Lane (Princeton, N.J.: Princeton University Press, 1950), p. 160. See also Allen, "The Automobile," in Allen et al., *Technology and Social Change,* p. 126, who reminds us that "interaction with urban dwellers, coupled with an extension of the radio, TV, and other inventions to the rural scene, has tended to urbanize some of the rural dweller's attitudes."

Urbanization and Its Derivations

Enough has been said to make it clear that the urbanization of American communities has been made possible by increased agricultural productivity and by the development of modern transportation and communication facilities. At the same time, it is equally clear that urbanization has had its own derivative effects and has itself brought about change in other facets of community life. Some of the effects of urbanization on American community life were discussed in Chapter 2 when we considered Wirth's analysis of urbanism as a way of life. However, the changes that occur as a community undergoes urbanization are not always considered to be desirable. Urbanization often brings in its wake problems of congestion and overcrowding, a wide variety of conditions that adversely affect human welfare, and difficulties in providing adequate governmental, educational, health, and welfare services.

The present writer is entirely aware that definitions of social, including urban, problems are relative and that one must always keep things in perspective. Edward C. Banfield, for example, is undoubtedly correct when he says that

> the plain fact is that the overwhelming majority of city dwellers live more comfortably and conveniently than ever before. They have more and better housing, more and better schools, more and better transportation, and so on. By any conceivable measure of material welfare the present generation of urban Americans is, on the whole, better off than any other large group of people has ever been anywhere. What is more, there is every reason to expect that the general level of comfort and convenience will continue to rise at an even more rapid rate through the foreseeable future.[25]

Nonetheless, many sociologists take the position that "a social problem exists when there is a sizeable discrepancy between what is and what people think ought to be." [26] Even though American urbanites may be better off now than ever before, millions of them nonetheless feel that many of our cities are less than desirable places to live, work, and play. Hence we must now examine some different types of planned community change and determine how they can be used to ameliorate community problems.

[25] Edward C. Banfield, *The Unheavenly City Revisited* (Boston: Little, Brown and Company, 1974), pp. 1–2.
[26] Robert K. Merton and Robert Nisbet, *Contemporary Social Problems,* 4th ed. (New York: Harcourt Brace Jovanovich, Inc., 1976), p. 7.

☐ TYPES OF PLANNED COMMUNITY CHANGE

City planning, community organization, and *community action and development* are three terms that frequently crop up in discussions of planned community change. Although these terms are sometimes used interchangeably, they refer to different processes of planned change that are used to cope with different types of problems.

City Planning

The city planner pursues several different goals. Therefore, the nature of city planning is somewhat difficult to specify. Nevertheless, the term *city planning* usually refers to the process by which cities and metropolitan areas are rehabilitated and renovated, as well as guided in their future development, as physical entities.[27] Problems of traffic congestion and inadequate transportation facilities, urban deterioration and blight, slum housing and suburban sprawl all come within the purview of the city planner. In attempting to cope with these and related problems, most city planners are concerned not only with the improvement of existing conditions but also with preventing new problems from arising as the urban area continues to grow. In addition, city planners from time to time may help to design entirely new communities, such as Radburn, New Jersey, and Greenbelt, Maryland.[28]

Although city planning focuses on the physical and ecological dimensions of urban problems, a growing number of city planners have voiced the idea that their activities are but a means to a larger end. In reviewing the assumptions on which city planning has traditionally rested, for example, Melvin M. Webber points out that

> For generations it has been generally understood that the physical environment was a major determinant of social behavior and a direct contributor to individuals' welfare. Having accepted professional responsibility for the physical environment, the city planner was thus accorded

[27] Lloyd Rodwin says essentially the same thing when he indicates that "The city planner is the professional advisor and diagnostician on the physical environment of the city—and especially on the problems and on the methods of making plans and of establishing a framework for public and private decisions affecting the physical environment." See his article "The Roles of the City Planner in the Community," in Charles R. Adrian (ed.), *Social Science and Community Action* (East Lansing: Michigan State University Press, 1960), p. 48.

[28] For a discussion of new communities see Chapter 3. See also Paul K. Conkin, *Tomorrow a New World: The New Deal Community Program* (Ithaca, N.Y.: Cornell University Press, 1959), esp. Part III; Arthur Hillman, *Community Organization and Planning* (New York: Macmillan Publishing Co., Inc., 1950), esp. pp. 111–20.

a key role as agent of human welfare: the clearly prescribed therapy for the various social pathologies was improvement of the physical setting. If only well-designed and well-sited houses, playgrounds, and community facilities could be substituted for the crowded and dilapidated housing and neighborhoods of the city's slum, then the incidence of crime, delinquency, narcotics addiction, alcoholism, broken homes, and mental illness would tumble.[29]

It is now recognized that the improvement of the city as a physical entity will not by itself solve all the problems faced by urban dwellers. This means that modern city planners are best viewed as members of one among several professions that can contribute to the solution of urban problems. Interest has been renewed in the bearing of physical planning on the achievement of the nation's broader health, welfare, and educational goals.[30]

A Brief History of City Planning.[31] City planning of one kind or another is probably as old as the city itself. As people began to cluster in cities there were certain conditions that had to be met if life in an urban milieu was to be both safe and pleasant. Among other things, streets had to be designed so as to allow access to public facilities and gathering places, and provisions had to be made for defending the city against armed attack: the latter requirement gave rise to the walled city and to the hilltop city built around a citadel. Likewise, more than one ruler ordered the construction of temples and other public buildings that stood as monuments to his own power, beneficence, and foresight. As a result, many of the great cities of antiquity were characterized by carefully planned buildings, parks, monuments, and plazas. Some of these cities retain their magnificence to this day.

The colonial period of American history was marked by a healthy interest in city planning.[32] Perhaps the most noteworthy attempt to create a fully planned city in the United States was that proposed by Major Pierre Charles L'Enfant for Washington, D.C. L'Enfant visualized

[29] Melvin M. Webber, "Comprehensive Planning and Social Responsibility," *Journal of the American Institute of Planners,* 29 (November, 1963), 233.
[30] See ibid., pp. 232–41; Harvey S. Perloff, "Common Goals and the Linking of Physical and Social Planning," in American Society for Planning Officials and the Community Planning Association of Canada, *Planning, 1965* (Chicago: American Society of Planning Officials, 1965), pp. 170–84.
[31] The following summary is necessarily very brief. For a beautifully prepared history of city planning in the United States see John W. Reps, *The Making of Urban America: A History of City Planning in America* (Princeton: Princeton University Press, 1965).
[32] See ibid., especially Chapters 2–7.

nothing less than a city of beauty and magnificence. It would be marked by spaciousness, broad garden-lined avenues radiating from central squares, and the balanced placement of public buildings, statues, fountains, and waterways.[33] Unfortunately, L'Enfant's ambitious plan did not reach maturation,[34] nor did similarly ambitious plans for Buffalo, Detroit, Indianapolis, and several other cities. There were several reasons for this, but the most important one seems to have been the failure of government to curb the ambitions of greedy landowners and speculators. To these individuals land and its development represented a means by which one could acquire private wealth rather than a precious commodity to be developed and used for the public good. Glabb explains the situation very well when he states that "in the struggle between the speculator and the architect, the planner, or the visionary, the speculator ordinarily won."[35] As a result, by the middle of the nineteenth century American cities did not bear the marks of planned beauty, efficiency, and order. Rather, they bore the marks of a society that had allowed considerations of private gain to determine the architecture of its buildings, the quality of its housing, the location of its public facilities, and the layout of its transportation routes.

Modern city planning emerged as a response to the deterioration and decay that has engulfed many of our cities. Although the history of modern city planning is long and involved, there are several landmarks that should be mentioned. One of these, the emergence of city planning as a professional endeavor, is usually traced to 1917. It was during this year that the American Institute of Planners, the major professional organization to which city planners belong, was founded. At the time of its inception, this organization had twenty-four members: as of 1965 it had a membership of approximately 4,000.[36]

Another significant development has been the growing involvement of the federal government in attempts to cope with the physical problems facing our cities. One particularly important piece of legislation in this regard was the Housing Act of 1949. This act, which was an outgrowth of earlier legislation, authorized the federal government to provide grants

---

[33] Charles N. Glabb and A. Theodore Brown, A History of Urban America (New York: Macmillan Publishing Co., Inc., 1967), pp. 251–53.

[34] See Lewis Mumford, The City in History: Its Origins, Its Transformations, and Its Prospects (New York: Harcourt Brace Jovanovich, Inc., 1961), pp. 403–9. For an on-the-spot assessment of the difficulties encountered in making L'Enfant's plan a reality see "Modifications of the Washington Plan (Nicholas King to Thomas Jefferson, September 25, 1803)," in Charles N. Glabb, The American City: A Documentary History (Homewood, Ill.: The Dorsey Press, 1963), pp. 38–42.

[35] Ibid., p. 34.

[36] American Institute of Planners, A Challenging Career for You: Urban Planning (Washington, D.C.: American Institute of Planners, 1965).

and loans to cities for the purpose of acquiring and redeveloping blighted residential areas.[37] It also made federal loans available to cities for the purpose of developing previously unused land. The federal government has made direct subsidies to low-income people in an effort to help them buy or rent decent housing, and it has helped to finance public housing projects, the construction of modern transportation facilities, and so on. These programs have met with varying degrees of success: some of them have been dismal failures. For example, in many cases our public housing projects have simply further ghettoized the poor and the disadvantaged. One of the most colossal failures in this regard was the Pruitt-Igoe project that was completed in St. Louis in 1955. This was a massive housing project that consisted of thirty-three buildings, each of which was eleven stories high. However, because of poor planning and inadequate funding, Pruitt-Igoe soon became completely unlivable, and "one by one, the buildings were simply abandoned by their tenants. Even the most down-and-out welfare recipients were unwilling to tolerate the degradation and the constant threat of personal danger." [38] As a result, in 1972 the Housing Authority blew up the two worst buildings. In 1973 the remaining buildings were demolished.[39]

Problems and Procedures in City Planning. City planning represents one means of bringing about planned community change. The competent city planner seeks through purposeful action to create a more satisfactory physical environment in which urbanites can live, work, and play. It is because of this that city planning is often viewed as a problem-solving profession along with social work, psychiatry, medicine, and the other helping professions.

To be more specific, there are several major problem areas of concern to city planners. First, they must wrestle continually with problems centering around transportation and traffic congestion. The private automobile is supreme in our society; as a result, our cities have become nerve-wracking asphalt jungles. This means that the city planner, along with traffic engineers, must engage in an endless search for new and more

[37] For a discussion of urban renewal and the 1949 housing act see Lawrence M. Friedman, *Government and Slum Housing: A Century of Frustration* (Chicago: Rand McNally & Company, 1968), esp. Chapter IV. The interested reader might also consult Herbert J. Gans, "The Failure of Urban Renewal: A Critique and Some Proposals," in Stephen Gale and Eric G. Moore (eds.), *The Manipulated City: Perspectives on Spatial Structure and Social Issues in Urban America* (Chicago: Maaroufa Press, 1975), pp. 199–212.
[38] Palen, *The Urban World*, p. 260.
[39] For a description and analysis of Pruitt-Igoe see Lee Rainwater, "The Lessons of Pruitt-Igoe," *The Public Interest* (Summer, 1967), 116–23; Lee Rainwater, *Behind Ghetto Walls* (Chicago: Aldine, 1970).

efficient methods of accommodating the ever-increasing volume of traffic.[40] Second, closely related to this problem is that of urban sprawl. William H. Whyte, for example, points out that "already huge patches of once green countryside have turned into vast, smog-filled deserts that are neither city, suburb, nor country, and each day—at the rate of 3,000 acres a day—more countryside is being bulldozed under." [41] The problems of urban sprawl and traffic congestion are completely intertwined. It was the automobile that made possible the suburbanization of American cities, and it is the automobile-driving suburbanite who both morning and night clogs our city streets and highways. Third, there is not a major city in the United States that has been completely exempt from problems of blight and deterioration, which manifest themselves in shabby slum housing, decayed buildings, and patches of unused land that become trash-strewn eyesores. Finally, there are many cities within which public facilities are woefully inadequate. Public buildings are inaccessible and overcrowded, parks and playgrounds fail to meet the needs of their users, and other public facilities are unsafe and/or outmoded.

There are several tools that city planners can use in their efforts to solve some of these problems. Usually the first step in city planning is to develop a comprehensive master plan. Very briefly, the master plan represents the planner's window to the future. Ideally, it is based on population projections, economic forecasts, and other estimates that give the planner some clue as to what will happen to the city as it continues to grow. The master plan of course should make specific proposals for the orderly development of unused land within the city. In addition, plans should be made for the improvement of transportation systems, the development and improvement of public facilities, and the rehabilitation of blighted areas. Last but not least, the master plan might well contain some proposals for beautifying the city, in addition to providing for the renovation of blighted and unsightly areas.[42]

Even the most carefully developed master plan is absolutely worthless unless some of its provisions can be implemented. However, the tools that the planner can use to achieve the goals outlined in the master plan are rather limited. About the most common method by which municipal

[40] For further discussion see Francis Bello, "The City and the Car," in The Editors of Fortune, The Exploding Metropolis (Garden City, N.Y.: Doubleday & Company, Inc., 1958), pp. 53–80; Lewis Mumford, The Highway and the City (New York: Mentor Books, 1963), esp. Chapter 22.
[41] William H. Whyte, Jr., "Urban Sprawl," in The Editors of Fortune, The Exploding Metropolis, p. 133.
[42] For a description of the typical master plan and a discussion of some of the limitations of master planning see Herbert J. Gans, "Regional and Urban Planning," in David Sills (ed.), International Encyclopedia of the Social Sciences (New York: Macmillan Publishing Co., Inc., 1968), Vol. XII, pp. 129–37.

governments attempt to assure the orderly development of land within their jurisdiction is through the enactment of zoning ordinances.[43] These ordinances simply specify the uses to which various tracts of land within the city may be put. One tract may be reserved for commercial development, another for light industry, a third for single-family dwelling units, and so forth. Ordinances of this type can be effective in achieving desirable community goals when they are used in conjunction with rigorously enforced building codes. Today many municipal governments have the power to set structural and safety standards for new buildings, and even to regulate architectural styles. These codes are enforced by requiring builders to obtain a building permit and by on-site inspections while construction is in progress. When zoning ordinances and building codes are used in combination, they allow the city and its planners (1) to control the uses to which urban lands are put and (2) to regulate the quality and appearance of buildings that are constructed within each zoning area.

Direct action is the other major tool that municipal governments can use in making the master plan a reality. The problems facing American cities will be ameliorated only if local governments, with the help of government at the state and federal levels, channel billions of dollars into well-conceived, well-thought-out programs to provide low-income people with decent housing and to provide the city with modern transportation systems and a variety of other public facilities. One tool that makes it possible for local government to carry out projects of this type is its right of eminent domain. Very briefly, this means that the government can requisition privately owned land, provided that its owner is paid a fair price. It is only through the exercise of this right that city government can acquire land for new highways, housing projects, parks, and other public facilities.

Obstacles to City Planning. The task of assuring the rational, orderly development of our cities and metropolitan areas is a difficult one.[44] Among other things, the city planner must constantly deal with vested interest groups. In most cities there are at least a few individuals who stand to lose if the master plan is implemented fully. This is particularly true in respect to slum clearance. Slum housing is frequently owned by

---

[43] For a thorough analysis of zoning in the United States see Richard F. Babcock, *The Zoning Game: Municipal Practices and Policies* (Madison: The University of Wisconsin Press, 1966).

[44] It should be pointed out that the terms *rational* and *orderly* are highly subjective. As we shall see later, some of the critics of modern city planning assign a very different meaning to the phrase "the rational and orderly development of our cities and metropolitan areas" than do most contemporary city planners.

private investors who are able to charge high rents while doing little to maintain or improve their property. Irwin T. Sanders is undoubtedly correct, however, when he points out that vested interest groups are not always motivated by a desire for personal gain.[45] Sometimes well-intentioned citizens demand programs and projects that are desirable in themselves but that do not dovetail with the master plan. For example, a group of citizens may urge the city government to locate a park on a plot of land that is earmarked for industrial development. When situations of this type arise, the city planner must exercise his or her public relations skills and present the master plan to the public in an open-minded but nonetheless persuasive manner.

An even greater problem that city planners must face lies in the fact that the area over which they have authority is frequently smaller than the area that requires unified planning. In short, the city planner's authority usually ends at the city limits, whereas the city as a physical entity does not. Rather, the city often merges into numerous suburban communities that are politically independent and that refuse to participate in any effort at metropolitan planning. Richard L. Meier points out some of the problems that this entails:

> Most of the best ideas for improving the city, including the siting of a new industry, the levying of a new tax, or the establishment of an institution for higher education, can be blocked by a handful of small communities that feel they would get nothing from a project for themselves, or fear that it might "hurt" them at some time in the future.[46]

So far efforts to cope with problems of this type have had only limited success. One of the most hopeful approaches has been the merger of various local governments into one overall metropolitan government. This in itself can be a tremendously difficult task. Very often the proposed consolidation is vigorously opposed by groups who fear an increase in taxes and a decrease in local autonomy.[47]

Critics of Current City Planning. City planning has been subjected to rather severe criticism during recent years. However, the alternative approaches that have been suggested by some of the most vocal critics

[45] Sanders, *The Community,* esp. p. 400.
[46] Richard L. Meier, *Developmental Planning* (New York: McGraw-Hill Book Company, 1965), p. 390.
[47] There is a vast reservoir of literature relating to metropolitan government and the difficulties that confront it. Some of this literature is reprinted in Philip B. Coulter (ed.), *Politics of Metropolitan Areas: Selected Readings* (New York: Thomas Y. Crowell Company, 1967), and in Michael N. Danielson (ed.), *Metropolitan Politics: A Reader* (Boston: Little, Brown and Company, 1966).

of city planning do not seem to be particularly feasible or practical themselves.

One of the most influential critics of city planning, and particularly urban renewal, is Herbert J. Gans.[48] Basically, Gans questions the goals of our urban renewal programs themselves. The current thrust of our urban renewal program is, in effect, to clear away slums in the central city and to replace them with expensive, high-rise apartment buildings, civic centers, and so on. In doing this, the hope has been that middle-class people would be lured back into the central city, that the tax revenue of the city would be increased, that private enterprise would be encouraged to invest in the central city, and that civic pride would be restored. However, Gans argues that the primary goal of urban renewal should be to properly rehouse slum dwellers. As he puts it, "the solution . . . is not to repeal urban renewal, but to transform it from a program of slum clearance and rehabilitation into a program of urban re-housing." [49]

That many slum dwellers do need help in obtaining better housing is beyond dispute. However, some of Gans's proposals for meeting the housing needs of the poor do not seem to be particularly feasible, as he himself seems to admit.[50] Specifically, he suggests that slum dwellers should be helped to move out of the central city slums and into older but well-maintained suburban areas. This could be done in several different ways. For example, the federal government could provide poor people who are in need of adequate housing with rent subsidies. Gans also suggests that new communities (see Chapter 3) should be built that are specifically designed to meet the needs of slum dwellers.

As we have already noted, there are several problems associated with Gans's proposals. Three of these are particularly important. First, because many of the people who would be relocated would be nonwhite, the net effect might well be to drive middle- and upper-class whites even farther out into the suburban fringe. In brief, Gans's proposals would do little or nothing to combat residential segregation. Second, unless the relocation of slum dwellers in suburban areas was very carefully supervised, the end result might well be to simply move the slums to the suburbs. Finally, some of Gans's proposals might have the same negative effects that he correctly attributes to our current urban renewal program. For example, Gans observes that, under our urban renewal programs, "entire neighborhoods have frequently been destroyed, uprooting people who had lived there for decades, closing down their institutions, ruining small

[48] See Gans, "The Failure of Urban Renewal," pp. 199–212.
[49] Ibid., p. 204.
[50] Ibid., see esp. pp. 208–9.

businesses by the hundreds, and scattering families and friends all over the city." [51] Gans argues that these problems can be overcome by moving people en masse. In brief, he would not move individual families but entire neighborhoods. However, there is no guarantee that neighborhood institutions and small businesses could survive the move. Furthermore, many of the people whom Gans proposes to relocate might refuse to move or might choose to move elsewhere.

The present writer thoroughly agrees with Gans that one of our nation's top priorities must be to help the poor and disadvantaged obtain decent housing. Furthermore, this writer is at a loss to suggest a strategy by which this might be done. It would appear that ultimately we must (1) provide every American family with enough income that they can afford decent housing and (2) rigorously enforce laws that forbid discrimination in the sale or rental of housing.

Another articulate and outspoken critic of city planning is Jane Jacobs. In the introduction to her widely read book, *The Death and Life of Great American Cities*, Jacobs tells us that

> This book is an attack on current city planning and rebuilding. It is also, and mostly, an attempt to introduce new principles of city planning and rebuilding, different and even opposite from those now taught in everything from schools of architecture and planning to the Sunday supplements and women's magazines. My attempt is not based on quibbles about rebuilding methods or hairsplitting about fashions in design. It is an attack, rather, on the principles and aims that have shaped modern, orthodox city planning and rebuilding.[52]

Jacobs deplores the practice of zoning cities in such a way that one area is reserved for residential purposes, another for commercial purposes, a third for industrial purposes, and so on. Rather, Jacobs argues that the strength of the city lies in its diversity. Furthermore, she maintains that in order to insure this diversity, four conditions have to be met [53]:

1. Districts or neighborhoods within the city must serve more than one function. For example, the ideal central business district would be one where we would find residences intermingled with department stores, small shops, small manufacturing firms, intimate restaurants, and so on. Among other things, this would insure that reputable people would be on the street at almost all hours of the day and night, and therefore

---

[51] Ibid., p. 201.
[52] Jane Jacobs, *The Death and Life of Great American Cities* (New York: Vintage Books, 1961), p. 3.
[53] Ibid., see pp. 151–221.

criminals and other people who represent a threat to public safety could be spotted and brought under control.

2. Most city blocks should be short. This would encourage people to use different routes to get where they are going. In the process they might well stop in small shops that they would not otherwise even know about (e.g., a small Mom and Pop grocery store). This, in turn, would enable these small shops to survive in the face of stiff competition from much, much larger firms.

3. Urban districts and neighborhoods must have a variety of different types of buildings, including some that are old. The reason that old buildings are important is that the rent on them is usually low. They therefore provide quarters for small businesses, social service agencies, art galleries, and other enterprises that otherwise could not afford to locate in the district or neighborhood. Furthermore, "old buildings . . . break the visual monotony, and they can house cozy stores that provide gossip and a place to leave your key as well as merely selling goods." [54]

4. The district or neighborhood must have a dense concentration of people. Among other things, this presumably gives the area vitality, liveliness, and diversity. In Jacobs's thinking, a dense concentration of people is something quite different than overcrowding.

In sum, Jacobs maintains that if these four conditions were met then cities and the districts of which they are composed would be lively, dynamic places full of people of all races, social classes, and ethnic backgrounds. Most importantly, cities would be safe because law-abiding people would always be around to contain behavior that represents a threat to other people's lives or property.

Jane Jacobs has her critics, one of the most knowledgeable of whom is Lewis Mumford.[55] Among other things, Mumford criticizes Jacobs for totally disregarding many of the good things that city planners try to promote. For example, there is value in spaciousness, openness, and orderliness. Similarly, busy, densely concentrated, diversified areas all too frequently are noisy, polluted, chaotic, and lacking in beauty. Mumford states his case well when he says that "one solitary walk through Harlem should have made Mrs. Jacobs revise her notions of the benefits of high density, pedestrian-filled streets, crosslines of circulation, and a mixture of primary economic activities on every residence block, for all these 'ideal' conditions are fulfilled in Harlem—without achieving the

[54] Palen, *The Urban World*, p. 285.
[55] See Lewis Mumford, "Home Remedies for Urban Cancer," in Louis K. Loewenstein (ed.), *Urban Studies: An Introductory Reader* (New York: The Free Press, 1971), pp. 385–404.

favorable results she expects of her prescription." [56] Finally, Jacobs's proposals for ameliorating the ills of the city are impractical: our cities have become too large and structurally differentiated for her approach to work.

Community Organization

Community organization is another approach to planned community change that we must briefly consider. One of the most widely accepted definitions of community organization states that it is the process of bringing about and maintaining "a progressively more effective adjustment between social welfare resources and social welfare needs." [57] This definition suggests that community organization is an activity that is carried on by social workers and by persons in closely related fields. These persons may be employed by the United Fund, community welfare councils, religious and other private agencies, and a variety of social action groups. In addition, many of the duties that experts in community organization perform on a full-time basis are among the part-time activities of caseworkers and group workers. Likewise, the definition given also suggests that the goals of community organization are usually achieved by bringing community resources to bear on its unmet needs. It is safe to assume that every community has some gaps in the health and welfare services that it provides for its citizens. At the same time, most communities have at least a few resources that can be used to fill these gaps.

With these preliminary comments in mind, we may examine some of the more concrete goals that the expert in community organization may pursue.[58] In so doing we must remember that community organization, like city planning, is a type of instigated social change. It represents a way to trying to modify and improve health and welfare services at the local level.

To be more specific, experts in community organization may define their goals in essentially three ways. First, they may see their task as

[56] Ibid., p. 392.

[57] Cited in Norman R. Moore, "The Practice of Community Organization," in Robert W. Klenk and Robert M. Ryan, *The Practice of Social Work* (Belmont, Calif.: Wadsworth Publishing Company, 1970), p. 235. For further discussion of definitions of community organization see Ernest B. Harper and Arthur Dunham, *Community Organization in Action: Literature and Critical Comments* (New York: Association Press, 1959), pp. 54–59, 63–64.

[58] The analysis presented is similar to that offered by Murray G. Ross. See his *Community Organization: Theory and Principles,* 2nd ed. (New York: Harper & Row, 1967), pp. 203–24. For a different approach see Jack Rothman, "An Analysis of Goals and Roles in Community Organization," *Social Work,* 9 (April, 1964), 24–31.

that of pursuing a very specific limited objective. If one is the director of the local United Fund, one may define one's job as that of raising a certain amount of money during the annual fund-raising campaign. Similarly, one may be aware of the need for a mental health center in one's community and direct one's efforts toward convincing other people that a facility of this type should be created. More generally, experts in community organization may define their goal as that of strengthening community health and welfare systems by creating a new agency, adding to the services rendered by a specific agency, or bringing about a specific reform in social work practice. In theory, one never does this by forcing the public or its social agencies to accept the proposed innovation. Rather, one supposedly attempts to involve the public and its social agencies in the decision-making process and in bringing about the desired change.

Second, experts in community organization may see their job as that of coordinating and strengthening social agencies that already exist. In larger communities, there often are several agencies that provide identical services and therefore compete for clients. For example, it is quite common to find that a department of child welfare, a guidance clinic, and a mental health center all furnish psychiatric services for children. At the same time, there may be other needs that are left unmet or that are not adequately met because the area of competence and responsibility of the various agencies has not been clearly defined. If this is the case, the community organization worker can encourage the competing agencies to develop a more satisfactory division of labor. The department of child welfare might agree to refer all children with severe behavioral disorders to the guidance clinic, the guidance clinic could refer its adult clients to the mental health center, and so forth. This simple reshuffling of clients can free each agency to render superior service in its area of competence.

The coordinative goals of community organization of course may flow in other directions. Instead of focusing on the waste and inefficiency caused by a duplication of services, experts in community organization may encourage several agencies to pool their resources in order to ameliorate a particular problem. In short, they might initiate a concerted interagency attack on a growing community problem such as juvenile delinquency, mental illness, or whatever. If workers are to achieve this type of coordination, they must elicit the support and participation of the appropriate agencies. The coordination of welfare services is something that can be done only by the agencies themselves. The most that workers can do is to encourage and facilitate the process of interagency cooperation.

Finally, another task of experts in community organization is to foster public involvement in solving social problems and in improving welfare services. There are two reasons why the "public involvement" component of community organization is becoming increasingly important. First, most welfare agencies must receive financial and other types of support from the communities in which they are located. It is safe to assume that taxpayers will tolerate the expenditures of public agencies only if they are convinced that these agencies are rendering valuable services. The same thing is true in respect to supporting private agencies. Experts in community organization can help to elicit this support by encouraging public participation in setting welfare goals and in ameliorating social problems. Second, many programs of social and economic rehabilitation demand public acceptance, support, and involvement if they are to be successful. Competent community organization workers have skills that can be used to secure this acceptance, support, and involvement.

Community Action and Community Development

The terms *community action* and *community development* refer to the voluntary efforts of local citizens to achieve a goal they desire for themselves, their neighborhood, or their community. As such, community action and community development share at least one thing in common with city planning and community organization: they too are approaches to planned community change and community problem solving.

Programs of community action and community development may be of several types. Two approaches to community action and community development that have elicited considerable interest are the *power bloc* approach that was advocated by the late Saul Alinsky and the community action program that was a part of the ill-fated War on Poverty. We shall examine these two approaches as a means of increasing our understanding of what community action and community development entail. Similarly, we must say something about community development as it is practiced in foreign countries.

Saul Alinsky and the "Power Bloc" Approach. There is probably no name more closely associated with a "radical" approach to community action than that of the late Saul Alinsky.[59] Basically, Alinsky argued that in a democracy the poor and the disadvantaged will be heard only if they organize themselves into effective "power blocs." His basic assumption was that the local power structure (i.e., "the establishment") will do little for the poor unless it is forced to do so. Therefore, the poor must become organized to the point that they can confront, negotiate, and bargain

[59] Alinsky outlined his basic approach in his *Reveille for Radicals* (Chicago: University of Chicago Press, 1946). For a very brief review of Alinsky's "power bloc" approach see Dentler, *American Community Problems*, pp. 84–87.

with this power structure on equal terms.[60] However, the poor usually cannot do this on their own. Rather,

> The mean and difficult job of building the organization must be handled by professionals who know how to deal with the apathy of the slum and who can find a way of bringing its disparate fragments together into a working whole for more often than not, the indigenous leaders of the slum area are out of touch with one another, and only very rarely do they possess the skills to set up a large organization and keep it running.[61]

This is where Alinsky and his associates entered the picture. It was their task to search out indigenous leaders, to help them create power organizations, and to teach them the skills entailed in the politics of confrontation. At the same time, Alinsky did not consider himself to be an outside agitator. Rather, he was convinced that the essence of democracy lies in a confrontation between the strong and the weak. He maintained that when he encouraged the use of direct action techniques such as picketing, rent strikes, and demonstrations, he was helping to make democracy more responsive to the needs of the people.

That the politics of confrontation can be an effective method of inducing change is indisputable. One needs only to read Charles E. Silberman's account of Alinsky's work in Woodlawn, an apathy-filled, problem-ridden Chicago slum, to be convinced of this.[62]

Nonetheless, the use of direct action techniques by the poor has both advantages and limitations. On the positive side, one cannot ignore the sense of purpose and accomplishment that active involvement can give disadvantaged people. At the same time, there is a constant danger that the militant or pseudo-militant use of power by the poor will deepen the distrust and misunderstanding that already exists between the rich and the poor, the white and the nonwhite. This is a risk that may have to be taken, however, because many communities refuse to extend assistance to their disadvantaged citizens on a voluntary basis. All too often the only way disadvantaged groups can obtain help with their problems is through the strong and effective application of power.[63]

[60] See ibid., p. 84.

[61] Charles E. Silberman, "Up from Apathy: The Woodlawn Experiment," *Commentary*, 37 (May, 1964), 54.

[62] Ibid., pp. 51–58.

[63] For a description of an approach to community problem solving similar to that advocated by Saul Alinsky see John A. Garcia, "Community Autonomy, Advocacy, and Representation: A Latino Community Organization Model," in Roland L. Warren (ed.), *New Perspectives on the American Community: A Book of Readings*, 3rd ed. (Chicago: Rand McNally & Company, 1977), pp. 512–21.

The Community Action Program. On August 20, 1964, Congress passed the Economic Opportunity Act. This Act supposedly provided for an all-out war on the poverty that touches the lives of millions of Americans. Among the more important programs that Congress approved were Headstart, the Job Corps, the Neighborhood Youth Corps, and Volunteers in Service to America (VISTA).[64] In addition, the Act authorized the President to establish the Office of Economic Opportunity, which would have responsibility for coordinating the antipoverty efforts of all federal agencies. One of the most significant features of the Economic Opportunity Act was that it authorized federal participation in community action programs.

The purposes of and the philosophy behind the community action program were best captured in President Johnson's "Message on Poverty," which he delivered to Congress on March 16, 1964:

> through a new community action program we intend to strike at poverty at its source—in the streets of our cities and on the farms of our countryside among the very young and the impoverished old.
>
> This program asks men and women throughout the country to prepare long-range plans for the attack on poverty in their own local communities.
>
> These are not plans prepared in Washington and imposed upon hundreds of different situations.
>
> They are based on the fact that local citizens best understand their own problems, and know how to deal with these problems.
>
> These plans will be local plans striking at the many unfilled needs which underlie poverty in each community, not just one or two. Their components and emphasis will differ as needs differ.
>
> These plans will be local plans calling upon all the resources available to the community—Federal and State, local and private, human and material.
>
> And when these plans are approved by the Office of Economic Opportunity, the federal government will finance up to 90 per cent of the additional cost for the first two years.
>
> The most enduring strength of our nation is the huge reservoir of talent, initiative, and leadership which exists at every level of our society.
>
> Through the community action program we can call upon this, our greatest strength, to overcome our greatest weaknesses.[65]

This statement contains a hint of what many persons hoped would become the two principal components of the Community Action Program.

[64] For a discussion of these programs see Walter A. Friedlander, *Introduction to Social Welfare,* 3rd ed. (Englewood Cliffs, N.J.: Prentice-Hall, Inc., 1968), pp. 324–32.
[65] *Message to the Congress of the United States on the Economic Opportunity Act of 1964,* by President Lyndon B. Johnson (March 16, 1964).

First, the legislation that authorized federal participation in community action programs called for the use of a variety of tools in attacking poverty at the local level. Among other things, participating communities were encouraged to create their own community action boards. These boards, in turn, were to enlist the cooperation of schools, welfare agencies, and other community resources in waging a grassroots war on poverty. Second, the act also required the "maximum feasible participation" of the poor in planning and executing programs financed by the Office of Economic Opportunity. Although no fixed standards were established, "a developing consensus, both within the agency (OEO) and in Congress, settled on a pattern by which at least one-third of the seats on a community action agency's governing board were to be held by directly selected representatives of the poor." [66] It is only because citizen involvement was required that we can consider the now defunct Community Action Program to be a form of community action as it has been defined in this book.

Although supposedly one of the basic purposes of the War on Poverty was to encourage each community to design programs uniquely suited to its own needs, most of the funds expended on the War on Poverty went into "national emphasis programs." One of the most popular of these was Headstart. This program, which is still in operation, gives preschool children from impoverished families an opportunity to enrich their academic and social skills before they enter grade school. Likewise, much of the money Congress allocated to the Office of Economic Opportunity was earmarked for national programs of health care, adult education, and legal aid services. As a result, little money was left for the funding of programs conceived at the local level.[67]

The War of Poverty, including the Community Action Program, was a dismal failure. This was partly due to technical problems such as the lack of adequate budgets and poor budgeting procedures. Likewise, the provision in the Economic Opportunity Act that called for the "maximum feasible participation" of the poor in planning and implementing programs at the local level led to "constant squabbling at the local level over who would control local OEO programs." [68] But most importantly the War on Poverty was poorly conceived. Joan Huber explains it well: "Where the war on poverty went wrong, in brief, was in its assumption that the attitudes and values of the poor are the cause of their poverty.

[66] David A. Grossman, "The Community Action Program: A New Function for Local Government," in Barnard J. Frieden and Robert Morris (eds.), Urban Planning and Social Policy (New York: Basic Books, Inc., 1968), pp. 441–42.
[67] Ibid., p. 444.
[68] Dennis E. Poplin, Social Problems (Glenview, Ill.: Scott, Foresman and Company, 1978), p. 259.

259

The poverty program was designed to change the poor rather than to change existing social arrangements that supported poverty." [69] In other words, the War on Poverty failed to attack the real causes of poverty such as race and sex discrimination, unemployment, unequal educational opportunities, and low wages.[70]

Within ten years of its inception, the War on Poverty had been almost totally abandoned. Funds were no longer available for local community action programs, and the national emphasis programs had been integrated into various departments of the federal government. For example, the Job Corps was incorporated into the U.S. Department of Labor and the Headstart program into the U.S. Department of Health, Education, and Welfare. The Office of Economic Opportunity still exists, but it makes little noise anymore.

Community Development in Foreign Countries. The terms *community action* and *community development* mean essentially the same thing. Sometimes, however, the latter term is used to refer specifically to those efforts that are made to assist people in the underdeveloped countries of the world to improve the conditions under which they live. Many of the underdeveloped countries lack even the most basic resources that are required to solve community problems. Neither money nor equipment are available for use in community projects, and the capacities of potential community leaders have never been developed. In these resource-barren communities, people represent the only tool that can be utilized in an effort to instigate community change. Community development focuses on the long-range development of this one resource.

A well-conceived community development program often has two goals. Certainly the overriding goal of community development is to encourage people to mobilize whatever resources they may have in an effort to improve conditions at the local level. In a real sense, community development represents a process by which community members are taught to carry out their own programs of planned change. There are many skills that must be learned, but the most important are those of working with other people for the common good, learning to utilize the abilities of indigenous leaders, and learning to make creative use of the meager resources available to the community. The "instructor" in this learning process is either a specialist in a particular field (e.g., agriculture or engineering) or a generalist who has a broad knowledge of the processes and techniques involved in community development. He or she

[69] Joan Huber, "The War on Poverty," in Joan Huber and H. Paul Chalfant (eds.), *The Sociology of American Poverty* (Cambridge, Mass.: Schenkman Publishing Company, 1974), p. 300.
[70] Ibid., p. 310.

may be an employee of the national government under whose jurisdiction the community falls, the government of another country, or a private philanthropic organization.

In addition to the basic goal of encouraging community members to work together in order to solve common problems, community development programs usually have a more specific objective: to build a road or a schoolhouse, to improve the community's water supply, to modernize agricultural practices, and so on. However, these concrete objectives are usually subservient to the goal of developing human capacities. The reason why experts in community development place such a strong emphasis on human capacities is made clear by Curtis and Dorothy Mial when they suggest that "since the job of building better communities is not likely ever to be finished, the real goal of community development cannot be the solution of any specific problem but the development of people who can continue to take leadership responsibly and wisely." [71]

In the last few years, community development has received some criticism. For example, although not completely discounting the value of community development, Khinduka has suggested that "local destinies, for the most part, cannot be decided locally. Nor can the major problems of a locality—poverty, unemployment, housing, and discrimination—be solved merely or mainly by mobilizing local efforts." [72] To put it differently, if the core problems facing human beings today are really to be solved, it will require more than simply changing the attitudes and values of those people who are confronted with the problem. Rather, it will require societywide economic development and the modification of those social structural arrangements that perpetuate poverty, unemployment, discrimination, and so on.

☐ SUMMARY

We began this chapter by assuming that there is an intimate relationship between community change and community problems. Indeed, all community problems have a cause, and sometimes this is a change in some aspect of community structure. Thus many of the problems that plague modern communities are the result of continuous and rapid change. Among the more important types of change that have given rise

[71] Curtis and Dorothy Mial, "Community Development—USA," *International Review of Community Development,* No. 4 (1959), 14. Irwin T. Sanders sheds further light on the nature of community development. See his "Theories of Community Development," *Rural Sociology,* 23 (March, 1958), 1–12.
[72] Shanti K. Khinduka, "Community Development: Potentials and Limitations," in Warren (ed.), *New Perspectives on the American Community,* p. 506.

to community problems are rapid population growth, industrialization, and the mass movement of people into large metropolitan areas.

From the welter of changes that have occurred at the community level, we have identified urbanization as being the most important. Not too many years ago, most Americans lived in small communities and were uniformly rural in their values, attitudes, and patterns of behavior. Today the majority of Americans live in large cities and metropolitan areas, and the lives of all Americans are touched by what might be called a metropolitan culture. Much the same is true in other countries throughout the world. We have argued of course that urbanization is best viewed as a derivative effect of other changes, the most important of which have been the agricultural revolution and the improvement of methods of transportation and communication. These changes can be traced to yet other types of change.

Finally, we have suggested that the only solution to most community problems is to stimulate yet further change. Indeed, the term *solve* implies that change is purposefully used to alleviate a problem. Sometimes the required change occurs spontaneously and the problem solves itself. However, most community problems do not simply disappear with the passage of time. If most of the problems that plague modern American communities are to be solved, the required changes must be instigated. Because of this, three different types of planned community change have been discussed in this chapter. Not all students of the community will agree with the distinctions the present writer has drawn among city planning, community organization, and community action and development. Although there is wide agreement as to the nature of city planning, the other three terms are often used interchangeably. Nonetheless, one of the purposes of this book is conceptual clarification, and the terms *city planning, community organization,* and *community action and development* supposedly do refer to different types of planned community change. At the same time, the rather rigid distinctions that have been drawn among these three types of planned change are useful for conceptual purposes only. In attempting to solve their problems, success will come only to those communities that utilize a proper blend of city planning, community organization, and community action and development.

BIBLIOGRAPHY

Alinsky, Saul. *Reveille for Radicals.* Chicago: University of Chicago Press, 1946.
Allen, Francis R. *Socio-cultural Dynamics: An Introduction to Social Change.* New York: Macmillan Publishing Co., Inc., 1971.
Babcock, Richard F. *The Zoning Game: Municipal Practices and Policies.* Madison: University of Wisconsin Press, 1966.

Batten, T. R. "The Major Issues and Future Direction of Community Development," *Journal of the Community Development Society,* **4** (Fall, 1973), 34–44.

Blizek, William L., and Jerry Cederblom. "Community Development and Social Justice," *Journal of the Community Development Society,* **4** (Fall, 1973), 45–52.

Brokensha, David, and Peter Hodge. *Community Development: An Interpretation.* San Francisco: Chandler Publishing Company, 1969.

Clinard, Marshall. *Slums and Community Development: Experiments in Self-help.* New York: The Free Press, 1966.

Contini, Edgardo. "Problem-Solving in the Realm of Urban Planning," *American Behavioral Scientist,* **18** (November–December, 1974), 201–10.

Dentler, Robert A. *American Community Problems.* New York: McGraw-Hill Book Company, 1968.

Donnison, David. "The Age of Innocence Is Past: Some Ideas about Urban Research and Planning," *Urban Studies,* **12** (October, 1975), 263–72.

Downs, Anthony. "The Successes and Failures of Federal Housing Policy," *The Public Interest,* **34** (Winter, 1974), 124–45.

Editors of *Fortune. The Exploding Metropolis.* Garden City, N.Y.: Doubleday & Company, Inc., 1958.

Ferman, Louis A. (ed.). "Evaluating the War on Poverty," *The Annals of the American Academy of Political and Social Science,* **385** (September, 1969), 1–156.

Friedman, Lawrence M. *Government and Slum Housing: A Century of Frustration.* Chicago: Rand McNally & Company, 1968.

Gans, Herbert J. "The Failure of Urban Renewal: A Critique and Some Proposals," in Stephen Gale and Eric G. Moore (eds.), *The Manipulated City: Perspectives on Spatial and Social Issues in Urban America.* Chicago: Maaroufa Press, 1975.

———. *People and Plans: Essays on Urban Problems and Solutions.* New York: Basic Books, 1968.

———. "Regional and Urban Planning," in David Sills (ed.), *International Encyclopedia of the Social Sciences.* New York: Macmillan Publishing Co., Inc., 1968.

Garcia, John A. "Community Autonomy, Advocacy, and Representation: A Latino Community Organization Model," in Roland L. Warren (ed.), *New Perspectives on the American Community: A Book of Readings,* 3rd ed. Chicago: Rand McNally & Company, 1977.

Gilmore, Harlan W. *Transportation and the Growth of Cities.* New York: The Free Press, 1953.

Glabb, Charles N., and A. Theodore Brown. *A History of Urban America.* New York: Macmillan Publishing Co., Inc., 1967.

Goodman, Percival, and Paul Goodman. *Communitas: Means of Livelihood and Ways of Life.* Chicago: University of Chicago Press, 1947.

Huber, Joan. "The War on Poverty," in Joan Huber and H. Paul Chalfant (eds.), *The Sociology of American Poverty.* Cambridge, Mass.: Schenkman Publishing Company, 1974.

Jacobs, Jane. *The Death and Life of Great American Cities.* New York: Vintage, 1961.

Khinduka, Shanti. "Community Development: Potentials and Limitations," in Roland L. Warren (ed.), *New Perspectives on the American Community: A Book of Readings,* 3rd ed. Chicago: Rand McNally & Company, 1977.

Kramer, Ralph M. *Participation of the Poor: Comparative Case Studies in the War on Poverty.* Englewood Cliffs, N.J.: Prentice-Hall, Inc., 1969.

Mumford, Lewis. *The City in History: Its Origins, Its Transformations, and Its Prospects.* New York: Harcourt Brace Jovanovich, Inc., 1961.

——. *The Highway and the City.* New York: Mentor Books, 1963.

——. "Home Remedies for Urban Cancer," in Louis K. Loewenstein (ed.), *Urban Studies: An Introductory Reader.* New York: The Free Press, 1971.

Ogburn, William F. "How Technology Causes Social Change," in Francis R. Allen et al., *Technology and Social Change.* New York: Appleton-Century-Crofts, 1957.

——. *On Culture and Social Change,* edited and with an introduction by Otis Dudley Duncan. Chicago: University of Chicago Press, 1964.

——. *Social Change.* New York: B. W. Huebsh, 1922.

Palen, J. John. *The Urban World.* New York: McGraw-Hill Book Company, 1975.

Perloff, Harvey S. "Common Goals and the Linking of Physical and Social Planning," in American Society for Planning Officials and the Community Planning Association of Canada, *Planning, 1965.* Chicago: American Society of Planning Officials, 1965.

Reps, John W. *The Making of Urban America: A History of City Planning in America.* Princeton, N.J.: Princeton University Press, 1965.

Rodwin, Lloyd. "The Roles of the City Planner in the Community," in Charles R. Adrian (ed.), *Social Science and Community Action.* East Lansing: Michigan State University Press, 1960.

Ross, Murray G. *Community Organization: Theory and Principles,* 2nd ed. New York: Harper & Row, 1967.

Sanders, Irwin T. "Theories of Community Development," *Rural Sociology,* **23** (March, 1958), 1–12.

Silberman, Charles E. "Up from Apathy: The Woodlawn Experiment," *Commentary,* **37** (May, 1964), 51–58.

Vitullo-Martin, Julia. "Liberals and the Myths of Urban Renewal," *Public Policy,* **19** (Spring, 1971), 355–72.

Webber, Melvin M. "Comprehensive Planning and Social Responsibility," *Journal of the American Institute of Planners,* **29** (November, 1963), 232–41.

PART III

Research and Community Study

□ In the preceding chapters we have considered essentially the same kind of information that is presented in most courses on the community. If there is anything new and unique about these chapters, it lies in the way they are organized. The remaining two chapters, however, deal with topics that are not always covered in courses on the community. Specifically, an effort is made to introduce the student to some of the most significant empirical studies of community life and to show how the sociologist does research on the community. This is done in the belief that instruction in research methods, if it is to be meaningful, must be incorporated into every course the student takes.

It is hoped that Chapter 10 will encourage the student to think about why research on communities is important. Among other things, we examine the relationship between research and theory building as two components of community study and consider the role that scientifically trained researchers might play in helping a community to solve its problems. Some attention is also focused on the question of whether a community, if it is selected carefully, can serve as a "sample" of the society and culture of which it is a part. Furthermore, in this chapter the reader is also introduced to some of the most widely heralded studies of community life. It must be stressed that these introductions are brief. The only satisfactory way to get acquainted with these studies is to read them on one's own.

In the concluding chapter of this book we explore some of the methods by which community studies have been conducted, i.e., through the use of participant observation, social surveys, and records and documents. Our emphasis is not on the techniques that each of these methodological approaches entails. Rather, consideration is given to the basic characteristics of each of these methods, what types of data they yield, and where their advantages and limitations lie. It is hoped that this chapter will be useful to students who wonder how social scientists "know what they know" and to those students who would like to begin exploring their own communities on a scientific level.

CHAPTER 10

□□□□□□□□□□
□
□
□
□
□
□
□
□
□
□

Research on Community Life

The construction of theories has a very important role to play in our quest for knowledge about communities. Without human ecology, social system theory, and the other approaches to community analysis we have discussed, our knowledge of community structure and process would consist of little more than a chaotic assortment of findings and observations. If these raw data are to constitute a meaningful whole, they must be organized into a coherent explanatory system. This is the function of theory, that is, to make clear the relationship between what might at first appear to be unrelated bits of information. At the same time, the mere construction of theoretical systems does not yield scientific knowledge. Rather, scientific knowledge is obtained by collecting and processing data in certain clearly prescribed ways. Because of this we must turn our attention to research as a component of community study.

□ RESEARCH AND COMMUNITY STUDY

During the hours in which they are awake, human beings constantly acquire information or "data." We read about community affairs in the newspaper, on Sunday drives we observe how "the other half" lives, and we communicate with our neighbors about topics of mutual interest. This does not mean, however, that all our knowledge is scientific or that anyone can do research. Thus the unique features of research as a method of acquiring knowledge must be explored.

The Nature of Research

Sometimes the meaning of a term seems so obvious that nobody takes time to define it. The term *research* apparently falls into this category. Most textbooks on methods of social research simply do not delve into the question of what research is or how it differs from other methods of gaining knowledge. One exception is an older textbook by Wilson Gee.[1] Although Gee does not offer his own definition of research, he does provide us with a sampling of those definitions that have been developed by other writers. Even though each author's definition is somewhat unique, there seems to be unanimous agreement that research involves "a searching, investigation, or inquiry, presumably of a careful nature, for new knowledge, or at least a new arrangement and interpretation of existing knowledge." [2] This is implied, for example, in Frederic A. Ogg's assertion that "man learns a good many things by accident—by simply stumbling upon them. In the main, however, he adds to his knowledge by definite, deliberate inquiry—by coming up against a question or a problem and casting about for an answer or solution. This process of conscious, premeditated inquiry we call research." [3]

We shall not attempt to derive our own definition of research. To do so would take us too far away from our main concern, i.e., *the bearing of research on community study*. Perhaps it will suffice to say that research entails the systematic collection of raw data that are, in turn, converted into findings and principles. We should also note that from an analytical standpoint research has two different facets. First, research involves the use of a wide variety of methods, procedures, and techniques. These are the tools that the researcher utilizes in his or her quest for empirically grounded knowledge. As such, they include the processes by which he or she collects, analyzes, and presents data. Second, the researcher is expected to incorporate certain values and ethical standards into his or her work. Persons who engage in any type of scientific research must attempt to be objective, to remain neutral on ethical and moral issues, and to evaluate their findings in a skeptical, critical manner.

The Functions of Research

Before we look at some of the methodological details of conducting research on community structure and process, there are some questions that must be raised. What benefits can be expected to flow from research

---

[1] See Wilson Gee, *Social Science Research Methods* (New York: Appleton-Century-Crofts, Inc., 1950). Chapter IV of Gee's book is entitled "The Meaning of Research."
[2] Ibid., p. 128.
[3] Cited in ibid., p. 127.

on community life? Why do social scientists spend time and money on studies of both rural and urban communities? These questions can be answered by examining the role that research plays in the construction of theoretical systems and the contributions it can make to the solution of community problems. We must also consider the proposition that research on particular communities can yield generalizations applicable to the larger society.

Theory and Research in Community Study. It is absolutely essential that we have good theories if meaningful research is to be conducted. Among other things, theory helps the researcher choose relevant problems for investigation and to organize and interpret data. At the same time, careful research is essential if one is to arrive at scientifically valid theories. There are several reasons why this is the case.

Perhaps the chief function of empirical research is that it helps us to differentiate between scientifically valid theories and other explanations of reality. Without research, for example, there would be no way to determine if cities do display a characteristic ecological structure, nor would it be possible to determine whether many other propositions that have been made about community life are valid. Sjoberg and Nett express essentially the same idea when they suggest that "theory, as a system of concepts or ideas, is of course, not unique to science but is basic to all systems of philosophy and religious thought."[4] However, they further explain that "an essential difference, perhaps the only one, between theories in science and in other belief systems lies in the method of validation employed. Scientific theories are necessarily subject to validation through empirical observation, not by fiat or on the basis of tradition."[5] This is not to imply that all or even most of our theories of community structure and process have been subjected to empirical test. Indeed, some of the most popular theories of community are too broad and loosely articulated to be put to such a test.

In addition to helping the student of community life decide which of his or her ideas can stand the test of science and which cannot, Robert K. Merton has suggested that research has several other implications for the theorist.[6] In the first place, any piece of research can potentially display what Merton refers to as a serendipity pattern. By this he means that the research may unearth findings that are both unanticipated and strategic and that call for the development of new

---

[4] Gideon Sjoberg and Roger Nett, A *Methodology for Social Research* (New York: Harper & Row, 1968), p. 28.
[5] Ibid., p. 28.
[6] Robert K. Merton, *Social Theory and Social Structure*, rev. ed. (New York: The Free Press, 1957), pp. 102–17.

theory.[7] To cite one example, it has been generally assumed that property values are permanently reduced when nonwhites move into an all-white neighborhood. However, research conducted by Gillette has suggested that this simply is not the case. If anything, the migration of nonwhites into a previously segregated neighborhood serves in the long run to increase property values.[8] Findings of this type not only raise questions concerning the validity of "commonsense" knowledge, but they also create a demand for new theory. The fact that the movement of nonwhites into a previously segregated neighborhood increases property values must be explained. Similarly, research findings often force the theorist to modify and improve his or her theories. Findings not incorporated into the theory may keep cropping up. When this happens, the theory eventually must be reformulated.[9]

Also, innovations in research methodology sometimes bring new theoretical problems and previously neglected areas of inquiry to our attention. During recent years, for example, it has once more become popular to do research on the ecological structure of cities and metropolitan areas. This renewed interest in human ecology can be attributed partially to the development of social area analysis as a methodological tool for studying the spatial structure of urban areas. Likewise, empirical research often forces the social scientist to define his or her concepts more carefully. As Merton puts it,

> the clarification of concepts, commonly considered a province peculiar to the theorist, is a frequent result of empirical research. Research sensitive to its own needs cannot easily escape this pressure for conceptual clarification. *For a basic requirement of research is that the concepts, the variables, be defined with sufficient clarity to enable the research to proceed,* a requirement easily and unwittingly not met in the kind of discursive exposition which is often miscalled sociological theory.[10]

Perhaps one reason why many of the concepts that are used by the student of community life are so fuzzy is that much of what has been written about community life consists of "discursive exposition."

[7] Ibid., pp. 103–8.
[8] Thomas L. Gillette, "A Study of the Effects of Negro Invasion on Real Estate Values," *The American Journal of Economics and Sociology,* **16** (January, 1957), 151–62. See also Noel P. Gist and Sylvia Fleis Fava, *Urban Society,* 6th ed. (New York: Thomas Y. Crowell Company, 1974), pp. 219–20. In a similar vein, B. Bruce-Briggs has collected data indicating that, contrary to popular opinion, it is not true that more and more Americans are being priced out of the housing market. See B. Bruce-Briggs, "The Cost of Housing," *Public Interest,* **32** (Summer, 1973), 34–42.
[9] Merton, *Social Theory and Social Structure,* p. 108.
[10] Ibid., p. 115. Italics in original.

Research and Community Problems. In Chapter 9 we considered some of the methods by which community problems can be ameliorated. However, the question of whether sociologists *can* and *should* bring their research skills to bear on the solution of community problems was ignored. Social scientific research can undoubtedly be used to find solutions to community problems. Among other things, the research can supply data on which intelligent decisions can be based and can locate and analyze resistance to any changes that the problem-solving activity might entail. That sociologists should use their research skills to help solve community problems is somewhat more debatable. Indeed, we have ignored the proposition that research should be utilized to cope with practical problems until now because it is controversial. Opinions on this issue range all the way from those of sociologists who feel that it would be unprofessional for them to get involved in the nitty-gritty of community problem solving to those who feel that it would be unprofessional for them not to become so involved.

Perhaps one reason sociologists are sometimes reluctant to use their research skills to help a community solve its problems lies in our failure to distinguish between "fact gathering" and research. Thus, in one instance with which the writer is familiar, a group of citizens asked a sociologist to assist them in pursuing a goal to which they were deeply committed. In this case the citizens sought to further school integration through a busing program and had a pressing need for information on the following questions:

1. How many students must be bused in order to assure that school A will have the same percentage of nonwhite students in its total student body as schools B, C, and D?
2. From which parts of the city should students be selected for busing? (Here the guiding criterion might be to keep at a minimum the average mileage students must travel between home and school.)
3. What will be the per pupil cost of instigating a busing program? For example, how many new buses will the school district have to buy?

In the writer's opinion, the sociologist cannot spend the hours that he or she devotes to professional activities on questions of this type, simply because they hold no promise of extending our knowledge of human society.[11] At the same time, there are questions centering around school desegregation that are both sociologically relevant and have a bearing on the practicalities of the problem itself. For example, it might well be

---

[11] Of course, sociologists may want to deal with such questions in their role as interested citizens.

asked whether rates of juvenile delinquency and detected mental illness among nonwhite students will increase or decrease if local schools are integrated. That is, will school integration reduce or enlarge the magnitude of other community problems? Likewise, sociologists should be able to answer the question that is asked again and again by middle-class parents: Will the presence in the classroom of deprived children lower the quality of education? Once sociologists have answered these questions through research, they should be able to provide an explanation for their findings regardless of what they might be.

It is only by exploring questions of this type that sociologists can make a meaningful contribution to the solution of community problems. Any intelligent citizen can learn to gather facts and answer questions similar to those raised in regard to busing. However, only a professionally trained person knows how to explore the larger implications of community problems and to see them in all their complexity. Furthermore, by viewing problems in a wide perspective, sociologists can often forge a link between their personal concern for community problems and their professional obligation to engage in research that expands our knowledge of human society.

The Community as a Sample. Our remarks have made it clear that research is an essential component of community study. Among other things, careful research must be conducted if sociologists are to derive accurate theories of community structure and process. Likewise, the present writer firmly believes that sociologists have some obligation to bring their research skills to bear on the solution of community problems. However, there is an even more important reason why sociologists select particular communities for intensive study. In short, it has sometimes been assumed that if sociologists choose their study communities with care, then these can serve as a mirror of the society and culture of which they are a part. If this is the case, then the community becomes in effect a sample from which sociologists can derive generalizations that apply to the larger society and culture. One of the leading spokesmen for the "community as sample" approach, Conrad M. Arensberg, makes this same point when he states that "the community has served as a sample or unit of observation for the study of a culture or society, as a locus or local embodiment of a wider or general social problem or phenomenon, as a testing ground for plans of change, amelioration, or development." [12]

Oddly enough, the merits of the "community as sample" approach have not been vigorously debated. Most students of the community seem to

[12] Conrad M. Arensberg, "The Community as Object and as Sample," *American Anthropologist*, **63** (April, 1961), 241.

agree that their findings can be generalized to the larger society and culture, assuming that the study community is carefully chosen. Presumably, some communities are more valid "samples" of their society and culture than others. "Communities are," according to Julian H. Steward, "parts of regions and nations. If the formulation of a problem studied in one community is to have significance for other communities or larger groups, the community must be selected on the basis of explicit criteria." [13]

Steward does not discuss the criteria that should be used in selecting a community to serve as a sample of the larger society and culture. However, Conrad M. Arensberg devotes an entire paper to this question.[14] According to Arensberg, such a community should possess four basic properties. Although these properties are rather complex, they can be summarized as follows:

1. If a community is to serve as an adequate sample of the larger society and culture, then to some degree it must be *representative* of that society and culture. If the larger society is built around several racial groups and several social classes, then members of each of these racial groups and social classes must be represented in the community. Likewise, if the society is characterized by a high division of labor, then the community must also have a high division of labor. More generally, if a community is to serve as a sample of the larger universe, there must be found within it all the roles and the statuses, the types of actors and the types of groups, that are found in the larger society.

2. If a community is to be an accurate mirror of the larger society, it must display a certain degree of *completeness*. At first glance it may appear that this requirement is almost identical to item 1. This, however, is not the case. Rather, Arensberg apparently means that the community must be distinguishable from other communities. In addition, it must possess, at least to some extent, all the units of organization typically found in the other communities of which the larger society is composed. If the "typical" community has both slums and suburbs, then both slums and suburbs must be present in the study community.

3. If the results of studies pertaining to a particular community are to be generalized to the larger society, then the study community must display a degree of *inclusiveness*. By this Arensberg means that the study community must possess many of the institutions and cultural traits typical of the larger society. If members of the study community tend to be much more urbane and cosmopolitan than other members of the

[13] Julian H. Steward, *Area Research: Theory and Practice* (New York: Social Science Research Council Bulletin 63, 1950), p. 44.
[14] See Arensberg, "The Community as Object and as Sample," pp. 241–64.

society, then the community will not do as a sample. Likewise, a community should not be selected as a sample of the larger whole if it lacks an institution that predominates in the larger society. Only a community that displays most of the cultural and institutional traits which characterize the larger society can serve as a microcosm of that society.

4. Finally, if a community is to serve as a valid sample of the larger society, it must display a degree of *cohesiveness* similar to that of the larger society. If the society is well integrated and closely knit, then the community must display these same traits. At the same time, those cleavages and disunities that characterize the larger society must be reflected in the study community. "A sample community must," according to Arensberg, "reflect both the unities and the fissions . . . of the whole society it mirrors." [15]

Presumably, the researcher who takes these four criteria into account in selecting a study community can assume that his or her findings will have applicability to other communities and to the larger society. By doing research on carefully selected communities, he or she can learn about the patterns of interaction and association, the cultural traits, and the personality types that characterize the whole society. At the same time, Arensberg does not argue that the study community must be an exact replica of the larger society. Numbers and proportions are not so important as the fact that the roles and statuses, cultural traits and social cleavages that typify the larger society are, to some extent, reflected in the study community.[16]

We have already pointed out that the community as sample approach has not been vigorously debated. However, the future of community study may well hinge almost entirely on whether a carefully selected community can serve as a sample of the larger society. If we conclude that each community is completely unique, then one of the primary reasons for studying the community is lost. Nothing can be learned about other communities or about the larger society by studying community A. On the other hand, if community A is in fact a microcosm of the larger society, then it represents an ideal setting in which to conduct research. A balanced view probably lies somewhere between these two extremes. Every community is unique to some extent, and it seems unlikely that any community can be found that faithfully and without distortion mirrors the larger society. On the other hand, it seems reasonable to assume that communities, like personality types, are to some extent a reflection of the society and culture of which they are a part. If the researcher uses a particular community to sample the larger society,

[15] Ibid., p. 260.
[16] See ibid., pp. 255–60.

his or her first task is to distinguish between those features that are unique to the local community and those that are local manifestations of the larger society and culture.

☐ THE VARIETIES OF COMMUNITY RESEARCH: A REVIEW OF THE LITERATURE

Before we examine some of the methods by which communities can be studied, a few of the more notable studies of community life should be examined briefly. This review is necessary for one reason: it will introduce the reader to the types of research problems that have engaged the attention of students of the community. Until we can visualize some of the questions that can feasibly be explored at the community level, our knowledge of research methods will do us little good. Space prevents us from considering all the community studies that have been published. *It also prevents us from dealing in great detail with the studies that we do consider.* The only fully satisfactory way to become acquainted with these studies is to read them on one's own. However, the reader who wishes to supplement the present review should consult the articles and chapters that have been written by Hollingshead, Steward, and Simpson.[17]

Research on Community Structure and Dynamics

One important type of community research focuses on community structure and dynamics. Because this type of research asks what life is like and how it is organized in particular communities, it might be argued that only those studies that fall into this category are representative of community research in the strictest sense of the word. Indeed, these studies do tend to be holistic, that is, they "have in common the effort to understand the community as a totality."[18] There are of course several different types of study that fall into this broad category.

Ethnographic Research. Ethnographic research represents one major approach to the study of community structure and dynamics. Indeed, the term *ethnographic* implies that the investigator attempts to describe the community, or at least certain areas of it, as a totality and to see the manifold and complex interrelations of its parts. One of the most famous

[17] See August B. Hollingshead, "Community Research: Development and Present Conditions," *American Sociological Review*, 13 (April, 1948), 136–46; Steward, *Area Research*, pp. 20–43; Richard L. Simpson, "Sociology of the Community: Current Status and Prospects," *Rural Sociology*, 30 (June, 1965), 127–49.
[18] Simpson, ibid., p. 129.

examples of an American community study that takes an ethnographic approach is the Lynds' study of Middletown, which, according to the researchers, "proceeds on the assumption that all the things people do in the American city may be viewed as falling under one or another of the following six main-trunk activities: Getting a living, making a home, training the young, using leisure in various forms of play, art, and so on, engaging in religious practices, engaging in community activities." [19] The fact that the Lynds devote several chapters to an analysis of each of these activities as they were carried out in an Indiana community during the mid-1920s makes it clear that they did seek to understand their study community as a whole. Other famous investigations that take an essentially ethnographic approach are James West's study of Plainville, a small Missouri farm community, and Redfield's studies of communities located on the Yucatan Peninsula.[20] Even though they focus on subcommunities rather than on an entire city, Wirth's study of *The Ghetto,* Whyte's *Street Corner Society,* and Herbert J. Gans's study of the *Urban Villagers* are definitely ethnographic in nature.[21]

During recent years, there has been a resurgence of interest in ethnographic studies of urban subareas. This is partly because cultural anthropologists have begun to apply their research techniques to the study of urban communities located in industrial societies such as the United States. We cannot possibly discuss every urban ethnography that has been published during recent years.[22] Nonetheless, by reviewing three exceptionally interesting studies we can gain some insight into how anthropological techniques can be applied to the study of modern urban communities and how the emerging field of urban anthropology can contribute to our understanding of community life.

One study that has earned a great deal of favorable comment is Elliot

[19] Robert S. Lynd and Helen Merrell Lynd, *Middletown: A Study in American Culture* (New York: Harcourt Brace Jovanovich, Inc., 1929), p. 4. The Lynd's second study, conducted during the mid-1930s, is also ethnographic in its approach and should not be ignored as a seminal contribution to community research. See *Middletown in Transition* (New York: Harcourt Brace Jovanovich, Inc., 1937).

[20] See James West, *Plainville, U.S.A.* (New York: Columbia University Press, 1945); Robert Redfield, *The Folk Culture of Yucatan* (Chicago: University of Chicago Press, 1941). We reviewed Redfield's work in Chapter 5.

[21] Louis Wirth, *The Ghetto* (Chicago: University of Chicago Press, 1928); William Foote Whyte, *Street Corner Society* (Chicago: University of Chicago Press, 1955); Herbert J. Gans, *The Urban Villagers* (New York: The Free Press, 1962).

[22] Four excellent studies are those of Joyce Aschenbrenner, *Lifelines: Black Families in Chicago* (New York: Holt, Rinehart and Winston, 1975); Ulf Hannerz, *Soulside: Inquiries into Ghetto Culture and Community* (New York: Columbia University Press, 1969); James C. Spradley, *You Owe Yourself a Drunk: An Ethnography of Urban Nomads* (Boston: Little, Brown and Company, 1970); Carol B. Stack, *All Our Kin* (New York: Harper & Row, 1974).

Liebow's analysis of *Tally's Corner*.[23] In this study Liebow furnishes the reader with an in-depth picture of the lower-class black male and of the cycle of failure and frustration that entraps him. Liebow makes the nature of this cycle clear when he indicates that "the streetcorner man does not appear as a carrier of an independent cultural tradition. His behavior appears not so much as a way of realizing the distinctive goals and values of his own subculture, or of conforming to its models, but rather as his way of trying to achieve many of the goals and values of the larger society, of failing to do this, and of concealing his failure from others and from himself as best he can." [24]

Another ethnographic study that has generated a considerable amount of interest is E. E. LeMaster's study of the *Blue-Collar Aristocrats*.[25] This study focuses on the life-styles of highly skilled and hence well-paid blue-collar workers who patronize the Oasis, a family tavern located in a relatively small (about 6,000 population) suburban community on the fringe of a large metropolitan area. Included among the "blue-collar aristocrats" are carpenters, plumbers, bricklayers, roofers, sheetmetal workers, and so on.[26] On several occasions, LeMasters refers to these people as the "blue-collar elite."

LeMasters's study is both thorough and interesting. He devotes chapters of his book to a discussion of the attitudes that these men have toward work, politics, race, and religion. He also gives us considerable insight into how these men, and sometimes their wives, view marriage, divorce, sex, and the changing roles of women. After reading LeMasters's study one feels that one is intimately acquainted with these people.

At the same time, LeMasters's study leaves the present writer with mixed emotions. On the one hand, LeMasters generates a wealth of ideas and hypotheses that certainly merit further investigation. For example, he suggests that we need research that attempts "to isolate the differences between the successfully divorced and the unsuccessfully divorced." [27] Similarly, he suggests that the wives of blue-collar workers are much closer to the middle-class in terms of their attitudes and values than are the blue-collar workers themselves.[28] This hypothesis deserves further testing, and, if it does hold up, then why it is a fact needs to be explained. On the other hand, there is some question in the present writer's mind

---

[23] Elliot Liebow, *Tally's Corner: A Study of Negro Streetcorner Men* (Boston: Little, Brown and Company, 1967).
[24] Ibid., p. 222.
[25] E. E. LeMasters, *Blue-Collar Aristocrats: Life-Styles at a Working-Class Tavern* (Madison: University of Wisconsin Press, 1975).
[26] Ibid., p. 3.
[27] Ibid., p. 78.
[28] Ibid., p. 197.

as to how many of America's "blue-collar elite" really fit LeMasters's description of the men and women who patronize the Oasis. The present writer has spent most of his life in medium-sized (15,000 to 50,000 population) western and mid-south communities where a significant proportion of the labor force has, in effect, been blue-collar aristocrats. Yet he would have to hypothesize that the life-styles of these people are very different than those of the people who patronize the Oasis.

A final ethnographic study that may well become a classic has been conducted by Gerald D. Suttles.[29] Suttles lived and worked for three years in a Chicago ghetto inhabited chiefly by blacks, Italians, Puerto Ricans, and Mexicans. Among the more interesting findings reported by Suttles are that the ghetto he studied (1) was rigidly segregated into smaller neighborhoods that provided safety and protection for their residents and (2) these neighborhoods tended to be organized around adolescent male peer groups, which, among other things, provided the neighborhood with protection from hostile outsiders.[30]

Research of Social Stratification. Another set of studies that focus on community structure and dynamics is made up of those investigating patterns of social stratification at the local level. The best known are three studies conducted by Lloyd Warner and his associates: a study of a New England town with a population of about 17,000 (Yankee City), a study of a southern town of about 10,000 population (Old City), and a study of a midwestern town with a population of about 6,000 (Jonesville).[31] The most striking feature of these studies is the thoroughgoing manner in which the investigators describe and explore the class system of each community. Among other things, Warner maintains that the six classes he identifies (upper-upper, lower-upper, upper-middle, lower-middle, upper-lower, and lower-lower) are real entities to which local residents themselves attach significance [32] and that these classes exist

---

[29] See Gerald D. Suttles, *The Social Order of the Slum: Ethnicity and Territory in the Inner City* (Chicago: University of Chicago Press, 1968).

[30] For a much earlier but nonetheless extremely important study of the social organization of the slum see Whyte, *Street Corner Society*.

[31] The Yankee City studies include, among others, W. Lloyd Warner and Paul S. Lunt, *The Social Life of a Modern Community* (New Haven: Yale University Press, 1941), and W. Lloyd Warner and Paul S. Lunt, *The Status System of a Modern Community* (New Haven: Yale University Press, 1942). The results of the Old City study are presented in Allison Davis, Burleigh B. Gardner, and Mary R. Gardner, *Deep South* (Chicago: University of Chicago Press, 1941), and those of the Jonesville study in W. Lloyd Warner and associates, *Democracy in Jonesville* (New York: Harper & Row, 1949).

[32] Warner and associates, *Democracy in Jonesville*, p. xiv.

throughout the country.[33] The latter contention has been subjected to vigorous criticism. For example, Bell and Newby claim that "some doubt can be thrown on the assumption that he satisfactorily analysed even that community's [Jonesville's] local stratification system. What Warner has done is to extrapolate a mistaken view of a local stratification system on the whole of American society." [34]

In the course of their research, Warner and his associates developed two indexes for determining the social rank that an individual holds.[35] The first of these, the Index of Status Characteristics, uses four variables to rank the individual—occupation, source of income, quality of housing, and the reputation of the person's residential area. Put very simply, the second index (the Index of Evaluated Participation) relies on local informants to "tell" the researcher where different individuals stand in the class structure. As such, it has much in common with the reputational approach to the study of community power (see Chapter 8). Both of these indexes draw our attention to significant aspects of social ranking, but both have been subjected to heavy criticism.[36]

Inasmuch as his work has been so heavily criticized on both theoretical and methodological grounds, one might well raise the question: Why even bother discussing Warner's work? Perhaps the most straightforward answer to this question is that Warner was a pioneer in the study of local stratificational systems and he has exerted great influence on subsequent research on social stratification.[37] Furthermore, there is a lesson to be learned from Warner's work: We all have blind spots of which we must constantly be aware. Warner was trained in anthropology and paid almost no attention to the rapidly growing body of sociological research on social stratification.[38] If he had acquainted himself with this literature,

[33] Ibid., pp. xix-xv.
[34] Colin Bell and Howard Newby, *Community Studies: An Introduction to the Sociology of the Local Community* (New York: Praeger Publishers, 1972), p. 191. Warner's contention that there are six classes and that they are real entities has also been questioned. See Ruth Rosner Kornhauser, "The Warner Approach to Social Stratification," in Reinhard Bendix and Seymour Martin Lipset (eds.), *Class, Status, and Power: A Reader in Social Stratification* (New York: The Free Press, 1953), p. 249.
[35] W. Lloyd Warner, Marchia Meeker, and Kenneth Eels, *Social Class in America* (Chicago: Science Research Associates, 1949).
[36] For example, see Harold W. Pfautz and Otis Dudley Duncan, "A Critical Evaluation of Warner's Work in Stratification," *American Sociological Review,* **15** (April, 1950), 205–15; Oswald Hall, "Review of Social Class in America," *American Journal of Sociology,* **56** (January, 1951), 366–68.
[37] Noel P. Gist and Sylvia Fleis Fava, *Urban Society,* 6th ed. (New York: Thomas Y. Crowell Company, 1974), p. 338.
[38] Bell and Newby, *Community Studies,* pp. 196–97.

he may well have avoided many of his pitfalls. This, of course, is not a criticism of anthropology or anthropologists per se. There are many times when sociologists are guilty of ignoring the work of anthropologists, economists, and so on. The result is that the quality of their work suffers.

There have been a number of other studies that investigate various aspects of stratification at the local level. One study often hailed as a classic is August Hollingshead's analysis of Elmtown.[39] In summarizing the findings of this study, Hollingshead states that

> On the basis of the data presented, certain tentative conclusions appear to be warranted. First, each of the five strata, as delimited by the procedures used, has a distinct subculture. Second, identification with a given class or stratum is dependent upon the possession of a constellation of appropriate traits. Third, the members of each class participate in community activities in significantly different ways from the members of other classes.[40]

Another analysis of stratification at the local level is Arthur Vidich and Joseph Bensman's study of Springdale, a small community in upstate New York.[41] This study is significant for two reasons. First, the authors improve on earlier studies by recognizing that various groups of approximately equal social rank may still differ markedly from each other in values and behavior. College professors, for example, may have little in common with local businesspeople, even though both groups may earn about the same income, live in the same neighborhood, and be ranked in about the same way by other members of the community. The Springdale study, unlike earlier ones, takes this horizontal dimension of social differentiation into account. Second, Vidich and Bensman recognize that Springdale is profoundly influenced by decisions made at the societal level and that local residents are in no way the "masters" of their own fate. One of the major weaknesses of earlier community studies lies in their failure to take into account the fact that modern communities are not isolated, self-contained entities. Rather, they are small nodes in that infinitely complex web of relationships we call mass society.

Research on Race Relations. A final type of study that focuses on community structure and dynamics is that which considers race relations at the local level. Among the most famous of these are John Dollard's *Caste*

[39] August B. Hollingshead, *Elmtown's Youth* (New York: John Wiley & Sons, Inc., 1949). Warner's Jonesville and Hollingshead's Elmtown are the same community.
[40] August B. Hollingshead, "Selected Characteristics of Classes in a Middle Western Community," *American Sociological Review*, **12** (August, 1947), 395.
[41] Arthur J. Vidich and Joseph Bensman, *Small Town in Mass Society* (Princeton, N.J.: Princeton University Press, 1958).

and Class in a Southern Town [42] and the study of Old City we referred to previously. Although both of these studies are concerned with social stratification, focusing as they do on caste and class structures in small southern communities, their greatest contribution is that they provide us with a thoroughgoing analysis of southern race relations in the pre-World War II era. To be more specific, *Deep South* presents an in-depth picture of the manner in which mechanisms of social control can be used to perpetuate a caste system of race relations, even though this entails the violation of values basic to a democratic society. This study also suggested that a caste system can be maintained only in an essentially rural setting and that the caste system of race relations found in the deep south would probably erode away as this region became more urbanized. The years that have passed since Davis and the Gardners collected their data suggest that they were prophets in a sense. Dollard's study is of particular interest in that it attempted, through the use of psychoanalytic techniques, to determine the psychological costs and consequences of racism. These costs are tremendously high. In his discussion of Dollard's work, for example, Maurice Stein tells us that this "study also deepens our concept of community disorganization in that it shows how an overtly orderly community can exact tremendous emotional penalties from its members. Actually, Southerntown dehumanizes both whites and Negroes so that members of the two castes respond to each other categorically instead of concretely." [43]

The Community as a Variable

About the most common research design in the social sciences is that which analyzes the relationship between two or more variables. It is usually assumed that a change in one variable is the cause of change in another variable. Community studies that utilize this research design are extremely common and therefore we must give some attention to them. There are, for example, a prodigious number of studies that investigate the influence of community size on behavior, attitudes, and values. Similarly, there have been studies that examine the community as it is influenced by changes in other facets of modern society.

Before we examine the studies that exemplify each of these research designs, however, it should be noted that some of the studies dealing with the correlation between community size and other variables should not be called community studies. They may not shed much light on com-

[42] John Dollard, *Caste and Class in a Southern Town* (New Haven: Yale University Press, 1937).
[43] Maurice R. Stein, *The Eclipse of Community: An Interpretation of American Studies* (Princeton, N.J.: Princeton University Press, 1960), p. 174.

munity structure, and the researchers who conduct them are frequently more interested in the dependent variable than they are in the community. A person who examines the correlation between fertility rates and community size, for example, is usually interested in demographic behavior rather than the sociology of community life. Nonetheless, studies of this type must necessarily be based on the assumption that there is something about communities that causes them to influence human behavior, attitudes, and values. Moreover, it behooves the student of community life to know how people who live in different types of communities think and act and, more importantly, to determine why community size does influence their behavior, attitudes, and values. These comments, of course, do not apply to studies that examine the impact of other variables on community structure and process. These studies are of great relevance to the student of community life because they help us to understand the causes of community change.

The Community as an Independent Variable. The ideal way to study the influence of community size on a dependent variable would be to record changes in the dependent variable as a particular community increases in size or undergoes the transition from rural to urban. Unfortunately, this could take decades and it would probably be impossible to determine whether change in community size really caused the change in the dependent variable. The latter change could be due to the effects of yet a third variable. So investigators who wish to explore the relationship between community size and other social phenomena are forced to compare communities of various sizes in terms of the dependent variable. Of course we cannot assume always that differences in community size really explain the observed differences in the dependent variable. It is always possible that the relationship is spurious.

In any event, literally hundreds of studies have utilized this research design, so many in fact that we cannot hope to review them all. As early as 1958 the National Opinion Research Center collected data indicating that persons who live in rural areas are on the whole less likely to join voluntary associations than are persons who live in urban areas.[44] Their children are also less likely to plan on attending college than are urban high school students.[45] Similarly, rural residents are not necessarily more religious than urban residents, but they tend to be more orthodox in their religious beliefs—they are more likely to believe in life after death,

[44] Charles R. Wright and Herbert H. Hyman, "Voluntary Association Membership of American Adults: Evidence from National Sample Surveys," *American Sociological Review*, 23 (June, 1958), 289–91.
[45] Joel I. Nelson, "Participation and College Aspirations: Complex Effects of Community Size," *Rural Sociology*, 38 (Spring, 1973), 7–16.

in heaven and hell, and in the devil.[46] Similarly, the Gallup Poll has found that rural people tend to be a bit more conservative in their attitudes toward abortion, the legalization of marijuana, and premarital sexual relations than urban people. They are also somewhat more conservative on issues pertaining to minority rights, and a slightly higher percentage of them (42 per cent versus 36 per cent) would favor a conservative over a liberal political party.[47]

Because they generate a certain amount of interest, studies of this type will probably continue to appear. There is reason to suspect, however, that studies examining the relationship between community size and other social phenomena will become less and less meaningful with the passage of time. Research conducted during recent years is making it increasingly evident that many of the hypothesized relationships between community size and other variables are quickly narrowing. This is not surprising. Studies of this type are based on the assumption that rural people are surrounded by a cultural milieu that is quite different from that within which urban people function. This assumption simply does not fit the facts of modern urban society. Furthermore, we must avoid the tendency to exaggerate the differences that apparently do exist between rural and urban people. Glenn and Hill put it well when they point out that "the predictive utility of the rural-urban variable is modest at best; 'overinterpretation' of rather small differences between percentages has often obscured the fact that on most issues the rural and urban populations each has almost as much internal differentiation in attitudes as does the total population." [48]

The Community as a Dependent Variable. Only a handful of studies have examined the influence that other variables can have on community life. However, the few studies that do utilize this research design are of utmost interest in that they shed light on some highly significant questions. For example, studies have been conducted that help us to understand what happens to small communities when they undergo rapid industrialization and experience heavy in-migration. Likewise, spe-

[46] Hart M. Nelsen, Raytha L. Yokley, and Thomas W. Madron, "Rural-Urban Differences in Religiosity," *Rural Sociology,* 36 (September, 1971), 389–96.
[47] See Norval D. Glenn and Lester Hill, Jr., "Rural-Urban Differences in Attitudes and Behavior in the United States," in Jacqueline Scherer (ed.), *Annual Editions: Urban Society* (Guilford, Conn.: The Dushkin Publishing Group, 1978), esp. p. 15. It should also be pointed out that governmental agencies continue to publish data on rates of fertility, mortality, crime, and so on by place of residence. No overall generalizations can be made about the relationship between these variables and size of community except that, in many cases, the difference between the rural and urban rates seems to be narrowing.
[48] Ibid., p. 20.

cialists in business and economic research have attempted to assess the impact the construction of new highways has on the economic life of communities. Some of these studies must now be examined.

A good place to start is with Lowell J. Carr and James E. Stermer's study of Willow Run, Michigan. In this study the authors indicate some of the things that can happen to a small community when it undergoes extremely rapid industrialization.[49] In 1941 Willow Run was chosen by the Ford Motor Company as the site of "the biggest mass-production bomber plant in the world." [50] Within several months Willow Run was deluged by tens of thousands of factory workers and faced the prodigious task of coping with this gigantic influx of population. The picture Carr and Stermer paint is a bleak one in which our ability to induce technological change far outstrips our ability to adjust to such changes:

> Willow Run demonstrated that the industrial culture's devices for creating social changes had far outrun its devices for readjusting to these changes. A bomber factory was certainly twentieth century. Political answers for technological questions and business as usual in the face of a crisis were both antediluvian and prescientific. Eighteen hundred trying to master the 1940's was the portent of Willow Run. It was a portent that boded no good for America in the atomic age.[51]

A closely related piece of research was Havighurst and Morgan's study of Seneca, Illinois, another war-boom community.[52] Apparently the people of Seneca reacted to the rapid changes that were thrust on them in much the same way as the people of Willow Run. This raises the possibility that the findings of these two studies can be generalized to other communities that are exposed to a similar pattern of change. In a somewhat different vein, Rudolf Haberle has analyzed the effects of industrialization on the organization of southern cities.[53] Although Haberle's paper does not present the results of field research, it makes it clear that industrialization has played a key role in bringing about change in the ecological and class structure of cities in the southern United States.

Sociologists have conducted relatively little research pertaining to the impact of new, multiple-lane highways on community life. However,

[49] Lowell Julliard Carr and James Edson Stermer, *Willow Run: A Study of Industrialization and Cultural Inadequacy* (New York: Harper & Row, 1952).
[50] Ibid., p. 8.
[51] Ibid.
[52] Robert J. Havighurst and H. Gerthen Morgan, *The Social History of a War-Boom Community* (New York: Longmans, Green and Co., 1951).
[53] Rudolf Haberle, "Social Consequences of the Industrialization of Southern Cities," *Social Forces*, 27 (October, 1948), 29–37.

this has been a favorite area of inquiry for specialists in business and economic research. Generally speaking, these studies suggest that new freeways have a favorable impact on property values and on the volume of business in the communities through which they pass.[54] The practice of bypassing communities with these freeways does not inevitably spell disaster for local businesspeople. For instance, in analyzing the effects of bypassing four Kansas communities with modern highways, Wagner concludes that "the more rapid the growth of the city's economy, the larger the city's size, the less will be the potential economic effect of a bypass highway on the sellers of highway-oriented goods on the old bypassed route." [55] Apparently the construction of a bypass does not in itself cause business reversals. However, if the local economy is already faltering then the bypass may indeed have an adverse effect on business. Similarly, in discussing the impact of highway relocation on Marysville, Washington, Garrison and his associates do not deny that some businesses may have suffered. However, they also point out that

> the construction of the by-pass highway has made Marysville a somewhat more desirable place to live from the standpoint of residential amenities. It is presumed that this is largely related to the removal of traffic from downtown Marysville streets. This may also be related to the greater ease of access to Everett and other places because of the new highway facility. This should affect the competitive position of Marysville as a site for residential building and consequently the available market for businesses located in Marysville.[56]

There are many other questions that could be asked concerning the impact of new highways on community life. Some of these rather definitely fall into the bailiwick of the sociologist. For example, does the construction of freeways hasten the suburbanization of smaller communities that are located near large cities? One would presume that it does, but little research has been conducted along this line. Likewise, we can assume that many other changes, in both people and communities, result from changes in transportation networks. Indeed, transportation has always had a profound impact on community life.

[54] For a summary of relevant findings see H. Kirk Dansereau, "Some Implications of Modern Highways for Community Ecology," in George A. Theodorson (ed.), *Studies in Human Ecology* (New York: Harper & Row, 1961), pp. 175–86.
[55] Hulse Wagner, *The Economic Effects of Bypass Highways on Selected Kansas Communities* (Lawrence: The University of Kansas Center for Research in Business, n.d.) p. 44.
[56] William L. Garrison et al., *Studies of Highway Development and Geographic Change* (Seattle: University of Washington Press, 1959), p. 109.

Research on Selected Aspects of Community Life

Today most community-oriented research focuses on very specific problems. To be more precise, two aspects of community structure and process have been subjected to intensive investigation during recent years. First, research on community power, leadership, and decision making continues to be exceedingly popular. Second, there has been a rather striking resurgence of interest in human ecology, although many of the recent studies have little in common with earlier studies.

Because many of the recent studies of community power, leadership, and decision making were considered in Chapter 8, anything further said at this point would be repetitious.[57] However, it might be well to review some of the more recent developments in human ecology inasmuch as modern ecological research differs in significant ways from that conducted during the 1930s. Specifically, modern ecologists do not spend so much time trying to isolate overall patterns of urban spatial organization as did their forerunners. Rather, the tendency today seems to be to focus on the spatial distribution of specific social or economic phenomena. A classic piece of research of this type was Otis Dudley Duncan and Beverly Duncan's study of residential segregation in the Chicago Metropolitan District.[58] Among other things, the Duncans found that persons of relatively high and relatively low socioeconomic status are more likely to be segregated from members of other socioeconomic groups than are persons of intermediate socioeconomic status, and that there is a direct relationship between socioeconomic status and the distance one lives from the center of the city. Of even greater importance is the fact that the Duncans developed several techniques for studying residential distribution and segregation that are simple but sophisticated.[59]

Another study along the same lines is Bahr and Gibbs's recent analysis of the relationship between residential segregation and other racial dif-

[57] Many of the articles on community power, leadership, and decision making have been reprinted and are readily available to the interested reader. For example, see Michael Aiken and Paul E. Mott, *The Structure of Community Power: An Anthology* (New York: Random House, Inc., 1970); Terry N. Clark (ed.), *Community Structure and Decision-Making: Comparative Analyses* (San Francisco: Chandler Publishing Company, 1968); Willis D. Hawley and Frederick M. Wirt (eds.), *The Search for Community Power* (Englewood Cliffs, N.J.: Prentice-Hall, Inc., 1968). See also Richard A. Schermerhorn, *Society and Power* (New York: Random House, Inc., 1961), pp. 87–105.

[58] See Otis Dudley Duncan and Beverly Duncan, "Residential Distribution and Occupational Stratification," *The American Journal of Sociology*, 60 (March, 1955), 493–503.

[59] Ibid., pp. 493–95.

ferences.[60] Although this is not an ecological study in the strictest sense of the word, Bahr and Gibbs do test the hypothesis that the greater the amount of residential segregation found in a metropolitan area, the greater will be the differences in the educational attainment of whites and blacks. In turn, there should be a direct relationship between the degree of educational differentiation and the amount of occupational and economic differentiation between the two groups. Surprisingly enough, this hypothesis cannot be confirmed, and Bahr and Gibbs are forced to conclude that "though subject to various interpretations, the findings suggest that the elimination of residential segregation by race would not bring about a decline (certainly not in a generation) in other forms of racial differentiation, a most important point in analyzing race relations as a social problem." [61]

Cross-cultural studies of ecological phenomena have also retained their popularity. A study by Fernando Peñalosa, for example, has suggested that the inverse-concentric-circle model purportedly characteristic of Latin American cities must be modified. In his study of three Mexican cities of moderate size (20,000 to 30,000 population) Peñalosa found that proximity to major arterials has a much stronger influence on the location of middle- and upper-class residences than does proximity to the central plaza. Since the two major arterials commonly found in Latin American cities bisect each other at the central plaza, the area inhabited by the elite therefore assumes the shape of a cross.[62] Similarly, Lois B. DeFleur has published an ecological study of juvenile delinquency in Cordoba, Argentina.[63] Basically, DeFleur found that the spatial distribution of juvenile delinquency in Cordoba is different from that found in the United States. Therefore, she concludes that a number of ecological studies will have to be performed before cross-cultural testing of social and cultural theories of juvenile delinquency can occur. We cannot arrive at adequate theories of juvenile delinquency until something is known about the spatial context in which it occurs and which groups have high rates of juvenile offenses. Ecological research provides us with this type of information.

Finally, social area analysis is still extremely popular. Because this approach was considered in Chapter 4, we shall not discuss it further.

[60] Howard M. Bahr and Jack P. Gibbs, "Racial Differentiation in American Metropolitan Areas," *Social Forces*, 45 (June, 1967), 521–32.
[61] Ibid., p. 532.
[62] See Fernando Peñalosa, "Ecological Organization of the Transitional City: Some Mexican Evidence," *Social Forces*, 46 (December, 1967), 221–29.
[63] Lois B. DeFleur, "Ecological Variables in the Cross-Cultural Study of Delinquency," *Social Forces*, 45 (June, 1967), 556–70.

However, it should be pointed out that literally hundreds of cities, both in the United States and in other countries, have been subjected to study by this method. The reader who wishes to examine some of these studies should refer to the bibliography appended to Janet L. Abu-Lughod's analysis of Cairo, Egypt,[64] and to Berry and Kasarda's 1977 book entitled *Contemporary Urban Ecology*.[65]

☐ SUMMARY

In this chapter we have considered the bearing of research on community study. It was suggested that research is essential if one is to arrive at adequate theories of community life and that it has a key role to play in any effort to solve community problems. Furthermore, we raised the possibility that findings derived from the study of specific communities can be generalized to other communities and to the larger society. The validity of the "community as sample" approach must, at this time, be left open to question.

More importantly, a tentative classification of community studies has been developed and the reader has been introduced to some of the outstanding studies of community life. The reader must have at least a passing acquaintance with these studies before our discussion of methods of community research will make much sense. At the same time, it should be clear that our review of community studies is by no means exhaustive. For every study we have cited, dozens more have gone unmentioned. Furthermore, it has been impossible to explore fully the few studies that have been reviewed. The only really satisfactory way by which the reader can grasp the significance of these studies is by examining them him- or herself.

It may be fitting to close this chapter with a few brief comments about the future of research on the community. Because of the growing complexity of communities in highly industrialized societies such as the United States, sociologists who do study communities will probably become increasingly specialized. Some will become specialists on urban ecology, some on community power structures, some on the ethnography of urban subareas, some on rural-urban differences, and so on. This may be good, although somebody must always be on hand to remind us that the community is a whole and should be viewed as such. Sociologists

[64] Janet L. Abu-Lughod, "Testing the Theory of Social Area Analysis: The Ecology of Cairo, Egypt," *American Sociological Review*, 34 (April, 1969), 210–12.
[65] Brian J. L. Berry and John D. Kasarda, *Contemporary Urban Ecology* (New York: Macmillan Publishing Co., Inc., 1977).

must not throw up their hands in resignation when confronted with the task of studying the modern urban community with all its complexities. Students of community life have an inescapable responsibility to bring their finest research skills to bear on understanding communities of this type, because within them are harbored the greatest problems and the most exciting potentials of modern society.

BIBLIOGRAPHY

Arensberg, Conrad M. "The Community as Object and as Sample," *American Anthropologist,* **63** (April, 1961), 241–64.

Aschenbrenner, Joyce. *Lifelines: Black Families in Chicago.* New York: Holt, Rinehart and Winston, 1975.

Bahr, Howard M., and Jack P. Gibbs. "Racial Differentiation in American Metropolitan Areas," *Social Forces,* **45** (June, 1967), 521–32.

Bell, Colin, and Howard Newby. *Community Studies: An Introduction to the Sociology of the Local Community.* New York: Praeger Publishers, Inc., 1972.

——— (eds.). *The Sociology of Community.* London: Frank Cass and Company, 1974.

Carr, Lowell Julliard, and James Edson Stermer. *Willow Run: A Study of Cultural Inadequacy.* New York: Harper & Row, 1952.

Davis, Allison, Burleigh B. Gardner, and Mary R. Gardner. *Deep South.* Chicago: University of Chicago Press, 1941.

Dollard, John. *Caste and Class in a Southern Town.* New Haven: Yale University Press, 1937.

Gans, Herbert J. *The Urban Villagers.* New York: The Free Press, 1962.

Glenn, Norval D., and Lester Hill, Jr. "Rural-Urban Differences in Attitudes and Behavior in the United States," in Jacqueline Scherer (ed.), *Annual Editions: Urban Society.* Guilford, Conn.: The Dushkin Publishing Group, 1978, pp. 12–20.

Hannerz, Ulf. *Soulside: Inquiries into Ghetto Culture and Community.* New York: Columbia University Press, 1969.

Harry, Joseph. "Urbanization and the Gay Life," *The Journal of Sex Research,* **10** (August, 1974), 238–47.

Havighurst, Robert J., and H. Gerthen Morgan, *The Social History of a War-Boom Community.* New York: Longmans, Green and Company, 1951.

Hollingshead, August B. "Community Research: Development and Present Condition," *American Sociological Review,* **13** (April, 1948), 136–46.

———. *Elmtown's Youth.* New York: John Wiley & Sons, Inc., 1949.

Konig, Rene. *The Community,* translated by Edward Fitzgerald. New York: Schocken Books, 1968.

Leeper, Joseph S. "The Future of Butte, Montana: A Special Kind of Uncertainty," *The Social Science Journal,* **14** (January, 1977), 111–17.

LeMasters, E. E. *Blue-Collar Aristocrats: Life-Styles at a Working-Class Tavern.* Madison: University of Wisconsin Press, 1975.

Liebow, Elliot. *Tally's Corner: A Study of Negro Streetcorner Men.* Boston: Little, Brown and Company, 1967.

Lynd, Robert S., and Helen Merrell Lynd. *Middletown: A Study of American Culture.* New York: Harcourt Brace Jovanovich, Inc., 1929.

————. *Middletown in Transition.* New York: Harcourt Brace Jovanovich, Inc., 1937.

Nelsen, Hart M., Raytha L. Yokley, and Thomas W. Madron. "Rural-Urban Differences in Religiosity," *Rural Sociology,* 36 (September, 1971), 389–96.

Nelson, Joel I. "Participation and College Aspirations: Complex Effects of Community Size," *Rural Sociology,* 38 (Spring, 1973), 7–16.

Pfautz, Harold W. (ed.), *Charles Booth on the City: Pattern and Social Structure.* Chicago: University of Chicago Press, 1968.

Roebuck, Julian B., and Wolfgang Frese. "The After-Hours Club: An Illegal Social Organization and Its Client System," *Urban Life,* 5 (July, 1976), 131–64.

Simpson, Richard L. "Sociology of the Community: Current Status and Prospects," *Rural Sociology,* 30 (June, 1965), 127–49.

Sjoberg, Gideon, and Roger Nett. *A Methodology for Social Research.* New York: Harper & Row, 1968.

Spradley, James C. *You Owe Yourself a Drunk: An Ethnography of Urban Nomads.* Boston: Little, Brown and Company, 1970.

Stack, Carol B. *All Our Kin.* New York: Harper & Row, 1974.

Stein, Maurice R. *The Eclipse of Community: An Interpretation of American Studies.* Princeton, N.J.: Princeton University Press, 1960.

Steward, Julian H. *Area Research: Theory and Practice.* New York: Social Science Research Council Bulletin 63, 1950.

Suttles, Gerald D. *The Social Order of the Slum: Ethnicity and Territory in the Inner City.* Chicago: University of Chicago Press, 1968.

Vidich, Arthur J., and Joseph Bensman. *Small Town in Mass Society.* Princeton, N.J.: Princeton University Press, 1953.

————, and Maurice R. Stein. *Reflections on Community Studies.* New York: John Wiley & Sons, Inc., 1964.

Warner, W. Lloyd, and associates. *Democracy in Jonesville.* New York: Harper & Row, 1949.

Warner, W. Lloyd, and Paul S. Lunt. *The Social Life of a Modern Community.* New Haven: Yale University Press, 1941.

————. *The Status System of a Modern Community.* New Haven: Yale University Press, 1941.

West, James. *Plainville, U.S.A.* New York: Columbia University Press, 1945.

Whyte, William Foote. *Street Corner Society.* Chicago: University of Chicago Press, 1955.

CHAPTER 11

□□□□□□□□ □
□
□
□
□
□
□
□
□
□

Methods of Community Study

There are several different methods by which communities can be studied. Among the most fruitful of these are participant observation, the social survey, and the use of documents. The applicability of these research methods to the study of community structure and process is the concern of this chapter.

In discussing the three major methods by which the community can be studied, we shall focus on the type of data each method yields, on what each demands of the investigator, and on the advantages and limitations inherent in each. We shall not present a series of practical instructions relating to the use of each method,[1] nor will we argue that the student of community life must choose either participant observation, the social survey, or documentary analysis as his or her basic approach to research. A competent investigator can and often should use all three approaches to further his or her investigation.

□ PARTICIPANT OBSERVATION

Participant observation is more closely identified with the study of communities than is any other method of research. Not only has participant observation been the dominant methodological approach used by anthro-

---

[1] There are a number of textbooks that give the reader specific instructions on conducting research. For example, see Earl R. Babbie, *The Practice of Social Research* (Belmont, Calif.: Wadsworth Publishing Company, 1975); John T. Doby (ed.), *An Introduction to Social Research,* 2nd ed. (New York: Appleton-Century-Crofts, 1967); Henry L. Manheim, *Sociological Research: Philosophy and Methods* (Homewood, Ill.: The Dorsey Press, 1977); Bernard S. Phillips, *Social Research: Strategy and Tactics,* 3rd ed. (New York: Macmillan Publishing Co., Inc., 1976).

pologists to study small, isolated communities, but also it has been utilized in conducting some of the most perceptive studies of American community life. Some of these studies were considered in Chapter 10 including the Lynds's famous studies of Middletown, Liebow's study of Tally's Corner, LeMasters's study of the blue-collar aristocrats, and Suttles's study of a Chicago ghetto. The popularity of participant observation as a method of studying the community lies in the fact that it can, when skillfully used, reveal aspects of community structure and process that cannot be uncovered in any other way.

Participant Observation: Definitions and Goals

There have been several good, relatively simple definitions of participant observation.[2] However, the nature of a rather complicated method of research cannot be explained in a few words. Rather, in explaining participant observation to the uninitiated, three comments are in order:

1. Participant observation represents a particularly effective way to study units of social organization such as "primitive societies, deviant subcultures, complex organizations, social movements, communities, and informal groups."[3] On the other hand, it does not lend itself to the collection of large amounts of statistical data. Studies that demand this type of data are best carried out by means of a social survey.

2. In participant observation the investigator assumes a role within the group or community he or she seeks to study. It is through his or her participation in community life that the investigator collects data and gains insight into community structure and process. This means that the role of the participant observer can be extremely demanding. It may be literally years before the investigator has observed enough to render a valid analysis of the community. During this time he or she must carefully build and maintain rapport with community members, conscientiously scrutinize the effects of his or her presence on their behavior, and keep elaborate field notes. Furthermore, the participant observer uses a variety of specific techniques to collect data. These include direct observation, interviewing, and the analysis of documents.[4]

3. In contrast to social surveys, studies that utilize participant observation are relatively unstructured. Indeed, one of the major advantages of this method of collecting data is that the investigator is free to capitalize

[2] For example, see Morris S. Schwartz and Charlotte Green Schwartz, "Problems in Participant Observation," *American Journal of Sociology*, **60** (January, 1955), 344.
[3] George J. McCall and J. L. Simmons, *Issues in Participant Observation: A Text and Reader* (Reading, Mass.: Addison-Wesley Publishing Company, 1969), p. 1.
[4] For a brief discussion of the techniques used in participant observation see ibid., pp. 61–64.

on unanticipated research opportunities as they present themselves and to make use of informants in the most strategic way possible.[5] At the same time, the unstructured quality of participant observation increases the risk that the investigator will spend a great deal of time collecting superfluous data. Unless the investigator keeps the ultimate goals of the study in mind, he or she could painstakingly record a great many observations that are of little use to anyone.

It is hoped that these comments make it clear that participant observation is that style of research in which the investigator collects data by actually living, working, or otherwise interacting with the study group. If the study focuses on the inner workings of a modern factory, he or she might well obtain a job as a factory worker. Similarly, in the course of studying a particular community, the investigator would take up residence in that community and observe it directly.[6] There are some types of data that can be collected only in this way.

Techniques of Participant Observation

Participant observation involves the use of several highly specialized research techniques. Some of these techniques must now be examined.

Direct observation is the core technique used in participant observation. Indeed, participant observation draws its strength from the fact that the investigator observes the community firsthand and witnesses the behavior of local residents in a variety of situations. Sometimes it is only because of this role as a direct observer that the investigator can gain a full appreciation of the subtleties of community life. This is especially true when an event occurs that is particularly dramatic but cannot be anticipated in advance. When events of this type occur, local residents may not be able to describe what really happened. To expect them to put their deepest feelings into words is simply asking too much.

Direct participation is another basic technique used by the participant observer. The difference between direct participation and direct observation should be clear. In direct participation, the investigator assumes a role within the study group and becomes directly involved in its activities. For example, if the investigator seeks to study ways of life in a particular

[5] See John P. Dean, Robert L. Eichhorn, and Lois R. Dean, "Observation and Interviewing," in Doby (ed.), *An Introduction to Social Research*, pp. 274–75.
[6] For two very insightful collections of essays in which a number of eminent researchers discuss various aspects of their own fieldwork experiences see Arthur J. Vidich, Joseph P. Bensman, and Maurice R. Stein, *Reflections on Community Studies* (New York: John Wiley & Sons, Inc., 1964), and George D. Spindler, *Being an Anthropologist: Fieldwork in Eleven Cultures* (New York: Holt, Rinehart and Winston, 1970).

ghetto, he or she would become a participating member of that ghetto. Similarly, if several local groups were at odds with each other over a highly significant issue (e.g., school integration), the investigator might become involved in the controversy as a means of getting an inside view of community conflict. A research procedure of this type can of course entail several dangers. Among other things, the investigator may well become so devoted to group purposes that he or she loses scientific objectivity and detachment. Likewise, in conducting research, the investigator may become so closely identified with one group that he or she permanently jeopardizes the chances of studying other groups.[7] Nonetheless, many proponents of direct participation maintain that these risks must be taken and that direct participation is the only way by which the sociologist can capture the full meaning and significance of group activities. It is hoped that participant observation helps us to see the truly human dimension of the phenomena we seek to understand.

There are several other research techniques used in participant observation. For example, the observer must do a great deal of interviewing. In this respect, McCall and Simmons draw a useful distinction between informant and respondent interviewing.[8] In informant interviewing, the investigator simply asks informed community members to tell about events that have happened and to interpret things the investigator has observed him- or herself. This type of interviewing is used with great frequency in participant observation simply because the investigator cannot directly observe everything that happens or always make sense out of what he or she does observe. The great challenge posed by informant interviewing is of course to get the informant "to report hard, particular facts so that the scientist can form his own, often quite different generalizations."[9] In respondent interviewing, on the other hand, the interviewee is not used as an assistant observer. Rather, the investigator seeks facts about the interviewee him- or herself. This type of interviewing is similar to that used in social surveys.

Finally, the participant observer must use a wide variety of documents and unpublished records. This includes statistical material that has been compiled and/or published by federal, state, or local governments as well as newspapers, minutes of meetings, and even personal diaries. Data of this type are of significant value to the participant observer, and indeed to any student of community life. Among other things, the use of data of this type can save the investigator a great deal of time and often

[7] See Colin Bell and Howard Newby, *Community Studies: An Introduction to the Sociology of the Local Community* (New York: Praeger Publishers, 1972), esp. pp. 66–67.

[8] McCall and Simmons, *Issues in Participant Observation*, p. 4.

[9] Ibid., p. 4.

represent the participant observer's only source of information pertaining to certain types of events. This is particularly true of events that happened so long ago that no informants can recall them.

Field Roles of the Participant Observer

One of the hallmarks of participant observation is that the investigator's behavior can have a profound impact on the type and quality of data he or she collects. Because of this a great deal of attention has been focused on the types of roles the investigator can assume. Two of the most insightful analyses along these lines are those offered by Raymond Gold and Robert Janes.

A Typology of Field Roles: Raymond Gold. Raymond Gold argues that there are essentially four roles that can be adopted by the participant observer.[10] These roles seem to lie along a continuum with the *complete participant* at one end and the *complete observer* at the other. Intermediate role types are the *participant-as-observer* and the *observer-as-participant.*

The investigator who conceals his or her true identity and purposes from those being observed is acting in the role of a *complete participant.* Rather than letting it be known that he or she is an investigator, he or she assumes the role behaviors appropriate to members of the group. The *complete observer*, on the other hand, refrains from interacting with group members and may not even make his or her presence known. Because members of the group are at most vaguely aware of the investigator's presence, the investigator presumably has little influence on their behavior. This research role is frequently used in studies of small-group behavior. In research of this type it is not uncommon for the investigator to observe a laboratory group through a one-way mirror or to eavesdrop systematically on group members in some other way. This role is not particularly useful when one is conducting a genuine field study. People quickly become aware that there is a stranger in their midst and seek an explanation for his or her presence. This is all the more true when the investigator's activities are unique or unusual, as may be the case if the stranger is also a participant observer.

Once these two field roles are clearly understood, then the other two roles can be easily explained. Thus the *participant-as-observer* role has much in common with the role played by the complete participant. The only major difference between the two roles is that in the participant-as-

---

[10] See Raymond L. Gold, "Roles in Sociological Field Observation," *Social Forces, 36* (March, 1958), 217–23.

observer relationship "both field worker and informant are aware that theirs is a field relationship." [11] This role is used with great frequency in field studies of community life. It is very common for the investigator to announce his or her purposes and intentions but then to blend into the fabric of local life as much as possible. On the other hand, the role played by the *observer-as-participant* has certain things in common with the role played by the complete observer. The investigator explains that he or she is conducting a field study but then tries, as much as possible, to remain aloof from direct participation in community events and activities. According to Gold, "the observer-as-participant role is used in studies involving one-visit interviews." [12] However, it is difficult to see why this has to be the case. A skilled investigator can explain his or her purposes to community members but still place emphasis on observation rather than participation.

The reasons why Gold and others have analyzed the roles that the participant observer can assume are more than purely academic. Rather, this type of analysis is of crucial importance, because the correlation between the role the investigator assumes and the type and quality of data he or she collects may be strong. For example, the "complete participant" is less likely to have a lasting influence on the behavior of community members than is the investigator who makes it known that he or she is conducting research. The reason for this is simple. On the whole, people feel more threatened by a person who, in effect, announces that he or she has come to observe them than by a person whom they think is a new colleague, neighbor, or whatever. The same advantage is inherent in the complete observer role, but for a different reason. In this case community members may not even be aware that there is a new person in their midst. At the same time, both of these roles do pose certain dangers. The complete participant, for example, can easily become so closely identified with the community and its members as to completely lose scientific objectivity and detachment. The complete observer, on the other hand, may remain so aloof and detached as to completely miss many of the subtleties of community life. But more serious than this are the ethical questions brought to the forefront by the practice of concealing one's identity from persons who are being studied. Most of us will say and do things in the presence of a person whom we think to be a new group member that we would not say or do if we knew that our behavior was to be the subject of a research report. The question of whether the investigator has a right to use information obtained by keeping his or her identity concealed is a difficult one indeed.

[11] Ibid., p. 220.
[12] Ibid., p. 221.

Many of these problems are avoided if the investigator reveals his or her identity and purposes to community members. If nothing else the investigator cannot be accused of being a spy or prying into other people's lives. At the same time, we have already hinted that the knowledge that they are being observed and studied may cause some people to modify their behavior. The tendency for community members to put their best foot forward and to conceal the less desirable aspects of their collective existence from the investigator would seem to be great.

The Community Role of the Participant Observer: Robert W. Janes. We have argued that the way in which an investigator enacts the role of an investigator is one variable that affects the type and quality of data the participant observer collects. Another writer, Robert W. Janes, has suggested that the manner in which community members define the investigator's place in the community also affects his or her ability to collect meaningful, accurate data. Because of this we now turn our attention to the "community role" of the participant observer.

To be more specific, in reporting on his field study of Riverville, a small midwestern town, Janes observed that "the community role of the author and his family apparently underwent a progressive redefinition in the course of their residence." [13] When the Janeses first arrived in Riverville they were treated of course as *newcomers*. During their tenure in this role the Janeses were given general information about Riverville and were subjected to careful scrutiny by community members. After spending a period of time in Riverville, Janes was finally "graduated" from his role as a newcomer. At this point local residents defined him as a *provisional member* and then as a *categorical member* of the community. In his role as a provisional member, Janes's occupation was examined very closely, as were his associational memberships and interests (i.e., church affiliation, club memberships, recreational interests, and so on). During this phase of his relationship with the community, local residents voluntarily supplied him with information about people and issues but "without any of the invidious intimations of later statements." [14] By the time that Janes had become accepted as a categorical member of the community, apparently local residents had concluded that his reasons for studying Riverville were legitimate and that it was safe to give him the "inside story" on local people and issues. However, it was not until Janes became defined as a *personalized member* of the community that he was able to establish "a continuing sense of rapport" with community members.[15]

[13] Robert W. Janes, "A Note on Phases of the Community Role of the Participant-Observer," *American Sociological Review,* **26** (June, 1961), 448.
[14] Ibid., p. 448.
[15] Ibid., p. 449.

In this role, Janes was able to get community members to discuss their personal thoughts, feelings, and attitudes with him. Finally, when Janes indicated that he had completed his research and would soon be leaving Riverville, he was assigned the role of *imminent migrant*. In this, the concluding stage of his relationship with the community, Janes found that his informants would offer him no new information about Riverville and its people. Rather, they were more interested in what he thought about the community. Indeed, the residents of Riverville appeared to be somewhat threatened by the Janeses' departure, perhaps because they knew that the die had been cast. Once Janes and his family left Riverville, nothing that they could do would have any influence on his conclusions.

Advantages and Limitations

The advantages and limitations of participant observation have been vigorously debated. Some investigators view it as the only method by which meaningful, valid data can be collected. To others its potentially subjective quality and the fact that it yields largely nonquantifiable data disqualify it as a respectable means of gathering data. Because the merits and deficiencies of participant observation have been so hotly contested, they must be spelled out.

The primary advantage of participant observation lies in the fact that there are certain types of data that can be unearthed only by the investigator who enters into close and continuous interaction with his or her informants. Some advocates of participant observation, for example, would argue that it is only through the field study that one can gain insight into the subtleties of human thought, action, and emotion. A long and highly structured interview is not a satisfactory way of uncovering these types of data, nor is such information available in census materials, courthouse records, or newspapers. Indeed, participant observation does allow the investigator to bring the truly human dimension into a study. It is this fact that apparently prompted Becker and Geer to state that "participant observation can . . . provide us with a yardstick against which to measure the completeness of data gathered in other ways, a model that can serve to let us know what orders of information escape us when we use other methods." [16] Some of the remarks that were made earlier in this chapter should make it clear that the present writer tends to concur with this statement, but with a few qualifications.

[16] Howard S. Becker and Blanche Geer, "Participant Observation and Interviewing: A Comparison," *Human Organization*, **16** (1957), 28.

There are of course other advantages inherent in participant observation. Many of these have been spelled out by Dean, Eichhorn, and Dean.[17] Certainly one of the cardinal advantages of participant observation lies in the fact that as the investigator conducts research, he or she is not wedded to a specific set of questions. Rather, the investigator is free to pursue the quest for knowledge in any seemingly profitable direction. He or she can assume that different informants know different things and can tailor questions to take these "knowledge differentials" into account.[18] This cannot be done when the interviewer is required to ask the same questions of everyone contacted, as is almost always the case in survey research.

At the same time, participant observation has its limitations as a methodological tool. These limitations are indeed serious in that they have a direct bearing on the validity of the data collected. Specifically, two objections to participant observation have been raised:

1. Several writers have noted the hazards that center around the fact that the participant observer becomes a part of the situation he or she is observing.[19] Among other things, the investigator may unavoidably influence the behavior of group members because his or her presence is a reality with which members of the group must cope. They may do this by restricting their conversation when the investigator is present, by "showing off" for the investigator, or by otherwise tailoring their behavior to fit the fact that they are being observed. Similarly, the investigator's close relationship with the study group increases the likelihood that his or her findings and conclusions will reflect a variety of biases. The investigator may identify more closely with one informant than with another and unintentionally may give undue weight to things said by informants he or she personally likes. Furthermore, because the investigator assumes a role within the study group, he or she eventually may grow blind to many of its unique features. The student of community life, for example, can easily come to believe that "the way things are done here is the way in which they are done everywhere." If and when this happens, the investigator has ceased to view the community from the vantage point of a disinterested and objective scientist and has come instead to view it as a community member would. Finally, the very nature of participant observation makes it almost impossible to check the original investigator's conclusions by replicating the study. Another investigator may be accus-

---

[17] See Dean, Eichhorn, and Dean, "Observation and Interviewing," pp. 276–79.
[18] See ibid., p. 275.
[19] For further discussion of this and similar problems see Morris S. Schwartz and Charlotte Green Schwartz, "Problems in Participant Observation," *American Journal of Sociology,* **60** (January, 1955), 343–53.

tomed to looking for different things than the original observer and will relate to informants in different ways.[20] These problems are compounded by the considerable amount of time that may elapse between the original and the replicatory study.

2. Participant observation has also been criticized on the grounds that it usually does not yield quantifiable data. In a sense, this criticism is well taken. Data that can be expressed in quantitative form are more easily presented than qualitative data, and they can be manipulated in such a way that the relationships between two or more variables are revealed. Furthermore, once such a relationship is established, its strength can be measured statistically (for example, by means of correlational analysis). This is usually not the case with data gathered by the participant observer. When the participant observer does manage to quantify observations, it is usually in the form of qualitative statements such as *more than* and *less than, above average* and *below average,* and so on.

Both of these criticisms of participant observation are of course valid. However, participant observation must be evaluated in terms of the uses to which it is put. Although many things can adversely affect the quality of data gathered by this method, at the present time it seems to be the only way by which one can get an *in-depth picture* of communities, subcultures, and complex organizations. Furthermore, it must be hoped that an unbridgeable chasm does not develop between those who favor participant observation and those who prefer the survey approach. As a matter of fact, participant observation can and should supply the investigator with the preliminary information and insight necessary before he or she can begin to test relationships by means of a social survey.

☐ THE SOCIAL SURVEY

When professional sociologists refer to a research project, they often mean a study in which data are gathered by systematically interviewing a large number of people. This is essentially what we mean by a social survey. Indeed, the social survey probably represents the most common method by which sociologists collect data.

[20] For a classic example of this one might compare Robert Redfield's study of Tepoztlan, Mexico, with that of Oscar Lewis, which was conducted some years later. See Robert Redfield, *Tepoztlan: A Mexican Village* (Chicago: University of Chicago Press, 1930); Oscar Lewis, *Life in a Mexican Village: Tepoztlan Restudied* (Urbana: University of Illinois Press, 1963). Both of these studies were discussed and evaluated in Chapter 5.

Characteristics of the Survey Approach

There are several ways by which the characteristics of a social survey could be explained. However, because we have just discussed participant observation, perhaps we can learn the most about the social survey by comparing it with participant observation. Our previous discussion should make it clear that three characteristics of participant observation stand out above all others in importance. First, in participant observation the investigator uses a small number of informants. These informants are hand-picked in terms of their ability to shed light on the research problem of interest to the investigator. Second, the investigator tailors questions to fit each informant. This is because the investigator recognizes that each informant can make a unique contribution to the understanding of the problem. Finally, the data collected by the participant observer are usually nonquantitative: they consist of a series of more or less factual statements made by both the informants and the investigator. The characteristics of a social survey are rather different. They may be summarized as follows:

1. In survey research the investigator collects data through interviews with a very large number of people. Sometimes this includes every member of the study population (e.g., all residents of Murray, Kentucky), but it is more common to draw a sample representative of the larger population (e.g., every tenth resident). This is done because conclusions based on interviews with a relatively small number of respondents can be just as valid as conclusions based on interviews with all members of the study population, assuming that the sample is carefully chosen. This means a considerable savings in both time and money. Furthermore, the survey researcher never hand-picks respondents. Rather, the goal is to determine what characteristics are typical of the study population; therefore the investigator chooses respondents at random. At the completion of fieldwork the survey researcher has normally interviewed a rather large number of people. The sample presumably mirrors the larger population and therefore provides a picture of that population. This is in distinct contrast to the method used by the participant observer. The participant observer frequently collects data from a small number of exceptionally well-informed, articulate people.

2. In survey research each respondent is asked the same questions and must answer these questions in terms of a few clearly defined categories. If this is not the case (i.e., if the questions are open-ended), then the investigator classifies the respondent's answers after the interview has been completed. There are advantages to this procedure. [21] Among other

---

[21] The so-called structured interview also has some serious disadvantages. For a discussion of both its advantages and disadvantages see Clair Selltiz et al., *Research*

things, it greatly simplifies the task of processing and analyzing the raw data. The investigator does not have to decide what the respondent "really said," nor does the investigator have to comb through a wide variety of statements relating to a number of diverse subjects. Rather, he or she simply counts the number of responses that fall into each category and presents the findings in tabular form. This again is a much different procedure than that used by the participant observer. In analyzing findings, the participant observer is faced with the enormous task of sorting through a wide variety of statements and personal observations and of organizing them in such a way as to test his or her hypotheses and theories. Most of the time it is impossible for the participant observer to present data in tabular form.

3. Finally, the survey approach is particularly suitable for testing hypotheses and theories. There are two reasons for this. First, we have already indicated that survey data are easily converted into quantitative form: one simply counts the number of respondents who are male or female, who favor or who are against a particular policy, or whatever. These data can then be cross-tabulated, that is, tables can be constructed to see if there is a relationship between an independent variable such as age, race, or sex and a dependent variable such as satisfaction with the community in which the respondents live. Second, in the social sciences most hypotheses either consist of a simple proposition or state a relationship between two or more variables.[22] In a study of attitudes toward local government, for example, we might hypothesize that people who live in small communities tend to disapprove of the city manager form of government. Likewise, we might also hypothesize that people of high socioeconomic status have more favorable attitudes toward city managers than do people of low socioeconomic status. If the survey researcher asks the right questions, he or she can easily test both of these hypotheses. To be more specific, the percentage of the total population that disapproves of the city manager form of government can easily be determined and the investigator can use correlational analysis to measure the relationship between socioeconomic status and attitudes toward city managers. Operations of this type cannot be performed with data collected by the participant observer. At most, the participant observer can report that it was his or her impression that most people

Methods in Social Relations, rev. ed. (New York: Holt, Rinehart and Winston, 1959), pp. 259–63.
[22] See Bernard S. Phillips, *Social Research: Strategy and Tactics,* 2nd ed. (New York: Macmillan Publishing Co., Inc., 1966). All references to Phillips in the pages that follow are from this edition of his book. See also Sanford Labovitz and Robert Hagedorn, *Introduction to Social Research* (New York: McGraw-Hill Book Company, 1971), esp. pp. 1–12.

disapprove of the city manager form of government. Likewise, the participant observer may be convinced that people of high socioeconomic status have more favorable attitudes toward city managers than do people of low socioeconomic status, but he or she usually cannot calculate statistics and construct tables to show that this is the case.

It should be clear that our purpose is not to criticize participant observation. Rather, we seek only to acquaint the reader with some of the basic properties of the social survey. To be more specific, we have indicated that the survey researcher collects data from a large number of randomly selected respondents, that all respondents are asked about the same questions, and that data collected by means of a survey lend themselves to the testing of hypotheses. This method of collecting data has many advantages.

The Outlines of Social Survey

We must examine the applicability of the survey approach to the study of communities. Before doing this, however, it might be helpful to trace the steps entailed in conducting a social survey. This review will be superfluous for the reader who is experienced in social research, but it may help the inexperienced person to understand the methodological procedures involved in conducting a social survey.

Delineating the Problem. The first step in any scientific investigation is to delineate a research problem. The investigator must decide what it is that he or she wishes to investigate and clearly indicate the nature of the study. When one first becomes interested in doing research one will have of course only a vague idea concerning the direction one's research might take. As time passes, however, one's preliminary "ideas must be translated into a precise statement of the research problem: preferably the investigator will before he begins his fieldwork, be able to specify one or more hypotheses which will guide his research." [23] If one's research problem is not delimited in this manner, one may make little progress toward completing the study.

There are several things that influence the investigator's choice of research problems. One of these is the availability of research funds. Although most agencies that support research do allow the investigator a considerable amount of freedom in defining a problem, they also insist that the research be relevant to their needs. In addition to funding, how-

---

[23] The characteristics of a good hypothesis are discussed in William J. Goode and Paul K. Hatt, *Methods of Social Research* (New York: McGraw-Hill Book Company, 1952), pp. 68–73.

ever, there are other things that should be considered in choosing a research problem. Some of these can make or break a study.

1. The investigator must carefully appraise the potential value of the research. The value of a study of course can be measured in several ways. For example, the student of community life might well ask whether the proposed research will fill a gap in our understanding of communities and/or whether it will test some of our theories of community structure and process. Phillips puts the case well when he states that "a wise choice of a scientific problem differs from an unwise choice in that it advances the goals of science; and unwise choice does not." [24] Similarly, the investigator might also consider whether a study will enhance our ability to solve community problems. If both of these questions can be answered in the affirmative, then the investigator is undoubtedly on the right track in terms of choosing a good research problem.

2. The investigator must also ask whether the proposed research is technically feasible. Is the problem suitable for study by means of a social survey? Can data be collected that will enable the investigator to test his or her hypotheses? It is one thing to jot down a list of hypotheses that capture one's interest and enthusiasm. It can be much more difficult to devise rigorous means to test them.

3. The investigator should always consider whether he or she has sufficient resources to carry out the research. If a social survey is the only feasible means by which the study can be conducted, then the investigator must recognize that the survey approach normally requires that interviewers be hired and trained. Likewise, the investigator must be well versed in questionnaire construction and statistical and computer analysis, and above all must possess a goodly amount of patience. An investigator who cannot provide these things might be well advised to try another type of research.

4. Finally, the investigator must be thoroughly dedicated to the research and firmly convinced that the problem is worth pursuing. It must be remembered that any type of research is difficult and demanding. If the problem and the research it entails do not ignite the investigator's enthusiasm and imagination, the research project will soon become a nightmare.

Research Design. Once the research problem has been delineated, the investigator must develop a research design. A research design simply specifies the procedures that will be followed in conducting the study. In survey research, for example, the research design must delineate the study population and indicate the methods that will be used in selecting

[24] Phillips, *Social Research*, p. 75.

a sample of respondents from this population. In addition, it should indicate the type of data collection instrument that will be used and how the raw data will be analyzed.[25] A good research design is one that is both thorough and detailed: careful attention to matters of research design is essential if one's study is to be successfully completed. Bernard S. Phillips, for example, tells us that "the attempt to formulate a research design very early in the development of the investigation can aid the scientist in achieving a more focused approach. In moving from problem definition to research design, the implications of the general research goals must be outlined in order to make decisions on specific procedures." [26]

Data Collection. After a research problem has been selected and the research design has been developed, the investigator must focus on the technicalities of conducting the survey. One usually begins by identifying the persons one intends to interview. As has already been indicated, one may decide to interview all members of the study population. In conducting most surveys, however, this is both impractical and unnecessary because a sample can be chosen that accurately reflects the entire population.

It is beyond the scope of this book to offer a detailed discussion of sampling procedures.[27] In most social surveys the investigator uses a random sample or some variation thereof. By this we mean that each member of the study population has an equal chance of being included in the sample. If this procedure is followed and if the sample is of the correct size, then the members of the sample should closely parallel the members of the study population in their characteristics and attributes. For example, if nonwhite females make up 20 per cent of the study population, then approximately 20 per cent of a carefully drawn sample will consist of nonwhite females. The same relationship between the sample and the study population should hold in terms of the variables on which the investigator wishes to collect data. It is only because of the tendency for a random sample to mirror the larger population that a sample survey can yield results as trustworthy as those obtained by a complete enumeration of the population.

[25] The things that should go into a good statement of research design are outlined in Delbert C. Miller, *Handbook of Research Design and Social Measurement*, 2nd ed. (New York: David McKay Company, 1970), pp. 3–6.
[26] Phillips, *Social Research*, pp. 77–78.
[27] There are a number of good discussions of types of samples and of sampling procedures. See Russell L. Ackoff, *The Design of Social Research* (Chicago: University of Chicago Press, 1953), pp. 83–126, and Leslie Kish, *Survey Sampling* (New York: John Wiley & Sons, Inc., 1965).

At about the same time that a sample is drawn, the investigator must also decide what information to obtain from respondents. We shall not deal with the technicalities of constructing and administering a satisfactory interview schedule.[28] However, as the investigator embarks on this phase of the research, there are several things to keep in mind. In the first place, he or she should remember that the interview schedule is a tool which helps to gather data that bear directly on the problem or hypotheses. Each time the investigator adds a question to the interview schedule he or she might well ask how it will contribute to the study. Second, the investigator must also give some thought to how respondents will react to the questions he or she proposes to ask them.[29] It is nonsensical to ask questions that respondents cannot or will not answer. In this regard, attention must be paid to questions that require the respondent to recall something (e.g., a previous year's income) and to those which touch on particularly sensitive topics (e.g., personal deviance, sexual behavior, and so on). Lastly, we might point out that there are a variety of norms that guide the experienced investigator in constructing an interview schedule.[30] These norms relate to the way in which questions are worded, the order in which they are presented to the respondent, and so forth.

Assuming that data are to be collected by means of an interview, the last step in the data collection phase is to administer the interview to all members of the sample. It is essential that the interviewer be highly skilled if valid, reliable data are to be obtained. Undoubtedly the most important skill the interviewer must possess is the ability to communicate. Indeed, Dean, Eichhorn, and Dean remind us that "the crux of a successful survey is the communication process that takes place in the interview." [31] This means that interviewers must be well trained and highly motivated. If these conditions are met and if the interview schedule has been carefully designed, then the investigator can have confidence in the findings. If they are not met, then the data may be worthless.

[28] Again, several good discussions are available. See Charles F. Cannell and Robert L. Kahn, "Interviewing" in Gardner Lindsey and Elliott Aronson, *The Handbook of Social Psychology*, 2nd ed., Vol. II (Reading, Mass.: Addison-Wesley Publishing Company, 1968), pp. 526–90.
[29] Leon Festinger and Daniel Katz (eds.), *Research Methods in the Behavioral Sciences* (New York: Holt, Rinehart and Winston, 1953), pp. 16–17.
[30] See Gideon Sjoberg and Roger Nett, *A Methodology for Social Research* (New York: Harper & Row, 1968), pp. 199–202.
[31] Dean, Eichhorn, and Dean, "The Survey," in Doby (ed.), *An Introduction to Social Research*, 2nd ed., p. 251.

Analysis and Presentation of Data. The analysis and presentation of one's findings constitute the final step in any research project. With the development of modern statistical techniques and of high-speed computers, the analysis of survey data has become rather complicated. However, the person who is new to survey research may find this task easier if he or she realizes that the logic of survey analysis is very simple: the investigator tries to determine what factors (independent variables) cause variation in the phenomena (dependent variables) being observed (e.g., the factors that cause some people to look askance at the city manager form of government). Sometimes this can be done only by controlling other factors that might cause a spurious relationship between the independent and dependent variables.

The way in which the investigator presents findings depends partly on publication plans. Every publisher has its own expectations concerning the length of the manuscript and the amount of technical detail included in it. Furthermore, the way the investigator prepares a report depends partly on whether he or she intends to disseminate the findings to professional colleagues or to the general public. On the whole, reports prepared for consumption by a professional audience deal more thoroughly with technical and methodological details than those that are to have a wider readership. This does not mean that the investigator can cut corners in preparing material for presentation to the general public. Anyone who is willing to wade through a research report has the right to know how and why the investigator arrived at his or her conclusions.

Social Surveys and Community Study

Little has been written during recent years concerning the use of social surveys in studying community life. Nonetheless, many of the earliest social surveys were essentially community studies. One thinks immediately, for example, of Charles Booth's monumental studies of London and its people.[32] Booth's seventeen-volume work was published between 1892 and 1896 and has been hailed by Sidney and Beatrice Webb as "the greatest statistical enterprise ever attempted by a private investigator at his own expense."[33] Likewise, B. S. Rowntree's almost equally famous surveys of York, England (circa 1900 and 1936), should not be forgotten, nor should the Pittsburgh Survey (1909–1914) conducted by Paul

[32] Charles Booth, *Life and Labour of the People in London* (London: Macmillan Company, Limited, 1902).
[33] Cited in Pauline V. Young, *Scientific Social Surveys and Research,* 3rd ed. (Englewood Cliffs, N.J.: Prentice-Hall, Inc., 1956), p. 13.

Kellogg.[34] The most noteworthy feature of these early community studies was their broad scope and richness of detail.

Today there is a tendency to use the survey approach to investigate very specialized problems. Needless to say, we cannot possibly discuss all the ways in which the survey approach can be used to study community life. However, some of the more important problems which can be investigated by means of a survey are the following:

1. A social survey is the only practical means by which quantitative data on the characteristics of the study population can be collected. It might be noted in passing that the U.S. Census is essentially a survey, the precision and richness of which make it an outstanding source of social, economic, and demographic data. It is also appropriate to use the survey approach to collect data on socioeconomic status, standards of living, and innumerable other characteristics of community members. When data of this type are collected, they are usually cross-tabulated with data pertaining to the respondent's behavior, attitudes, or values.

2. A social survey also lends itself to the collection of data relating to social participation and the use of community services. Data on associational membership, church attendance, use of public facilities, and involvement in local politics can all be gathered by means of a survey. To cite one example, Babchuk and Booth have collected data pertaining to the membership of Nebraska's adult population in voluntary associations.[35] Likewise, the University of Kentucky's Bureau of Community Services has published data on reading and library use in Lexington, Kentucky. These data, taken from interviews with a sample of 484 respondents, reveal that the residents of this city read more than one might expect [36] but that many of them never use the public library.[37] Data of this type are usually collected in order to test hypotheses, some of which can be rather significant. It could be hypothesized, for example, that there is a relationship between community size and participation in voluntary associations, the use of libraries and other public facilities, or attitudes toward community improvement projects. The significance that can be attached to studies of this type depends of course on the degree to which they shed light on theories of community or help us in finding solutions to community problems.

3. The social survey is a useful tool for collecting data on patterns

---

[34] Dates in parentheses indicate the year in which the surveys were conducted. All of these studies are discussed in ibid., pp. 9–24.

[35] See Nicholas Babchuk and Alan Booth, "Voluntary Association Membership: A Longitudinal Analysis," *American Sociological Review,* 34 (February, 1969), 31–45.

[36] Dennis E. Poplin, *Reading and Library Use in Lexington, Kentucky* (University of Kentucky: Kentucky Community Series Number 30, November, 1964), p. 9.

[37] Ibid., Tables 29 and 30.

of interaction. For example, several surveys have been conducted that shed light on patterns of neighboring in cities and metropolitan areas.[38] Generally speaking, these studies indicate that nonfamilial, primary group ties are stronger and more viable than we once thought. In all fairness, however, we must point out that William H. Key used survey data to test the hypothesis that the amount of "neighboring" decreases as the size of a community increases. Key's hypothesis was borne out.[39] The survey approach can also be used to determine the amount of interaction among the various racial, ethnic, religious, and status groups found in the modern community.

4. Perhaps the most important value of the survey approach is that it enables us to collect data on the attitudes and perceptions of community members. Among other things, surveys can be designed that shed light on people's attitudes toward local government, local schools, local welfare agencies, or any other group, institution, or program. Likewise, ways have been developed to measure a person's attitude toward the community in which he or she lives. Especially to be noted in this regard are Claud A. Bosworth's *Community Attitude Scale* and Donald R. Fessler's *Community Solidarity Index*.[40] The latter scale is particularly interesting in that it measures a person's opinion of his or her own community. In a similar vein, Schulze, Artis, and Beegle have developed a scale that enables us to determine the degree of satisfaction that people feel with their own community.[41] We can use a scale of this type to determine if there is any relationship between community satisfaction and whether people are likely to migrate, to engage in deviant behavior, and so on. Finally, the survey approach can be used to collect data pertaining to the perceptions held by community members. In doing research on community power structures, for example, we often ask our respondents who, in their opinion, holds power and makes the key decisions in their community.

[38] For example, see Wendell Bell and Marion T. Boat, "Urban Neighborhoods and Informal Social Relations," *American Journal of Sociology*, 62 (January, 1957), 391–98, and Joel Smith, William H. Form, and Gregory P. Stone, "Local Intimacy in a Middle-Sized City," *American Journal of Sociology*, 60 (November, 1964), 176–84.
[39] William H. Key, "Urbanism and Neighboring," *The Sociological Quarterly*, 6 (Winter, 1965), 379–85.
[40] Both scales are reproduced in Miller, *Handbook of Research Design and Social Measurement*, pp. 193–201. Bosworth's scale was originally presented in his Ph.D. dissertation (University of Michigan, 1954), whereas Fessler's scale was first published in his article "The Development of a Scale for Measuring Community Solidarity," *Rural Sociology*, 17 (June, 1952), 144–52.
[41] Rolf Schulze, Jay Artis, and J. Allan Beegle, "The Measurement of Community Satisfaction and the Decision to Migrate," *Rural Sociology*, 28 (1963), 279–83.

Other facets of community life can be studied by the survey researcher. However, the preceding discussion gives the reader some idea of the type and range of data that can be collected by this method. It should be remembered, of course, that relatively few surveys are of interest to the student of community life. All too often we fail to distinguish between research *on* communities and research that is only tangentially related to community study.

☐ DOCUMENTS AS DATA

The use of participant observation and/or the survey approach allows the investigator to collect data on many different research problems. The only limitation on the topics that the investigator can explore are those imposed by social norms. There are some things people think and do that are simply not revealed to a stranger. However, the investigator should also realize that he or she can often unearth a wealth of *data compiled by other people*. The use of documents as sources of data is of paramount importance in social research.

In most communities these types of data are available in abundance. One thinks immediately, for example, of documents of a historical nature. With a little searching, the investigator can frequently locate histories of the community, of some of its organizations, and of some of its leading families. These histories may be compiled by private citizens, or their compilation may be an official function of the mayor's office, a club secretary, or someone else. In some research projects the use of historical materials is absolutely essential if one is to understand the community and its present configurations. The present grows out of the past. At the same time, the investigator who has little or no training in the use of historical documents should proceed with care. Historical documents range all the way from those whose credibility and authenticity are beyond question to those that are completely fraudulent. There are a number of books and articles that spell out guidelines for determining the value of historical materials.[42]

In addition to formal histories, a host of official and semiofficial records is usually available to the student of community life. Included are records relating to vital events (births, deaths, marriages, and divorces), school

---

[42] See especially Louis Gottschalk, "The Historian and the Historical Document," in Louis Gottschalk, Clyde Kluckhohn, and Robert Angell, *The Use of Personal Documents in History, Anthropology and Sociology* (New York: Social Science Research Council Bulletin 53, 1945), pp. 28–47; and Jacques Barzun and Henry F. Graff, *The Modern Researcher,* rev. ed. (New York: Harcourt Brace Jovanovich, Inc., 1970), esp. pp. 99–128.

attendance, property transactions, arrests, and so forth, as well as governmental budgets, the annual reports of social agencies, and the minutes of various meetings. Sometimes records of this type are kept for years so that the investigator can study changes in the variables of interest. Likewise, the local newspaper is a potentially valuable source of data. The uses to which its articles, editorials, letters to the editor, and even advertisements can be put is limited only by the investigator's creativity. This does not mean, however, that there are no hazards inherent in the use of newspapers as sources of scientific insight. The contents of the typical newspaper are carefully selected, and the publisher's primary goal is to produce a document that will be widely read. This means that some community-relevant activities and events do not get newspaper coverage whereas other events and activities are overdramatized.

Finally, the U.S. census of population is an invaluable source of information for the student of community life. Perhaps the only way for an inexperienced investigator to familiarize him- or herself with its contents is by browsing through its many volumes. If a person is interested in a particular Standard Metropolitan Statistical Area, for example, some of the more important items of information that can be gleaned from the census of population are as follows:

1. The total population of the SMSA, cross-classified by age, sex, and race.
2. Number of persons in the labor force, classified by employment status (employed, unemployed) and cross-classified by race and sex.
3. Occupational composition of the labor force (number of persons in professional, technical, and managerial occupations, in clerical and sales occupations, etc.), by sex and race.
4. Median number of years of schooling completed by persons twenty-five years of age and over, cross-classified by sex and race.
5. Median income of families and unrelated individuals.

These data are published for all communities having a population of 2,500 or more. The U.S. Bureau of the Census publishes more detailed data for Standard Metropolitan Statistical Areas. Furthermore, for the SMSAs these data are available not only for the metropolitan area as a whole but also for each of its census tracts. These, according to the Bureau of the Census, are "small, permanently established, geographical areas into which large cities and their environs have been divided for statistical purposes." [43] Normally, census tracts have a population of 4,000 or more

[43] U.S. Bureau of the Census, *Census Tract Manual*, 5th ed. (Washington, D.C.: U.S. Government Printing Office, 1966), p. i.

and are relatively homogeneous in terms of their demographic, social, and economic characteristics. Thus the investigator who knows how to use the U.S. census of population has a wealth of information at his or her fingertips. This information can serve as background data for a social survey or a field study or as the raw data for a demographic analysis of the community. Materials taken from the U.S. census of population can often be supplemented by those contained in the U.S. censuses of housing, business, manufactures, and even agriculture.

The competent investigator must be able to locate data of the type we have just described. These data can reduce greatly the amount of time and money required to conduct certain types of studies. Similarly, if the event being studied occurred in the distant past, historical documents are the investigator's only source of information. It is, however, not enough simply to locate such data. The investigator must also know how to make correct use of them. Many records and documents are not compiled for scientific purposes, and the compiler may or may not be motivated to produce a record that is accurate and unbiased. Thus the U.S. Bureau of the Census is staffed by highly trained specialists who seek to gather and compile data that accurately reflect the demographic, economic, and social characteristics of the U.S. population. On the other hand, the writer of a history may have a variety of motives in addition to that of presenting an unbiased account of past events. One may write a book in order to justify the position of some individual or group with which one is identified or one may "spice" up one's work so that it will have a wide readership.

To determine the degree of authenticity and credibility that can be accorded a document is no easy task. However, Louis Gottschalk suggests four general rules that might be kept in mind as the investigator attempts to assess the validity of a historical document.[44] First, if the documentarian or recorder made his or her report immediately after the event occurred, it may be more accurate than one recorded after a considerable amount of time had elapsed. With the passage of time one's memory fades and facts get distorted. Second, one should also consider the motives of the person who compiled the document. If the writer compiled the document in order to aid his or her own memory, it may be more accurate than if it was compiled to impress a superior (e.g., a commanding officer) or to propagandize a particular group. Third, Gottschalk advances the proposition that "the fewer the number for whose eyes the document was meant (i.e., the greater its *confidential nature*) the more 'naked' its contents are likely to be." [45] This means in

[44] Gottschalk, "The Historian and the Historical Document," p. 16.
[45] Ibid., p. 16. Italics in original.

effect that if the documentarian's goal was to reach a mass audience, then he or she may have been forced to embellish the report with drama, to draw conclusions that appealed to the audience, and so forth. The value of the document as an objective source of data may therefore be decreased. Finally, documents compiled by experts on the matter under investigation are generally superior to those compiled by laymen. The expert is likely to see more things and to be able to interpret more accurately what he or she does see than is the person with an untrained eye.

It is important to note that Gottschalk is a historian and that his primary goal is to provide us with guidelines for determining the credibility of historical documents. However, he maintains that "the same four rules would seem to hold true for human documents exploited by any of the social studies." [46]

☐ OTHER APPROACHES

In addition to participant observation, the social survey, and the use of documents as data, there are a variety of other research approaches and tools that can be used to study community life. One such tool is content analysis. Put most simply, content analysis entails the scientific analysis of communications media and documents. [47] For example, in studying changing patterns of political leadership in a community, a researcher could tabulate the number of times that the mayor's office as opposed to the city council is mentioned in local newspapers over a specified period of time (e.g., 1945 to 1975). Oral history represents yet another tool by which we can gain insight into the community. In oral history, people, and particularly older individuals, are interviewed concerning their recollection of past events. Once enough people are interviewed, a general picture, or pattern, may begin to emerge. Finally, archeologists can analyze the remains of communities and peoples of the past and shed light on what early community life was like and how it has changed through time. [48] By looking at the past through the eyes

[46] Ibid., p. 16.
[47] For a dramatic illustration of the uses to which content analysis can be put see Milton Rokeach, Robert Homant, and Louis Penner, "A Value Analysis of the Disputed Federalist Papers," *Journal of Personality and Social Psychology*, 16 (October, 1970), 245–50. Through their research, the investigators were able to establish that it was Madison, rather than Hamilton, who wrote twelve of the Federalist papers, the authorship of which was in dispute.
[48] For a collection of readings that shed light on how archeology can contribute to our understanding of communities see Ruth Tringham, (ed.), *Urban Settlements:*

of the archeologist, we can very often enhance our understanding of the present, and of the future.

☐ SUMMARY

Research on community life has always been a vital part of sociology. Indeed, some of the community studies cited in Chapter 10 have become classics and are among the richest documents produced by sociologists. At the same time, the methods by which we study community life are not inherently different than those by which we study other forms of social organization. The three major ways sociologists can collect data are through *participant observation*, the *survey approach*, and the *analysis of documents and records*.

A question may arise as to which of these methods should be used to conduct a community study. However, Bernard S. Phillips makes it clear that this is probably a meaningless question:

> Not all of the beliefs surrounding social research have their origins in popular culture. In fact, some of the erroneous ones are propounded by social researchers themselves. One of these is that one given method of research is *ipso facto* better than other methods, regardless of the problem under investigation.[49]

In short, one's choice of method should be governed by one's choice of a research topic. Certainly each method yields a different type of data and is uniquely suited for the investigation of particular types of problems. We have seen that participant observation allows the investigator to get an in-depth view of groups, institutions, and communities, that the survey approach lends itself to the collection of quantitative data on the characteristics and attitudes of community members, and that documents and records are often the investigator's only source of information about the past. If the investigator wishes to conduct an in-depth, statistically rigorous study, the use of all three methodological approaches may be necessary.

Be this as it may, it is entirely appropriate that the last section of this book deals with methods of research. A backward glance will reveal that our chief concern has been with theories of community. On more than one occasion, however, it has been pointed out that good theories

---

The Process of Urbanization in Archeological Settlements (Andover, Mass.: Warner Modular Publications, 1973).

[49] Phillips, *Social Research*, p. 5.

are a product of good research, and vice versa. Thus during the past few decades students of community life have developed a number of theoretical systems that potentially help us to understand communal phenomena. During the same period of time an untold number of community studies have been conducted. Yet those of us who regard the community as a worthy object for study still face the challenge of bringing theoretical relevance to our research and of subjecting our theories to rigorous testing. If students of the community do not meet this challenge, then they can expect some rather devastating criticism to be aimed in their direction.

BIBLIOGRAPHY

Babbie, Earl R. *The Practice of Social Research.* Belmont, Calif.: Wadsworth Publishing Company, 1975.

Bell, Colin, and Howard Newby. *Community Studies: An Introduction to the Sociology of the Local Community.* New York: Praeger Publishers, 1972.

Dean, John P., Robert L. Eichhorn, and Lois R. Dean. "Observation and Interviewing," in John T. Doby (ed.), *An Introduction to Social Research,* 2nd ed. New York: Appleton-Century-Crofts, 1967.

Fessler, Donald R. "The Development of a Scale for Measuring Community Solidarity," *Rural Sociology,* 17 (June, 1952), 144–52.

Gibbs, Jack P. *Urban Research Methods.* Princeton, N.J.: D. Van Nostrand Company, Inc., 1961.

Gold, Raymond L. "Roles in Sociological Field Observations," *Social Forces,* 36 (March, 1958), 217–23.

Janes, Robert W. "A Note on Phases of the Community Role of the Participant Observer," *American Sociological Review,* 26 (June, 1961), 446–50.

Key, William H. "Urbanism and Neighboring," *The Sociological Quarterly,* 6 (Winter, 1965), 379–85.

Labovitz, Sanford, and Robert Hagedorn. *Introduction to Social Research.* New York: McGraw-Hill Book Company, 1971.

Manheim, Henry L. *Sociological Research: Philosophy and Methods.* Homewood, Ill.: The Dorsey Press, 1977.

McCall, George J., and J. L. Simmons. *Issues in Participant Observation: A Text and Reader.* Reading, Mass.: Addison-Wesley Publishing Company, 1969.

Miller, Delbert C. *Handbook of Research Design and Social Measurement,* 2nd ed. New York: David McKay Company, Inc., 1970.

Phillips, Bernard S. *Social Research: Strategy and Tactics,* 3rd ed. New York: Macmillan Publishing Co., Inc., 1976.

Schulze, Rolf, Jay Artis, and J. Allen Beegle. "The Measurement of Community Satisfaction and the Decision to Migrate," *Rural Sociology,* 28 (1966), 279–83.

Schwartz, Morris S., and Charlotte Green Schwartz. "Problems in Participant Observation," *American Journal of Sociology,* 60 (January, 1955), 343–53.

Spindler, George D. (ed.). *Being an Anthropologist: Fieldwork in Eleven Cultures*. New York: Holt, Rinehart and Winston, 1970.

Vidich, Arthur J., Joseph Bensman, and Maurice R. Stein, *Reflections on Community Studies*. New York: John Wiley & Sons, 1964.

AUTHOR INDEX

SUBJECT INDEX

□□□□□□□□□□□□□□□